Frederick the Great's
Philosophical Writings

Frederick the Great's
Philosophical Writings

Edited by Avi Lifschitz

Translated by Angela Scholar

PRINCETON UNIVERSITY PRESS

Princeton & Oxford

Published by Princeton University Press
41 William Street, Princeton, New Jersey 08540
99 Banbury Road, Oxford OX2 6JX

press.princeton.edu

All Rights Reserved
Library of Congress Control Number: 2020945331
First Paperback Printing, 2024
Paperback ISBN 9780691258911
Cloth ISBN 9780691176420
ISBN (ebook) 9780691189369

British Library Cataloging-in-Publication Data is available

Editorial: Ben Tate and Josh Drake
Production Editorial: Nathan Carr
Text Design: Pamela L. Schnitter
Jacket/Cover Design: Pamela L. Schnitter
Jacket/Cover Credit: Frederick II (1712-1786), steel engraving, from *Portrait Gallery of Eminent Men and Women of Europe and America* by Evert A. Duyckinck, published by Henry J. Johnson, Johnson, Wilson & Company, New York, 1873. Glasshouse Images / Alamy Stock Photo
Production: Danielle Amatucci
Publicity: Alyssa Sanford and Amy Stewart
Copyeditor: Francis Eaves

Generously supported by the Research Center Sanssouci, Potsdam

CONTENTS

INTRODUCTION

I. MONARCH AND AUTHOR

In 1794, Christoph Meiners, a conservative professor of philosophy at the University of Göttingen, warned that the writings of Frederick II ('the Great'), the recently deceased king of Prussia, possessed a dangerous potential and should, therefore, be treated with the utmost caution. Distinguishing between 'real, ill-timed, and false Enlightenment', Meiners warned that Frederick's published works should not be made openly accessible to peasants. In the king's writings one could read that the people, rather than God, were the ultimate source of royal authority, and that rulers were but the state's servants, who must fulfil various duties to their subjects. Exposing minds 'untrained in thinking' to such ideas was, for Meiners, an example of ill-timed, wrongheaded Enlightenment.[*]

Meiners was not alone: well into the nineteenth century, the king's numerous writings were an integral part of his image, strikingly distinguishing him from previous and contemporary rulers. Voltaire, a long-time collaborator and correspondent, noted that Frederick was the last incarnation of a writing and publishing monarch: the article 'Salomon' in Voltaire's *Questions sur l'Encyclopédie* (1770–74) began with a reference to Frederick as the only present-day Solomon 'who will very rarely be imitated'.[†] Particularly in the decades immediately preceding and following his death in 1786, Frederick's works formed part of a significant debate over the limits of state power and the proper extension of the freedom of thought and expression. It was only in the second half of the nineteenth century and throughout the twentieth that Frederick's image became increasingly focussed on his military and political exploits, while relatively little attention was paid to his writings.

---

[*]Meiners, *Ueber wahre, unzeitige, und falsche Aufklärung und deren Wirkungen* (Hanover: Helwingsche Hofbuchhandlung, 1794), 87–88. On Meiners's political theory, see Morgan Golf-French, 'Bourgeois Modernity versus the Historical Aristocracy in Christoph Meiners' Political Thought', *The Historical Journal* 62.4 (2019), 943–66.

[†]Voltaire, 'Salomon' (*Questions sur l'Encyclopédie*), in *Œuvres complètes de Voltaire*, ed. Theodore Besterman, Nicholas Cronk, et al. (Geneva and Oxford: Voltaire Foundation, 1968–2020), vol. 43, 199–211 (here 199–200). Henceforth *OCV*, followed by volume and page numbers.

The present English selection of Frederick's writings constitutes an attempt to shift the balance between philosophy and political action in the monarch's image. Its underlying principle is that the act of writing and publishing was not only window-dressing, a mere instrument allowing the king to present himself as an eighteenth-century incarnation of a Platonic philosopher-king, a Solomon, or a Marcus Aurelius. Far from acting from the outset as a shrewd manipulator of the European republic of letters, Frederick initially suffered the unforeseen consequences of the publication of works he had not intended for public consumption. Over time, he honed his authorial skills as well as his attitude to the print market and the public criticism that inevitably accompanied any publication.* If it was only gradually that the king came to terms with the lack of control over the reception and interpretation of his published works, eventually he managed to turn this unusual activity to his advantage.

Furthermore, this edition is not confined to the king's most obviously political works. The choice of a wide range of texts on a variety of topics and in several genres reflects another key argument underlying this project: Frederick's notions of kingship and service to the state cannot be fully comprehended as long as we concentrate on the narrowly 'political'. A more rounded reconstruction of his ideas of rulership can only be achieved through a serious engagement with his views on morality, the pursuit of self-love, and philosophical (rather than political) debate in the public sphere, alongside essays focussed more squarely on political theory. The writings collected here are philosophical in the eighteenth-century sense of the adjective, referring to a variety of topics and disciplines we would today classify across the humanities as well as the social and natural sciences.†

The spectacle of an absolutist ruler who wrote and published prolifically was rare and extraordinary indeed: writing for the public at large was an occupation beneath the dignity of hereditary monarchs. The crowned heads of Europe could easily commission advisers, ministers, and men of letters to convey specific messages in case of need, while writing directly to individuals or circumspect groups of addressees. In the eighteenth century, several monarchs, such as Catherine II of Russia or Stanisław August Poniatowski

---

*Avi Lifschitz, 'The Pitfalls of a Communication Process: Frederick II of Prussia as Public Author despite Himself', in Jonas Gerlings, Ere Nokkala, and Martin van Gelderen (eds), *Processes of Enlightenment: Essays in Honour of Hans Erich Bödeker*, Oxford University Studies in the Enlightenment (Liverpool: Liverpool University Press, forthcoming).

†See also Shiru Lim, 'Frederick the Great and Jean Le Rond d'Alembert on Philosophy, Truth, and Politics', *The Historical Journal* 61.2 (2018), 357–78.

of Poland-Lithuania, were engaged in extensive correspondence with renowned authors, the equivalents of modern public intellectuals; but most monarchs who were writers signalled their amateur status in the field of philosophy.

Frederick, however, identified himself as an intellectual from the age of sixteen, when he signed a letter as *Fédéric* [sic] *le philosophe*:* throughout his career he never shied away from situating himself in the intellectuals' own arena. For him, stooping to publish in the eighteenth-century print market was not only a magnanimous act of patronising the arts or demonstrating one's sharp wit. It involved exposing oneself inescapably to all aspects of contemporary publishing, especially its disagreeable elements: unflattering reviews, refutations, *ad hominem* attacks, pirated and mutilated editions, and witnessing one's arguments taken out of context. Another unusual feature of Frederick's authorship is the reputation his works enjoyed (or suffered) and their subsequent use in debates on political reform, Enlightenment, censorship, freedom of conscience, and the remit of governmental power. Radicals and conservatives alike have referred to the innovative aspects of writings by a monarch who presided over one of the most absolutist regimes in eighteenth-century Europe.

II. Making Prussia great

Upon his birth on 24 January 1712, Crown Prince Frederick became destined to rule over a clutter of widely dispersed hereditary territories centred on the Mark Brandenburg with its capital Berlin, an electorate of the Holy Roman Empire, and East Prussia, an eastern Baltic territory ruled by Brandenburg's electors since 1618 (with its capital in Königsberg, today's Kaliningrad). Frederick's grandfather, Elector Frederick III of Brandenburg (r. 1688–1713), acquired in 1701 the title of King in (rather than of) Prussia, his eastern territory that lay outside the Holy Roman Empire, thereby becoming Frederick I. Frederick's father, Frederick William I (r. 1713–40), known as the Soldier King, enacted wide-ranging administrative reforms that rendered the military the most significant arm of the state. Restructuring recruitment procedures and creating regionally based regiments, Frederick William I also elevated the military hierarchy above the courtly order of precedence and welded army and state together. As Brandenburg was still recovering from the devastating impact of the Thirty Years' War (1618–48), both Frederick I and Frederick William I were generally wary of extensive military adventures. The

*Reinhold Koser, *Friedrich der Große als Kronprinz* (Stuttgart: Cotta, 1886), 135.

Soldier King left his son Frederick II a relatively small aggregate of territories (with c. 2,380,000 inhabitants), of second or third order in international relations, yet in sound financial health and possessing a large army (c. 82,000) for its size.*

In the process of administrative consolidation under Frederick's predecessors, Brandenburg-Prussia became one of the most centralized political entities in Europe: the traditional estates were rarely convened, the nobility (or Junkers, as they were later to be styled) was tightly bound to the service of the state through the military, and regional affairs were largely subject to direct administration from Berlin. In the early eighteenth century, Berlin was a relatively small town compared to international entrepôts such as London, Paris, or Naples, with a pronounced military presence. In addition, roughly a fifth of its inhabitants around 1700 belonged to the 'French Colony' of Protestant (Huguenot) refugees expelled from Louis XIV's France following the revocation of the Edict of Nantes (1685), a community possessing legal and religious privileges of self-administration.† In 1700, Gottfried Wilhelm Leibniz convinced the elector of Brandenburg to establish a local Society of Sciences, which enhanced the outward projection of cultural prominence worthy of a kingdom in the making. After the elector had acquired a Prussian crown in 1701, the institution remained underfunded and largely neglected. Frederick William I regarded most intellectual activities as unnecessary expenditure—a point he publicly made by appointing his court jesters as presidents of the Society of Sciences.‡ In 1723, Christian Wolff, the most renowned philosopher in the German-speaking lands, was expelled by Frederick William I from the University of Halle at the instigation of the conservative wing of the Pietist movement.

The same attitude was expressed in the Soldier King's approach to ostentatious (and expensive) representation, and in the education of his children. The latter, and especially Crown Prince Frederick, were inculcated in the principles of austere Calvinism of a Pietist brand. Tutors had to minimise the

---

*Bernd Sösemann and Gregor Vogt-Spira (eds), *Friedrich der Große in Europa. Geschichte einer wechselvollen Beziehung*, 2 vols (Stuttgart: Franz Steiner, 2012), vol. 2, 410–11.

†Sibylle Badstübner-Gröger et al., *Hugenotten in Berlin* (Berlin: Union Verlag, 1988), 476.

‡C.G.A. von Harnack, *Geschichte der Königlich Preußischen Akademie der Wissenschaften zu Berlin*, 4 vols in 3 (Berlin: Reichsdruckerei, 1900), vol. 1.1, 220–25. See also Avi Lifschitz, *Language and Enlightenment: The Berlin Debates of the Eighteenth Century* (Oxford: Oxford University Press, 2012), 66–73, and idem, 'Les concours de l'Académie de Berlin, vecteurs de transferts intellectuels franco-allemands, 1745–1786', in Claire Gantet and Markus Meumann (eds), *Les Échanges savants franco-allemands au XVIIIᵉ siècle: transferts, circulations et réseaux* (Rennes: Presses Universitaires de Rennes, 2019), 205–18.

prince's exposure to classical civilisation, literature, and the fine arts. Religion-based ethics together with modern history and geography were Frederick's prescribed fare, although his Huguenot tutor, Jacques Égide Duhan de Jandun, introduced the crown prince to ancient and modern literature in French and helped him to build up a sizeable clandestine library. To his father's chagrin, Frederick also managed to refine his musical skills: he became an accomplished flautist, who would continue to perform and compose music throughout his reign.*

Early on, it became evident that the independently minded crown prince had very different leanings from his father. Frederick's fascination with French literature, philosophy, and music was not lost on the king, who frequently abused his son both privately and publicly at court. (Frederick would go on to compose his entire corpus of writings, as well as the vast majority of his correspondence, exclusively in French.) The escalating tension between father and son reached its zenith in 1730, when the crown prince saw a wholesale escape from Brandenburg-Prussia as the only way out of his predicament. During a royal visit in south-west Germany, Frederick attempted to flee camp near Steinsfurt, assisted by his confidant Hans Hermann von Katte. The ultimate destination of the naively planned and ill-executed flight was Britain, ruled by Frederick's uncle George II (also elector of Hanover). Easily captured, the crown prince and his accomplice were incarcerated, court-martialled, and charged with desertion. While the judges initially protested that they were in no position to declare a sentence on their future superior by God's grace, Frederick William I insisted on trying the crown prince and shaped the legal procedure. He changed the court's sentence for Katte to capital punishment, decreeing that the imprisoned Frederick be forced to observe the execution of his close friend. Shaken by the affair, Frederick had to repent according to his father's protocol of absolution, which included the administration of a military regiment in Ruppin.

Adding to existing tensions, Frederick William I scuppered his wife's plans for a double Prussian–British wedding. According to the queen's design, Frederick was to marry a British princess while the Prince of Wales would marry one of his sisters. The king, suspicious of his Hanoverian relations and pressured by agents of the Holy Roman Emperor in Vienna, insisted on marrying the crown prince to Elisabeth Christine of Brunswick-Bevern, and his elder sister Wilhelmine to Margrave Frederick of Brandenburg-Bayreuth, both of a substantially lower rank than the in-laws desired by queen and crown

---

*Sabine Henze-Döhring, *Friedrich der Große. Musiker und Monarch* (Munich: C. H. Beck, 2012).

prince. Frederick, whose homoerotic preferences came to be no secret in eighteenth-century Europe, shared a residence with his wife only as crown prince at Rheinsberg Castle in the north of Brandenburg (1736–40), where he also initiated his correspondence with Voltaire and other men of letters. After his accession, Frederick became completely estranged from his wife, who was confined mainly to Schönhausen Palace outside the capital. Frederick, meantime, spent most of his time in Potsdam (especially in the second half of his reign). They had no offspring: Frederick was succeeded by his nephew.[*]

The extreme conflict between father and son came to dominate the biographical literature on Frederick as a probable explanation of much of his conduct upon acceding to the throne, on 31 May 1740. While following his father in eschewing elaborate court ceremony, the first years of Frederick's reign saw him abolishing torture, minimising the use of capital punishment, relaxing censorship, initiating new commercial enterprises, enacting extensive legal reforms, and re-establishing the derelict Society of Sciences as a Royal Academy—now presided over by a renowned physicist (Pierre Louis Moreau de Maupertuis, who transferred to Berlin from the Academy of Sciences in Paris).[†] Moreover, the young king reversed his father's dismissal of Christian Wolff, who returned triumphantly to the Prussian University of Halle in December 1740. In the 1740s, Frederick also built the small Sanssouci palace outside Potsdam, where he convened philosophical and musical soirees for his confidants. Asylum was offered to authors persecuted to varying degrees in France due to their writings, including Voltaire, La Mettrie, the Marquis d'Argens, and the Abbé de Prades. The young king commissioned the first self-standing opera house in Europe, built next to a new royal library in the centre of Berlin. His policy of extended religious toleration would later give rise to a large Catholic church (St Hedwig, inaugurated in 1773) at the same Forum Fridericianum on the main east–west axis of Berlin, a symbolic gesture of toleration unparalleled in eighteenth-century European capitals.

These measures alone would have sufficed to accentuate the perception that Brandenburg-Prussia was becoming a very different entity under the newly minted king. The break with precedent extended, however, well beyond cultural preoccupations and internal politics. Frederick abandoned another hallmark of his predecessors' politics: support for the Holy Roman Emperor in

---

[*]On Frederick's sexuality, see Thomas Biskup, 'Der kinderlose "roi philosophe". Herrschertugend und Sexualmoral', in Sösemann and Vogt-Spira (eds), *Friedrich der Große in Europa*, vol. 1, 21–35; Tim Blanning, *Frederick the Great: King of Prussia* (London: Allen Lane, 2016), 50–71 and 175–80.

[†]See, in this volume, Frederick's ardent critique of torture in the *Dissertation on the Reasons for Establishing or Repealing Laws*, pp. 102–3.

Vienna. This traditional policy had been accompanied by the acceptance of client status for much of the time, and the consequent recognition that Brandenburg-Prussia was a second-rate European power that could only extract favours or subsidies from larger states, mostly in return for military assistance. A few months after Frederick's accession, in October 1740, the death of Emperor Charles VI left the Habsburg dynasty vulnerable, for the heir to the throne was female, Maria Theresa. Though Charles had sought to secure her succession to the Habsburg hereditary lands through the so-called Pragmatic Sanction, opposition could be anticipated, and as a woman his daughter was unable to become Holy Roman Emperor. In December 1740, Frederick took a momentous step that would shape his reign, by marching his troops into the Habsburg province of Silesia, to the south-east of Brandenburg. Despite their best efforts, the Austrians could neither defend nor reclaim the large, rich, and well-populated territory in the First and Second Silesian Wars (1740–42; 1744–45). These conflicts, and the wider European War of the Austrian Succession (1740–48), of which they formed part, were concluded by treaties granting international recognition to Prussia's control of its new province.

Habsburg efforts to regain Silesia did not cease, however, leading to the reversal of traditional international alliances and the formation of an anti-Prussian coalition including France, Russia, and Austria, as well as much of the Holy Roman Empire. The ensuing Seven Years' War (1756–63), arguably the first global war, is renowned elsewhere as the occasion of the British seizure of large swathes of French colonial territory in North America and in the Indian sub-continent; in Germany it has been known as the Third Silesian War. Having failed to pre-empt a struggle against three much larger powers surrounding Brandenburg-Prussia, the middle-aged Frederick now underwent another formative experience, supported only by British subsidies and troops. A series of important early successes, notably the victories at Rossbach over a combined Franco-Imperial army (November 1757), over the Austrians in the following month at Leuthen, and at Zorndorf against Russia (August 1758), gave way to significant losses in what became an attritional struggle, including the Russian occupation of East Prussia (1758–61) and a raid on Berlin. After a major defeat at the battle of Kunersdorf (August 1759), Frederick even contemplated suicide; towards the end of 1761, the Prussian army significantly dwindled and it was not clear whether the state would survive in its existing form. The death of Tsarina Elisabeth in January 1762 transformed Frederick's fortunes: under her successor, the Prussophile Peter III, Russia withdrew from East Prussia and Pomerania, and concluded a peace with Brandenburg-Prussia. In the Treaty of Hubertusburg that brought an end to the Seven Years' War in central Europe (February 1763), Austria renounced all claims to Silesia.

If the overall result of this wide-ranging conflict was a restoration of the *status quo ante*, it was Prussia which triumphed as the de facto victor, having survived intact a lengthy, devastating struggle against the mightiest land-based powers in Europe. Now firmly dubbed 'the Great', Frederick made a concerted effort to rebuild his domains and finances. Even if Prussia's increased weight in international affairs did not equal that of the larger European powers, from the 1740s onwards it could compete with Austria for domination in Germany—for example, in the War of the Bavarian Succession (1778–79) and again in the crisis of the League of Princes (Fürstenbund) after 1784.* In the first partition of Poland (1772) Brandenburg-Prussia gained territorial contiguity across the southern shore of the Baltic by annexing West Prussia, the province that had divided Brandenburg and Pomerania from East Prussia: Frederick and his successors were henceforth kings of, rather than in, Prussia. Upon his death on 17 August 1786, the much enlarged and internationally esteemed Prussia was a rather different state from the scattered and barely defensible electorate-cum-kingdom Frederick had inherited in 1740.

III. POLITICAL CONDUCT AND PHILOSOPHICAL WRITINGS

These political and military feats may account for Frederick's status as a 'great' king of Prussia, a designation he endorsed and amplified through a variety of means.† In this respect, did his writings constitute much more than an instrument of shrewd self-promotion? The question has been frequently raised, due to the perceived contradiction between Frederick's political agency and his philosophical writings. Historians have tried to plumb the depths of what they saw as an abyss separating Frederick the Enlightenment author, ally of the French *Encyclopédistes*, and the absolutist king of Prussia who had no compunction about launching first a war of conquest in Silesia and then a parti-

---

*Cf. H. M. Scott, 'Aping the Great Powers: Frederick the Great and the Defence of Prussia's International Position 1763–86', *German History* 12.3 (1994), 286–307.

†On Frederick's orchestration of his own 'greatness', see Jürgen Luh, *Der Große. Friedrich II. von Preußen* (Munich: Siedler, 2011); Thomas Biskup, *Friedrichs Größe. Inszenierungen des Preußenkönigs in Fest und Zeremoniell 1740–1815* (Frankfurt: Campus, 2012); Katrin Kohl, 'Publizistische Inszenierung von Größe. Friedrichs Schriften als Medium des Ruhms', in *Friederisiko: Friedrich der Große. Die Essays*, ed. Stiftung Preußische Schlösser und Gärten (Munich: Hirmer, 2012), 26–35.

tion of Poland-Lithuania, maintaining the nobility's traditional privileges, and tightening the already firm link between military and society.

The controversy over conflicting elements of Frederick's reign and personality reflects, to a large extent, the broader debate over Enlightened Absolutism.* This epithet has been applied to monarchs who embarked, in the second half of the eighteenth century, on a series of reforms from above that ostensibly mirrored Enlightenment values: enacting religious toleration and minimising church involvement in civil affairs, reforming an often brutal penal system, initiating the unification and codification of laws across their territories, and creating the foundations of a centralised, academically trained state apparatus. Such reforms, executed to differing degrees and purposes by Frederick II, Catherine II of Russia, Joseph II of Austria and other rulers in this period, were not intended to introduce popular representation or to create the beginnings of modern liberal democracies. On the contrary, the increasing consolidation of legislative and executive power in the hands of a single ruler was regarded as a prerequisite for the success of such reforms, which frequently depended on undermining the power of the traditional intermediary bodies between monarch and subjects (nobility, church, and estates). Especially after the Second World War, the historiographical debate over Enlightened Absolutism involved a large measure of scepticism concerning the so-called 'enlightened' nature of absolutist reforms. In its extreme version, the absolutist monarchs were depicted as cynically exploiting a contemporary zeitgeist to extend their authority, override the privileges of self-administering corporations, and engage in resource-draining, disastrous warfare.

This line of criticism was not, however, the exclusive preserve of modern historians. Shortly after the Napoleonic wars, the reactionary author Carl Ludwig von Haller argued that Frederick II, in a manner characteristic of other reforming monarchs, deviously used whatever he had learned from natural law theorists to empower himself and extend the reach of his supposedly modernised state. For Haller, this amounted to painting a false philosophical veneer over the most egotistic and despotic regime of the time. But it was also a perilous game, for some of the ideas Frederick advocated in public

---

*Two nineteenth-century accounts of Frederick within this framework are Wilhelm Roscher, *Politik: Geschichtliche Naturlehre der Monarchie, Aristokratie und Demokratie* (Stuttgart: Cotta, 1892), 286–92, and Reinhold Koser, 'Die Epochen der absoluten Monarchie in der neueren Geschichte', *Historische Zeitschrift* 61 (1889), 246–87. On Enlightened Absolutism, see the essays in H. M. Scott (ed.), *Enlightened Absolutism: Reform and Reformers in Later Eighteenth-Century Europe* (Ann Arbor, MI: University of Michigan Press, 1990), and in Gabriel B. Paquette (ed.), *Enlightened Reform in Southern Europe and its Atlantic Colonies, c. 1750–1830* (Farnham: Ashgate, 2009).

could also be appropriated by radicals and revolutionaries.* More recent accounts have been less ideological, and in many cases more appreciative of Frederick's reign. Yet the chasm between the ruler's conduct and the author's writings has remained ominously deep. In his renowned work of 1924 on reason of state, Friedrich Meinecke saw Frederick's reign as a protracted struggle between humanitarian philosophical drives (*ethos*) and pragmatic, at times crude power politics (*kratos*), even if the king's function as ruler always preceded his philosophical persona.† Some sixty years later, this Janus-faced interpretation dominated Theodor Schieder's biography of Frederick, subtitled 'a kingship of contradictions'.‡ The frequent resort to such terms as 'antinomy', 'irreconcilability', or 'contradiction' where Frederick and his writings are concerned betrays a basic assumption about the link between the written word and political action: if it cannot be demonstrated that Frederick pursued in practice the principles apparently avowed in his writings, the philosophical works must have been duplicitous masks in a ball of realpolitik.§

Several points should be borne in mind in response to this line of argumentation. The first is that the king's writings deserve to be analysed and studied on their own terms, whether they were compatible with his political conduct or not. When approaching Frederick's works, we would do well to ask why they were considered so surprising at the time as to attract such a broad range of responses. What were the intellectual strands that moulded the king's works? Who did Frederick engage with and reply to? An analysis of the substance of the king's writings does matter for the intellectual history of the eighteenth century (and beyond), irrespective of the function of such works

---

*Haller, *Restauration der Staats-Wissenschatft, oder Theorie des natürlich-geselligen Zustands, der Chimäre des künstlich-bürgerlichen entgegengesetzt*, 6 vols, 2nd edn (Winterthur: Steiner, 1820), vol. 2, 188–92. On Haller, see Béla Kapossy, 'Karl Ludwig Haller's Critique of Liberal Peace', in Béla Kapossy, Isaac Nakhimovsky, and Richard Whatmore (eds), *Commerce and Peace in the Enlightenment* (Cambridge: Cambridge University Press, 2017), 244–71; idem, 'Words and Things: The Language of Reform in Wilhelm Traugott Krug and Karl Ludwig von Haller', in Susan Richter, Thomas Maissen, and Manuela Albertone (eds), *Languages of Reform in the Eighteenth Century* (London: Routledge, 2019), 384–404. Tim Blanning counters the cynical view of Frederick in his contribution to Scott (ed.), *Enlightened Absolutism*, 265–88, and in his recent biography, *Frederick the Great*.

†Friedrich Meinecke, *Die Idee der Staatsräson in der neueren Geschichte* (Munich: Oldenburg, 1924), 1–20; 350–73.

‡Theodor Schieder, *Friedrich der Große. Ein Königtum der Widersprüche* (Frankfurt am Main: Propyläen, 1983), abridged as *Frederick the Great*, trans. Sabina Berkeley and H. M. Scott (London: Longman, 2000).

§See, most recently, Andreas Pečar, *Die Masken des Königs. Friedrich II. von Preußen als Schriftsteller* (Frankfurt am Main: Campus, 2016).

within their most immediate political contexts. It highlights the legitimate ways of presenting oneself as pursuing specific lines of action, while enabling us to understand how contemporaries perceived—and used—Frederick's philosophical writings to various purposes.

The king's analytical acumen may not have equalled Immanuel Kant's, but philosophical originality of the first order was never his purpose: a philosopher-king was a creature very different from an academic philosopher. Yet while the king argued that he never wished to construct philosophical systems, and did not lay claim to unparalleled originality, he did concoct a unique synthesis out of modern and ancient ingredients through constant dialogue with some of the best minds of the French Enlightenment. It is his personality and status that made his writings startling, at times shocking, as well as the sheer quantity and diversity of his works (collected in thirty substantial volumes of the widely accessible Preuß edition).* Over more than half a century, Frederick composed discourses, reviews, histories, plays, dialogues of the dead, satirical pamphlets, and—importantly—philosophical poems and epics (his preferred genre of intellectual self-expression) on top of a sprawling correspondence with poets, philosophers, mathematicians, and other men of letters. The variety, volume, and thematic range of Frederick's philosophical authorship attests in itself to its significance in his life; he frequently complained about his uncurable addiction to philosophising and versifying.[†] If he had merely wished to boast of his superior intellectual ability and advertise himself as a *roi-philosophe*, much less would have been required to make the point.

Furthermore, Frederick's works merit serious attention regardless of his sincerity, or disingenuousness, at the time of writing—psychological notions that are anyhow outside the historian's usual province.[‡] Once again, we could do worse than listen to the king's contemporaries in this respect. Upon the appearance of Frederick's first published work, *Anti-Machiavel*, it was not only the incongruity between its apparent endorsement of international morality and the invasion of Silesia that puzzled readers. They were primarily

---

***Œuvres de Frédéric le Grand*, ed. Johann David Erdmann Preuß, 30 vols (Berlin: Decker, 1846–56). This edition is freely accessible online at http://friedrich.uni-trier.de/ (accessed 14 March 2020). Henceforth *OFG*, followed by volume and page numbers.

[†]An early example can be found in Frederick's letter to Voltaire, 12 June 1740 (D2233), *OCV* 91:205.

[‡]See Quentin Skinner's distinction between recoverable discursive intentions and irretrievable psychological motives in 'Motives, Intentions and Interpretation', in *Visions of Politics*, 3 vols (Cambridge: Cambridge University Press, 2002), vol. 1: *Regarding Method*, 90–102. On self-imposed constraints and the question of sincerity, see Skinner, 'Augustan Party Politics and Renaissance Constitutional Thought', *Visions of Politics*, vol. 2: *Renaissance Virtues*, 344–67.

perplexed by the curious phenomenon of a publishing monarch. As the Duc de Luynes observed at the French court, 'a prince who establishes publicly and almost under his own name such wise principles of government, which are nevertheless so rarely practised in a precise manner, contracts in a way an engagement with the public that is very difficult to realise to its fullest extent'.* The Duc de Luynes's puzzle did not concern a tension between the content of Frederick's work and his political conduct, but rather the young king's willingness to impose severe constraints on the remit of his publicly legitimate action. Genuine or dissimulating as Frederick may have been at the time of writing, his works acquired an independent lease on life in the public sphere.[†]

IV. SOCIAL CONTRACT VERSUS DIVINE GRACE

The final key to exorcising the ghost of the supposedly irresolvable contradiction between the king's printed ideas and his political agency is the recognition that the contrast is not as sharp as it has usually been portrayed. Frederick would have been the first to confirm that the notion of kingship portrayed in his writings was a regulative ideal rather than a realistic account of eighteenth-century politics. Moreover, it was far from a self-denying, idealistic conception of government.

As early as the first chapter of the *Anti-Machiavel*, Frederick wrote down the ideas with which he has become identified ever since: the king was the first servant of the state, and royal authority originated in a social contract.[‡] While references to a social contract were made already in his first publication, as late as 1777 the term *pacte sociale* appeared seven times in Frederick's *Essay on the Forms of Government*. If these major aspects of Frederick's

---

*Charles-Philippe d'Albert, duc de Luynes, *Mémoires du duc de Luynes sur la cour de Louis XV (1735–1758)*, ed. Louis Dussieux and Eudore Soulié, 17 vols (Paris: Firmin-Didot, 1860–65), vol. 3, 267. On the composition and publishing circumstances of the *Anti-Machiavel*, see Werner Bahner and Helga Bergmann's introduction in *OCV* 19:1–101; Christiane Mervaud, *Voltaire et Frédéric II: une dramaturgie des Lumières, 1736–1778* (Oxford: Voltaire Foundation, 1985), 89–120; Shiru Lim, 'Philosophical Kingship in Eighteenth-Century Europe: Frederick II, Catherine II, and the *philosophes*', PhD dissertation, University College London (UCL), 2018, 59–111; Lifschitz, 'Pitfalls of a Communication Process'.

†See section VI below.

‡'The Sovereign, far from being the absolute master of the people who are under his domination, is himself only their first servant.' (*Anti-Machiavel*, p. 15 below) On this occasion the servant is a *domestique*, but Frederick used alternately the terms *serviteur* (in the 'Political Testament' of 1752 and in the 1777 *Essay on the Forms of Government*, *OFG* 9:225, 238) and *ministre* (1757, *OFG* 27:303). He also compared the role of the first servant of the state to that of a magistrate (*magistrat*) on behalf of the people (*OFG* 9:225).

political theory, the ruler's servitude to the state and the appeal to a social contract, have usually been seen as discrete elements, they essentially stem from the same seventeenth-century model developed by theorists such as Thomas Hobbes and Samuel Pufendorf. (The latter served Frederick's grandfather, the first 'king in Prussia', as royal historiographer and privy councillor.)*

In their major works, *Leviathan* (1651) and *De iure naturae et gentium* (1672), Hobbes and Pufendorf respectively wished to counter republican arguments about the advantages of self-governing communities. Another prominent target of these contractarian theorists was the monarchomach literature of the sixteenth and seventeenth centuries, which grounded political authority in an original contract as a way of justifying rebellion or dethronement if the monarch had neglected his duties towards his subjects (originally enshrined in the foundational pact).[†] Despite some theoretical differences, both Hobbes and Pufendorf separated the state from its ruler and the citizens alike; their version of the social contract was more authoritarian than other contemporary or subsequent constructs. They rejected the idea that the people, as if they had originally formed a single person, could negotiate the terms of the initial contract: one of Hobbes's theoretical innovations was to argue that a 'multitude' of individuals constituted itself as a single body only through their joint submission to a government.[‡] The foundations of the modern concept of an impersonal state are thus to be found, according to Quentin Skinner, in a seventeenth-century theory that was absolutist and secular in its implications due to the elevation of the state above all traditional powers demanding spiritual or civic allegiance. In their use of social contract theory, Hobbes and Pufendorf rejected contemporary notions of popular sovereignty.[§]

---

*On the differences between Pufendorf's historical works and Frederick's own accounts of his dynasty, see Christopher Clark, *Time and Power: Visions of History in German Politics from the Thirty Years' War to the Third Reich* (Princeton, NJ: Princeton University Press, 2019), 72–117; cf. Pečar, *Masken des Königs*, 33–81.

†Quentin Skinner, 'The State', in Terence Ball, James Farr, and Russell L. Hanson (eds), *Political Innovation and Conceptual Change* (Cambridge: Cambridge University Press, 1989), 90–131; idem, 'From the State of Princes to the Person of the State', in *Visions of Politics*, vol. 3: *Renaissance Virtues*, 368–413.

‡Chapter 17 in Hobbes, *Leviathan*, ed. Noel Malcolm (Oxford: Oxford University Press, 2012), II.i, 254–57. For Pufendorf's version: *Of the Law of Nature and Nations*, trans. Basil Kennet (London: Sare, Bonwicke, Goodwyn, et al., 1717), Book VII, ch. 2, 476.

§Skinner, 'From the State of Princes', 405.

Frederick usually presented his political ideas in lapidary form, frustratingly sparing where sources are concerned.* Yet the main elements of Hobbesian-Pufendorfian contract theory are clearly present in his works: in particular, it is difficult to ignore their pronounced secular and absolutist overtones. Such similarities should not, however, diminish the shockwaves Frederick's own writings sent through eighteenth-century Europe. Not only was it the first time that a hereditary king took pen to paper to announce such principles in his own voice; Frederick also added to his contract theory a distinctly modern flavour concerning the pursuit of self-love, to be discussed in the next section of this Introduction.

Royal authority, the king argued, originated in the people's decision to renounce their natural liberties in exchange for security of life and possessions, safeguarded by a ruler they appointed. Frederick did not allow, of course, any opt-out mechanisms justifying rebellion under special circumstances or subjecting the ruler's executive decisions to institutional supervision by representatives of the people. The monarch alone represented the state, Frederick insisted, by uniting in his person the will of the people.† Nevertheless, he carefully demarcated the political sphere in his writings. While pointing to the well-being of the people as the ruler's main duty, he interpreted such welfare in a flexible manner, especially concerning the citizens' opinions and beliefs: Frederick repeatedly exhorted his subjects to seek their salvation and happiness in any way they saw fit. This encouragement was paralleled by his account of the areas left outside the original contract. As subjects' opinions and beliefs could never have formed part of the pact, they should be of no concern to modern governments either.

> One would have to be insane to imagine that men have ever said to a fellow man: 'We are raising you above ourselves, because we like to be slaves, and we are giving you the power to direct, as you will, our thoughts.' On the contrary, they said: 'We need you to uphold the laws we wish to obey, to govern us wisely, and to defend us; we demand of you, moreover, that you respect our freedom.' The verdict [on freedom of thought and belief], then, is given, without appeal; and such toler-

---

*As Frederick usually read classical and modern philosophy in French, the most probable conduit was Jean Barbeyrac's French translation of Pufendorf's *De iure naturae et gentium* under the title *Le Droit de la nature et des gens* (Amsterdam: Henri Schelte, 1706). On Barbeyrac's background in the Huguenot community in Berlin, see Sieglinde Othmer, *Berlin und die Verbreitung des Naturrechts in Europa* (Berlin: De Gruyter, 1970), 60–90; Fiammetta Palladini, *Die Berliner Hugenotten und der Fall Barbeyrac* (Leiden: Brill, 2011).

†*Essay on the Forms of Government and the Duties of Sovereigns*, p. 199 below.

ance, moreover, is so favourable to the society where it is established, that it ensures the good fortune of the State. (*Essay on the Forms of Government and the Duties of Sovereigns*, p. 205 below)

This explicit endorsement of contract theory by a ruling monarch was, no doubt, unique at a time of kingship by God's grace. Although fellow monarchs shared some of Frederick's convictions and enacted similar reforms, none went so far as to reject publicly the religious aspect of kingship. And if Frederick took up major elements of Hobbes and Pufendorf's contract theory, his writings clearly constituted a break with a different line of argumentation for absolute monarchy.

Apologists for this form of government used to argue that while tyrants ruled arbitrarily, legitimate kings were restrained by their allegiance to the law of God, natural law, and the fundamental laws of their kingdom. Royal power was, however, as absolute as a father's right over his offspring or God's control of his creation. James VI and I of Scotland and England, the last European monarch before Frederick to write extensively on political theory, declared in a speech to the English Parliament in 1610 that 'Kings are not only God's Lieutenants upon earth, and sit upon God's throne, but even by God himself they are called Gods'.‡ Relying on the Bible and referring to recent religious wars in which monarchs were declared heretics, James argued that even if the king failed to rule according to divine laws and those of the realm, only God could hold him to account.§ James's library contained a copy of Jean Bodin's *Six livres de la république* (1576), where he may have encountered some aspects of his own notion of absolute sovereignty. While Bodin did not exclusively discuss monarchies, he insisted that sovereignty 'is not limited in power, or in function, or in length of time'.¶ Elective monarchs or kings who ruled on behalf of the estates did not enjoy absolute sovereignty, for 'the main point of sovereign majesty and absolute power consists of giving the law to subjects in general without their consent'.** A century later, Jacques-Bénigne Bossuet, the renowned propagandist for Louis XIV's absolutist regime, made

---

‡'Speech to Parliament of 21 March 1610', in King James VI and I, *Political Writings*, ed. Johann P. Sommerville (Cambridge: Cambridge University Press, 1995), 181 (modernised orthography).

§See also 'The Trew Law of Free Monarchies', ibid., 62–84.

¶Bodin, *On Sovereignty*, ed. Julian H. Franklin (Cambridge: Cambridge University Press, 1992), Book I.8, 3; *Les Six Livres de la République/De Republica libri sex*, Book I, ed. Mario Turchetti and Nicolas de Araujo, preface by Quentin Skinner (Paris: Classiques Garnier, 2013), 448–49. In Bodin's theory, unlike those of James VI and I or, subsequently, Bossuet, biblical precedent did not play a central role.

**On Sovereignty*, 23.

a similar point by grounding the practical unaccountability of the monarch in biblical examples and a 'particular providence' directly intervening in human affairs (in *Politique tirée des propres paroles de l'Écriture sainte*, posthumously published in 1709).*

Frederick, on the other hand, had no time for biblically grounded, divinely warranted justifications of absolute monarchy. Time and again he employed the social contract as a secular source of royal authority which could nevertheless be reconciled with religious belief. In 1770, replying to an attack on contemporary monarchs, Frederick insisted that he was not writing in defence of God-given royal authority.

> We would surrender to the author such titles as 'images of the Divinity' or 'God's representatives on earth', which one attributes to kings so improperly. Kings, like the rest of us, are men; they do not enjoy the exclusive privilege of being perfect in a world where nothing is so. They bring to the throne, upon which an accident of birth has placed them, their timidity or their resolution, their energy or their idleness, their vices or their virtues; and in a hereditary monarchy it must of necessity be the case, that Princes with very differing characters succeed one another. (*Examination of the* Essay on Prejudice, p. 177 below)

Unsurprisingly, this critique of kingship by divine grace and the turn to contract theory were not meant to resuscitate republican notions of self-governance. If at times Frederick seemed to present himself as a so-called republican or patriot king, it was only in so far as some of the goals ascribed to a virtuous monarch coincided with those of classical republics. Such an ideological coincidence remained, however, on a rather superficial level: that of the glory and the flourishing of the *patria*. Beyond this register, Frederick followed closely the critics of classical republicanism, emphasising repeatedly that the well-being of his subjects took precedence over self-governance and its institutional safeguards.

Indeed, Frederick disdained the republican stress on formal procedures for the maintenance of self-rule. His *Essay on the Forms of Government* (1777) is, if anything, an essay against the theoretical fixation with forms of government from antiquity to the eighteenth century. In this treatise, he made an

*'It is again God who establishes reigning houses. He said to Abraham: "Kings shall come out of thee", and to David: "The Lord will make thee a house," and to Jeroboam: "If thou art faithful to me, I will make thee a house, as I did for David."': Bossuet, *Politics Drawn from the Very Words of Holy Scripture*, ed. Patrick Riley (Cambridge: Cambridge University Press, 1990), 245; *Politique tirée des propres paroles de l'Écriture sainte*, ed. Jacques Le Brun (Geneva: Droz, 1967), 272.

argument similar to Hobbes's point in chapter 21 of *Leviathan*, about the citizens of the republic of Lucca. According to Hobbes, while these ardent republicans could emblazon the word *Libertas* in great characters on the turrets of Lucca, a private citizen there did not enjoy greater liberty or 'immunity from the service of the Commonwealth' than in Constantinople, under the Ottoman sultan.* This point would later be reworked by early liberal theorists such as Benjamin Constant, who distinguished in 1819 between a 'liberty of the ancients', focussed on the communal freedom of small city-states, and modern freedom, predicated on individual liberty in commercial society.† While Frederick did not provide any institutional guarantees for individual freedom beyond the rule of law, he did make a similar distinction between past and present. More generally, however, forms and institutions of government—especially the free state espoused by republicans—were of no great consequence in his writings. Monarchy could be the best form of government or the worst, Frederick argued, depending on the way it was administered and whether it promoted the well-being of its subjects.

V. Luxury, happiness, and self-love

Despite presenting the unusual spectacle of a hereditary monarch who explicitly expounded such ideas while corresponding with the most renowned French *philosophes*, Frederick espoused neither the radical materialism associated with his contemporaries Claude Adrien Helvétius or Paul-Henri Thiry, baron d'Holbach, nor Jean-Jacques Rousseau's contract theory, which placed a premium on popular sovereignty. The king also did not take up, unlike Rousseau and other eighteenth-century authors, the vision of a self-denying and frugal kingship that had been elaborated by François de Salignac de La Mothe-Fénelon in *Télémaque* (1699), one of the best-selling and most influential books in eighteenth-century Europe.

Fénelon wrote this didactic account of the adventures of Ulysses's son, Telemachus, as tutor to the Duke of Burgundy, second in line and later heir-apparent to Louis XIV's throne (before his untimely death in 1712). *Télémaque* contrasted glory-driven, bellicose rulers of an ancient Roman mould with those committed to promoting the common good of a largely agricultural polity—free of luxury, modern commerce, urban corruption, and expensive

---

*Hobbes, *Leviathan*, ed. Malcolm, II.i, 332.
†Constant, 'On the Liberty of the Ancients Compared with that of the Moderns', in *Political Writings*, ed. Biancamaria Fontana (Cambridge: Cambridge University Press, 1988), 308–28.

wars (a de-militarised image of Spartan austerity). Widely interpreted as a vehement critique of Louis XIV's wars and his ostentatious culture of representation, *Télémaque* prompted its author's fall from royal grace and exile to
his northern diocese. Fénelon also managed to attract Bossuet's ire (and the
Vatican's censure) for his endorsement of a disinterested love of God beyond
any hope for personal salvation or happiness, requiring the total elimination
of self-interest. In Fénelon's work, the ancient republican critique of self-
interest in the name of the *patria* was the political incarnation of a pure,
wholly disinterested love of God.*

It is indeed easy to mistake Frederick's emphasis on the ruler's duties to
his subjects and an impersonalised state for a Fénelonian-republican critique
of modern politics and commercial society. Perhaps because we know that
Frederick's mother admired *Télémaque* and discussed the book with her son,
literature on the king has tended to over-emphasise the subsequent impact of
Fénelon's notions of frugality and the absolute prioritisation of the public over
the self.† In his seminal biography of Frederick, Theodor Schieder argued that
Fénelon provided the model for benevolent kingship in the *Anti-Machiavel*;‡
Meinecke has suggested that Frederick's ideal of service to the state was inspired
by either Fénelon, Pierre Bayle, or a form of Calvinist self-denial that Frederick
could never completely shake off, hard as he may have tried.§

The king's ideas were, however, altogether more realistic: they were well
adjusted to modern reason of state and commercial politics.¶ Frederick argued

---

*See Patrick Riley's introduction to Fénelon, *Telemachus*, ed. Patrick Riley (Cambridge: Cambridge University Press, 1994), xiv–xv, and his 'Fénelon's "Republican" Monarchism in *Telemachus*', in
Hans Blom, John Christian Laursen, and Luisa Simonutti (eds), *Monarchisms in the Age of Enlightenment* (Toronto: University of Toronto Press, 2007), 78–100.

†Ernst Bratuscheck, *Die Erziehung Friedrichs des Großen* (Berlin: Georg Reimer, 1885), 27–28;
Eduard Zeller, *Friedrich der Große als Philosoph* (Berlin: Weidmannsche Buchhandlung, 1886),
237–38.

‡Schieder, *Friedrich der Große*, 105; *Frederick the Great*, 77. Schieder notes that Frederick contrasted at the outset of chapter VII of *Anti-Machiavel* an angelic Fénelon with a demonic Machiavelli
(see p. 27 below). The purpose of this juxtaposition was, however, surely to dismiss both views of morality as exaggerated and non-practical. (See also the conclusion of Frederick's *Dissertation on the Reasons
for Establishing or Repealing Laws*, p. 106 below.)

§Meinecke, *Idee der Staatsräson*, 350–51. A rare exception, emphasising the modern elements in
Anti-Machiavel (from a political perspective) is Isaac Nakhimovsky, 'The Enlightened Prince and the
Future of Europe: Voltaire and Frederick the Great's *Anti-Machiavel* of 1740', in Kapossy, Nakhi-
movsky, and Whatmore (eds), *Commerce and Peace*, 44–77.

¶The present edition is dedicated to Frederick's major philosophical works. If any evidence of his
adroit perception of realpolitik is required, it can be found in his political correspondence (from the
early Natzmer Letter of 1731 onwards) and in analyses such as *Considerations on the Present Condition
of the Body Politic of Europe* (1738, *OFG* 8:1–30) or the 'Political Testaments' of 1752 and 1768 (repro-

that a healthy dose of luxury oiled the springs of commerce, manufacture, and (indirectly) even agriculture. More generally, he was well aware of the substantial distance separating his own age from Machiavelli's: he did not condemn the latter's *Prince* only to endorse central tenets of Renaissance (or ancient) republicanism. Referring to the qualitative difference between modern standing armies and the mercenaries employed by the miniature rulers (*principini*) of Italian city-states, Frederick argued that the enormous costs of modern warfare provided a powerful incentive for the maintenance of peace. Furthermore, a modern economy founded on the division of labour allowed eighteenth-century states to operate much more efficiently than self-governing republics, where each citizen was also potentially a soldier.

> The unique advantage of this [earlier] arrangement was that the military cost nothing in times of peace, but that, when the call to arms sounded, every citizen became a soldier, whereas, at present, these roles are separate: the farmer and the manufacturer each continues his own work, without interruption, while that section of the citizens destined to defend the others performs its duty. [. . .] It thus follows from our modern practice that our wars are shorter than those of our forebears, less ruinous to the lands that provide the theatre of war, and that we owe to the great expense that wars involve those brief moments of peace that we enjoy, and which, moreover, the exhaustion of the great powers will probably lengthen. (*Examination of the* Essay on Prejudice, p. 176 below)

These views originated in Frederick's (as yet under-studied) engagement with the European luxury debate, where he positioned himself at the ideological pole opposite to Fénelon's. The eighteenth-century luxury debate was not only, or even mainly, confined to political economy: it was a controversy over the values of a modern, commercial, and globalised society, as well a discussion of human nature and its basic instincts. The debate gave rise to the first enthusiastic apologies for an economy based on the division of labour, relentless growth, and inequality—as well as to blistering critiques of modern civilisation such as Jean-Jacques Rousseau's *Discourse on Inequality* (*Discours sur l'origine et les fondements de l'inégalité parmi les hommes*, 1755).* Initially

duced in the original French in Gustav Berthold Volz (ed.), *Die politischen Testamente Friedrichs des Grossen* (Berlin: Reimar Hobbing, 1920)).

*The literature on the luxury debate is vast. A partial list would include Albert Hirschman, *The Passions and the Interests: Political Arguments for Capitalism before Its Triumph* (Princeton, NJ: Princeton University Press, 1977); István Hont and Michael Ignatieff (eds), *Wealth and Virtue: The* linked to the Quarrel of the Ancients and the Moderns around the turn of the century, over the comparable merits of classical and modern literature, the luxury debate gradually diverged from the early Quarrel on account of its more explicit emphasis on politics and ethics.* Moralists of either Christian or republican leanings (or both, in Fénelon's case) criticised luxury as the untrammelled pursuit of self-interest and its prioritisation over the common good. They usually recommended overcoming self-regarding instincts by focussing on human reason, God's grace, or future salvation. Their opponents recognised, however, that the passions held sway over fragile human reason, and professed agnosticism concerning future rewards and punishments. Damned or saved in another life, human beings had to pursue their self-love in this world, since they could not do otherwise—and because the satisfaction of such passions gave rise to unprecedented economic and cultural prosperity. For its advocates in different forms, such as Bernard Mandeville, Voltaire, Montesquieu, David Hume, and Adam Smith, luxury became a proxy for modern culture *tout court*: Hume, for example, renamed his essay 'Of Luxury' (1752) as 'Of Refinement in the Arts' (1760).

Connotations and overtones were significant in this context, following centuries of denunciations of luxury as sinful voluptuousness. The prerequisite for this condemnation was a sharp distinction between the necessary and the superfluous: for the critics, almost anything beyond basic and peaceful subsistence, preferably in a rural setting, was yet another sprig in the tangled thicket of luxury—from commercial commodities to technological advances to intellectual endeavours. The adherents of modern luxury attempted to undermine such notions by re-defining luxury as the simple pursuit of human happiness and improvement in this world (rather than the next)—or 'the use of riches and industry to acquire a more comfortable existence', as luxury was

---

Shaping of Political Economy in the Scottish Enlightenment (Cambridge: Cambridge University Press, 1983); Christopher Berry, *The Idea of Luxury: A Conceptual and Historical Investigation* (Cambridge: Cambridge University Press, 1994); Maxine Berg and Elizabeth Eger (eds), *Luxury in the Eighteenth Century: Debates, Desires and Delectable Goods* (Basingstoke: Palgrave, 2002); Pierre Force, *Self-Interest before Adam Smith: A Genealogy of Economic Science* (Cambridge: Cambridge University Press, 2003); István Hont, *Jealousy of Trade: International Competition and the Nation-State in Historical Perspective* (Cambridge, MA: Harvard University Press, 2005); John Shovlin, *The Political Economy of Virtue: Luxury, Patriotism, and the Origins of the French Revolution* (Ithaca, NY: Cornell University Press, 2007).

*On Ancients vs Moderns, see (among many other items) Joan DeJean, *Ancients against Moderns: Culture Wars and the Making of a* Fin de siècle (Chicago: University of Chicago Press, 1997); Anne-Marie Lecoq (ed.), *La Querelle des Anciens et des Modernes* (Paris: Gallimard, 2001); Levent Yilmaz, *Le Temps moderne: variations sur les anciens et les contemporains* (Paris: Gallimard, 2004); Dan Edelstein, *The Enlightenment: A Genealogy* (Chicago: University of Chicago Press, 2010).

defined in 1765 in the *Encyclopédie*.* Within the pro-luxury camp, this moderate pursuit of comfort and self-love was seen as an agent of civilisation and peace, as suggested in Montesquieu's vision of 'sweet commerce' (*doux commerce*) in *De l'esprit des lois* (1748).† Early societies, biblical or classical, may have been virtuous, but were also uncouth and poor in comparison to eighteenth-century Europe.

The main challenge facing pro-luxury authors was whether and how to condone the negative aspects of the modern pursuit of self-love, namely increasing inequality, a perceived neglect of collective values, and the escalating urbanisation of traditionally agricultural societies. As István Hont succinctly summarised the opposing views, 'For its critics, luxury was the product of extreme inequality, the sacrifice of the countryside for the cities, the cause of depopulation, the nemesis of courage, honour and love of country. For its defenders, luxury was an engine of population growth, higher living standards, the circulation of money, good manners, the progress of the arts and the sciences, and, last but not least, the power of nations and the happiness of citizens.'‡ The broader intellectual shift around 1740 towards a firm focus on material and cultural improvement—both regarded as luxury by its detractors—has been identified by John Robertson as the Enlightenment's coming of age.§

While Voltaire joined the fray in the early 1730s, his involvement in the luxury debate intensified in 1736—exactly when his correspondence with Frederick was launched. At this point the twenty-four year old crown prince was open to different poetic and philosophical influences: his first letter to Voltaire mentions (beyond several of Voltaire's own plays) Corneille, Lefranc de Pompignan, and Jean-Baptiste Rousseau. Frederick was also interested in the broadly Leibnizian philosophy of Christian Wolff, expelled by his father from the Prussian University of Halle: the crown prince sent Wolff's works,

---

*Jean-François de Saint-Lambert, 'Luxe', in *Encyclopédie, ou Dictionnaire raisonné des sciences, des arts et des métiers*, ed. Denis Diderot and Jean-Baptiste le Rond d'Alembert, vol. 9 (Neuchâtel: Faulche, 1765), 763–71 (at 763).

†'Commerce cures destructive prejudices, and it is an almost general rule that everywhere there are gentle mores, there is commerce and that everywhere there is commerce, there are gentle mores.': Montesquieu, *The Spirit of the Laws*, trans. A. M. Cohler, B. C. Miller, and H. S. Stone (Cambridge: Cambridge University Press), Book 20, ch. 1, 338.

‡István Hont, 'The Early Enlightenment Debate on Commerce and Luxury', in Mark Goldie and Robert Wokler (eds), *The Cambridge History of Eighteenth-Century Political Thought* (Cambridge: Cambridge University Press, 2006), 379–418 (at 380).

§Robertson, *The Case for the Enlightenment: Scotland and Naples 1680–1760* (Cambridge: Cambridge University Press, 2005), 8–9 and 28–44.

in French translation, to Voltaire.* Given his well-known philosophical pre-
dilections, Frederick's years as crown prince were marked by a political struggle in which Wolffian philosophy was used by an Austrian-Saxon faction as
a bait to catch the crown prince's attention. The attempt to turn Frederick
more firmly towards Wolff, spearheaded by the Saxon diplomat Ernst Christoph von Manteuffel, was accompanied by the latter's secret activities on behalf of the Viennese court and intended to counter French intellectual impact on Frederick.[†] Very quickly, however, Voltaire and the prince royal of
Prussia established a mutually beneficial, vigorous exchange, while Wolffian
philosophy gradually receded from Frederick's horizon (partly due to its lukewarm reception by Voltaire).[‡] Frederick became ever more appreciative of
Voltaire's views and flattered by his senior correspondent's frequent encomia.
In the late 1730s, Voltaire assumed the mantle of Frederick's intellectual tutor,
while endorsing in public the pursuit of self-love in a series of interventions
in the luxury debate.

Commerce, toleration, and the flourishing arts—all seen as effects of
the benign pursuit of luxury—had already stood at the centre of Voltaire's
Lettres philosophiques (1734), which presented an idealised image of England
following the author's sojourn in London from 1726 to 1728. The *Lettres*
were concluded by an attack on Pascal, who—together with other austere
Jansenists—was condemned for his Augustinian view of a fallen human nature. The 25th Letter, on Pascal, was an affirmation of the human condition
in the here and now: for Voltaire, God must have created human beings with
all their current instincts in place, including their basic penchant for self-love.
Explicitly attacking the doctrine of original sin, Voltaire declared 'that self-
esteem is the same in all men, and is necessary to them as the five senses; that
this self-esteem was given to us by God that we might preserve ourselves'.[§]
This was not, however, an endorsement of an uninhibited pursuit of pleasure.
Voltaire noted that reason and moral principles, provided by religion or other
sources, mitigated the basic instincts of our nature, even if they could never

*Frederick to Voltaire, 8 August 1736 (D1126), in *OCV* 88:28–31; Frederick to Voltaire, December 1736/January 1737 (D1247), ibid., 186.

[†]Koser, *Friedrich als Kronprinz*, 140–45; Johannes Bronisch, *Der Mäzen der Aufklärung. Ernst
Christoph von Manteuffel und das Netzwerk des Wolffianismus* (Berlin: De Gruyter, 2010), 72–122;
idem, *Der Kampf um Kronprinz Friedrich. Wolff gegen Voltaire* (Berlin: Landt, 2011).

[‡]Voltaire to Frederick, 26 August 1736, in *OFG* 21:9. On the notable intensity of their exchange in
1736–38, see Mervaud, *Voltaire et Frédéric II*, 71–90.

[§]Letter 25 in Voltaire, *Philosophical Letters; Or, Letters Concerning the English Nation*, ed. John
Leigh, trans. Prudence Steiner (Indianapolis: Hackett, 2007), 103.

override the healthy pursuit self-love. The contrast with Pascal or Fénelon's search for a purer, disinterested human condition was clear.

In the mid-1730s, Voltaire and his lover, Émilie du Châtelet, studied Alexander Pope's defence of fallen human nature in his *Essay on Man* (1733–34). Voltaire also appreciated the pro-luxury points in Jean-François Melon's *Essai politique sur le commerce* (1734), yet another endorsement of modern commerce against calls for austere virtue. In 1735–36 du Châtelet was working on a translation of Bernard Mandeville's *Fable of the Bees* (1714), subtitled 'Private Vices, Public Benefits', a major apology for the pursuit of luxury and self-love. Du Châtelet, in collaboration with Voltaire, attempted to remove Mandeville's more radical views from his endorsement of modern culture, for example his insistence that human beings had no natural inclinations beyond self-interest. In du Châtelet's version, natural virtue was tightly linked both to the common good and to a healthy pursuit of self-love: the latter was no longer a 'private vice'.* This also became the theme of the final chapters of Voltaire's posthumously published *Traité de métaphysique* (completed in 1736): some of its draft chapters were sent to Frederick in 1737.†

In summer 1736, when Frederick first contacted Voltaire, the latter was writing *Le Mondain*—his most renowned intervention in the luxury debate. The uproar caused by its pirated publication prompted Voltaire to issue a *Défense du mondain* in 1737. In biting rhymed verses, Voltaire ridiculed anyone advocating a return to a biblical, classical, or any other bygone golden age of noble austerity. *Le Mondain* was a hymn to the present 'iron age' of global commerce and modern living standards, from basic comforts to painting, music, and the popping corks of champagne bottles (a recently developed product).‡ While *Le Mondain* immediately became scandalous for its portrayal of Adam and Eve as a boorish couple with long dirty nails and frazzled hair, living indigently in Eden, the poem's clear target was Fénelon's *Télémaque* (explicitly discussed towards its end). Voltaire consistently revaluated and lavished praise on the terms most intensely condemned by Fénelon: abundance, luxury, superfluity, and softness (*mollesse*). These were, for Voltaire, the surest guarantors of

---

*Felicia Gottmann, 'Du Châtelet, Voltaire, and the Transformation of Mandeville's *Fable*', *History of European Ideas* 38.2 (2012), 218–32. Du Châtelet's version of Mandeville's *Fable* is available as an appendix in Ira O. Wade, *Studies on Voltaire: With Some Unpublished Papers of Mme du Châtelet* (Princeton, NJ: Princeton University Press, 1947).

†See W. H. Barber's introduction to the *Traité* in *OCV* 14:384–87, 409–11.

‡*OCV* 16:295–303. See Haydn Mason's introduction to *Le Mondain* (ibid., 273–88); Nicholas Cronk, 'The Epicurean Spirit: Champagne and the Defence of Poetry in Voltaire's *Le Mondain*', *Studies on Voltaire and the Eighteenth Century* 371 (1999), 53–80; Wade, *Studies on Voltaire*, 49–56.

industry and prosperity in modern Europe. The poem's most famous line, 'Le superflu, chose très nécessaire' (The superfluous, such a necessary thing), was not just a succinct, memorable slogan.* The equivalence Voltaire drew between the necessary and the superfluous undermined the entire differentiation between nature and artifice, or between basic subsistence and luxury—a distinction underpinning all contemporary critiques of modernity.

These insights, at both the psychological and political levels, appear in the very first letters and poems Voltaire sent Frederick in 1736. Encouraging the young Hohenzollern to cultivate his passion for philosophy and poetry—and to philosophise in verse—Voltaire also emphasised that learning should not come at the expense of a worldly, engaged lifestyle that involved the pursuit of self-love: Frederick should not become a pedantic scholar or sacrifice his political calling on the altar of philosophy.† In a rhyming poem for Frederick (August–September 1736), Voltaire proposed a new role model to the crown prince: the biblical King Solomon, whom Voltaire would compare again to the mature Frederick in the 1770s. If Voltaire and Frederick did not regard the Bible as a blueprint for modern politics, they knew well how to make use of it when opportunity called. Voltaire could not ignore the case of a rare king of Israel renowned not only for his wisdom and philosophical authorship, but also for generating unprecedented prosperity and wealth. Both modern Europe and Solomon's kingdom linked distant continents through naval commerce, powered by a benevolent pursuit of luxury and 'abundance'.‡ This term, now associated with Solomon and recommended as a political goal to Frederick, was one of the concepts derided by Fénelon and revaluated in *Le Mondain* of the same year as the poem to the crown prince. In Voltaire's *Défense du mondain* against his (and luxury's) critics, Solomon featured as an exemplary king who employed luxury in the service of national well-being and his own happiness.§ Solomon also ruled over a sizeable kingdom, which allowed Voltaire to make the point that luxury was wholesome in states possessing a large territory but detrimental to small republics.¶

---

*OCV 16:296.

†'The illustrious [seventeenth-century Swedish] Queen Christina abandoned her kingdom to look for the arts; govern, Sir, and let the arts come looking for you.' (Voltaire to Frederick, 26 August 1736, in OFG 21:8) For an exhortation to continue writing rhymed verse, see Voltaire to Frederick, [12?] October 1737 (D1375), in OCV 88:380.

‡'Le Mondain', lines 22–29 (OCV 16:296); 'Au Prince Royal de Prusse', lines 71–75 (ibid., 380).

§'Défense du mondain' (early 1737), lines 113–19, OCV 16:308–9.

¶'Sachez surtout que le luxe enrichit / Un grand État, s'il en perd un petit.' ('Défense du mondain', OCV 16:306.)

Voltaire thus made, in 1736–37, a concerted effort to link the defence of luxury and modern commerce to the figure of an earthly philosopher-king pursuing his self-love while promoting the well-being of his state. Frederick had to become 'le Salomon du nord', as Voltaire would crown him after his accession to the throne.* Most significantly, through Solomon's example Voltaire suggested to Frederick that governing in the interest of the state, like the pursuit of learning, should not come at the expense of personal pleasure.

> These are the lessons a sage king should follow
> Knowledge, after all, without joy of life is hollow.
> Everything aims at happiness, as God did intend,
> Knowledge is a means; it must lead to an end.
> A know-all king who does not know the art supreme
> Of making his people happy and being himself content
> Is like a rich miser, tied firmly to his gold,
> Piling up a treasure that is hidden and useless [. . .]
> The more a king is learned, the more he loves his own glory.[†]

Voltaire's point was reiterated a few months later, in a letter to Frederick attached to a copy of his *Défense du mondain*. In the *Défense* itself and in Voltaire's letter, cultural and material magnificence—'commonly called *luxury*'— underpinned political greatness, rather than threatening public spiritedness.[‡] Even before receiving these texts, Frederick indicated his broad agreement ('my ethics, Sir, matches yours very well'): the pursuit of happiness and self-love was beneficial when free of excess and abuse.[§]

The significance of this early exchange, from summer 1736 to winter 1737, cannot be overstated. To a large extent, it was a more formative and enduring experience than Voltaire's subsequent sojourn in Potsdam as Frederick's guest, from 1750 to 1753: physical proximity brought about mutual coolness and even hostility. Assuming in the late 1730s the role of unofficial instructor of the crown prince at the latter's enthusiastic invitation, Voltaire actualised the sort of educational relationship imagined by Fénelon between the young prince Telemachus and his tutor, Mentor, while preaching to his own pupil a very different philosophical sermon. Accompanied by an exchange of newly composed writings and a playful discussion of contemporary authors,

---

*Voltaire to Frederick, 16 November 1743 (D2887), *OCV* 93:25.

[†]'Au Prince Royal de Prusse' (September–October 1736), lines 76–89, *OCV* 16:381–82.

[‡]Voltaire to Frederick, January 1737 (D1251), *OCV* 88:190.

[§]Frederick to Voltaire, 16 January 1737 (D1261), *OCV* 88:205. See also Voltaire's programmatic letter of 15 October 1737 about ethics (D1376), ibid., 381–85.

the correspondence with Voltaire introduced Frederick to the main pro-luxury arguments concerning state and self. Instead of useless hoarding (a potential reference to Frederick's father), a ruler should make money circulate through investment and extensive commerce; trade stood at the basis of flourishing economies; and it was founded on the healthy pursuit of one's own glory. King Solomon allegedly showed the way by aligning his own 'joy of life' (material, intellectual, and sexual) with national well-being, rendering his subjects happy through the benign pursuit of self-love. Frederick would later de-emphasise only a single element of Voltaire's vision of modern monarchy: the almost exclusively peaceful means by which the ruler should pursue his goals, due to the moderating effects of culture and international trade (*doux commerce*).

Ample evidence of this broader outlook can be found in Frederick's writings from the *Anti-Machiavel* of 1740 all the way to the 1770s. Emphasising the financial and military advantages of large commercial monarchies over ancient or Renaissance city-states, Frederick made this point by reference to the terms that had attracted Fénelon's most violent censure.

> *Luxurious* living, which is born of *abundance*, and which causes *wealth* to circulate through the bloodstream of a State, makes a great kingdom flourish; it is *luxury* which supports industry, and it is *luxury* that increases the needs of the rich, so as to bind them, through these same needs, to the poor. (*Anti-Machiavel*, p. 47 below; editor's emphases.)

The rapid pace at which the crown prince appropriated Voltaire's pro-luxury stance, endorsing the pursuit of natural human instincts, did not necessarily (or only) reflect youthful intellectual infatuation with a famous interlocutor. Frederick was fully aware of the compatibility between the pro-luxury stance and modern monarchies rather than small republics. As Montesquieu would argue in 1748, large monarchies were best suited to promote and reward the quest for honour and esteem: 'Republics end in luxury; monarchies, in poverty.'*

After Jean-Jacques Rousseau had skilfully revived elements of the Fénelonian ideology in the 1750s, Frederick renewed his public allegiance to the pro-luxury camp in essays on the themes of Rousseau's early *Discourses*. In his *Discourse on the Usefulness of the Sciences and the Arts within a State* (1772), the king responded to Rousseau's thesis that the arts and the sciences were

---

*Montesquieu, *Spirit of the Laws*, 1.VII.4, 100. Cf. Horst Dreitzel, *Monarchiebegriffe in der Fürstengesellschaft*, 2 vols (Cologne: Böhlau, 1991), 2:732–35.

luxuries that had originated in the vanity of their practitioners. For Rousseau, enjoyment of the arts could only come at the expense of political prowess, because they necessarily diverted citizens' attention from the single-minded pursuit of the common good.* For Frederick, however, scientific inventions and cultural achievements were unquestionable markers of national glory. As such, they have always been generated by the benevolent pursuit of self-love and social esteem. If Rousseau had argued that the Roman republic was all but lost once its citizens started studying virtue instead of practising it, Frederick replied that the Romans truly came into their own when Cicero, Virgil, and Livy produced their masterpieces.†

Already in the *Anti-Machiavel*, servitude to the state was not predicated on idealistic self-abnegation. Contrary to the portrayals of ancient republican virtue by Fénelon, Rousseau, and even Montesquieu, Frederick never grounded the ruler's proper action in the elimination of his ambition or self-love. He made a clear distinction between *l'intérêt*—material gains pursued with no regard to the common good, usually rendered in this edition as 'self-interest'—and *amour-propre*, a healthy love of self that was a fundamental element of morality and benevolent kingship. (In this volume, *amour-propre* is translated as 'self-love' if not left in the original French.) The fullest elaboration of the link between self-esteem and the common good, the lesson learned from Voltaire in the late 1730s, can be found in Frederick's *Essay on Self-Love, Considered as a Principle of Morality* (1770). Although it may have also been a reply to works written in the late 1760s, the king's *Essay on Self-Love* certainly addressed some of the main themes in Rousseau's *Discourse on Inequality* (1755). Rousseau had contrasted self-love (*amour-propre*), which he saw as an excessive drive for recognition and domination, with a benign care of the self or basic self-preservation (*amour de soi-même*). Self-love was the corruption of the natural instinct for self-preservation, Rousseau argued, because it depended on the affirmation of one's worth by others.‡

---

*Rousseau, 'Discourse on the Sciences and Arts', in *The Discourses and Other Early Political Writings*, ed. Victor Gourevitch (Cambridge: Cambridge University Press, 1997), 1–28.

†*OFG* 9:195–207. Voltaire made a similar link between cultural and political glory in seventeenth-century France in *Le Siècle de Louis XIV*, published in 1751 during his sojourn in Prussia. See Nicholas Cronk's introduction to Voltaire, *Le Siècle de Louis XIV* (Paris: Gallimard, 2018), 7–29.

‡'*Amour-propre* is only a relative sentiment, factitious, and born in society, which inclines every individual to set greater store by himself than by anyone else, inspires men with all the evils they do one another, and is the genuine source of [social] honour.' (Rousseau, *Discourses*, 218). On German discussions of similar themes, see Friedrich Vollhardt, *Selbstliebe und Geselligkeit: Untersuchungen zum Verhältnis von naturrechtlichem Denken und moraldidaktischer Literatur im 17. und 18. Jahrhundert* (Tübingen: Niemeyer, 2001).

For Frederick, this could not be farther from the truth, because 'the examples that we have of the greatest absence of self-interest [*désintéressement*] stem from the principles of self-love.' (p. 146 below) The key to the proper regulation of self-love was understanding that others' interests could be conceived as one's own, and aligning one's self-love with the common good. This was a form of Stoic *oikeiosis*, the rational extension of self-love to gradually encompass one's family and fellow citizens. Here, in 1770, Frederick went beyond Voltaire, advocating a Hellenistic view of happiness as a perfect peace of mind. The pursuit of such mental tranquillity would teach us not to attach ourselves too strongly to tempestuous passions, which—if we could not satisfy them—might only trouble us. According to the mature Frederick, 'there is no other felicity in this world [. . .] than peace of mind' (p. 143 below). The king was well aware that his 'peace of mind' (*la tranquillité de l'âme*) was highly reminiscent of the equivalent term in ancient Epicurean philosophy, *ataraxia*, and its Stoic version, *apatheia*. This royal resuscitation of pagan ethics was complemented by a ringing condemnation of those who could not reconcile self-love and fellow-feeling. First and foremost among Frederick's targets were the monotheistic faiths, charged with advocating the wrong sort of ethics. The anchoring of morals in a wrathful God or in divine rewards and punishments was a serious obstacle to the proper motivation of virtuous action.

> How many degenerate Christians there were who corrupted the pure morality of antiquity! Greed, ambition, and fanaticism filled the hearts of those who professed the renunciation of the world, and destroyed all that simple virtue had established. History teems with such examples. In summary, with the exception of a few recluses who were both pious and useless to society, the Christians of today are no better than were the Romans of the time of Marius and Sulla; but, of course, I am restricting this parallel purely to the comparison of morals. (*An Essay on Self-love, Considered as a Principle of Morality*, p. 140 below)

> Come now, cowardly Christians, let fears of eternal fire
> Prevent you from indulging your criminal desires,
> Your austere virtue is nothing more than show.
> But we, who renounce all future rewards,
> Who do not believe in your eternal torments,
> Who have never let self-interest [*l'intérêt*] sully our sentiments;
> It is the good of mankind, it is virtue that moves us.
> (*Epistle XVIII: To Keith, on the Vain Terrors of Death and the Fears of Another Life*, p. 115 below)

Frederick's rehabilitation of self-love as an ethical principle was, therefore, meant to offer an alternative to virtue as self-denial, which the king attributed to the motley crew of Christians, ancient republicans, Fénelon, and Jean-Jacques Rousseau.* According to Frederick, self-love could generate on its own all the sociable and patriotic drives usually deemed virtuous. It is disinterestedness in the guise of self-abnegation and withdrawal from this world that Frederick saw as detrimental to both individual health and the social fabric.

The largely Stoic channelling of healthy self-love into the pursuit of the common good linked Frederick's notions of patriotism and state service to his endorsement of luxury and pleasure. The efficacy of monarchical government depended on the king's alignment of his natural love of esteem with the well-being of the state. Once this balance had been achieved, he could openly base his rule on an initial social contract. Peculiar as this synthesis may have been, it did not involve a purely idealistic or 'humanitarian' view of politics, as Meinecke and others have suggested.† The king's function as the first servant of the state was by no means governed by a self-denying principle of pure morality, contrary to reason of state. It was part and parcel of an eighteenth-century conception of modern kingship in commercial society, which Frederick developed early on with Voltaire and retained throughout his career—despite subsequent changes of authorial tone and register. While the *Anti-Machiavel* differs from most of his mature work in its youthful enthusiasm and lack of executive experience, Frederick would keep emphasising distinct elements of his early philosophical ideas on different occasions and for a variety of purposes.

VI. PUBLIC CRITICISM AND ROYAL ACCOUNTABILITY

Yet did this modern synthesis amount to more than an apology for despotism in the name of public happiness? It did differ from earlier philosophical invocations of a social contract in the service of absolutist rule, due to another specific aspect of Frederick's notion of kingship. This was a point on which

---

*Frederick was not aware of Rousseau's later, more positive re-conceptualisation of self-love (which resembled his own) in *Émile, or On Education* (1762). See Avi Lifschitz, 'Adrastus versus Diogenes: Frederick the Great and Jean-Jacques Rousseau on Self-Love', in idem (ed.), *Engaging with Rousseau* (Cambridge: Cambridge University Press, 2016), 17–32.

†Meinecke, *Idee der Staatsräson*, 354–56. Eduard Zeller compared Frederick's sense of obligation to the state to Kant's disinterested moral duty, while recognising an irresolvable tension with the king's endorsement of the pursuit of self-love (Zeller, *Friedrich als Philosoph*, 69–70).

he repeatedly insisted, even if it was not formally codified in contemporary Prussia: the accountability of the monarch to his people.

> He [the Prince] is no more than the first servant of the State, obliged to act with probity, with wisdom, and with total disinterest, as if at any moment he were to be held to account for his administration by his subjects. (*Essay on the Forms of Government and the Duties of Sovereigns*, p. 205 below)

The king's emphasis on accountability was closely linked to his stance on censorship, the freedom of thought, and public debate. It is by allowing a generous measure of free discussion—rather than establishing institutional checks and balances—that the government could become well informed, the better to align its conduct with the citizens' wishes or well-being. According to Frederick, the ruler had no leverage over his subjects' belief systems, which were outside the remit of the original social contract: therefore, he could tolerate unflattering views of his government as long as they were not accompanied by disobedience or disorder.

It is indeed in the public sphere that the king could be held to account, a lesson Frederick learned from unflattering responses to the *Anti-Machiavel* (1740) and the illicit publication of his scurrilous philosophical poems (1760). Shrewdly transforming his initial resentment of the unregulated international print market into a major tenet of his philosophy, the king eventually presented the uncontrollable character of the public sphere as an informal check on his political conduct. Well aware of his unique role as a writing and publishing monarch, Frederick mobilised open criticism to his advantage by construing it as a logical extension of his subjects' freedoms of worship and belief. For Frederick, only public opinion—a significant phenomenon in the second half of the eighteenth century, following a major expansion of readership and the print market—could constrain the utterances and actions of rulers.*

---

*On public opinion and debate in print, especially in Germany, see Jürgen Habermas, *The Structural Transformation of the Public Sphere*, trans. Thomas Burger and Frederick Lawrence (Cambridge, MA: MIT Press, 1989), 71–117; Anthony J. La Vopa, 'Conceiving a Public: Ideas and Society in Eighteenth-Century Europe', *Journal of Modern History* 64.1 (1992), 79–116; Andreas Gestrich, *Absolutismus und Öffentlichkeit. Politische Kommunikation in Deutschland zu Beginn des 18. Jahrhunderts* (Göttingen: Vandenhoek & Ruprecht, 1994); James Van Horn Melton, *The Rise of the Public in Enlightenment Europe* (Cambridge: Cambridge University Press, 2001); T.C.W. Blanning, *The Culture of Power and the Power of Culture: Old Regime Europe 1660–1789* (Oxford: Oxford University Press, 2002), 194–232; Ursula Goldenbaum (ed.), *Appell an das Publikum. Die öffentliche Debatte in der deutschen Aufklärung 1687–1796* (Berlin: Akademie Verlag, 2004).

The link between the limits of absolute power and the norms restricting the public use of language was made explicit in Frederick's *Essay on German Literature* (1780). In this misinformed critique of contemporary German culture, the king floated the possibility of a reform of pronunciation that would render the German language more melodic, in a manner similar to Romance languages. Yet Frederick immediately added that such a reform, even if decreed by the Holy Roman Emperor and all his electors, would have no practical effect. The people, 'who are the arbiters of language in every country, would continue to pronounce words in the usual way'. The obvious reply to the imperial edict would be that the emperor himself was subject to the rules of grammar, controlled as they were by impersonal public use.*

This reference to popular use as defiance of political imposition did not remain an isolated anecdote in a text ostensibly addressing literary issues. In 1784, Immanuel Kant appropriated Frederick's parallel between the constraints imposed upon authors by the public use of language and the political limitations that public opinion placed upon the king. In his essay *What Is Enlightenment?*, Kant's argument for the freedom of thought and expression drew on Frederick's point that rulers must allow their subjects to define freely what was necessary for their own salvation. For this purpose, the philosopher of Königsberg quoted back at Frederick his own phrase from the *Essay on German Literature*, 'Caesar is not above the grammarians'.

> It indeed detracts from his majesty if he interferes in these affairs by subjecting the writings in which his subjects attempt to clarify their religious ideas to governmental supervision. This applies if he does so upon his own exalted opinions—in which case he exposes himself to the reproach: *Caesar non est supra Grammaticos*—but much more so if he demeans his high authority so far as to support the spiritual despotism of a few tyrants within his state against the rest of his subjects.†

It is tempting to read Kant's *What Is Enlightenment?* as a panegyric to Frederick, almost a funerary oration written two years before the king's death. Rhetorically asking whether he lived in an enlightened age, Kant famously replied, 'No, but we do live in an age of *enlightenment*.' As far as the obstacles to man's emergence from self-incurred immaturity were being overcome,

---

*"De la Littérature Allemande; des defauts qu'on peut lui reprocher; quelles en sont les causes, et par quels moyens on peut les corriger', in *OFG* 7:120.

†Kant, *Political Writings*, ed. Hans Reiss, trans. H. B. Nisbet (Cambridge: Cambridge University Press, 1991), 58.

'our age is the age of enlightenment, the century of *Frederick*'.* An idealised image of the Prussian king was held up as a shining model of toleration and free public debate, showing 'how freedom may exist without in the least jeopardising public concord and the unity of the commonwealth'.† Yet the praise Kant showered on Frederick was heavily qualified: it depended upon a certain course of action, announced and enacted by Frederick himself. If the king—or his successors, a more likely target for Kant in 1784—deviated from this path, the 'greatness' with which Kant endowed the king of Prussia would fade away. Kant did in this essay precisely what the king had advocated in his political writings: he publicly held Frederick to account in front of his subjects by referring to his published work, regardless of whether Frederick was sincere at the time of writing.

It was not a coincidence that of Frederick's profuse output, Kant chose to quote from the *Essay on German Literature*. This was a relatively recent example of a work by the ageing king that immediately drew almost universal denunciation from German men of letters, academics, and even Frederick's own civil servants.‡ The year 1784 also witnessed Frederick's unprecedented invitation of public views on a new code which would unify legislation across all Prussian provinces. In the final decade of Frederick's reign, residents of Brandenburg-Prussia took pride in the relative freedom of local discussions of politics, which was not lost on foreigners as well. The British physician John Moore, visiting Berlin in the 1770s, was surprised to find 'ticklish' political issues discussed openly 'with as little ceremony as at a London coffee-house'. This applied even to pamphlets attacking the king's role in the first partition of Poland.§ Count Mirabeau, who was on a diplomatic mission in Berlin in 1786–87, credited the recently deceased king with extensive toleration of religious minorities and public discussion. He was particularly impressed by the cultural and material prosperity of the Jewish community in Berlin, despite the existing legal discrimination against Jewish subjects. Frederick, like Voltaire, was not particularly well disposed towards the Jews; Mirabeau essentially praised the benevolent effects of his passivity in this respect. By letting

*Ibid. (original emphases).

†Ibid., 59.

‡Erich Kästner, *Friedrich der Große und die deutsche Literatur* (Stuttgart: Kohlhammer, 1972); Horst Steinmetz (ed.), *Friedrich II., König von Preußen, und die deutsche Literatur des 18. Jahrhunderts* (Stuttgart: Reclam, 1985). Cf. Tim Blanning, 'Frederick the Great and German Culture', in Robert Oresko, G. C. Gibbs, and H. M. Scott (eds), *Royal and Republican Sovereignty in Early Modern Europe: Essays in Memory of Ragnhild Hatton* (Cambridge: Cambridge University Press, 1997), 527–50.

§Moore, *A View of Society and Manners in France, Switzerland, and Germany*, 2 vols (London: Strahan and Cadell, 1779), vol. 2, 187.

the Jews pursue their cultural and economic self-improvement, the king rendered them 'useful' citizens of Prussia.* As to public debate, if Frederick did not allow complete freedom of expression, especially on military affairs, he at least extended it well beyond its usual confines elsewhere. At the end of the late king's reign, according to the French observer, his policies in this regard had spread beyond Prussia's borders.

> With the exception of a very small number of German states ruled by imbecile tyrants, today one can discuss across Germany, at least in a theoretical manner, any issue of theology, philosophy, economy, and politics; a book, for which one would have been burnt at the stake before the reign of the disseminator of enlightenment, is publicly printed and sold. Great shame is brought on anyone wishing to repress or punish with violence the freedom of thought. [. . .] This is the incommensurable benefit that the rest of Europe, as much as Germany, has reaped from Frederick's example.†

These testimonies and many others override what is arguably the most renowned critique of Frederick in this context.‡ The status of the critic, Gotthold Ephraim Lessing (one of the founding fathers of modern German literature), has lent substantial weight to the assertion that the king's much-touted freedom of expression was merely a cynical ploy. Having left Prussia in 1760 (though still visiting Berlin from time to time), Lessing ridiculed from Hamburg the famous 'Berlin freedom' which amounted 'solely and only to the freedom of publishing as much nonsense against religion as one wishes; an honourable man must be ashamed to make use of such a liberty'. Proper self-expression in political matters would be duly chastised, demonstrating that

---

*'Here is what a single man has brought about, without the help of legislation. One should well reflect how generous goodwill (*libérale bienveillance*) on behalf of the government made this great work happen.': Honoré Gabriel Riquetti, comte de Mirabeau, *De la monarchie prussienne sous Frédéric le Grand*, vol. 5 (London, 1788), 58. Mirabeau's focus on a few Berlin-based families did not capture the serious discrimination still suffered by most Jews in Prussia; see Tobias Schenk, *Wegbereiter der Emanzipation? Studien zur Judenpolitik des "Aufgeklärten Absolutismus" in Preußen (1763–1812)* (Berlin: Duncker & Humblot, 2010).

†Mirabeau, *De la monarchie prussienne*, vol. 5, 348.

‡For an overview of public discussion in Prussia in the early 1780s, see Horst Möller, *Vernunft und Kritik. Deutsche Aufklärung im 17. und 18. Jahrhundert* (Frankfurt am Main: Suhrkamp, 1986), 281–307; James Schmidt's introduction in idem (ed.), *What Is Enlightenment? Eighteenth-Century Answers and Twentieth-Century Questions* (Berkeley, CA: University of California Press, 1996), 1–44; Blanning, *Frederick the Great*, 335–400.

xl   INTRODUCTION

Prussia was 'the most slavish state in Europe'.* Although Lessing's correspondent, the Berlin publisher-author Friedrich Nicolai, was in a much better position to exercise judgement, his reply to Lessing's accusation has rarely
been noted. Despite the existing constraints, in Prussia one could write much
more freely against despotism and for the rights of the people than in Austria,
Nicolai argued, referring to reports about the confiscation of Moses Mendelssohn's *Phädon* in Vienna. (The Berlin-based Mendelssohn, a close friend and
literary collaborator of Lessing and Nicolai, was a major protagonist in Mirabeau's account of the local Jewish community.)† More generally, Nicolai
made a distinction between political and scholarly freedom (*politische/geleh-
rte Freiheit*). In an absolute monarchy, 'where I take no part in government',
there could be no full political freedom: this applied to Prussia and Austria
alike. Under Frederick, however, Nicolai and his fellow authors felt they enjoyed extensive scholarly freedom to write, publish, and debate. By comparison, Nicolai replied to Lessing, their Austrian peers lived in scholarly slavery.†

    Both Nicolai in 1769 and Kant in 1784 referred to an almost complete
scholarly freedom, the intellectual liberty to engage in free discussion of political and religious matters in the public sphere. Indeed, the qualification 'as
a scholar' appears time and again in Kant's *What Is Enlightenment?* where
freedom is concerned. Kant tightly linked 'the public use of reason', which
must remain free at all times, to one's capacity 'as a scholar' in the realm of
written and printed debate, dichotomously separating it from one's professional activities as a clergyman, an officer, or a tax collector. Distilling a theoretical statement from the conditions in Brandenburg-Prussia of his time,
Kant distinguished between the public and private use of reason in a manner that mirrored Nicolai's differentiation, fifteen years earlier, between scholarly and political freedom.

> The *public* use of man's reason must always be free, and it alone can bring
> about enlightenment among men; the *private use* of reason may quite
> often be narrowly restricted, however, without due hindrance to the
> progress of enlightenment. But by the public use of one's own reason I

---

    *Lessing to Nicolai, 25 August 1769, in Lessing, *Sämtliche Schriften*, ed. Karl Lachmann and Franz
Muncker (Leipzig: Göschen, 1904), 17:298.
    †Also in Mirabeau, *Sur Moses Mendelssohn, sur la réforme politique des Juifs, et en particulier sur la
révolution tentée en leur faveur en 1753 dans la Grande Bretagne* (London, 1787).
    †Nicolai to Lessing, 29 August 1769, in *Sämtliche Schriften*, 19:315. Under Frederick II's successor,
Frederick William II, the remit of censorship was significantly extended in an edict of 19 December 1788. In 1794, Nicolai's journal *Allgemeine Deutsche Bibliothek* was proscribed in several Prussian
provinces, although it had been sold in 1792 to a non-Prussian publisher. (Möller, *Vernunft und Kritik*,
283.)

mean the use which anyone may make of it as *a man of learning* [*als Gelehrter*] addressing the entire *reading public*. What I term the private use of reason is that which a person may make of it in a particular *civil* post or office with which he is entrusted.*

Contrary to modern connotations, for Kant the duly restricted private use of reason concerned one's official function within the state, a notion parallel to Nicolai's political freedom. The public use of reason was, on the other hand, the equivalent of Nicolai's scholarly freedom to address an audience of readers in print (in Kant's German phrasing, 'das ganze Publikum der Leserwelt'). Complimentary as Nicolai and Kant were of the king, they both put their finger on the sorely missing elements in Frederick's Prussia: citizens' participation in government through any sort of representative mechanism, and firm institutional guarantees of individual freedom. Indeed, Nicolai and Kant's distinction between the political and the scholarly matched, to a large extent, Frederick's own vision of accountability in the public sphere. This did not primarily concern affairs of state, but rather philosophy in its broader eighteenth-century sense, including political thought, belles-lettres, the sciences, and the fine arts. Despite Frederick's novel re-conceptualisation of kingship, he championed a paternalistic view of the state whereby citizens could make their voice heard in printed form, 'as scholars', hoping that the government would take heed.

It is thus no wonder that, in 1784, members of the Prussian intelligentsia chose to interpret Frederick's unusual public consultation on a new legal code as a first step towards constitutionalism—which, with any luck, would include guarantees of personal freedom. In *What Is Enlightenment?* of the same year, Kant allowed himself a brief foray into legislative matters, noting hopefully that 'the attitude of mind of a head of state who favours freedom in the arts and the sciences extends even further, for he realises there is no danger even to his *legislation* if he allows his subjects to make *public* use of their own reason and to put before the public their thoughts on better ways of drawing up laws, even if this entails forthright criticism of the current legislation'.† This optimism was, alas, short-lived. Even the draft legal code of the mid-1780s balanced traditional privileges with declaratory statements about the popular foundation of the state and the duties of its rulers. Further watered down under Frederick's successor, it would subsequently be published

---

*Kant, *Political Writings*, 55 (original emphases). On similar early modern distinctions between political and personal freedom, see Dreitzel, *Monarchiebegriffe* 1:128–31.

†Kant, *Political Writings*, 59 (original emphases).

as the *Allgemeines Landrecht* of 1794.* Ultimately, Frederick's idiosyncratic tightrope walk proved too unstable to last: in the absence of a written constitution or representative bodies, his reforms depended on his own person. Mirabeau's tribute to Frederick concerning the toleration of the Jews could thus be read, after the king's death, as criticism: 'Here is what a single man has brought about, without the help of legislation'—or beyond the remit of existing legislation.†

It would be a mistake, however, to conclude retrospectively that the institutional shortcomings of eighteenth-century Prussia render Frederick's writings mere theoretical distractions from a highly despotic reality. Even if we chose to discount contemporaries' pride in their relative freedom of thought and expression, in the most extensive religious toleration in Europe, or in a vigorous public sphere, we should still appreciate the genuinely original elements in the king's writings. His works included an unprecedented royal endorsement of social contract theory, an attack on the divine right of rulers, and a new conceptualisation of the monarch's role in a commercial society based on the pursuit of self-love and luxury (rather than a Calvinist or quasi-republican espousal of self-denying kingship). On the ethical and the religious fronts, Frederick's promotion of the freedom of worship and opinion was accompanied by his peculiar endorsement of largely pagan ethics and a sharp critique of the foundations of Christian morality.‡ All these aspects of the king's authorial labour, as represented in this edition, constituted an integral part of his political agency, publicly placing constraints on his conduct. As cynical and self-seeking as Frederick may have been, his philosophical writings matter also because contemporaries used them as a means of holding him to account in the public sphere, 'as scholars'—and Frederick listened sometimes, if not at all times, to such voices. Finally, the pieces collected here might explain why, regardless of his sincerity or the situation on the ground, eighteenth-century readers and subsequent authors regarded Frederick II as a unique, innovative, and potentially dangerous king—as Christoph Meiners portrayed him a few years after his death.

---

*On the transformation of the draft legal code (*Gesetzbuch*) of the mid-1780s into the 1794 *Allgemeines Landrecht*, see Günter Birtsch, 'Reformabsolutismus und Gesetzesstaat: Rechtsauffassung und Justizpolitik Friedrichs des Großen', in Günter Birtsch and Dietmar Willoweit (eds), *Reformabsolutismus und ständische Gesellschaft. Zweihundert Jahre Allgemeines Landrecht* (Berlin: Duncker & Humblot, 1998), 47–62; Thomas Finkenauer, 'Vom Allgemeinen Gesetzbuch zum Allgemeinen Landrecht—preußische Gesetzgebung in der Krise', *Zeitschrift der Savigny-Stiftung für Rechtsgeschichte* (Germanistische Abteilung) 113 (1996), 40–216.

†See the first note in p. xxxix above.

‡This critique was more attenuated in his reviews of d'Holbach's works in 1770.

PRINCIPAL EVENTS AND PUBLICATIONS

Note: the items in bold indicate written works.

1712 Birth of Frederick of Brandenburg-Prussia on 24 January, son of Crown Prince Frederick William and his wife, Sophie Dorothea of Hanover.

1713 Frederick's father is crowned as King Frederick William I in Prussia, Frederick becomes crown prince. The Peace of Utrecht concludes the War of the Spanish Succession.

1714 Frederick's grandfather, Elector Georg Ludwig of Hanover, accedes to the British throne as George I.

Bernard Mandeville, *The Fable of the Bees*.

1715 Death of Louis XIV, king of France. His reign provided the theme for Voltaire's *Le Siècle de Louis XIV* (1751), conflating cultural flourishing with political greatness.

1727 Frederick's uncle is crowned George II of Great Britain and Ireland.

1728 **Voltaire, *Henriade*.**

1730 Frederick's failed attempt to escape to England. Detention in Küstrin; execution of the crown prince's friend and accomplice, Hans Hermann von Katte.

1732 Frederick released from Küstrin; becomes regiment commander in Ruppin and Nauen.

1733 Frederick's marriage to Elisabeth Christine of Braunschweig-Wolfenbüttel-Bevern.

1733 **Alexander Pope, *Essay on Man*.**

1734 **Montesquieu, *Considerations on the Greatness and Decadence of the Romans* (*Considérations sur les causes de la grandeur des Romains et de leur décadence*).**

Voltaire, *Lettres philosophiques*.

Jean-François Melon, *Essai politique sur le commerce*.

1736 Frederick settles in Rheinsberg Castle in the north of Brandenburg; launches his correspondence with Voltaire.

Voltaire, *Le Mondain*.

1737 **Voltaire, *Défense du mondain*.**

1739 Exchange with Voltaire on *Anti-Machiavel*.

1740 Death of Frederick William I; the crown prince becomes King Frederick II in Prussia on 31 May 1740.

Maria Theresa inherits the Austrian crown; War of the Austrian Succession (until 1748).

First Silesian War (until 1742).

Frederick II, *Anti-Machiavel*.

1742 **Frederick II, *Memoirs for the History of the House of Brandenburg* (*Mémoires pour servir à l'Histoire de la Maison de Brandebourg*).**

1744 Second Silesian War (until 1745).

1747 Inauguration of Sans-Souci Palace.

1748 **Montesquieu, *On the Spirit of the Laws* (*De l'esprit des lois*)**

1749 **Frederick II, *Dissertation on the Reasons for Establishing or Repealing Laws* (*Dissertation sur les raisons d'établir ou d'abroger les lois*).**

1750 Voltaire in Potsdam (until 1753).

Jean-Jacques Rousseau, *Discourse on the Sciences and the Arts* (*Discours sur les sciences et les arts*).

1751 **Voltaire, *The Century of Louis XIV* (*Le Siècle de Louis XIV*).**

First volume of the French *Encyclopédie*.

1755 **Jean-Jacques Rousseau, *Discourse on the Origin and Foundations of Inequality among Men* (*Discours sur l'origine et les fondements de l'inégalité parmi les hommes*).**

1756 Seven Years' War (Third Silesian War, until 1763).

Voltaire's universal history, *Essai sur les mœurs*.

1759 **Voltaire, *Candide*.**

1760 George II of Great Britain dies; succeeded by George III.

Illicit publication in France of Frederick's *Œuvres du philosophe de Sans-Souci*; Frederick publishes a modified, authorised version under the title *Poësies diverses*.

1762 Elisabeth of Russia dies (January), succeeded by Peter III who concludes a peace treaty with Prussia. Peter III assassinated (July), succeeded by Catherine II.

Frederick grants Rousseau asylum in Prussian-governed Neuchâtel.

Jean-Jacques Rousseau, *Émile* **and** *On the Social Contract* **(***Du contrat social***).**

1763 Peace of Hubertusburg concludes the Seven Years' War in central Europe.

D'Alembert visits Berlin and Potsdam.

Voltaire, *Treatise on Tolerance* **(***Traité sur la tolérance***).**

1764 **Cesare Beccaria,** *On Crimes and Punishments* **(***Dei delitti e delle pene***).**

1765 Death of Holy Roman Emperor Francis I, succeeded by Joseph II who co-rules with his mother Maria Theresa.

1767 **Moses Mendelssohn,** *Phaedo, or on the Immortality of the Soul* **(***Phädon, oder Über die Unsterblichkeit der Seele***).**

1770 **Frederick II,** *Essay on Self-Love, Considered as a Principle of Morality* **(***Essai sur l'amour-propre envisagé comme principe de morale***);** *Examination of the* **Essay on Prejudice (***Examen de l'***Essai sur les préjugés).**

1772 The first partition of Poland between Russia, Austria, and Prussia. West Prussia annexed; Frederick assumes the title of King of Prussia.

1774 Louis XV of France dies, succeeded by Louis XVI.

1775 American Revolutionary War (until 1783).

1776 American declaration of independence.

Adam Smith, *An Inquiry into the Nature and Causes of the Wealth of Nations.*

1778 War of the Bavarian Succession (until 1779). Deaths of Voltaire and of Rousseau.

1780 Maria Theresa dies; Joseph II sole ruler in Austria.

1781 **Immanuel Kant,** *Critique of Pure Reason* **(***Kritik der reinen Vernunft***).**

1784 Launch of public discussion in Prussia of a draft law code.

Immanuel Kant, *What Is Enlightenment?* **(***Was ist Aufklärung?***).**

1785 Formation of the League of Princes (Fürstenbund) against Austria, under Frederick's leadership.

1786 Death of Frederick II on 17 August; succeeded by Frederick William II.

Mirabeau in Berlin and Potsdam.

NOTE ON THE TEXTS

The notes to each translated text are prefaced by a brief history of its publication or, in the case that it remained unpublished, the context of its composition and circulation. The translation follows the version of the texts in the magisterial nineteenth-century edition of Frederick's works, *Œuvres de Frédéric le Grand*, ed. Johann David Erdmann Preuß, 30 vols (Berlin: Decker, 1846–56), which is based on a careful comparison of the published works with manuscripts still extant in the mid-nineteenth century. Preuß's edition (henceforth *OFG*, followed by volume and page number) is freely accessible online at http://friedrich.uni-trier.de/

The only exception is the *Dialogue of the Dead between Madame de Pompadour and the Virgin Mary*, considered by Preuß irredeemably lost (*OFG* 14:1), but rediscovered in the late 1990s. It is translated from the recovered text in Frederick II, *Totengespräch zwischen Madame de Pompadour und der Jungfrau Maria*, ed. Gerhard Knoll (Berlin: Berlin Verlag, 2000).

The references to Frederick's correspondence with Voltaire concerning some of the texts are usually to *Œuvres complètes de Voltaire*, ed. Theodore Besterman, Nicholas Cronk, et al. (Geneva and Oxford: Voltaire Foundation, 1968–2020; henceforth *OCV*).

Frederick the Great's
Philosophical Writings

1

Dissertation on the Innocence
of Errors of the Mind

I consider myself obliged, Monsieur, to justify to you my present inactivity
and to give you some account of the use I am making of my time. You know
my interest in, and indeed my passion for, philosophy, which attends, faithfully, my every step. A number of my friends, who know this to be my over-
riding predilection—and either to humour me, or because they themselves
take pleasure in it too—often engage me in speculative talk on questions of
physics, metaphysics, or ethics. Our conversations are usually of little interest,
since they revisit well-known topics that are either commonplace or unworthy of the enlightened attention of true scholars. The conversation I had yesterday evening with Philante, however, appeared to me to be worthier of
note: it concerned a subject that both interests and divides almost the whole
of the human race. I thought at once of you. It seemed to me that I owed you
this conversation. On my return from my walk with him, I went straight up
to my room; and, with my thoughts still fresh and my mind still full of our
own, earlier, discussion, I recorded it on paper, as faithfully as I was able. I beg
you, Monsieur, to tell me what you think of it, and if I am fortunate enough
to have earned it, the sincerity of your response will be the reward for my efforts. I will, if you do not find my work displeasing, be amply rewarded.

Never was weather lovelier than yesterday: the sun blazed more beautifully
than usual, the sky was so tranquil that no trace of a cloud, however distant,
was to be seen. I had spent the whole morning studying, after which, to re-
fresh my ideas a little, I joined Philante for a walk.[1] We spent quite some time
agreeing as to the great good fortune enjoyed by the human race, to which,
however, the majority of them are quite oblivious, insensible as they are to the
pleasures of beautiful sunshine and air that is tranquil and pure. Having
passed in this way from one consideration to another, we noticed, at last, that
our conversation had prolonged, infinitely, our walk, and that it was imperative we curtail it if we were to reach home before darkness fell. Philante, who
noticed this first, blamed me; I defended myself by saying that his conversation

always seemed to me so agreeable that I took no account of time when I found myself in his company, and that I had believed there would be time enough to think of returning home when we saw the sun go down.

'What? See the sun go down?' he replied. 'Are you a Copernican? And are you going to adopt popular forms of expression, not to mention Tycho Brahe's errors?'[2]

'Wait a moment!' I retorted, 'You're going a bit too fast. For a start, this is a conversation between friends, not a philosophical debate, and if I have sinned by misrepresenting Copernicus, my error must be forgiven me as readily as was Joshua's, who stops the sun in mid-course, and who, being divinely inspired, must certainly have been conversant with the secrets of nature.[3] At that particular moment, moreover, Joshua was speaking as ordinary mortals do, whereas I am talking to an informed and enlightened man, who, for his part, understands me, in one way or another, quite as well as I do him. But since you are attacking Tycho Brahe, please allow me, just for a moment, to attack you in return.

'It seems to me that your enthusiasm for Copernicus is very marked indeed: for a start, you call down curses upon all those who find themselves thinking differently from him. I should like to think that he is right; but can we be quite sure of this? What guarantee do you have? Has nature, has its author, persuaded you of the infallibility of Copernicus? As for me, all I see is a system, an arrangement, in other words, of what Copernicus observed, so adjusted as to match the workings of nature.'

'Whereas I,' replied Philante warmly, 'what I see there is truth.'

'Truth? And what do you mean by truth?'

'I mean', he said, 'actual evidence, as it is provided by things and facts.'

'And what is it to know the truth?' I continued.

'To know the truth', he replied, 'is to have succeeded in establishing an exact correlation between our ideas and things that really do exist or that have existed, between facts past or present, and the ideas we have of them.'

'In that case, my dear Philante,' I said, 'we can hardly flatter ourselves we know any truths at all, since they are, almost all of them, in doubt; and, according to the definition you yourself have just offered me, there are only, at the very most, two or three truths that are indisputable. The evidence of our senses, which is the nearest thing we have to certainty, is not without its own uncertainties. Our eyes deceive us when they present to us, from a distance, a tower that is round, but which we find, as we draw near it, to be square. We sometimes think we hear sounds that are, in fact, a mere product of our imagination, and which depend on nothing more than some faint impression made upon our ears. The sense of smell is no less deceptive than are the other senses: we sometimes imagine, while walking in the woods and the fields, that we catch the scent of flowers, when, on the contrary, there are none. And even now, while I am talking to you, I notice, from some blood that is oozing from my hand, that a midge has stung me; the fervour engendered by our conversation has made me oblivious to pain, the sense of touch has let me down. If, then, the least unreliable of our faculties proves to be so powerfully so, how can you speak with such certainty of those abstract matters with which philosophy is concerned?'

'Because', retorted Philante, 'they are plain for all to see; because Copernicus's system is confirmed by experience: the movements of the planets are charted there with admirable precision, eclipses are calculated with wonderful accuracy; in other words, it is a system that explains, perfectly, the mysteries of nature.'

'But what would you say,' I replied, 'if I showed you a system that is clearly very different from yours, and which, according to a principle that is obviously false, explains the same miraculous events as does that of Copernicus?'

'By which I assume you mean the mistakes made by the Malabars', said Philante.

'It was of their mountain, indeed, that I was going to speak to you. But, however many inaccuracies it involves, this system, my dear Philante, illustrates perfectly the astronomical workings of nature; and it is astonishing that, on the basis of a belief as absurd as is that of supposing the sun to be wholly occupied in encircling a large mountain situated within the lands of these barbarians, their astronomers were able to predict so accurately the same revolutions and the same eclipses as your Copernicus.[4] The mistake made by the Malabars is crude, that made by Copernicus is perhaps less obvious. But perhaps we will see, one day, a new philosopher, full of self-importance and puffed up with arrogance over some wholly insignificant discovery he claims to be the basis of a new system, dismiss the Copernicans and the Newtonians as a mere swarm of miserable little creatures who do not even deserve to have their errors corrected.'

'It's quite true', said Philante, 'that new philosophers have always had the right to supplant their forebears. Descartes demolished the sainted schoolmen and was, in turn, demolished by Newton, who himself only awaits the appearance of some worthy successor to suffer the same fate.

'Might it not be the case', I continued, 'that all we need in order to establish a new system is self-love? From this elevated sense of his own merit there emerges, in the philosopher, a conviction as to his own infallibility, out of which he forges his system. He starts by believing blindly in whatever it is he wishes to prove; he seeks reasons that will give it an air of plausibility, and from this there emerges an inexhaustible source of error. He ought, on the contrary, on the basis of various observations he has made, to begin by retracing his steps from one consequence to the next, and then to observe, quite simply, where these would lead, and what the result would be. One would be less taken in by such a process and, through following in the timid footsteps of circumspection, would learn, wisely, how to doubt.'

'Your philosophers would have to be angels,' objected Philante vehemently, 'for where would one find a man without prejudice and perfectly impartial?'

'In other words,' I replied, 'to be in error is our lot in life.'

'God forbid!' retorted my friend, 'We are made for truth.'

'If you have time and patience enough to listen to me,' I replied, 'I will easily persuade you of the contrary. And, since we are very close to home now, let us sit down on this bench, for I fear that our walk has tired you.'

Philante, who is not a good walker, and who had made progress rather as a result of absent-mindedness and habit than from any deliberate intention, was delighted to sit down. We settled ourselves calmly and quietly, and I continued, more or less as follows.

'I have told you, Philante, that to be in error is our lot in life; I must now persuade you of this. The error that afflicts us has more than one source. It seems that we were not destined by the Creator to possess much learning, nor to advance very far into the realms of knowledge; he has placed the truths we seek in chasms so deep that our feeble minds cannot reach them, and has surrounded them with a dense thicket of thorns. The road to truth is bordered with precipices on every side; it is impossible to know, if one is to avoid such dangers, which path to follow; and if one is fortunate enough to have passed beyond all of this in safety, one finds further along one's way a labyrinth, so sinuous and convoluted that even Ariadne's magic thread would be of no assistance there, and from which there is no escape.[5] Some chase after a ghost, an impostor, who deceives them with false promises, and offers them, as valid currency, money that is counterfeit; they lose their way, like travellers who, as night falls, follow, lured on by their light, mere will-o'-the-wisps. Others guess at these secret truths; they believe they have stripped nature of her veil, they conjecture and they suppose; and this is, it must be conceded, an area in which the philosophers have made great advances. But these truths are located so far from our sight that they become doubtful, and acquire, through their very distance from us, an equivocal air. There is scarcely one that has not been disputed. This is because there is not one of them that is not two-faced: looked at from one side, such a truth appears incontestable; looked at from the other, it is falsehood itself. Summon up every argument for and against that your reason offers you, weigh them all up carefully, consider, reflect; you will still not be able to reach a decision, so certain it is that the only thing that lends substance to opinions arrived at by men is the number of probabilities involved. If some probability, whether for or against, escapes their notice, they choose the wrong course of action, and since the human imagination can never offer them, with equal force, both the arguments for and those against, they always decide out of weakness, and are blind to the truth.

'Let us suppose that a town is situated on a plain, that this town is quite extensive, and that it consists of a single street; let us suppose, too, that a traveller who has never heard of this town arrives there, and from such a direction that all that he notices, initially, is its great length: seeing it, as he does, from one angle only, he will judge it to be immense, a judgement that is completely false, because, as we have seen, it consists of only one street. The same holds good for truths: if we consider them piecemeal and leave aside the ensemble they form, we will reach a sound judgement as to this or that particular part, but will be in considerable error as to the whole. If we are to arrive at some knowledge of an important truth, we must first have assembled a good supply of simple truths that lead us to, or serve as stepping stones that take us towards, the composite truth we seek: it is this, once again, that evades us. It is not of mere conjecture that I speak, but of evident, certain, and irrevocable truths. Looking at things from a philosophical point of view, we know nothing at all; we can only guess at certain truths, we form the vaguest notion of them; and we adopt a particular tone of voice when speaking of or using certain terms we call scientific, terms whose resonance pleases our ears, and which our minds believe they understand. But, taken all in all, they offer the imagination only confused and convoluted ideas, so that our philosophy is reduced to a habit we have of employing expressions that are obscure, terms we scarcely understand, and to a profound meditation as to effects whose causes remain perfectly unknown to us and completely hidden. The pitiable totality of these musings is dignified with a grand title, that of most excellent philosophy, which its author presents to the world, with all the arrogance of a charlatan, as a discovery of the greatest rarity and of the greatest value to humankind. Should curiosity prompt you to inform yourself further as to this discovery, you would expect to find things of great import. What injustice that you should even entertain such a hope! No, this discovery, so rare, so precious, amounts to nothing more than the invention of a new word, more barbarous even than any that has so far appeared; this new word, according to our charlatan, explains marvellously some as yet undiscovered truth, and reveals it to be more brilliant than daylight itself. Observe, examine, divest his idea of the trappings of the terms that cover it, and you will find nothing there: only, as before, darkness, only shadows. It is mere ornament, which disappears, and which destroys, along with itself, its illusory, its wholly false, glamour.

'True knowledge of the truth must be quite different from what I have just described to you. It ought to be possible to identify the causes of everything; it ought to be possible, by returning to first principles, to know them and to discover their essence. This is what the philosopher-poet Lucretius understood so well, and it is what led him to say, "Felix, qui potuit rerum cognoscere causas!"[6] But the number of first principles of existing entities and the resources of nature are either too immense or too small to be observed by and known to philosophers. From this there follow disputes about atoms, about the infinite divisibility of matter, about plenitude or the void, about movement, about the manner in which the world is governed: so very many and such very thorny questions, which we will never resolve.[7] It would appear that a man's life is his own; it seems to me that I am master of my own person, that I can sound my own depths, that I know myself. But I do not know myself; it has not yet been decided if I am a machine, an automaton set in motion by the Creator's hands, or if I am a free being, independent of this Creator. I sense that I possess the ability to move, but I don't know what movement is, whether it is an accident or whether it is a substance. One learned scholar insists it is an accident, another swears it is a substance; they argue, courtiers laugh at them, the idols of the earth despise them, and the people ignore them, them and the subject of their quarrels. Would you not agree that to employ your reason in matters so incomprehensible and so abstract is to divert it from the proper sphere of its activity? It seems to me that the human mind is not capable of such vast knowledge. We are like men who, finding themselves drifting slowly along a coast, imagine that it is the mainland that is moving, and do not suspect that it is they themselves who are moving. Matters are, however, quite the opposite of what they believe to be the case: the shore is immobile, and it is they who, driven by the wind, are in motion. Our self-love will always prevail; we attach to everything we cannot understand the epithet of obscure, and everything becomes unintelligible to us, once it is beyond our grasp. It is nevertheless this, it is the way our minds work, that renders us incapable of acquiring any great knowledge.

'There are eternal truths, that is beyond dispute. But, if we were truly to understand these truths, if we were to know them in every detail, we would need a million times more memory than mankind possesses; we would need to be able to devote ourselves entirely to the study of a single truth. This would require a life the length of Methuselah's, and even longer, a life of speculation, rich in experience; it would require, in short, an attentiveness that is beyond our capabilities. Consider, in view of all this, if it was the Creator's intention to fashion us as people possessed of intelligence and skill, given, in particular, the obstacles to this that also seem to emanate from his will; while experience teaches us that we possess little ability, little application, that our genius is not sufficiently transcendent to penetrate the first, the eternal truths, and that our memory is neither capacious nor reliable enough to be burdened with all the knowledge required for this noble and exacting study.

'There is another obstacle, too, that prevents us from arriving at a full knowledge of the truth, one with which men themselves have encumbered the path that leads there, as though this path were in itself too easy. This obstacle derives from the prejudices instilled by education. The greater part of mankind adheres to principles that are clearly false: their physics is faulty, their metaphysics worthless, while their morality derives from a sordid self-interest, and from a boundless attachment to worldly things. But there is one great virtue that they do have, and that is the wisdom of foresight, which makes them look to the future, and thus to provide, well in advance, for the well-being of their family. As you can imagine, the logic employed by this kind of person is consistent with the rest of their philosophy, and therefore pitiable. The art of reasoning resides, for them, in being the only one to have a voice, in deciding everything themselves, and in permitting no reply. These small-time family legislators busy themselves, from the start, with ideas that they wish to inculcate into their progeny; father, mother, all the relatives, strive to perpetuate their own misapprehensions: no sooner are the children out of the cradle than their elders are at pains to give them some notion of the ghostly monk and the werewolf.[8] These priceless pieces of knowledge are usually followed by others that are equally important: schooling plays its part here, too; you must work your way through the visions of Plato in order to arrive at those of Aristotle, while with a single leap and a bound you are initiated into the mysteries of the vortex. You leave school, your memory laden with words, your mind stuffed with superstition and filled with respect for a great deal of ancient nonsense. The age of reason arrives, at which point either you shake off the yoke of error, or you even surpass your parents. If they were one-eyed, you become blind; if they believed certain things because they imagined they believed them, you will believe them out of obstinacy. In due course, the example of so many people, all of whom adhere to a particular opinion, is enough to carry you along with them; their approbation lends them authority in your eyes; their very number adds weight to this; so that popular error makes converts, and prevails. Over the course of time, these errors become ineradicable, as deeply rooted as those of a young sapling, whose stem is bent double by the force of the wind, but which, in the fullness of time, raises its lofty head to the clouds above and presents to the woodman's axe an unassailable trunk. "Quite so!" you will reply, "My father always said as much, as I have myself for some sixty, no, seventy years now; why on earth would you suppose that I begin, after all this time, to argue differently? As for the suggestion that I become a schoolboy again and work as your apprentice, I would rather creep along, earth-bound, as we mortals have always done, than become a second Icarus and rise with you into the air.[9] Don't forget his fall: such are the wages of new-fangled ideas and such is the punishment that awaits you. Obstinacy is often accompanied by prejudice, while a certain barbarousness, also known as false zeal, never fails to broadcast, far and wide, its tyrannical maxims."'

Such are the effects that attend the prejudices acquired in childhood; they take deeper root then, thanks to the pliability of the brain at this tender age. The earliest impressions are the most lasting and the most vivid, and all subsequent reasoning, however powerful, can only appear cold in comparison.

'So you see, my dear Philante, that to be in error is the lot of mankind. You no doubt understand, after all that I have just explained to you, that one would have to be very full of oneself and of one's own opinions if one were to believe oneself above error, and very secure in one's own saddle if one were to dare to attempt to unseat others.'

'I begin to see, to my great astonishment,' replied Philante, 'that human error cannot, for the most part, be overcome by those who are infected with it. I have listened to you attentively and with pleasure, and have taken careful note, unless I am much mistaken, of the causes of error that you have pointed out to me. These are, so you said, the great distance beyond our sight where truth resides, our lack of knowledge, the weakness and inadequacy of our minds, and the prejudices instilled by education.'

'Spoken to perfection, Philante, you have a truly divine memory, and if God and nature deigned to form a mortal capable of embracing their sublime verities, that mortal would assuredly be you, who combine with this vast memory a lively mind and a sound judgement.'

'No more compliments, thank you,' replied Philante. 'I prefer philosophical argument to praise. This is not the moment to indulge in panegyrics, but rather, on behalf of all scholars, to make a proper public apology and reparation for our pride and a confession of our ignorance.'

'I will second you with the greatest pleasure, Philante, when we are called upon to acknowledge our profound and crass ignorance. I confess to this most willingly: I would even go so far as to embrace Pyrrhonism, for it seems to me that one does well to have no more than an equivocal faith in what we call the truths of experience. You've made a good start, Philante. Scepticism does you no disfavour. Pyrrho, at the Lyceum, would not have spoken differently from you.[10]

'I have to confess to you, for my part,' I continued, 'that I am something of an adherent of the Academy;[11] I consider things from every angle, I remain undecided and in doubt, which is the only way to guard oneself against error. Such scepticism does not help me to advance by gigantic—by truly Homeric— steps towards the truth I seek; but it saves me from the pitfalls of prejudice.'

'And why are you so afraid of error,' retorted Philante, 'you, who are its most eloquent apologist?'

'Alas!' I said to him, 'There exists error that is of such sweetness that one prefers it to truth itself; these errors fill you with pleasing thoughts, they shower you with good things that you do not possess, that you will never enjoy, they sustain you in the midst of adversity and, at the point of death itself, when you are about to lose all that you have and life itself, they offer you still, as though these were within your grasp, blessings greater than those you are losing, and torrents of pleasures whose joys and delights are capable of sweetening even death itself, and making it lovable, if such a thing were possible. I remember, as to this, a story I was told about a madman; perhaps it will be of some compensation to you for my long and didactic discourse.'

'My silence', Philante replied, 'is no doubt in itself sufficient indication that I am listening to you with pleasure, and that I am curious to hear your story.'

'I will do as you wish, Philante, on condition that you will not regret having caused me to prattle.

'There was once, in a mental asylum in Paris, a madman—a man of very good birth, who caused his whole family the utmost distress because of the derangement that afflicted his brain. He was perfectly sensible on every subject except that of his own beatitude: in which happy state—surrounded by hosts of cherubim, seraphim and archangels, with whose immortal souls he sang all day long in concert—he was blessed with beatific visions, paradise was his dwelling-place, the angels his companions, and manna from heaven his only food. This most contented of lunatics continued to enjoy perfect happiness in the asylum, until, most unfortunately for him, a doctor or surgeon came to pay a pastoral visit to the insane. This doctor suggested to the family that he cure this blessed man. As you can well imagine, he was engaged at once, and no expense was spared that would enable him to surpass himself, and, indeed, to perform miracles. In the end, to cut a long story short, either through bleeding or by means of other remedies, he succeeded in restoring the madman to a state of perfect good sense. He, however, amazed at finding himself no longer in heaven, but in an apartment not unlike a dungeon, and surrounded by people bearing no resemblance at all to angels, took against, and indeed completely lost his temper with the doctor. "I was happy in heaven," he said, "and you had no right to make me leave it; I hope that, for your pains, you find yourself condemned to inhabit, really and truly, the land of the damned in hell."

'From which you can see, Philante, that there are such things as auspicious errors; and I could easily persuade you that they are harmless.'

'I should like that very much,' said Philante, 'and, besides which, we are dining late this evening, so that we have, at our disposal, another three hours at least.'

'I won't need quite as long as that', I replied, 'to say all that I have to tell you; I will tax my own time rather than your patience.

'You agreed, a moment ago, that error is involuntary in those who are infected by it; they believe themselves to be in possession of the truth, and they are mistaken. They may be pardoned for this, since, according to what they themselves believe, they are certain about the truth; they themselves are of good faith; it is appearances that are against them; they take the shadow for the substance. Consider again, if you would, that the motive of those who fall into error is laudable: they seek the truth, they lose their way, and if they fail to find the truth, it was not their wish to do so: they lacked guides, or, which is worse, had bad guides. They sought the path that leads to truth, but their powers were insufficient for them to arrive there. Could one blame a man who drowns while fording an immensely wide river that he would not have had the strength to cross? Only someone without a vestige of humanity would not mourn his sad fate; rather, we should pity a man so full of courage, capable of a plan so generous and so bold, for not having received sufficient help from nature; his boldness would seem worthy of a happier fate, and his ashes would be watered with tears. Every thinking person must make an effort to know the truth; such efforts are worthy of us, even when they surpass our powers. It is a great enough misfortune for us that these truths are impenetrable. We must not exacerbate this by pouring scorn on those who are shipwrecked while discovering this new world: they are noble Argonauts,[12] who expose themselves to danger for the greater safety of their compatriots, while the lot of those who wander in lands of the imagination is certainly very hard. The air in these countries does not suit us, we do not speak the language of the inhabitants, and we do not know how to cross the quicksands we find there.

'Believe me when I say, Philante, that we must be tolerant of error: it is a subtle poison, one that slips into our hearts without us noticing. I, who am talking to you, am not sure of being free of it. Let us never fall prey to the ridiculous pride of those infallible scholars whose every word must be taken as an oracle. Let us be full of indulgence for the most palpable errors, and let us show tolerance for the opinions of those with whom we live in society. Why would we disrupt the sweetness of the ties that unite us, simply for the sake of an opinion about which we ourselves lack conviction? Let us not set ourselves up as champions of an unknown truth, and let us leave to the imagination of each person the freedom to construct the story of his own romance. The days of legendary heroes, of miracles and chivalrous exploits are over. Don Quixote is still admired in the pages of Miguel de Cervantes; but as to the Pharamonds, Rolands, Amadis, Gandalins: they would now attract the ridicule of all reasonable people, while the knights who would like to follow in their footsteps would suffer the same fate.[13]

'Reflect again that, if we were to banish error from the universe, we would need to exterminate the whole of the human race. Believe me, I continued, it is not our way of thinking on speculative matters that could influence the happiness of society, but, rather, the way in which we act that does so. By all means be an advocate of Tycho Brahe's system, or of that of the Malabars; I will gladly forgive you, as long as you retain your humanity. But, were you to be the most orthodox of all doctors, if your character were cruel, harsh, and barbaric, I would always detest you.'

'I am in entire agreement with your views on this matter,' Philante replied.

As he spoke, we heard, quite close by, a muffled noise, like that of someone muttering abusive words. We turned round and were astonished to see, by the light of the moon, our chaplain, not two steps distant from us, and who had probably heard the greater part of our conversation.

'Ah! It's you, Father,' I said. 'How comes it that we encounter you so late?'

'Today is Saturday,' he replied. 'I came here in order to compose my sermon for tomorrow, when I heard something of what you were saying, which led me to listen to the rest. Would to heaven, and for the good of my soul, that I had heard nothing! You have aroused righteous anger in me, you have scandalised my believer's ears, sacred sanctuaries, as these are, of our ineffable truths. Non-believers, profane, as you are, who prefer—alas for bad Christians!—humanity, charity, and humility, to the power of faith and to the sanctity of our belief. As for you, you will be cursed and thrown into the cauldrons of boiling oil that are ready and waiting for you and your kind, that is, for the damned.'

'Oh! but if you please, Father,' I replied, 'we did not so much as touch on matters of religion just now; we were concerned merely with philosophical topics that are of no particular importance; and, unless you were to promote Tycho Brahe and Copernicus to the ranks of the Fathers of the Church, I do not see that you have any grounds for complaint.'

'Away with you; that's quite enough for now,' he said. 'I'll be preaching to you tomorrow, and God knows with how glad a heart I'll be sending you to the devil.'

We were about to reply, but he left us abruptly, continuing all the while to mutter something under his breath that we could not quite make out. I thought it was a saintly sigh of regret, but Philante fancied he had heard various eloquent curses drawn from one of the Psalms of David.[14]

We came away from this encounter, mortified by what had happened, and troubled as to what we should do now. It seemed to me that I had said nothing that need shock anyone, and that what I had advanced on behalf of human error was in conformity with pure reason, and, in consequence, with the principles of our most sacred religion, which commands us to suffer one another's shortcomings, and not to shock or upset the weak. I felt at ease as to my own feelings; the only thing that gave me cause for anxiety was the manner of thinking among the deeply devout. One knows only too well how far they will go when carried away, and how capable they are of being prejudiced against innocence itself, especially when they take it upon themselves to spread alarm against those to whom they have taken a dislike. Philante reassured me as well as he could, and we retired after supper, both of us reflecting, I think, on the subject of our conversation and on our unfortunate encounter with the priest. I went straight up to my room, and spent the better part of the night relating to you all that I was able to remember of our conversation.

2

Anti-Machiavel, or a Study of Machiavelli's *The Prince*

FOREWORD

Machiavelli's *The Prince* is to morality what Spinoza's work is to faith: Spinoza undermined the very foundations of faith, and attempted nothing less than the demolition of the entire edifice of religion; Machiavelli corrupted politics, and set out to destroy the teachings of sound morality. The errors of the former were nothing more than errors of speculation; those of the latter concerned practical matters. It so happened, nevertheless, that the theologians sounded the alarm, and called for arms to be taken up against Spinoza, that his work was formally refuted, and that the Divinity was upheld against his attacks; whereas Machiavelli was merely harassed by a few moralists, and, in spite of them and of his pernicious morality, has maintained his reputation in political science up until our own times.

I venture to defend humanity against this monster, whose aim it is to destroy it; I venture to confront sophism and crime with reason and justice; and I have dared to present my reflections on Machiavelli's *The Prince*, chapter by chapter, so that the poison is followed, immediately, by the antidote.

I have always regarded Machiavelli's *The Prince* as one of the most dangerous works to have been disseminated throughout the world: it is a book that must, inevitably, fall into the hands of princes and of those who have some interest in politics; it is only too easy for an ambitious young man, whose heart and judgement are not as yet sufficiently formed for him to distinguish good from evil, to be corrupted by maxims that encourage his passions.

But if it is pernicious to corrupt the innocence of an individual who has little influence over public affairs, it is all the more so to pervert princes whose duty it is to govern people, to administer justice, and to offer an example of justice to their subjects; and to offer, through their goodness, their magnanimity, and their mercy, a living image of the Divinity.

The floods that ravage whole countries, the thunder and lightning that reduce entire towns to cinders, the deadly plague that ruins whole provinces, none of these are as destructive of the world as are the vicious morality and the uncontrolled passions of kings. Heaven-sent scourges last only a short time; their ravages are confined to certain countries, and the damage they cause, although grievous, is, in time, made good; but the crimes of kings impose suffering, over many years, upon whole nations.

Just as kings have the power, when they so choose, to do good, so may they, when they so decide, do evil. And how wretched is the lot of their people when they have everything to fear from the abuse of a sovereign power, when their goods are prey to the greed of the prince, their freedom to his whim, their peace of mind to his ambition, their safety to his treachery, and their life to his cruelty! Such is the tragic picture of a state ruled by a prince whose character Machiavelli wants to form.

I must not end this foreword without addressing a few words to people who believe that Machiavelli was describing what princes do, rather than what they ought to do: a view which, because it is satirical, has pleased many people.

Those who have delivered such a decisive sentence on sovereigns have, doubtless, been persuaded by the example of various bad princes, who were contemporaries of Machiavelli, and are mentioned by the author; and also by the lives of various tyrants who have attracted the opprobrium of all humanity. I beg these censorious people to reflect that, since the attractions of a throne are very powerful, one would need more than ordinary virtue to resist them, and that it is not surprising, therefore, that among the numerous ranks of princes, bad ones are to be found among the good. Among the Roman emperors, which include men such as Nero, Caligula, and Tiberius, the whole universe remembers, with joy and relief, the hallowed names of the virtuous Titus, of Trajan and Antoninus.[1] It is, in other words, a manifest injustice to attribute to a whole body what applies only to some of its parts.

We should preserve, in history, only the names of good princes, and allow the names of the others to perish, for ever, along with their indolence, their injustice, and their crimes. The history books would, in truth, be the poorer for this, but humanity would profit from it; while the honour of being a notable figure in history, and of seeing one's name preserved for future centuries, and on into eternity, would be no more than a right and proper reward for virtue. Machiavelli's book would no longer infect schools of politics; we would despise his constant self-contradictions, and the world would be persuaded that the true political art of kings, founded on justice, prudence, and goodness alone, is in every way preferable to the system, incoherent and full of horrors, that Machiavelli has had the insolence to offer to the public.

CHAPTER I[2]

If we are to argue our position coherently, we must begin by exploring the nature of the subject we wish to discuss; and we must, moreover, return to its origins, in order to establish, as far as one can, its first principles. It will be easy, thereafter, to assess the course of the argument, and all the consequences that follow from it. Before, therefore, noting the differences between states, Machiavelli ought, it seems to me, to have examined the origin of princes, and the reasons that have been successful in persuading free men to submit themselves to rulers.

Perhaps it would not have been appropriate, in a book in which he proposed to pronounce on crime and tyranny, to make mention of what ought to destroy tyranny. It would have been an example of bad faith on Machiavelli's part to say that people have found it necessary, for their peace of mind and preservation, to have judges to settle their differences, protectors to defend them against their enemies and to support them in the possession of their goods, to have sovereigns to combine all their separate interests into a single common interest; and that, from among their own number, the people have chosen, to govern them, those whom they believed to be the most wise, the most equitable, the most disinterested, the most humane, and the most courageous.

It is, then, one might conclude, justice that must be the prime objective of a sovereign; it is, in other words, the welfare of the people he governs that he must put before every other consideration. What, then, becomes of the concepts of self-interest, of greatness, of ambition, and of despotism? It transpires that the sovereign, far from being the absolute master of the people who are under his domination, is himself only their first servant.

Since I have taken it upon myself to refute, in detail, his pernicious principles, I reserve the right to discuss them as and when the subject of each chapter provides me with the opportunity to do so.

I must, however, say that, in general, what I have related as to the origin of sovereigns shows the actions of usurpers to be more shocking than if we were to judge them simply by their violence, since they wholly contravene the intention of the people, who created sovereigns to protect them, and who have accepted submission to these sovereigns on this condition alone; they do not merely obey the usurper, they sacrifice themselves and everything they have, to satisfy the greed and all the whims of a tyrant. There are, therefore, only three legitimate ways of becoming the ruler of a country: through succession, through election by the people who hold power, or through conquest, by means of a just war, of enemy territory.

I ask those for whom this work is intended not to forget these comments on the first chapter of Machiavelli, since they are the mainspring that governs the reflections that follow.

CHAPTER II[3]

Mankind shows a certain respect, which borders on superstition, for everything that is ancient; and when the rights of inheritance are combined with the power that antiquity exercises over men, there is no yoke, however heavy, that we bear more readily. I am, therefore, far from denying Machiavelli's opinion, one that all the world will allow him, that hereditary kingdoms are the easiest to govern.

I will simply add that hereditary princes are greatly sustained in the position they hold by the intimate connection that exists between them and the most powerful families in the state, most of whom owe their property and their rank to the ruling house; and whose own fortune is so bound up with that of the prince that they cannot allow his fortunes to decline without becoming all too aware that their own fall would be the certain and necessary consequence of this.

At the present time, the numerous troops and the powerful armies that princes maintain, both in peacetime and in war, contribute considerably to the security of states, in that they limit the ambitions of neighbouring princes. They are naked swords, which ensure that all other swords remain sheathed.

But it is not enough that the prince should be, as Machiavelli puts it, *di ordinaria industria*; I should also like him to aspire to making his people happy. A contented nation will not dream of revolution; a nation that is content fears losing its prince, who is also its benefactor, more than does the sovereign himself fear losing his power. The Dutch would never have risen up against the Spanish if the tyranny of Spain had not reached such heights that it was impossible for the Dutch to be more wretched than they already were.

The kingdoms of Naples and Sicily passed more than once from Spanish hands into those of the emperor, and from the emperor to the Spanish. These conquests were always very easily achieved, since both rulers were equally harsh, and since the people always hoped to find that their new masters were liberators.

What a difference there was between these Neapolitans and the people of Lorraine! When the latter were obliged to change their rulers, all Lorraine wept; they were sorry to lose the offspring of the dukes who, for so many centuries, had been in possession of their flourishing country, and among whom we find many who were so notable for their benevolence that they deserved to be held up as an example to kings. Duke Leopold's memory was still so dear to the people of Lorraine that, when his widow had to leave Lunéville, the people, as one, threw themselves to their knees before her carriage, and the horses had several times to be stopped; only weeping could be heard, and only tears could be seen.[4]

CHAPTER III[5]

The fifteenth century, when Machiavelli lived, was still a barbarous time, when the baneful triumphalism of conquerors, as well as certain striking actions which, because of their magnificence, commanded respect, were set above gentleness, fairness, mercy and all the other virtues. At the present time, I note that we prefer humanity to all the qualities of a conqueror, and we are scarcely subject, any more, to the mad impulse to encourage and praise the cruel passions that hasten the destruction of the world.

I wonder what it is that inclines a man to aggrandise himself, and how it is that he can form the intention of building his own power upon the wretchedness and destruction of other men, and how he can believe that he will make himself illustrious by inflicting nothing but misery on others. The new conquests of a sovereign do not make the states he already possesses more opulent nor more rich, his people do not profit by them, and he is in gross error if he imagines that he will become the happier for them. How many princes have conquered, through their generals, lands that they themselves never see! These are, then, as it were, imaginary conquests, which have very little reality for the princes who caused them to be made. Many people have to be made wretched in order to gratify the fantasies of a single man, who often does not deserve, even, to be well known.

But let us suppose that this conqueror makes the whole world submit to his rule. Once this world has been well and truly conquered, will he be able to govern it? However great a prince he is, he is nothing more than a very limited human being; he will scarcely be able to remember the names of his provinces, and his greatness will serve only to make manifest his insignificance.

It is not the size of the country over which a prince rules that bestows fame upon him, and it will not be the acquisition of a few more leagues of territory that will make him famous, unless we are to believe that the more acres of land a man possesses, the more esteemed he will be.

Machiavelli's error on the matter of the fame of conquerors may have been widespread in his time, but his malice was certainly not so. There is nothing more shocking than the measures he suggests for preserving what has been conquered; if we were to examine them carefully, there is not a single one which is just or reasonable. 'You must', says this wicked man, 'eliminate the whole tribe of princes who reigned before your conquest.' Can we read such a precept without shuddering with horror and indignation? This precept tramples underfoot everything that is holy and sacred in the world; it opens up the way to all criminality, in order to promote self-interest. What! If an ambitious man takes possession, through violence, of the states of a prince, is he to have the right to have the prince assassinated or poisoned? But this same conqueror, by acting in the way he does, introduces into the world a practice that can only contribute to his own downfall; another conqueror, more ambitious and more skilful than he, will retaliate in the same way, will invade his states, and will have him put him to death with the same cruelty as he himself put to death his predecessor. The age in which Machiavelli lived provides only too many examples of this: have we not seen Pope Alexander VI, on the point of being deposed for his crimes; his abominable bastard son, Cesare Borgia, stripped of every land that he had invaded, and dying in misery; Galeazzo Sforza, assassinated in the central precinct of the church in Milan; Ludovico Sforza, the usurper, dead in France imprisoned in an iron cage; the princes of York and Lancaster destroying each other turn and turn about; the Byzantine emperors assassinated, in turn, by each other, until, at last, the Turks took advantage of their crimes and extinguished their feeble power?[6] If today, in Christian countries, there are fewer revolutions, this is because principles of sound morality are beginning to prevail more widely; men are more cultivated, they are less ferocious, and perhaps we owe this to the men of letters who have brought refinement to Europe.

Machiavelli's second maxim proposes that the conqueror take up residence in his new States. There is nothing cruel about this; it appears even to be wise in some respects. We must, nevertheless, reflect that the disposition of most States ruled by great Princes is such that they cannot easily abandon the centre without the whole State being affected; Princes are the motive force in the body of the State, so they cannot abandon the centre without causing the extremities to decline.

The third political maxim states that "Groups of settlers must be sent to, and established in, the newly conquered territories, in order to secure their loyalty", a maxim that the author derives from the practice of the Romans. But it does not enter his mind that if the Romans, when they established colonies, had not also sent their legions there, they would soon have lost their conquered territories. Nor does it occur to him that, in addition to founding these colonies and deploying these legions, the Romans also knew how to form alliances. The Romans, in the happy era of the republic, were the wisest brigands who have ever laid waste the whole earth; they preserved through prudence what they had acquired through injustice. In the end, nevertheless, the Romans experienced what every usurper experiences: they were, in turn, oppressed.

Let us now consider whether these colonies, during whose establishment Machiavelli makes his Prince commit so much injustice, are as useful as the author claims. Either you establish powerful colonies in a recently conquered country, or you establish weak ones. If these colonies are strong, you considerably weaken your own population, and you displace many of your new subjects, which diminishes your power. If you send less capable people to colonise the conquered territory, they will guarantee that your possession of it will be inadequate; and thus, without gaining much, you will have heaped misfortune on those you have expelled.

It would be much better, therefore, to send into a country that has just been conquered troops who, through discipline and good order, will not be able to oppress the people, nor be a burden to the towns where they are garrisoned. This is better politics, but it was unknown in Machiavelli's time: Sovereigns then did not maintain large armies; troops were for the most part nothing but gangs of bandits, who survived usually only through violence and pillage. No one at that time knew anything about troops that are continually, even in times of peace, in service; also unknown were military storehouses, barracks, and a thousand other regulations, which protect a State during peacetime, both against its neighbours and even against the soldiers paid to defend it.

"A Prince must make overtures to, and protect, the neighbouring Princelings by sowing dissension among them, in order to promote or weaken whomsoever he wishes." This is Machiavelli's fourth maxim, and so it was that Clovis, the first barbarian King to convert to Christianity, acted. He was imitated in this by several equally cruel Princes. But what a difference there is between these tyrants and a man of integrity who chooses, rather, to mediate between these Princelings, to solve their differences amicably, to win their confidence through his probity, by giving evidence of total impartiality in the midst of their disagreements, and, on his own part, through his perfect disinterestedness! His wisdom would make him the Father of his neighbours rather than their oppressor, and his rank and status would protect them rather than ruin them.

It is true, moreover, that Princes who tried, through violent means, to elevate other Princes were themselves put down; our own century has provided two examples of this. The first is that of Charles XII, who placed Stanisław on the throne of Poland, and the other is more recent.[7] From which I conclude that the usurper will never deserve fame, that assassins will always be loathed by all humankind, that princes who commit injustice and violence against their new subjects will alienate—instead of winning—hearts and minds, that it is never possible to justify crime, and that all those who wish to excuse it are reasoning as badly as does Machiavelli. To deploy the art of reasoning against the welfare of humanity is to wound oneself with a sword that has been given to us only so that we may protect ourselves.

Chapter IV[8]

If we are to reach a sound judgement as to the particular character of each nation, we must compare them one with another. Machiavelli in this chapter compares the Turks with the French, two nations very different in customs, morals, and opinions; he examines the reasons that make any conquest of the Turkish empire difficult to achieve, but easy to maintain; he points out, at the same time, what could contribute to the easy subjugation of France, but also what would, by fomenting there endless strife, threaten continually the peace of mind of its conqueror.

The author considers things from one point of view alone: he is concerned only with the make-up of governments; he seems to believe that the power of the Turkish and Persian empires was founded solely on the total enslavement of these peoples, and on the elevation of one man alone to be their leader. His idea is that total despotism, well-established, is the most sure means that a prince could have if he is to reign without trouble, and if he is to oppose, vigorously, his enemies.

In Machiavelli's time, nobles and other great men were still regarded in France as lesser sovereigns, who, in one way or another, shared the power of the prince. This gave rise to divisions; it strengthened factions, and fomented frequent revolts. I do not know, however, whether or not the great sultan is more susceptible to dethronement than is a French king. The only difference between them is that a Turkish emperor is usually strangled by his janissaries, while those French kings who have died were assassinated by monks, or by various monsters schooled by the monks. But, in this chapter, Machiavelli is speaking of revolutions in general rather than of particular instances; and although he has, in truth, discovered various intricacies in what is a very complex mechanism, he has not, it seems to me, examined the fundamentals.

The differences in climate, diet, and education that men experience produce a profound difference in their ways of living and thinking; therein, for example, lies the difference between an Italian monk and a Chinese man of letters. The character of a deeply thoughtful but melancholic Englishman is quite unlike the proud courage of a Spaniard; while a Frenchman as little resembles a Dutchman as does the liveliness of a monkey the composure of a tortoise.

It has always been observed that a particular characteristic of oriental peoples is their fidelity to their ancient customs, which they hardly ever abandon. Their religion, unlike that of Europeans, makes them, in some manner or other, unsympathetic to the endeavours against their own rulers of those they call infidels, and makes them avoid, carefully, anything that could damage their religion and overturn their government. This is what, in their country, assures the security of the throne rather than that of the monarch; for the monarch is often dethroned, while the empire is never destroyed.

The particular character of the French, quite unlike that of the Muslims, was wholly, or at least in part, the cause of the frequent revolutions that have taken place in their kingdom; frivolity and changeability have formed the character of this agreeable nation. The French are restless, licentious, and only too prone to boredom; their love of change for change's sake has shown itself even in the most serious matters. It appears that the cardinals, hated and respected by the French, and who, one after the other, have ruled this empire, have profited from the maxims of Machiavelli, in order to disempower the nobility, and have profited also from a knowledge of the particular character of their nation, in order to deflect those frequent upheavals through which the fickleness of the French has always threatened their sovereigns.

The policy followed by Cardinal Richelieu had no aim other than that of diminishing the power of the nobility in order to increase that of the king, and of making the latter the foundation of all the different elements in the state. He succeeded so well in this that in France today there remains no vestige of the power of the aristocracy and the nobility, nor of that power that the kings claimed was abused by the nobility.

Cardinal Mazarin, following in the footsteps of Richelieu, suffered much opposition, but prevailed; he stripped the parlement, moreover, of its prerogatives, so successfully that, today, this institution is a mere ghost, still imagining sometimes that it could again acquire a body, although it is usually made to repent of this error.[9]

The same policy that led ministers to establish absolute despotism in France taught them how to indulge the frivolity and inconstancy of the nation, in order to make it less of a threat to them. A thousand frivolous pursuits, trifles, and pleasures altered the genius of the French nation, to such an extent that they who had for so long fought great Caesar, who so often threw off the imperial yoke, who called on the assistance of foreigners during the time of the Valois, formed a league against Henri IV, and cabals during the reign of minors, these French, I say, have done nothing in our days but follow the tide of fashion, alter minutely their tastes, despise today what they admired yesterday, introduce inconstancy and frivolity into all they do, and are always seeking new mistresses, new places, new amusements, and new follies. Nor is this everything, since powerful armies and numerous fortresses have ensured, for ever, the French kings' rule over France, so that they have nothing to fear at present from civil war, any more than they need fear the ambitions of their neighbours.

CHAPTER V[10]

'There is', says Machiavelli, 'no more certain means of securing a free state that one has conquered, than to destroy it.' It is the most sure means of avoiding the risk of revolt. An Englishman was mad enough to kill himself some years ago in London; a note was found on his table, in which he justified what he had done, and in which he indicated that he had taken his own life to avoid ever becoming ill. Such is the case, too, of a prince, who ruins a state in order not to lose it. I am not discussing humanity with Machiavelli: to do so would be to profane virtue. We should, rather, refute Machiavelli with his own idea, self-interest: the god of politics and crime, the very soul of his book.

You say, Machiavelli, that in order to secure its possession, a prince must destroy a free country he has recently conquered. I ask you, however: to what end did he undertake this conquest? You will tell me that it was to increase his power, and to prove himself more formidable. This is what I wanted to hear, in order to prove to you that, by following your maxims, he does quite the opposite; for this conquest costs him dear, and he goes on to ruin the only country that could make amends for his losses. You will acknowledge that a country that has been laid waste, and emptied of its inhabitants, cannot, through his possession of it, make a prince powerful. I believe that a monarch, even should he possess the vast deserts of Libya and of Barca, would not in himself be formidable, and that a million panthers, lions, and crocodiles cannot equal a million subjects, wealthy towns, navigable ports filled with ships, industrious citizens, soldiers, and everything that a well-populated country produces. Everyone agrees that the power of a state does not depend on the extent of its borders, but on the number of its inhabitants. Let us compare Holland with Russia: as regards Holland, you will see there only barren and marshy islands which rise from the bed of the sea, a small republic which is only forty-eight leagues in length and forty in width. But this little body is all sinews and energy, there is a large population, and the people are industrious, powerful, and very rich; it has thrown off the yoke of Spanish rule, which at that time was the most formidable monarchy in Europe. This republic's trade stretches to the ends of the earth, it is second in consequence only to the monarchies, it can, in times of war, field an army of fifty thousand men, not to mention a numerous and well-maintained fleet.

Cast, on the other hand, your eyes on Russia: a vast country comes to view, a world that resembles the universe when it emerged from chaos. It borders, on one side, Greater Tartary and the Indies, and on the other, the Black Sea and Hungary; its borders extend as far as Poland, Lithuania, and Courland; and, to the north-west, Sweden. Russia is more or less three hundred German miles in width, and more than five hundred miles in length; the country is rich in corn, and provides, as to food, all the necessities of life, principally around Moscow and towards Lesser Tartary. Nevertheless, in spite of all these advantages, it has at the very most fifteen million inhabitants. This nation, which is only now beginning to become a presence in Europe, is scarcely more powerful than Holland in land and sea forces, and is much inferior to it in wealth and resources.

The power of a state does not depend on the extent of its land, nor on its possession of a vast uninhabited area or of an immense desert, but on the wealth and number of its inhabitants. It is, then, in the interests of a prince to populate the country, to make it flourish, and not to lay it waste, nor to destroy it. If Machiavelli's malice horrifies us, his reasoning arouses our pity; he would have done better to learn sound reasoning than to teach us his monstrous politics.

'A prince must establish his residency in a newly conquered republic.' This is our author's third maxim; it is more moderate than the others; but I have pointed out in my third chapter the objections that may be raised against it.

It seems to me that a prince who, with just cause for making war, has conquered a republic, should be content with having punished it, and should subsequently restore to it its freedom; but very few people would think in this way. As to those who think otherwise, they could preserve their possession of it by establishing strong garrisons in the principal areas of their new conquest, leaving, moreover, the people to enjoy total freedom.

How foolish we are! We want to conquer everything, as though we had the time to possess everything, and as though our time here on earth were infinite; our life passes too quickly, and often when we believe we are working for ourselves alone we are working only for ungrateful and unworthy successors.

CHAPTER VI[11]

If men were without passions, Machiavelli could be forgiven for wanting to provide them with some: he would be a new Prometheus who would steal the celestial fire to give life to automata. In practice, things are not quite thus, for no man is without passions. When they are moderate they are the very soul of society; but when they are allowed free rein, they are its destruction.

Among the many emotions that tyrannise our souls, none is more deadly to those who are driven by it, nor more inimical to humanity, nor more fatal to the peace of the world, than unlimited ambition, and the overweening desire for false fame and glory.

An individual who has the misfortune to be born with such a disposition is more wretched even than he is mad. He is mindless of the present, and lives only for the future; nothing on earth can satisfy him, and the absinthe of ambition always mingles its bitterness with the sweetness of his pleasures.

A prince who is ambitious is less fortunate than a commoner, for his madness is proportionate to his rank, and is thus more intractable, less defined, and more insatiable. If honours and rank feed the passions of commoners, provinces and kingdoms nourish the ambition of monarchs; and since it is easier to acquire responsibilities and employment than it is to conquer kingdoms, commoners are better able than are princes to find satisfaction.

Machiavelli advances as examples Moses, Cyrus, Romulus, Theseus, and Hiero;[12] we could very easily lengthen his list by including the founders of sects, such as Muhammad in Asia, Manco Cápac in America, Odin in the North, and the many members of such sects throughout the whole world.[13] May the Jesuits of Paraguay permit me to offer them here a small mention, which can only be to their glory, by including them among the lawgivers![14]

The bad faith with which the author presents these examples merits our attention; it is, indeed, imperative to uncover all the subtleties and all the seductive ruses employed by our deceiving author.

Machiavelli presents ambition only in its most favourable light, if, that is, it has one; he speaks only of those ambitious people who have been blessed with good fortune; but he maintains complete silence about those that have been victims of their own passions. This can only be considered a huge deception; indeed, there is no denying that Machiavelli plays in this chapter the role of a criminal and a charlatan.

Why, when he speaks of the lawgiver of the Jews, of the first monarch of Athens, of the conqueror of the Medes, of the founder of Rome, all of whose successes matched their intentions, does Machiavelli not add the example of several leaders who met with misfortune, in order to show that, if ambition makes some men succeed, it also destroys a greater number? Was there not a certain John of Leiden, leader of the Anabaptists, who was tortured, burned with a red-hot iron, and then hanged in an iron cage in Münster?[15] If Cromwell himself was fortunate, was not his son dethroned, and did he not see his father's exhumed body carried to the gibbet?[16] Did not three or four Jews, who claimed to be the messiah, suffer the extreme penalty, and did not the last of them, after becoming a Muslim, end by being employed as a kitchen boy to the Turkish sultan?[17] If Pepin dethroned his king with the approval of the pope, was not Henry I, duke of Guise, who also wanted to dethrone his own king, with the same approval, assassinated?[18] Have there not been more than thirty religious leaders, and more than a thousand other ambitious people, who in the end met with violent deaths?

It seems to me, moreover, that it was ill-considered of Machiavelli to place Moses alongside Romulus, Cyrus, and Theseus. Either Moses was inspired or he was not. If he was not, which we have no reason to suppose, we must regard him as a simple impostor, who was using God rather as poets use their own gods, as a device when they lack a dénouement. Moses was, moreover, if we are looking at things from a human perspective, so little skilful that he led the Jewish people for forty years along a path that they could easily have covered in six weeks; having profited so little from the wisdom of the Egyptians, he was, in this regard, much inferior to Romulus and Theseus, and to other such heroes. If Moses was inspired by God, as he certainly believed himself to be, we can regard him only as the blind agent of the all-powerful Divinity; and, as the leader of the Jews, he was, from this point of view, much inferior as a man to the founder of the Roman empire, to the Persian king, and to those heroes who achieved through their own courage and their own strength greater things than Moses achieved with the immediate assistance of God.

I must confess, in general and without bias, that a great deal of courage, genius, skill, and leadership would be needed if one were to equal the men of whom we have just spoken; but I do not know if the epithet 'virtuous' applies to them. Courage and skill are found, equally, among both highwaymen and heroes; the sole difference between them is that the conqueror is an illustrious thief while the ordinary thief is an obscure wretch; the former, as a reward for his violence, gets laurels, the latter the noose.

It is true that, whenever we wish to introduce something new into the world, a thousand obstacles present themselves to prevent it from happening, and that a prophet who leads an army will make more converts than he would by argument alone.

It is true that the Christian religion was, when it depended on disputation for its survival, weak and oppressed, and that it spread throughout Europe only after it had shed a great deal of blood; it is true, nevertheless, that it is possible to disseminate new opinions and new ideas without much difficulty. How many religions, how many sects, have been introduced with the greatest ease! There is nothing more helpful than fanaticism for endowing new ideas with credibility, and it seems to me that Machiavelli has taken too decisive a tone on this matter.

It only remains for me to make a few remarks on the example of Hiero of Syracuse, which Machiavelli offers to those who wish to increase their power through the help of their friends and of their armies.[19]

Hiero rid himself of his friends and his soldiers, who had helped him realise his ambitions; he formed new friendships, and he raised fresh troops. I maintain, in spite of Machiavelli and other renegades, that Hiero's politics was very poor, and that it is much wiser to place your trust in troops whose courage you have experienced, and in friends whose fidelity you have put to the test, than in strangers on whom you cannot rely. I leave it to the reader to take this argument further; those who detest ingratitude, and who are fortunate enough to know true friendship, will not remain silent on this matter.

I must, however, warn the reader to pay attention to the different meanings Machiavelli gives to certain words. Let no one be deceived when he says, 'Without the opportunity to practise it, virtue melts into thin air.' This must mean, according to him, that, unless circumstances are favourable, cheats and adventurers will not know how to use their talents; it is only the prevalence of crime that can explain the obscurities of our author.

It seems to me, in general, and in order to conclude this chapter, that the only occasion when an individual can, without committing some criminal action, achieve royal status, is when he is born into an elective kingdom, or when he saves his fatherland.

Sobieski in Poland, Gustav Vasa in Sweden, and the Antonines in Rome, are heroes of both kinds; let Cesare Borgia be the model of the Machiavellians; mine is Marcus Aurelius.[20]

CHAPTER VII[21]

If you compare M. Fénelon's prince with that of Machiavelli, you will observe in the former a man of integrity, generosity, justice, fairness, and of all the virtues, in a word, taken to an extraordinary level; we are, perhaps, when we say that wisdom is appointed to watch over the government of the world, speaking of people of a pure intelligence of this kind.[22] You will see in Machiavelli's prince wickedness, treachery, perfidy, betrayal, and every possible crime. He is, in a word, a monster such as hell itself could scarcely have produced. But if, while reading *Telemachus*, it seems to us that our nature is close to that of the angels, it appears, when we read Machiavelli's *The Prince*, that it is close, rather, to the demons of hell. Cesare Borgia, duke of Valentinois, is the person on whom the author models his prince, and whom he has the impudence to cite as an example to those who rise in the world through the help of their friends or by force of arms. It is, therefore, vital to know what Cesare Borgia was, so that we may form an impression both of this hero, and of the author who is extolling him.

There is no crime that Cesare Borgia did not commit; he had his brother, his rival in fame and love, assassinated, before the very eyes, almost, of his own sister; he had the Swiss guards of the pope massacred, in an act of vengeance against some Swiss people who had offended his mother; he stripped cardinals and wealthy men of their possessions, in order to satisfy his own greed; he robbed the duke of Urbino of the Romagna, of which he was the ruler, and had d'Orco, his own cruel and tyrannical deputy, put to death; he ordered the assassination in Senigallia, in a frightful act of treachery, of several princes whose existence he believed to be damaging to his own interests; he had a Venetian lady, of whom he had taken advantage, drowned. How many more cruel acts were committed under his orders, and who could count the total number of his crimes? Such was the man whom Machiavelli prefers to all the great spirits of his own age and to all the heroes of antiquity; such was the man whose life and actions he finds worthy to serve as an example to those whom fortune favours.

But I must attack Machiavelli in greater detail, so that those who think as he does will find no more subterfuges, and no more hiding places, for their malice.

Cesare Borgia based his plans for self-aggrandisement on the dissension between the princes of Italy. If it is my aim to rob all my neighbours of their possessions, I must first weaken them; and in order to weaken them I must set them at odds with one another: such is the logic of the scoundrel.

Borgia wanted to secure some support; it was therefore necessary that Pope Alexander VI should grant a marriage dispensation to Louis XII, in exchange for his support. This is how, in contempt of the whole world, so many politicians acted; they were thinking only of their self-interest when they appeared to be most concerned with the interests of heaven. If Louis XII's marriage was of the sort that could be brought to an end, the pope ought to have ended it, assuming that he had the power to do so; if the marriage was not of this kind, nothing should have persuaded the head of the Roman church to bring it to an end.

Borgia was determined to surround himself with creatures of his own making; for this purpose he corrupted the House of Urbino with gifts. Let us not dwell on Borgia's crimes, and let us overlook his corrupt practices, if only because they bear some faint resemblance to good deeds. Borgia wanted to rid himself of several princes from the houses of Urbino, Vitelozzo, Oliverotto da Fermo, etc.; and Machiavelli says he was wise enough to make them come to Senigallia, where, treacherously, he had them put to death.

To betray the good faith of one's fellow men, to employ vile trickery, to be treacherous, to lie and to assassinate: this is what our Professor of Villainy calls wisdom. But I wonder if it is wise for a man to demonstrate how to betray good faith, and how to commit perjury. If you overturn good faith and your own word of honour, what guarantee will you have of any human loyalty? If you betray others, fear betrayal; if you give examples of assassination, fear the actions of your own followers.

Borgia appointed that cruel man d'Orco to be the governor of the Romagna, in order to suppress some unrest there. Borgia brutally punished those whose vices were much less considerable than his own. Borgia, the most violent of usurpers, the most false of perjurers, the most cruel of assassins and poisoners, condemned to the most frightful punishment some petty criminals, some restless spirits who, simply, on a small scale and as far as their limited capacity allowed, imitated the ways of their new master.

The Polish king, whose death has just caused such unrest in Europe, acted much more consistently and decently towards his subjects in Saxony.[23] Saxon law condemned adulterers to be beheaded. I will not go into the origin of this barbarous law, which seems more appropriate to Italian jealousy than to German patience. Any unfortunate who had broken this law was condemned. Augustus was supposed to sign the death warrant; but Augustus had an understanding of love and of humanity; he pardoned the criminal, and he repealed a law which, tacitly, condemned himself too.

His behaviour was that of a sensitive and humane man; but whenever Cesare Borgia meted out punishment he did so tyrannically and ferociously. In the end Borgia had the cruel d'Orco torn to pieces; d'Orco had, faithfully, carried out Borgia's plans, and Borgia destroyed him in order to make himself agreeable to the people by punishing the agent of his own barbarity. The full weight of tyranny is never heavier than when the tyrant attempts to clothe himself with the appearance of innocence, and when oppression is cloaked with law.

Borgia, anticipating what might happen after the death of his father, the pope, began by liquidating all those whom he had stripped of their possessions, so that the new pope could not make use of them against him. Take note of the cascade of crimes! To finance our expenses we need possessions; to acquire them we need to strip them from their owners; and to enjoy them securely we need to exterminate these owners: this is the reasoning of the highwayman.

In order to poison several cardinals, Borgia invited them to a meal at his father's house. He and the pope in error took a poisoned drink: Alexander VI died, Borgia escaped, but only to drag out a wretched existence, a well-deserved recompense for poisoners and assassins.

Such is the prudence, the cleverness and the virtue that Machiavelli is never tired of praising. The famous bishop of Meaux, the distinguished bishop of Nîmes, the eloquent panegyrist of Trajan, could not have spoken more fulsomely of their heroes than did Machiavelli of Cesare Borgia.[24] If his praise had taken the form simply of an ode, or of a rhetorical figure, we might praise its subtlety, while detesting his choice of subject; but, on the contrary, this is a political treatise, one that is to be handed down to future generations. It is a deeply serious work, in which Machiavelli is so impudent as to speak in praise of the most abominable monster that hell has spewed upon the earth. Machiavelli, thus, exposes himself, calmly and coolly, to the hatred of the human race.

CHAPTER VIII[25]

To refute Machiavelli I need use only his own words. What more shocking could I report of him than that he is here offering a rule-book to those whose crimes elevate them to supreme greatness? Such is the title of this chapter.

If Machiavelli were teaching crime, if he were imparting the principles of treachery in a university of traitors, it would not be surprising if he dealt with matters of this kind: but he is speaking to all mankind. For, since an author who has his works printed is communicating with the whole universe, he is speaking, above all, to those men who ought to be the most virtuous of men, since it is they who are destined to govern the rest. What could be more infamous, more insulting, than to teach them treachery, perfidy, and murder? One would hope, rather, for the good of the human race, that examples such as those of Agathocles and Oliverotto da Fermo, whom Machiavelli takes pleasure in citing, were for ever unknown.[26]

The examples of an Agathocles or of an Oliverotto da Fermo might well nurture in a man whose instincts incline him to wickedness a dangerous seed, which is implanted within him without his knowing it. How many young people there are who have ruined their minds by reading novels, who only saw and only thought like Gandalin or Médor![27] There is something of an epidemic in this way of thinking, if I may express myself thus, which spreads from one mind to another. That extraordinary man, that adventurer-king, a fine example of ancient chivalry, that wandering hero, all of whose virtues, carried to excess, degenerated into vices, Charles XII, in a word, nurtured within himself from his earliest years the history of the life of Alexander the Great, and many of the people who knew personally this Alexander of the North insist that it was Quintus Curtius Rufus who laid waste Poland, that Stanisław became king after the model of Abdolonymus, and that the battle of Arbela gave rise to the defeat of Poltava.[28]

But, if I may be permitted to pass from such great examples to lesser ones, it appears to me that, when it is a question of the history of the human mind, differences in rank and possessions disappear; kings are only men, and all men are equal. It is a question only of certain impressions or of small differences which, in general, have placed certain external trappings on the human mind.

All England knows what happened in London some years ago. A somewhat mediocre comedy was being put on whose title was *Thieves and Knavish Tricks*;[29] this play was a representation of various cunning tricks and frauds used by thieves. It so happened that many people, on leaving the theatre, noticed the loss of their rings, their snuff-boxes, and their watches. The author of the play had, in other words, acquired disciples so quickly that they were putting his lessons into practice in the very stalls of the theatre. This proves well enough, it seems to me, how pernicious it is to offer bad examples.

Machiavelli's first remarks on Agathocles and on Fermo examine the reasons that allowed them to continue to rule in their small states, notwithstanding their cruelty. The author attributes this to the fact of their having carried out these cruel acts at an opportune moment: so that to be prudent in barbarity, and to be a tyrant consequently, means, according to Machiavelli's politics, to carry out suddenly and at the same time every violent act and every crime that one judges to be in one's own interest.

Order the assassination of all those whom you find suspect, and whom you distrust, as well as those who declare themselves your enemies; but do not delay in taking revenge. Machiavelli approves of acts that resemble the Sicilian Vespers as well as the terrible St Bartholomew's Day massacre, where acts of cruelty were committed such as make humanity tremble.[30] This monster thinks nothing of the horror of these crimes, provided they are committed in a way that impresses the people, and terrifies them when they are fresh in their minds; and he gives as the reason for this that such impressions vanish more easily from the public mind than do the impressions created by the continuing and successive cruelties committed by princes: as though it were not equally wicked to put to death a thousand people in a day or to have them assassinated over a period of time.

It is not enough simply to refute the shocking morality of Machiavelli; we must also convict him of deceitfulness and bad faith.

It is, in the first place, false to assert, as Machiavelli does of Agathocles, that he enjoyed in peace the fruits of his crimes. He was, on the contrary, almost always at war with the Carthaginians; he was forced, even, to abandon in Africa his army, who slaughtered his children after his departure; and he himself died of a poisoned drink which his grandson gave him. Oliverotto da Fermo perished through the treachery of Borgia, a suitable recompense for his crimes; and as this happened a year after he usurped the throne, his fall appeared so rapid as to seem fore-ordained as the punishment that the public's hatred had in store for him.

The example of Oliverotto da Fermo should not, then, have been adduced by the author, since it proves nothing. Machiavelli would have liked crime to have been successful, indeed he flatters himself that it offers various good grounds for validating his view, or at least a palpable argument to adduce in its favour.

But let us suppose that crime can be committed without repercussions, and that a tyrant can commit wickedness with impunity: even if he does not fear a tragic death, he will be equally wretched at finding himself the object of the opprobrium of the human race: he will not be able to stifle the inner witness that his own conscience presses upon him; he will not be able to silence that powerful voice that makes itself heard even by kings on their thrones; he will not be able to avoid that deadly melancholy that will invade his imagination, and act as his hangman in this world.

We have only to read the life of a Dionysius of Syracuse, of a Tiberius, of a Nero, of a Louis XI, of the tyrant Vasilyevich, etc; and we will see that these monsters, all of them furious and insane, ended in the most wretched manner possible.[31] A cruel man is by nature misanthropic and full of bile; if from his earliest years he does not oppose this unfortunate bodily disposition, he cannot fail to become insane and furious. If, therefore, there were no justice on earth and no Divinity in heaven, it would be the more necessary that men be virtuous, since virtue both unites them and is absolutely necessary for their preservation; and since, moreover, crime can only make them wretched, and destroy them.

CHAPTER IX[32]

The love of freedom is the sentiment most vital to our existence; all men, equally, from the most civilised to the most barbaric, are imbued with this sentiment; for, since we are born without chains, we aspire to a life lived without constraint. It is this spirit of independence and of pride that has given the world so many great men, and has created republican government, which establishes a kind of equality among men, and brings them closer to their natural condition.

Machiavelli offers, in this chapter, various sound political maxims to those who, with the agreement of the leaders of a republic, are rising to supreme power. This is almost the only case in which he allows his subject to be a man of integrity, but, unfortunately, this situation almost never arises. The republican spirit, excessively jealous of its freedom, is offended by anything that can shackle it, and rebels against the very idea of a master. We know of a number of nations in Europe which have thrown off the yoke of tyranny in order to enjoy independence; but we know of none who, after enjoying freedom, have subjected themselves willingly to slavery.

A number of republics have, over the course of time, reverted to despotism; it would appear, even, that this is an inevitable misfortune, one that awaits them all. For, how could a republic resist for ever all the forces which undermine its freedom? How could a republic contain for ever the ambitions of the great men it is nourishing within its bosom? How could it, over a long period of time, guard against the seductive promises and the obscure actions of its neighbours, and against the corruption of its own people, so long as self-interest remains all-powerful among men? How could it hope always to emerge successful from the wars it will have to undergo? How could it anticipate the unfortunate conjuncture of circumstances that threaten its liberty, those critical and decisive moments, and those products of chance that favour the bold and the corrupt? If the army is under the command of cowardly and timid generals, it will be a prey to its enemies; and if it has at its head audacious and brave men, they will, having served in times of war, be dangerous in times of peace.

Almost all republics have risen from the abyss of tyranny to the heights of liberty, and they have nearly always fallen back again from liberty into slavery. The same Athenians who, during the time of Demosthenes, insulted Philip of Macedon, grovelled before Alexander; those same Romans who, after the expulsion of the kings, detested royalty, suffered patiently, several centuries later, all the cruelties of their emperors; and those same Englishmen who put Charles I to death, because he had encroached upon their rights, bowed their proud and courageous heads to the arrogant power of their lord protector. It is not, therefore, that these republics have given themselves masters by choice, but that opportunistic men, aided by favourable circumstances, have, against their will, subjugated them.

Just as men are born, live for a time, and die from illness or old age, so, too, republics come into being, flourish for a few centuries, and perish at last through the boldness of a citizen or through the arms of their enemies. Everything has its day; all empires and even the greatest monarchies survive only for a while; all republics sense that this moment will come, and they look upon every family that is too powerful as the germ of the illness that will deliver in time their death blow.

Republicans who are truly free will never be persuaded to accept a master, by which I mean even the best possible master; for, as they will always tell you, 'It is better to be dependent on the law than on the whim of a single man.'

Chapter X[33]

Since the time when Machiavelli was writing *The Prince*, the world has changed so much that it is almost no longer recognisable. If an able captain of the time of Louis XII reappeared in our own days, he would be entirely disorientated: he would see that war is waged, now, with huge armies, which can scarcely be fed during a campaign, and which are maintained during peacetime as in war; whereas, in his time, in order to make an attack and to carry out large-scale operations, a handful of men was enough, and the troops were disbanded after the end of the war. Instead of iron armour, lances, and matchlock guns, he would find regulation uniforms, rifles, bayonets, as well as new methods of pitching encampments, of laying siege, and of engaging in battle; and he would find the task of provisioning the troops every bit as essential in our time as was that of overcoming the enemy in former times.

But what would Machiavelli himself say, if he could observe the new politics of Europe, and note the number of great princes who play a part at the present time in the world, but were of no account previously; and if he saw the power of kings firmly established, the negotiating methods of sovereigns, and the balance of power now established in Europe that has led to the alliance of various considerable princes, an alliance, moreover, undertaken to oppose the ambitious, and whose sole aim is peace in the world!

All these things have produced a change so general and so universal that they render most of Machiavelli's maxims irrelevant to our modern politics. That is what this present chapter principally demonstrates. I must give some examples of this.

Machiavelli assumes 'that a prince whose country is extensive, and who has, moreover, much money and many troops, can sustain and defend himself with his own forces, and without the assistance of any ally, against the attacks of his enemies'.

I must, however, venture to contradict this assumption: I will go even further, and maintain that a prince, however formidable he is, would be unable, on his own, to withstand powerful enemies, and that he needs, necessarily, the help of various allies. If the most formidable, the most powerful prince in all Europe, if Louis XIV, was on the point of succumbing during the War of the Spanish Succession; and if, for want of allies or alliances, he could scarcely any longer withstand the league of so many kings and princes, who believed that they could overwhelm him, how much more likely is it that a sovereign less powerful than Louis XIV could not, without considerable risk, remain isolated and in want of strong alliances?

It is said, and is often repeated, without much thought, that treaties are ineffectual, since all their provisions are almost never fulfilled, and since the parties concerned are no more scrupulous in this matter in the present century than they were in any other. My reply to those who think in this way, is that they will find, I have no doubt, ancient and even very recent examples of princes who have not fulfilled their obligations to the letter; but that it is always, nevertheless, advantageous to enter into treaties. For every ally you acquire, you will have one enemy the less, and, even if your allies are of no help to you, you will force them to observe a strict neutrality.

Machiavelli discusses, next, the *principini*, those miniature sovereigns, who, ruling only small states, cannot raise an army in the field. The author insists that they must fortify their capital cities, so that they can retreat there with their troops in times of war.

The Italian princes whom Machiavelli is discussing here, are, properly speaking, hermaphrodites, at the same time sovereigns and individuals; they play the part of great noblemen only in front of their servants. The best possible advice to give them would be, it seems to me, to lower in one way or another the very high-flown opinions they have of their own status, the excessive reverence that they have for their ancient and illustrious lineage, and the inexhaustible enthusiasm that they have for their coats of arms. People of good sense say that such princelings would do better to present themselves in society merely as gentlemen of leisure, to get down, once and for all, from the stilts on which their pride has elevated them; to maintain, at the very most, a guard powerful enough to chase thieves from their castles, should it happen that there were thieves hungry enough to seek nourishment there; and also to raze to the ground their ramparts and walls and everything that could give their residence the appearance of a fortress.

Here are the reasons: most princelings, especially those in Germany, ruin themselves through their expenditure, which is excessive in proportion to their revenues, and to which they are driven by their vain and intoxicating notions of grandeur; they do damage to themselves only to keep up the honour of their house; they embark out of vanity on the road that leads to misery and the workhouse; even the younger son of a younger son in a privileged family aspires, in one way or other, to resemble Louis XIV; he builds his Versailles, he keep his mistresses, and he maintains his armies.

There is, at the present moment, a certain prince, the scion of a great house, whose notions of grandeur are highly refined, and who maintains just for his own use every kind of armed unit that forms part of the household of a great king, a force that, in miniature, is so strong that you would need a microscope to identify each unit; his army would, perhaps, be strong enough to stage a battle in the theatre at Verona.[34]

I have said, moreover, that the princelings were unwise to fortify their residences, and for a perfectly straightforward reason: they are not in danger of being besieged by their peers, since neighbours more powerful than themselves intervene from the start in their disputes, and offer mediation which they are not in a position to refuse; thus, instead of spilled blood, two strokes of a pen are enough to end their little quarrels.

What use, then, are their fortresses? Even if they were strong enough to withstand their small enemies in a siege as long as the siege of Troy, they would not survive a siege of Jericho against the armies of a powerful monarch. If, moreover, a major war breaks out in a neighbouring area, they are not in a position to remain neutral, for neutrality will cause them to be totally ruined; while if they do adhere to the cause of one or other of the belligerents, their capital city becomes a battleground for the prince in question.

The impression Machiavelli gives us of the free imperial cities of Germany is quite different from their present situation; a single explosive charge, and a mere command, even, from the emperor, would be enough for him to become master of these cities. They are all of them badly fortified, most of them having ancient walls, flanked now and then with big towers, and surrounded by dykes that are almost entirely filled in with collapsed earth. These cities have very few troops, and those they maintain are badly disciplined; their officers are, for the most part, either the dregs of Germany, or old men in no fit state to serve. Some of the imperial cities have quite good artillery; but this would not be enough to withstand the emperor, who is accustomed, often enough, to making them aware of their weakness.

In a word, making war, doing battle, attacking or defending fortresses, these are the concerns only of great sovereigns; and those who, without their power, try to imitate them, resemble the man who, imitating the sound of thunder, believed himself to be Jupiter.[35]

CHAPTER XI[36]

I see in antiquity very few priests who became sovereigns. It seems to me that, among all the peoples of whom we still have some slight knowledge, only the Jews have had a succession of despotic pontiffs. It is not surprising that, in the most superstitious and the most ignorant of all primitive nations, the religious leaders should, in the end, have seized control over the management of affairs of state; but it seems to me that, everywhere else, priests concerned themselves only with their proper duties. They made sacrifices, they drew a salary, they had some prerogatives; but they neither advised nor governed; and it is, I think, because they neither held views that might disunite the people, nor had powers to abuse them, that there was never among them any religious war.

At the time when, during the decline of the Roman empire, Europe was in a state of barbarous anarchy, everything was divided into a thousand small sovereign states; many bishops made themselves into princes; indeed, it was the bishop of Rome himself who set the example. It seems that, under these ecclesiastical governments, the people must have lived contentedly enough; for elected princes, princes raised to sovereignty in their later years, princes, in other words, whose estates were very limited as were those of such churchmen, needed to deal with their subjects prudently, if not for religious reasons then at least for political ones.

It is certainly the case, however, that no country swarms with beggars more than do those that are ruled by priests; it is these countries that offer us the touching sight of all the miseries of mankind. These are not countries where poor wretches, attracted by the generosity and the alms of their sovereigns, resemble nothing so much as insects who attach themselves to the rich, and who crawl along in the wake of opulence. Rather, half-starved beggars in these countries are deprived of the necessities of life by the charity of their sovereign—the priests—who wish to avoid the corruption and abuse which people are accustomed to wherever there is abundance and plenty.

It is, without doubt, upon the laws of Sparta, where money was forbidden, that the principles of most ecclesiastical governments are based, except that the prelates reserve for themselves the use of all the good things of which their subjects are deprived. How blessed, they say, are the poor, for they will inherit the kingdom of heaven! And since they want everyone to be saved, they are careful to impoverish everyone.

Nothing ought to be more edifying than the history of the leaders of the church and of the vicars of Jesus Christ; we expect to find there examples of saintly and irreproachable morals. On the contrary, however, all that we find there are obscenities, outrageous behaviour, and scandal; nor can we read the lives of the popes without being appalled, time and again, by their cruelty and their perfidy.

We find there, writ large, their ambition directed towards the increase of their temporal and spiritual power, their greed devoted to diverting to their own families the means of subsistence intended for the ordinary people, in order to enrich their nephews, their mistresses, or their bastards.

Those little given to reflection find it odd that the people suffer, with so much docility and patience, the oppression of this kind of sovereign, that they do not open their eyes to the vices and excesses of churchmen, and that they endure from a tonsured head what they would never tolerate from a head crowned with laurels. This phenomenon appears less strange to those who know the power that superstition wields over fools, and the power that fanaticism exercises over the human mind; they know that religion is an ancient machine that will never wear out, one that has always been used to ensure the loyalty of the people, and to curb the intractability of the human spirit; they know that error can blind the shrewdest of men, and that nothing succeeds better than the politics of those who enlist heaven and hell, God and the damned, in order to achieve their aims. So certain it is that religion itself, the purest source of all that is good, often becomes, through wholly deplorable abuse, the origin and the source of our ills.[37]

The author identifies, judiciously, what it was that contributed most to the increased power of the Holy See. The main reason he gives for this is the skilful conduct of Alexander VI, the pontiff who took cruelty and ambition to extreme lengths, and who knew nothing of justice except what served his self-interest.[38] And so, if it is true that one of the wickedest men ever to wear the tiara was that same man who most increased papal power, what must we think of Machiavelli's heroes?

This chapter ends with an encomium of Leo X, whose ambition, debauchery, and irreligion are common knowledge.[39] Machiavelli does not, explicitly, praise him for those qualities, but he nevertheless pays court to him: such princes deserve such courtiers. If he had praised Leo X only as a mighty prince, and as a patron of the arts, he would have been right; but he praises him as a statesman.

CHAPTER XII[40]

Variety prevails throughout the universe: men differ in character and temperament, while nature establishes a similar variety, if I dare to express myself thus, in the character of states. When I speak of the character of a state I mean, in general, its situation, its extent, the size and nature of its population, its commerce, customs and laws, its strengths and weaknesses, its wealth, and its resources.

These differences in the character of governments are appreciable, and indeed, if we descend to the details, infinite; and, just as doctors do not possess a secret remedy, one that treats all illnesses and all dispositions, so politicians cannot prescribe general rules whose application is appropriate to all forms of government.

This reflection leads me to examine Machiavelli's thoughts on foreign troops and on mercenaries. Our author rejects their use entirely, citing a number of examples on the basis of which he claims that mercenaries have been more damaging than they have been helpful to the states that have used them.

It is certainly the case, and experience has taught us this, that, in general, the best troops in a state are drawn from its own population. We could confirm this view with the example of the brave resistance of Leonidas at Thermopylae,[41] and, above all, with that of the extraordinary progress of the Roman empire, and of the power of the Arabs. Machiavelli's maxim is therefore applicable to every nation that is well enough populated to provide a sufficient number of soldiers for its defence. I am persuaded, as is our author, that a state can only be poorly served by mercenaries, and that the loyalty and courage of soldiers with possessions in a country far outstrip the loyalty and courage of mercenaries. It is, above all, dangerous to allow one's subjects to languish in inaction and to become soft and effeminate, at a time when fighting and the hardships of war are making seasoned soldiers of their neighbours.

It has been noted, more than once, that states that are emerging from civil war are infinitely superior to their enemies, because in a civil war everyone is a soldier, people are valued for their worth rather than for the favours shown them, every talent flourishes, and men habitually display all their skill and courage.

There are, however, cases that appear to be exceptions to this rule. If kingdoms or empires do not produce a great enough number of men as are required for an army and to replace the casualties of war, they are of necessity obliged to have recourse to mercenaries, as the only means of making up for the deficiencies of the state.

One can find, therefore, measures to alleviate most of these difficulties and by doing what Machiavelli finds damaging in such a militia: foreigners can be combined, judiciously, with nationals, so as to prevent the former from making up a separate force, and in order to instil in them the same discipline and loyalty; while the greatest care is given to ensuring that the number of foreigners does not exceed that of nationals.

There is a king in the North whose army is made up of such a combination of troops, and who is in consequence no less powerful and formidable.[42] Most European troops, indeed, are made up of both nationals and mercenaries: those who till the earth, and those who live in the towns, in return for a particular tax that they pay for the maintenance of the troops who are to defend them, no longer go to war. The soldiers, who are drawn from the worst section of the populace, useless people who prefer idleness to work, debauchees who seek the licence and impunity of the soldiery, feather-brained young people, disobedient to their parents, who enrol out of empty-headedness: all of them have as little liking for, and as little attachment to, their leaders as do the foreigners. How different these troops are from the Romans, who conquered the world! Desertions, so frequent in our day in all armies, were unknown in the Roman world; men who fought for their families, for their household gods, for the Roman people, and for all that they held most dear in this life, never thought of betraying, through a cowardly desertion, so many causes at one and the same time.

What assures the security of the great princes of Europe is that their troops are more or less equal, so that they have, in that respect, no advantage over one another. It is only Swedish troops who are, at one and the same time, citizens, peasants, and soldiers; but, when they are at war, almost no one remains within the country to till the land. Their power, therefore, is in no way formidable, since they cannot fight for long without damaging themselves more than do their enemies.

So much for the mercenaries. As to the way in which a great prince must wage war, I find myself wholly at one with Machiavelli. A great prince must, in practice, take entire responsibility for the conduct of his troops, and he must stay with his army, as he does within his residence; his self-interest, his duty, his reputation, everything commits him to this. Just as he is at the helm of distributive justice, so he is equally the protector and defender of his people; he must look upon the defence of his subjects as one of the most important objectives of his administration, one which he must entrust to no one but himself. His own interests seem, necessarily, to demand of him that he be present, in person, with his army, since every order that is issued comes from him, and so that plan and execution follow one from the other with the utmost rapidity. His presence, moreover, puts an end to any dissension among his generals, so deadly to armies, and so damaging to the interests of the leader. It introduces, too, better order into anything that concerns stores, ammunition, and all the supplies of war, without which even a Caesar, at the head of a hundred thousand soldiers, would never achieve anything. As it is the prince who decides to engage in battle, it seems only right that it should be for him also to direct the conduct of the war, and to communicate, through his own presence, a spirit of valour and confidence to his troops. He is at their head only to be an example to them.

But, you will object, not everyone is born a soldier, and many princes have neither the talent, nor the experience, nor the necessary courage, to lead an army. I concede that this is, indeed, the case. Such an objection need not, nevertheless, greatly discomfort me; for there is always, in an army, a sufficient number of competent generals, so that the prince has only to follow their advice. For a war will always go better this way than when the general is under the supervision of a minister, who, not himself being in the army, is not in a position to make judgements, and who often makes it impossible for even the most skilful general to give evidence of his capabilities.

I will finish this chapter by drawing attention to a remark made by Machiavelli which appears to me very remarkable. 'The Venetians,' he says, 'wary of the duke of Carmagnola, who was in command of their troops, were obliged to cause him leave this world.'

I must confess that I do not understand what it is to be obliged to cause someone to leave this world, unless this means to betray him, poison him, or to assassinate him. It is in this way, by moderating his language, that our Doctor of Crime believes he can make the blackest and most culpable actions appear innocent.[43]

The Greeks were in the habit of using circumlocutions when they spoke of death, because they could not bear, without an inner feeling of dread, to contemplate the terrible fact of mortality. Machiavelli, for his part, finds other words for crimes, because his heart, in revolt against his mind, cannot allow him to digest, raw, the terrible morality he teaches.

How regrettable it is to blush when you reveal yourself to others just as you are, and when you flee the opportunity to examine yourself!

CHAPTER XIII[44]

Machiavelli pushes hyperbole to its utmost extremity when he maintains that a wise prince would rather die alongside his own troops than prevail, with foreign help, in battle.

I doubt if a man in danger of drowning would lend an ear to those who claim that it is unworthy of him to owe his life to anyone but himself, and that he ought, therefore, to prefer to die rather than to catch hold of the rope or the stick that others, in order to save his life, are proffering him. Experience tells us that the first concern of men is their self-preservation, and the second their well-being; which entirely destroys our author's bombastic and false reasoning.

If we go deeper into this maxim that Machiavelli offers us, we will find, perhaps, that it is only excessive jealousy that inspires princes. It is, nevertheless, the jealousy of these same princes towards their generals or towards auxiliaries upon whom, for fear of having to share their glory, they did not wish to depend, that was always very damaging to their own interests. An infinite number of battles has been lost for this reason; petty jealousy, indeed, has often done more damage to princes than has the greater number or the superiority of their enemies.

Doubtless, a prince must not, when he wages war, use only auxiliary troops; he must himself be an auxiliary, and must ensure that he gives as much help as he receives. Here is what wisdom tells him: put yourself in a position where you need fear neither your enemies nor your friends; but if you have entered into a treaty, you must be faithful to it. For as long as the Empire, England, and Holland allied themselves against Louis XIV, for as long as Prince Eugène and Marlborough were united, they were the victors; but once England abandoned her allies, Louis XIV immediately recovered.[45]

Those powers that can manage without mixed or auxiliary troops would do well to exclude them from their armies; but since few European princes are in such a situation, it seems to me that they take no risks when they use auxiliaries, as long, that is, as the nationals exceed the auxiliaries in number.

Machiavelli was writing only for minor princes, and I confess that I see scarcely anything but minor ideas in his work; there is nothing great or true about him, because he is not a man of integrity.

Whoever wages war solely on behalf of another, can only be weak; whoever wages war in alliance with others, is very strong.

Leaving aside the war that the allies waged against France in 1701, the enterprise whereby three kings of the North stripped Charles XII of some of his German territories was also carried out by troops under different leaders, but who were linked by alliances;[46] and the war of 1734, which France began under the pretext of supporting the rights of the king of Poland (who was constantly being elected and constantly being dethroned), was waged by the French and the Spanish in alliance with the Savoyards.[47]

What, after so many examples, is Machiavelli left with, and what is the meaning of the allegory of the arms of Saul, which, when he had to fight Goliath, David refused because of their great weight?[48] This is mere whipped cream. I confess that auxiliaries sometimes inconvenience princes; but I wonder if princes do not, voluntarily, inconvenience themselves when, thereby, they win towns and provinces.

When it comes to the question of auxiliaries, Machiavelli attempts to pour venom on the Swiss who are in the service of France; I must say a word or two about these worthy troops, for it is beyond doubt that the French have won more than one battle with their help, that they rendered signal service to the French, and that if France were to dismiss the Swiss and the Germans who are serving in its infantry, its armed forces would be much less formidable than, at the present moment, they are.

So much for Machiavelli's errors of judgement; let us turn now to his moral errors. The bad examples that Machiavelli offers to princes are born of malice, and we cannot accept this. He refers, in this chapter, to Hiero of Syracuse, who, believing that his auxiliary troops were as dangerous to keep as to dismiss, had them all torn to pieces. Such facts, when we find them in history books, horrify us; but it is an outrage when we see them included in a book that must have been written for the instruction of princes.

Cruelty and barbarity are often fatal to private individuals, who are, therefore, generally speaking, horrified by them; but princes, whom Providence has placed at such a distance from the destinies of ordinary men, have much less aversion to them, since they have no need to fear them. So that all those who govern men must be taught to have the greatest distaste for all those abuses that they can themselves perpetrate through the use of their unlimited power.

CHAPTER XIV[49]

There is a kind of pedantry, one that all professions have in common, which comes only from the greed and intemperance of those who practise these professions. A soldier becomes a pedant when he is too concerned with minutiae, when he is boastful, or gives himself over to acting the Don Quixote.

Machiavelli's immoderation here exposes his prince to ridicule: he takes this point so far that he wants his prince to be nothing but a soldier; he makes of him a total Don Quixote, whose imagination is filled solely with battlefields, entrenchments, the methods of besieging different places, the making of demarcation lines, and the mounting of attacks.

But a prince fulfils only half of his calling if he concerns himself solely with the profession of war; it is clearly false that he must be, only, a soldier, and we might, indeed, remember what I said about the origin of princes in the first chapter of this work. Princes are, by the nature of their office, judges; and if they are also generals, that is of secondary importance. Machiavelli's prince is like the gods of Homer, who are portrayed as very strong and powerful, but never equitable. Our author knows nothing of the teachings of justice; he knows only self-interest and violence.

Our author, indeed, puts forward nothing but petty ideas; his narrow mind is concerned only with subjects relevant to the politics of princelings. Nothing is more feeble than the case he makes for recommending that princes should hunt: he is of the opinion that princes will learn in this way how to acquire knowledge of the geography and the main routes of their own country.

If a French king, or a Holy Roman Emperor, wanted, in this way, to acquire knowledge of his states, he would need to spend as much time hunting as it takes the universe to bring about the great revolution of the stars.

I hope I may be allowed to go into greater detail, here, on a matter that will be a kind of digression, on the question of hunting; and since this is a pleasure that is an almost universal passion among the aristocracy, among noblemen and kings, especially in Germany, it seems to me that it merits some discussion.

Hunting is one of those sensual pleasures that exercise the body but do nothing for the mind. It involves a passionate desire to pursue some beast or other, and a cruel satisfaction in killing it. It is a pastime that strengthens and refreshes the body, but leaves the mind lying fallow and uncultivated.

Hunters will, no doubt, reproach me for taking too serious a tone on these matters, and for being too severe a critic; they will say that I resemble those priests who, since they alone have the privilege of speaking from the pulpit, can, without fear of contradiction, say anything they like.

I will not avail myself of this privilege; I will simply put forward, in good faith, the specious arguments that enthusiasts for hunting advance. They will tell me, first of all, that hunting is the noblest and most ancient pleasure enjoyed by men; that the biblical patriarchs, and many great men even, have been hunters; and that, by hunting, men continue to exercise over animals the same right that God Himself deigned to grant to Adam.

But, because something is old, it is not necessarily better, above all when it is carried to excess. Great men have been, I must admit, passionate about hunting; and they have had their faults as well as their weaknesses. Let us, however, imitate what was great about them, and not what was petty.

The patriarchs went hunting; this is well established; I must confess, also, that they married their sisters, and that polygamy was customary in their time. But these worthy patriarchs, in hunting as they did, only exhibited the barbaric character of the times in which they lived: they were uncouth and grossly ignorant. They were idlers, too, who, not knowing how to occupy themselves, and, in order to kill the time that hung heavily on their hands, took their boredom, as it were, for a walk, and went hunting; so that they wasted in the woods, in pursuing animals, time which they had neither the ability nor the wit to spend in the company of reasonable people.

I wonder if these are examples to be imitated, and if such uncouthness is what civilises us, or if it is not, rather, the task of enlightened centuries to serve as a model for those that follow.

Whether or not Adam was given power over the beasts is not the question I am asking; what I do know, very well, is that we are more cruel and rapacious even than the beasts, and that we exercise, most tyrannically, this power that we claim. If anything should give us an advantage over the animals, this must be our power of reasoning; and those who usually declare themselves in favour of hunting, have nothing in their heads but horses, dogs, and all sorts of animals. They are sometimes very uncouth, and it is greatly to be feared that they will become as inhuman towards men as they are towards animals, or that, at the very least, the cruel habit of inflicting suffering, with total indifference, will make them less sensitive to the misfortunes of their fellow men. Is that the pleasure of which the nobility speaks so highly? Is that the activity they claim to be so worthy of a thinking being?

It will be objected that hunting is good for the health; that experience has shown us that those who hunt live to a great age; that it is a harmless pleasure, one that suits great noblemen, since it spreads their grandeur far and wide, dispels their woes, and, in times of peace, offers them visions of war.

I am far from condemning moderate exercise; but let us be careful: exercise is a necessity only for those who over-indulge. There is no prince who has lived longer than did the Cardinal de Fleury or the Cardinal Jiménes de Cisneros, or the last pope.[50] These three men, however, did not hunt. Must we, moreover, choose an occupation whose only merit is that it promises us a long life? Monks live longer, usually, than do other men: must one, therefore, become a monk?

My point is not that a man should draw out his days in useless idleness until he reaches the age of Methuselah; but that the more time he has given to reflection, the more fine and worthy his actions will be, and the more he will have lived.

Hunting is, moreover, of all the pleasures that there are, the one that is the least appropriate for princes. They could display their rank in a hundred ways that would be of greater use to their subjects; and if it should happen that an over-abundance of game was harmful to country people, the task of destroying these animals could perfectly well be undertaken by hunters paid for this purpose. Princes should, properly speaking, be concerned only with the task of informing themselves, and with governing, in order to acquire even more knowledge, so that they might form a view of their own profession that would make them act well subsequently.

I must add, especially in reply to Machiavelli, that, in order to be a great leader, it is not necessary to be a hunter. Gustavus Adolphus, Turenne, Marlborough, Prince Eugene, all of whose qualities as eminent men and skilful generals are beyond dispute, were, none of them, hunters; nor do we read anywhere that Caesar, Alexander or Scipio hunted.[51]

We can, when out walking, reflect more judiciously and more profoundly on the geography of a country in relation to the art of war than when we are distracted by partridges, hunting dogs, stags, a pack of all kinds of animals, and the thrill of the chase. A great prince who led the second campaign in Hungary, risked, through having lost his way when hunting, being made prisoner by the Turks.[52] Hunting ought to be forbidden even in the army, since during a march it can cause great disorder.

I conclude, therefore, that it is permissible for princes to go hunting, provided they do so only rarely, and in order to distract them from their serious and sometimes very sad duties. I do not, I repeat, forbid any respectable pleasure; but the need to govern well, to ensure that the state flourishes, to protect and promote the success of all the arts, is, without doubt, the greatest pleasure of all; and woe to him who needs other pleasures!

CHAPTER XV[53]

What painters and historians have in common is that they have to copy nature. The former portray the features and complexion of men; the latter their characters and actions: but there are painters so eccentric that they portray nothing but monsters and devils.

Machiavelli portrays the universe as hell, and all human beings as the damned; you might say that this writer about politics, out of a particular form of hatred, tried to slander the whole of humankind, and that he has taken it upon himself to annihilate virtue, in order, perhaps, to make all the inhabitants of this continent resemble himself.

Machiavelli maintains that it is not possible to be wholly good in this world, so wicked and corrupt is the human race; while I, for my part, maintain that if one is not to perish, one must be wise and good. Men are, in general, neither wholly good nor wholly bad; but everyone, whether good, bad, or mediocre, will unite in their support of a powerful prince who is both skilful and just. I would rather wage war against a tyrant than against a good king, rather against a Louis XI than a Louis XII, rather against a Domitian than a Trajan; for the good king will be well served, while the tyrant's subjects will desert to my army.[54] If I go to Italy in order to take on, with ten thousand men, an Alexander VI, half of Italy will be on my side; if I go there with forty thousand men, in order to take on an Innocent XI, all Italy will rise up and destroy me.[55] In England, no wise and good king has ever been dethroned by a large army; and all their bad kings have been worsted by rivals, who did not even go to war with four thousand regular soldiers. Do not, in other words, meet wickedness with wickedness, but with dauntless virtue: you will, if you do so, make your own people as virtuous as you are, your neighbours will try to imitate you, and the wicked will tremble.

CHAPTER XVI[56]

Two famous sculptors, Phidias and Alcamenes, made, each of them, a statue of Minerva;[57] the Athenians had to choose the more beautiful, which was to be placed on the top of a column. Both statues were shown to the public: that of Alcamenes won the greater number of votes; the other, it was said, was too crudely worked. Phidias, undismayed by the people's decision, requested that, since the statues had been made to be placed on a column, they should, both of them, be put there; whereupon Phidias's statue won the prize.

Phidias owed his success to the study of visual form and proportion. Politics, too, needs to observe proportionality: different places demand different rules; to attempt to apply a rule universally would be to vitiate it; what would be admirable for a great kingdom would not be suitable for a small state. Luxurious living, which is born of abundance, and which causes wealth to circulate through the bloodstream of a state, makes a great kingdom flourish; it is luxury which supports industry, and it is luxury that increases the needs of the rich, so as to bind them, through these same needs, to the poor.

If some maladroit politician decided to ban luxurious living in a great state, that state would sink into idleness; luxury, on the contrary, would destroy a small state. Money that leaves a country in greater quantities and proportion than returns to it would cause the delicate body to succumb to consumption, so that it would inevitably waste away and die.[58] It is, therefore, an indispensable rule for every politician that he never confuse small states with large ones, and this is where Machiavelli in this chapter sins grievously.

The first error with which I must reproach him is that he understands the word 'generosity' in too vague a sense. He does not distinguish between generosity and prodigality. 'In order to do great things,' he says, 'a prince must not only appear to be generous, he must also be so.' I know of no hero who has not been generous. It would be the essence of miserliness to say to the people, 'Expect nothing of me, I will always reward you inadequately for your services'; to say this would be to extinguish the enthusiasm that every subject instinctively feels for serving his prince.

It is, without doubt, only a thrifty man who can be generous: only he who manages his own goods prudently can do good to others.

Everyone is familiar with the example of Francis I, king of France, whose excessive expenditure was the cause, in part, of his misfortunes. Francis I's pleasures consumed all the resources that attended his princely splendour; he was not generous but, rather, prodigal; and at the end of his life he became a little miserly; instead of managing his resources carefully he put treasure into his coffers.[59] But it is not treasures which are out of circulation that are needed, but, rather, ample revenues. Any individual, any king, who knows only how to accumulate and how to hoard money, understands nothing: money must be made to circulate if true wealth is to be created. The Medici acquired sovereignty in Florence only because the great Cosimo, father of his country, but a simple merchant, was skilful and generous.[60] A miser is nothing more than a small-minded individual, and I think, too, that Cardinal de Retz is right when he says that, in matters of importance, one must never think of money. The sovereign who puts himself into a position where he can acquire much revenue, by favouring the commerce and manufacturing industry of his subjects, is one who can, therefore, spend much money wisely: he will be loved and valued.

Machiavelli says that generosity will earn a prince nothing but contempt: this is what a moneylender might say; but ought a man who has taken it upon himself to offer advice to princes say it?

CHAPTER XVII[61]

The most precious responsibility with which princes are entrusted is the life of their subjects. A prince's office gives him the power either to condemn the guilty to death or to pardon them. He is the supreme arbiter of justice.

Good princes regard this much-vaunted power that they hold over the lives of their subjects as the most onerous duty conferred by the crown. They know that they, too, are men, as are those on whom they must pass judgement; they know that wrongs, injustice, and injury can be remedied in this world, but that a hastily imposed death sentence is an irreparable evil. They tend towards severity only to avoid the laxer discipline which they foresee if they behaved otherwise; they take these painfully difficult decisions only in cases that are desperate; like the case of the man, who, feeling gangrene in his limb, and in spite of the tenderness he feels towards himself, decides to have it cut off, in order to preserve, and to save, by means of this painful operation, at least the rest of his body.

Machiavelli treats such serious, grave, and important matters as mere trifles. According to him, human life counts for nothing; self-interest, the only god he worships, counts for everything. He prefers cruelty to clemency, and he advises those who have recently become sovereigns to disregard, much more than others do, the stigma of being cruel.

It is the hangman who puts Machiavelli's heroes on the throne, and who keeps them there. When our political thinker looks for examples of cruelty, it is with Cesare Borgia that he takes refuge.

Machiavelli quotes, once again, some verses that Virgil puts into the mouth of Dido; but this quotation is entirely misplaced, because Virgil makes Dido speak in precisely the same way as Jocasta is made to speak in the tragedy *Oedipus*.[62] The poet makes these figures speak in language that is appropriate to their character. It is not, in other words, Dido's authority, it is not Jocasta's authority, that should be appropriated for use in a political treatise; what is needed is the example of great men and virtuous men.

Our political author recommends, above all, that the soldiery be sub-jected to strict discipline; he contrasts Scipio's indulgent approach with Hannibal's severity; he prefers the Carthaginian to the Roman, and quickly concludes that severity is the motive force of order and discipline, and therefore of victory for an army. Machiavelli does not on this occasion act in good faith, for he chooses Scipio, the mildest of all the generals as far as discipline is concerned, in order to set him against Hannibal and to favour strict discipline.

I concede that good order cannot exist in an army without strict discipline; for how can libertines, debauchees, scoundrels, cowards, chancers, beasts who are nothing but coarse automata, be held to their duty, if they are not given pause by fear of punishment?

All I ask of Machiavelli on this matter is moderation: that he should un-derstand that, while clemency inspires goodness in a man of integrity, at the same time wisdom does not incline him any the less to severity. But his se-verity is like that of a skilful pilot; we see him taking down the masts and the rigging of his ship only when he is forced to do so by the imminent dan-ger to which storm and tempest expose him.

There are occasions when one must be strict, although never cruel. I would rather, in battle, be loved by my soldiers than feared.

I come now to Machiavelli's most fallacious argument. He says that, since most people are inclined to ingratitude, changeability, dissimulation, coward-ice, and greed, a prince acts more wisely if he makes himself feared rather than loved; that love encourages a sense of obligation, which malice and the baseness of the human race make very fragile, whereas the fear of punishment inspires in people a much greater attachment to duty; that men can be mas-ters of their goodwill, but not of their fear; and, therefore, that a wise prince will depend upon himself rather than upon others.

I do not deny that there are in the world men who are ungrateful and who dissimulate; I do not deny that severity is from time to time very useful. But I would suggest that every king whose policies have no purpose other than that of inspiring fear will only reign over cowards and slaves; that he will not be able to expect great acts from his subjects, because everything that is in-spired by fear and timidity has always had this outcome. I maintain that a prince who has the gift of making himself loved will reign over the hearts of his subjects, since they see their own interest lies in having him as their lord and master, and that there are a great many examples, in history, of great and fine acts performed out of love and loyalty. I maintain, as well, that the fashion for sedition and revolution seems to have entirely disappeared in our days. We see no kingdom, except for England, where the king has the slightest reason to be fearful of his people; and in England, even, the king has nothing to fear, unless it is he himself who stirs up the storm.

I conclude, therefore, that a prince who is cruel is more at risk of being betrayed than an easy-going prince, since cruelty is intolerable, and we soon tire of being afraid, and because, after all, goodness is always lovable, and we do not grow tired of loving it.

It is much to be hoped, then, for the happiness of the world, that princes should be good without being too indulgent, so that goodness in them would always be a virtue, and never a weakness.

CHAPTER XVIII[63]

Machiavelli, the tutor of tyrants, dares to assert here that princes can deceive the whole world by dissembling: it is on this point that I must begin my refutation of him.

Everyone knows how curious the public is; the public is a creature that sees everything, hears everything, and discloses everything it has seen and heard. If, out of curiosity, it examines the conduct of private individuals, it does so to distract itself from its idleness; but when it makes judgements about the character of princes, it does so out of its own self-interest. Princes, then, are exposed more than are any other men to the study and the judgement of the world. They are like the stars, on which a whole army of astronomers has focussed its telescopes and its astrolabes. The courtiers who watch the princes notice everything; a single gesture, a glance, a look, betrays them, and the public make inferences as to what they are thinking;[64] in a word, just as the sun cannot disguise its sunspots, so a great prince cannot hide his vices and his true character from the eyes of so many observers.

Even if the mask of dissimulation were to hide for a while the natural deformities of a prince, he would not be able to wear this mask continuously, but would remove it sometimes, even if only to breathe; and even one such occasion would be enough to give satisfaction to the curious.

Guile and dissimulation, therefore, will in vain grace the lips of the prince; deceit in his speech and his actions will be of no avail to him. Men are not to be judged by what they say; that would always lead one to error; rather, their actions should be compared one with another, and then with their words: in the face of repeated examination of this kind, falsehood and dissimulation will never prevail.

It is only if we act in accordance with our true selves, that we act well; we must in actual fact be of the character that we want the whole world to suppose us to be; if not, he who believes he is deceiving the public is himself deceived.

Sixtus V, Philip II, and Cromwell, were, all of them, widely thought to be hypocritical and enterprising, but never virtuous.[65] A prince, however cunning he is, and even if he were to follow all Machiavelli's maxims, cannot turn his crimes into a virtue that he does not possess.

Machiavelli does not argue any better when he turns to the reasons that must incline princes to deceit and hypocrisy. The ingenious and false parallel he draws with the old story about centaurs proves nothing; for, even if the centaur had had a form that was half-human and half-horse, would it follow from this that princes must be both wily and ferocious?[66] Someone must really want to preach a particular theory about crime, if they resort to such weak and irrelevant arguments.

But we come now to an argument more specious than any we have as yet seen. Machiavelli, the teacher of politics, says that a prince must combine the qualities of a lion and of a fox; of the lion, in order to rid himself of wolves, and of the fox, in order to be cunning; and he concludes, 'This demonstrates that a prince is not bound to keep his word.' Here, indeed, is a conclusion without premises: our Doctor of Crime, is he not ashamed of himself for garbling in this way his lessons in impiety?

If I wished to introduce probity and good sense into Machiavelli's muddled thoughts, here, more or less, is how I might render them. The world is like a game of cards, played by honest men, but also by rascals who cheat. If a prince, therefore, who must take part in this game, is not to be deceived, he must know how to cheat at cards, not because he would ever indulge in such a practice himself, but so that he will not be deceived by others.

Let us return to the blunders of our author. 'Since all men', he says, 'are scoundrels, who never keep their word, you are not obliged, any more than they are, to keep yours.' Here, for a start, is a contradiction; for the author says, a moment later, that men who dissemble will always find others who are so simple that they may be deceived. How is this consistent with what he has just said? All men are scoundrels, and yet you will find men so simple that they may easily be deceived!

It is, moreover, not at all the case that the world is made up only of scoundrels. One must, indeed, be very misanthropic if one cannot see that in any society there are many honest people, and that the greater number of them is neither good nor bad. But if Machiavelli had not supposed the whole of humanity to be wicked, upon what would he have based his abominable maxim? Even if we were to assume that all men are as wicked as Machiavelli claims, it would not follow that we must imitate them. If Cartouche steals, loots, and assassinates, I conclude that Cartouche is a wretch who must be punished, and not that I should model my conduct on his.[67] If there were no more honour or virtue in the world, as Charles the Wise said, it would be to princes that we would have to look, in order to recover any traces of them.[68]

After our author has proved the need for crime, he tries to encourage his disciples by asserting how easy it is to commit it. 'Those who understand the art of dissembling', he says, 'will always find men who are so simple that they may be deceived', which comes down in the end to this: your neighbour is a fool and you are clever; you must, therefore, deceive him because he is a fool. Such are the syllogisms for which Machiavelli's pupils were hanged and broken on the wheel in the Place de Grève.[69]

Machiavelli, not satisfied with having demonstrated, according to his own way of thinking, the ease with which crime may be committed, raises next the joys of treachery; but what is deplorable about this is that Cesare Borgia, the most wicked and the most perfidious of men, Machiavelli's hero Cesare Borgia, was, in truth, thoroughly wretched. Machiavelli is careful not to mention him at this point. He needs to give examples; but where would he find them, except from the registers of criminal trials, or from the history of wicked popes and Neros? He asserts that Alexander VI, the most false of men, the most impious man of his age, always succeeded in his deceitfulness, because he knew very well how weak and credulous men are.

I venture to assert that it was not so much the credulity of men, but rather certain events and certain circumstances which, sometimes, ensured the success of Alexander VI's plans; above all, the contrast between French and Spanish ambitions, the dissension and hatred within Italian families, and the passions and general weakness of Louis XII contributed no less to this outcome.

Deceitfulness, if one takes it too far, is even a failure of style in politics. I cite the authority of a great politician: Don Luis de Haro, who said of Cardinal Mazarin that he had one great failing, politically speaking: that he always was deceitful. When this same Mazarin wanted to involve M. de Fabert in a disgraceful negotiation, Marshal de Fabert said to him, 'Permit me, my lord, to refuse to deceive the duke of Savoy, especially since the matter in question is a mere trifle; I am known everywhere as an honest man; keep my probity in reserve, therefore, for an occasion when what is at stake is the safety of France.'[70]

I am not, at this moment, talking about honesty or virtue; but, if we consider only the self-interest of princes, I say that it is very bad politics on their part to be deceitful, and to fool everybody: they deceive only once; and once is enough to lose the trust of all princes.

A great power recently set out in a manifesto the reasons for its actions, and acted subsequently in a manner entirely inconsistent with what it had set out.[71] I confess that behaviour as striking as this is wholly destructive of confidence: the more immediate the contradiction, the more gross it is. The church of Rome, to avoid such contradictions, has wisely fixed a probation period, of one hundred years following their death, for those it places among the number of the saints; thanks to which, the memory of their faults and of their excesses dies with them; those who witnessed their lives, and those who could testify against them, are no longer alive, so nothing contradicts the aura of saintliness wanted for the public.

I hope I may be pardoned for this digression. I confess, moreover, that there are troublesome, although necessary, circumstances in which a prince cannot avoid breaking his treaties and alliances. But he must distance himself from them honourably, by warning his allies in good time, and, above all, by never going to such lengths, unless the safety of his people, and overwhelming necessity, oblige him to do so.

I will end this chapter with a single reflection. We must note the ease with which vices multiply in the hands of Machiavelli. He wants an unbelieving king to crown his unbelief with hypocrisy; he thinks that the people will be more moved by the piety of a prince than they will be disaffected by the ills they suffer at his hands. There are people who agree with Machiavelli; to me it seems that one should always be indulgent towards errors of theory, so long as they do not bring in their wake the corruption of the heart; and that the people will prefer a prince who is a non-believer, but who is a man of integrity and who assures their well-being, to an orthodox believer who is a scoundrel and evil-doer. It is not what a prince thinks, but what he does, which makes men content.

CHAPTER XIX[72]

The passion for systematic thought has not been the privileged folly of philosophers only; it has also become that of political thinkers. Machiavelli is more infected by it than anyone else: he wants to prove that a prince needs to be wicked and deceitful; these are the sacramental words of his religion. Machiavelli has all the malice of the monsters felled by Hercules, but he has not their strength; we do not, then, need Hercules's club to knock Machiavelli down. For, what is more simple, more natural, and more appropriate in princes than justice and goodness? I do not think it is necessary to exhaust oneself in putting forward arguments to prove this. Our political thinker must, therefore, and of necessity, lose the argument by maintaining the contrary. For if he maintains that a prince, already established on his throne, must needs be cruel, deceitful, treacherous, etc., there would be no gain at all in teaching him to be wicked. And if he wants to endow a prince who is seizing the throne with all these vices, the author, in order to make the prince's usurpation secure, gives him advice whose effect will be to cause every sovereign and every republic to rise up against him. For, how can a private individual achieve sovereignty except by dispossessing a sovereign prince of his states, or by usurping the authority of a republic? This is certainly not how the princes of Europe understand matters. If Machiavelli had composed a collection of ruses for the use of thieves, he could not have produced a more culpable work than this.

I must, however, give an account of several false arguments that appear in this chapter. Machiavelli claims that a prince becomes odious to his subjects when he unjustly seizes their property, and violates the honour of their wives. It is obvious that a prince who is self-seeking, unjust, violent, and cruel is bound to be hated by, and to make himself odious to, his people. But this is not always the case when it comes to love affairs. Julius Caesar, who was called in Rome the husband of every wife and the wife of every husband; Louis XIV, who very much loved women; Augustus I, king of Poland,[73] who shared women with his subjects: these princes were not hated because of their love affairs; and Caesar was assassinated, with the Romans' love of freedom thrusting so many daggers into his side, because he was a usurper, and not because he was a libertine.

On the subject of the expulsion of the kings of Rome, the attempt on the virtue of Lucretia will, perhaps, be cited in support of Machiavelli's view, and against my argument. But my reply is that it was not the love of the young Tarquin for Lucretia, but the violent manner in which he made love, that caused the uprising in Rome; and that, since this act of violence reawakened in the people memories of other violent acts committed by the Tarquins, they considered, seriously, taking vengeance; if, that is, the story of Lucretia is not a fiction.[74]

I do not say this to excuse the love affairs of princes, which can be morally evil; I have tried here to show only that they did not cause sovereigns to be hated. Love among good princes is considered a pardonable weakness, provided it is not accompanied by injustice. One can make love, as did Louis XIV, as did Charles II, king of England, as did King Augustus; but neither Nero nor David should be imitated.

Here is, as it seems to me, a contradiction in terms. Machiavelli requires that 'a prince make himself loved by his subjects, in order to avoid plots against him'; while in chapter XVII he says that 'a prince must aim, above all, to make himself feared, since he can count only on what depends upon himself, which is not at all the case where the love of the people is concerned'. Which of these represents the true opinion of the author? He speaks in oracles, so that we can interpret him as we wish; but this oracular language, it should be said in passing, is the language of rogues.

I must say here, in general, that conspiracies and assassinations hardly ever occur in the world of today; princes are, as to that, safe. These crimes are out of date; they have gone out of fashion, and the reasons that Machiavelli gives for this are sound; there is, at the very most, only the fanaticism of a few ecclesiastics which can make them commit, out of their pure fanaticism, so dreadful a crime. Among the good things Machiavelli says on the matter of conspiracies, there is one that is very good, but which, coming from him, is bad. Here it is: 'A conspirator', he says, 'is troubled by his apprehension of the punishment that threatens him, while kings are supported by the majesty of their dominion and by the authority of the law.' It seems to me that Machiavelli, our political theorist, is not the person to pronounce on law, he for whom self-interest, cruelty, despotism, and wrongful seizure of power find their way into everything. Machiavelli does what the Protestants do: they use the arguments of non-believers against the trans-substantiation of the Catholics, and they use the same arguments that the Catholics use in support of trans-substantiation, to defeat non-believers.

Machiavelli, then, advises princes to make themselves loved, and to school themselves to that end, in order to win over, equally, the goodwill of the nobles and of the people; he is right to advise them to delegate to others anything that could arouse the hatred of one or other of these two groups of people, and to appoint, to this end, magistrates to arbitrate between the people and the noblemen. He offers as a model the government of France. This man, an outrageous friend of despotism and of the wrongful seizure of power, thinks well of the authority that the parlements of France had in former times![75] It seems to me that, if there is a form of government whose wisdom one could offer as a model, it is that of England: there, Parliament is the arbiter between the people and the king, and the king has unlimited powers to do good, but none to do harm.

Machiavelli enters now into a lengthy discussion of the life of the Roman emperors, from Marcus Aurelius until the two Gordians.[76] He attributes the cause of the frequent changes in the empire to corruption; but this was not the only cause. Caligula, Claudius, Nero, Galba, Otho, and Vitellius all came to a grievous end, without having bought Rome, as did Didius Julianus.[77] Corruption was in the end one more reason for assassinating emperors; but the real cause of these revolutions was the form of government. The Praetorian Guards became what were later the Mamluks in Egypt, the Janissaries in Turkey, and the Strelitzes in Muscovy. Constantine broke up the Praetorian Guard skilfully; but in the end the misfortunes of the empire exposed its leaders, once again, to assassination and poisoning.[78] I will point out that only wicked emperors died violent deaths; whereas a Theodosius died in his bed, and a Justinian lived happily for eighty-four years.[79] I must insist upon this. There were almost no bad princes who lived happily, and Augustus knew peace only when he became virtuous.[80] The tyrant Commodus, successor to the divine Marcus Aurelius, was put to death, in spite of the respect in which his father was held. Caracalla could not maintain his position for long, because of his cruelty. Severus Alexander was killed through the betrayal of Maximinus Thrax, who was held to be a giant, and Maximinus, having roused everyone against him because of his barbarous acts, was, in turn, assassinated.[81] Machiavelli claims that Maximinus died because of the contempt aroused by his low birth. Machiavelli is quite wrong: a man who rises to power through his own courage no longer has relatives; we think only of his power, and not of his birth. Pupienus was the son of a village blacksmith, Probus of a gardener, Diocletian of a slave, Valentinian of a rope-maker: they were all highly respected.[82] Sforza, who conquered Milan, was a peasant; Cromwell, who subjected England to his rule, and made all Europe tremble, was the son of a tradesman; the great Mohammed, founder of the most flourishing religion in the whole world, worked as a boy in a shop; Samo, the first king of the Slavs, was a French tradesman; the famous Piast, whose name is still revered in Poland, was elected king while still wearing clogs, and he lived and was respected for many a long year.[83] How many generals, how many ministers and chancellors have been of common birth! Europe is full of them, and is all the better for it, for such positions are given on merit. I do not say this in order to despise the blood of Widukind, Charlemagne, and Otto;[84] I must, on the contrary, and for more than one reason, love the noble blood of heroes; but I love, still more, merit.

We ought not to forget here that Machiavelli is greatly mistaken in thinking that, in the time of Severus, it was enough to treat the military carefully in order to maintain power. The history of the emperors contradicts this. The more carefully the unruly Praetorian Guard was treated, the more they felt their own power; and it was as dangerous to pander to them as it was to try to repress them. The military are not today to be feared, because they are all divided into small units who watch over each other, because kings appoint all those who work for them, and because the power of law is better established. The Turkish emperors are only exposed to this danger because they have not yet learned how to use such policies to their own advantage. The Turks are slaves of the sultan, and the sultan is the slave of the Janissaries. In Christian Europe, a prince must treat equally well everyone that is under his command, without the discrimination that causes jealousies fatal to his interests.

The example of Severus, offered by Machiavelli to those bent on taking power, is therefore every bit as bad as would the example of Marcus Aurelius be useful to them. But how can we present, together, as models, Severus, Cesare Borgia, and Marcus Aurelius?[85] To do so is to unite wisdom and the purest virtue with the most terrible wickedness.

I cannot finish without emphasising, yet again, that Cesare Borgia, with his so cunning cruelty, came to a very bad end; and that Marcus Aurelius, that philosopher wreathed with laurels, always good, always virtuous, never experienced, to the day of his death, any reversal of fortune.

CHAPTER XX[86]

In pagan times Janus was portrayed with two faces, which indicated the perfect knowledge he had of the past and of the future. The image of this god, taken allegorically, can very easily apply to princes. They must, as did Janus, look backwards into the history of all the centuries that have passed, and which provide them with salutary lessons in conduct and duty; they must also, like Janus, look forward, with clear-sightedness, and with the strength and good judgement which brings together everything that is relevant, and discerns in present states of affairs those that must follow.

Machiavelli puts five questions to princes, both to those who will have made new conquests and to those for whom policy requires only that they make their existing possessions secure. Let us consider what better ideas a prudent judgement can suggest, by combining the past with the future, and by making decisions on the basis always of reason and justice.

Here is the first question: should a prince disarm a people he has conquered, or not?

One must always reflect on how far the conduct of war has changed since Machiavelli's time. It is always well-disciplined armies, more or less strong, who provide protection for their country; a mere collection of armed peasants would be the object of scorn. If, sometimes, during a siege, the citizens take up arms, the besieging forces will not tolerate this, and, to contain them, will threaten them with bombardment and red-hot cannonballs. It appears, moreover, that it is prudent in a conquered town to disarm the citizens in the first instance, especially if they pose some sort of threat. The Romans who had conquered Great Britain, and who could not maintain the peace there, because of the turbulent and bellicose nature of the people, took the decision effectively to emasculate them, in order to temper their wild and bellicose instincts; this, as Rome had hoped, succeeded. The Corsicans are a handful of men, as courageous and steadfast as the English; they can be tamed, I believe, only by wisdom and goodness. In order to preserve sovereignty in Corsica, it seems to me absolutely necessary that the inhabitants be disarmed and their customs moderated. I will say, in passing, on the subject of the Corsicans, that we can see, from their example, what courage and strength the love of freedom gives to men, and how dangerous and unjust it is to oppress it.

The second question concerns the confidence a prince, after making himself master of a new state, should have either, on the one hand, in those of his new subjects who have helped him to become their leader, or, on the other, in those who have remained faithful to their legitimate prince.

When a town is captured through intelligence and through the treachery of various citizens, a prince would be most unwise to trust the traitors, who will probably betray him; and he must assume that those who have been faithful to their former masters will also be so to their new sovereign; for they are, usually, wise heads, householders who have property in the country, people who like good order, and to whom every change is unwelcome: one must, nevertheless, not trust anyone too readily.

But let us suppose for a moment that an oppressed people, forced to bear the yoke of a tyrant, were to call upon another prince to govern them. I think that the prince should repay in every way the confidence accorded to him, and that if he fails to repay, on this occasion, those who have entrusted to him all they hold dear, that would be a most unworthy sign of ingratitude and one that would certainly sully his reputation. William, prince of Orange, maintained until the end of his life his friendship for, and his confidence in, those who had placed in his hands the reins of government in England; while those who were opposed to him abandoned their fatherland, and followed King James.[87]

In elective kingdoms, where most elections are corrupt, and where, whatever we say about it, the throne goes to the highest bidder, I believe that the new sovereign will find the means, after his elevation, to buy those who have been opposed to him, just as he won the favour of those who elected him. Poland offers us examples of this: the throne is trafficked so crudely there that you might think that it had been purchased in public, in the market-place. The generosity of a Polish king sweeps aside all opposition; he is the master of the art of winning over the great families by granting them estates, whole counties, and other offices. Nevertheless, since, on the matter of gifts, the Poles have very short memories, it is necessary often to return to the charge. The republic of Poland is, in a word, like the Danaïdes' barrel:[88] even the most generous king will in vain shower gifts upon his people; he will never satisfy them. Nevertheless, as a king of Poland has a great many favours to bestow, he can use his resources economically by bestowing gifts only when he has need of the families whom he is enriching.

Machiavelli's third question concerns, in essence, the security of a prince in a hereditary kingdom: whether it would be better for him to maintain unity or discord among his subjects.

This question could perhaps have arisen at the time of Machiavelli's ancestors in Florence; but I do not think that any politician now would raise it in this form, crudely and without qualification. I need quote only the fine and well-known fable of Menenius Agrippa, by means of which he reunited the Roman people.[89] Republics, however, must maintain, in one way or another, jealousy among their members, for if neither party watches over the other, the government becomes a monarchy.

There are princes who believe that disagreements among their ministers are necessary, to protect their own interests; they think that they are less likely to be deceived by men who are constantly on the watch, one upon the other, through mutual hatred. But, if such hatred has this effect, it also produces an effect that is very dangerous; since, instead of the ministers having to work together in the service of the prince, it often happens that, with the intention of harming each other, they thwart one another continually, and that in the course of their individual quarrels they damage the interests of the prince and the safety of the people.

Nothing, then, contributes more to the strength of a monarchy than the intimate and inseparable union of all its members; which it must be the aim of a wise prince to promote.

The answer I have just given to Machiavelli's third question can, up to a point, provide a solution to his fourth problem; let us, however, examine and judge, briefly, whether a prince should encourage factions against himself, or if he should win the friendship of his subjects.

To create enemies in order to fight them is to fashion monsters simply in order to defeat them; it is more natural, more reasonable, and more human to make friends. Blessed are the princes who know the sweetness of friendship! Still more blessed are those who deserve the love and the affection of their people!

We come now to Machiavelli's last question, which is to say: whether a prince should have fortresses and citadels, or whether he ought to raze them to the ground.

I believe I have already, in my tenth chapter, expressed my opinions as regards princelings; let us move now to the conduct of kings.

In Machiavelli's time, the world was in a state of general ferment; a spirit of sedition and revolution reigned everywhere; there was nothing but party strife and tyrants: frequent and continual revolutions obliged princes to build citadels on the heights above towns in order to contain, in this way, the restless spirit of the inhabitants.

Since Machiavelli's barbarous times, either because men have become weary of destroying one another, or because sovereigns wield a more despotic power over their states, there is no more talk of sedition and revolution, and one might even say that this spirit of restlessness, having exhausted itself, has reached at present a state of tranquillity; so that citadels are no longer needed to assure the loyalty of towns and countries. This is, however, not the case when it comes to fortifications intended to provide assurance against enemies, the better to make secure the peace of the state.

Armies and fortresses are of equal usefulness to princes, since they can confront their enemies with their armies, and, if a battle is lost, the army can be saved by the artillery in their fortresses; while the siege that the enemy is mounting against their fortress gives them time to regroup, and to raise further forces, which they can, if they raise them in time, use to lift the enemy siege.

The recent wars in Flanders between the emperor and France made scarcely any progress, thanks to the great number of fortified sites.[90] Battles involving one hundred thousand men waged against another hundred thousand men led to no more than the capture of one or two towns; in the next campaign the adversary, having had the time to make good his losses, reappeared once again, and what had been won the previous year was again in dispute. In countries where there are many fortified sites, armies occupying over two miles of ground can fight for thirty years, and, if they are fortunate, win, at a cost of twenty battles, ten miles of terrain.

In open country, the outcome of a battle or of two campaigns may decide the fortunes of the victor, and give him sway over whole kingdoms. Alexander, Caesar, Genghis Khan, and Charles XII owed their victories to finding few fortified sites in the countries they conquered; the conqueror of India mounted only two sieges during his glorious campaigns; the arbiter of Poland mounted no more.[91] Eugene, Villars, Marlborough, and Luxembourg were great military leaders; but, in a way, fortresses took the edge off the brilliance of their successes.[92] The French know very well how useful fortresses are, for, from Brabant to the Dauphiné, there stretches, in effect, a double chain of fortified sites; the French frontier towards Germany is like the open jaws of a lion, which offer two rows of threatening teeth that seem to want to swallow up everything.

I have said enough to demonstrate the principal uses of fortified towns.

Chapter XXI[93]

This chapter of Machiavelli contains both good and bad. I will point out, in the first instance, Machiavelli's mistakes; I will support what he says that is good and praiseworthy; and I will hazard, subsequently, my own opinions on some subjects that are relevant to these topics.

Machiavelli offers the conduct of Ferdinand of Aragon and of Bernard of Milan as models for those who want to distinguish themselves in great enterprises and unusual and extraordinary actions.[94] He seeks a similar distinction in the boldness and rapidity with which such enterprises are carried out. Actions of this kind are great, I agree; but they are praiseworthy only in so far as the conqueror's action is just. 'You who boast of ridding the world of thieves,' said the Scythian emissaries to Alexander, 'you are yourself the greatest thief on earth, for you have robbed, pillaged, and laid waste all the nations you have conquered. If you are a god, you must provide for the welfare of mortals, and not rob them of everything they have; if you are a man, never forget what you are.'[95]

Ferdinand of Aragon was not satisfied simply with constantly waging war, but used religion as a veil to conceal his intentions; he forswore what he had solemnly pledged; he spoke always of justice, and acted always with injustice. Machiavelli praises in him everything that is blameworthy.

Machiavelli offers, in the second place, the example of Bernard of Milan to suggest to princes that they should reward and punish in a grandiose way, in order that all their actions should have the mark of greatness stamped upon them. Generous princes will not want for a good reputation, especially when their liberality arises from nobility of spirit, and not from self-regard.

Such goodness of heart can make them greater than can all the other virtues. Cicero said to Caesar, 'You have no greater power at your command than that of ensuring the safety of so many citizens; nor is there anything more worthy of your goodness than your desire to do so.'[96] The punishment, then, that a prince inflicts should always be less grave than the offence warrants, and the rewards he gives should always be disproportionately generous.

But here is a contradiction: our Doctor of Politics requires, in this chapter, that his princes hold to their alliances, while in his eighteenth chapter he formally relieves them of the duty of keeping their word. He behaves as do those fortune-tellers who say to some that white is black, and to others that black is white.

Although Machiavelli's reasoning is poor on everything we have just mentioned, he speaks well on the necessary prudence which princes must employ in order not to enter lightly into arrangements with other princes more powerful than they are, and who could, instead of helping them, destroy them.

This is what was known by a great prince in Germany, who was respected in equal measure by his friends and by his enemies. The Swedes invaded his territory when he was absent, with all his troops, lending assistance in the Lower Rhine to the emperor, in the war the latter was waging against France. The prince's ministers advised him, when they heard the news of this sudden invasion, to call on the tsar of Russia for help. But the prince, more far-seeing than they, replied that the Muscovites were like bears that must not be unleashed, lest one be unable to put them back in chains; he took upon himself, generously, the task of vengeance, and had no reason to regret it.[97]

If I lived in the next century, I would certainly extend this chapter with various reflections that might be appropriate; but it is not my place to judge the conduct of modern princes, especially since, in this world, we must know when it is appropriate to speak and when to remain silent.

Machiavelli deals with the question of neutrality as wisely as he does with that of alliances of princes. Experience has long shown that a prince who remains neutral exposes his country to the hostility of two belligerents; that his states become a theatre of war, and that he always loses by remaining neutral, without any substantial gain.

There are two ways in which a prince can increase his power: one is by conquest, when a warrior prince pushes forward, by force of arms, the frontiers of his dominion; the other is through good government, when an enterprising prince causes all the arts and all the sciences to flourish, which makes his states more powerful and more civilised.

Machiavelli's whole book is filled with advice only about this first way of increasing a prince's power. Let us now say something about the second way, which is more innocent, more just, and every bit as effective as the first.

The arts that are most necessary to life are agriculture, commerce, and manufacturing; those that do most honour to the human mind are geometry, philosophy, astronomy, rhetoric, poetry, painting, music, sculpture, architecture, engraving, and everything we understand under the rubric of fine arts.

Since every country is quite different, there are those whose strength consists in agriculture, others in viticulture, others in manufacturing, and others in commerce; in some countries these skills even flourish together at one and the same time.

Sovereigns who choose this mild and agreeable way of increasing their power must study, above all, the make-up of their own country, in order to ascertain which of these skills are the most likely to succeed, and which they must, therefore, most encourage. The French and the Spanish have noticed that commerce was not flourishing in their countries, and for this reason they have pondered on the best way of ruining English commerce. If they succeed in this, France will increase her power to a much greater extent than the conquest of twenty towns and a thousand villages would have been able to achieve, and England and Holland, the two most beautiful and richest countries in the world, will decline imperceptibly, as does a sick man who is dying of consumption.

Those countries whose wealth depends on grain and vines have two tasks they must undertake: the first is to clear, carefully, for cultivation all available land, in order to use profitably even the poorest soil; the second is to take care to achieve greater, much larger revenues, cheaper transport for their merchandise, and the ability to sell it at a better price.

So far as manufactured goods of all kinds are concerned, they are perhaps what is most useful and most profitable to a state, since, through them, the needs and the taste for luxury of the people are satisfied, and their neighbours must even pay tribute to their industry; on the one hand, the manufactures stop money from leaving the country, and on the other, they bring money in.

I have always believed that a shortage of manufacturing caused, in part, those remarkable migrations from the countries of the North, the migrations of the Goths and Vandals, who so often flooded into the countries of the South. During those distant times, in Sweden, in Denmark, and in the greater part of Germany, the skills of the people were confined to farming and hunting; cultivable land was divided between a certain number of landowners, who farmed it and gained their sustenance from it.

But since the human race has always been particularly fertile in these cooler climates, it so happened that there were twice as many inhabitants in a country than could be supported by working the land; so that the younger sons of good families formed gangs; they became, of necessity, illustrious brigands; they laid waste other countries, and dispossessed the leaders of these countries. We also observe that the barbarians in the eastern and western empires demanded, in general, only cultivable land, so as to provide for their subsistence. The countries of the North are no less populated now than they were then; but since luxury has very happily multiplied our needs, it has given rise to manufacturing and to all those skills that support entire peoples, who would otherwise have to seek their means of survival elsewhere.

These ways of making a state prosper are like the talents entrusted to the wisdom of the sovereign, which he must put out on loan, and invest profitably. The clearest indication that a country is under wise and benevolent government is when the fine arts are born and flourish there; they are like flowers that spring up in a fertile land and under a favourable sky, but which drought and the harsh north winds destroy.

Nothing renders a reign more illustrious than do the arts that flourish under its protection. The age of Pericles is as famous for the great geniuses who lived in Athens as it is for the wars which the Athenians waged at that time.[98] The age of Augustus is better known through Cicero, Ovid, Horace, Virgil, etc. than through the proscriptions of Augustus, that cruel emperor, who owes, after all, a great part of his reputation to the lyre of Horace.[99] The age of Louis XIV is more celebrated thanks to Corneille, Racine, Molière, Boileau, Descartes, Le Brun, and Girardon than by the crossing of the Rhine, which has been so much over-praised, or by the sieges where Louis was present in person, or by the battle of Turin, which M. de Marsin, on the orders of the Cabinet, caused the Duc d'Orléans to lose.[100]

Kings bestow honour on mankind when they offer rewards and distinctions to those who bring it most honour, and when they encourage those fine minds which strive to increase our knowledge, and which devote themselves to the cause of truth.

Blessed are the sovereigns who themselves cultivate the arts and sciences, who think like Cicero, the Roman consul, liberator of his country and father of eloquence, 'Literature educates the youth, and enchants the aged. It adds lustre to prosperity; gives comfort in adversity; and in solitude, during travels, in every time, in every place, in our houses and in others' houses, brings sweetness to our lives.'[101]

Lorenzo de' Medici, the greatest man of his nation, brought peace to Italy and restored its arts and sciences; his probity gained him the confidence of every prince.[102] Marcus Aurelius, one of the greatest emperors of Rome, was as fortunate a warrior as he was a wise philosopher, and combined the strictest moral conduct with his advocacy of such morality. Let us finish with these words: 'A king who is led by justice has the universe as his temple; and its sacrificial priests are men of goodwill and virtue.'[103]

CHAPTER XXII[104]

There are two sorts of prince in this world: those who see with their own eyes, and themselves govern their states; and those who rely on the good faith of their ministers, and who allow themselves to be governed by those who have gained influence over their minds.

Sovereigns of this first kind are, as it were, the soul of their states: the burden of government rests upon them alone, as does the world on Atlas's back; they administer domestic matters, as they do foreign affairs; they occupy at one and the same time the posts of lord chief justice, supreme commander, and minister of finance. They have—like God, who uses an intelligence superior to that of men to carry out His wishes—far-seeing and diligent people to carry out their plans and to complete in detail their grand designs; these ministers are, properly speaking, instruments in the hands of a wise and skilful master.

Sovereigns of the second kind sink, as it were, through lack of spirit or through natural indolence, into indifference and lethargy. If the state, on the point of failure owing to the weakness of the sovereign, needs to be supported by the wisdom and energy of a minister, the prince in such a situation is nothing but a ghost, but a necessary ghost, for he represents the state; all that can be hoped for is that he has made a good choice.

It is not as easy as one thinks for a sovereign to grasp in full the character of those he intends to employ on matters of state; for it is as easy for private individuals to adopt disguises before the eyes of their masters, as it is difficult for princes to hide their inner thoughts from the eyes of the public.

After all, if Sixtus V was able to deceive seventy cardinals, who must have known him, how much the easier it is, and for an even greater reason, for an individual to ambush a far-sighted sovereign who lacks opportunities to divine his intentions.[105]

A prince with wit and intelligence can without difficulty judge the cleverness and ability of those who serve him; but it is almost impossible for him to make sound judgements as to their good faith and lack of self-interest.

We often see men who, in the absence of circumstances that give them away, appear to be virtuous, but who abandon virtue as soon as it is tested. In Rome, no one spoke ill of Tiberius, Nero, or Caligula before they came to the throne; perhaps their wickedness would have remained dormant if it had not been activated by some occasion that awakened their viciousness.

There are men who combine great intelligence, subtlety, and talent with a soul that is dark and ungrateful; there are others who are good-hearted and generous.

Princes who are wise have usually preferred to employ men who are good-hearted and kind in managing internal affairs of state. On the other hand, they preferred to use those who were more subtle as their negotiators. For, since their only concern was to maintain law and justice in their states, it was enough that their appointees should be fair and just; and if they had to win over their neighbours and to spin a web of intrigues, we can well understand that probity is less needed than skill and wit.

It seems to me that a prince cannot enough reward the loyalty of those who serve him with enthusiasm; there is a certain sense of justice in us which inclines us to gratitude, and which must be respected. Moreover, the interests of the nobles require absolutely that they reward with generosity, and that they punish with leniency; for those ministers who understand that it is virtue that creates their good fortune will certainly not resort to crime, and they will naturally prefer the benevolence of their master to corrupt involvements abroad.

The path of justice and of wisdom in this world come together perfectly, then, on this matter, and it is unwise and harsh, for want of rewards and generosity, to put the loyalty of ministers to a dangerous test.

There are princes who fall into error in another way, which is just as dangerous: they change ministers on the merest whim, and they punish the slightest irregularity in their behaviour much too harshly.

The ministers who work most closely with the prince, after they have been in their post for some time, are not able entirely to hide their faults from him; the more observant the prince, the more easily he takes their measure.

Sovereigns who are not philosophical soon become impatient; they take against the weaknesses of those who serve them; they disgrace and ruin them.

Princes who reflect more deeply, know men better: they know that they are all only too human, that there is no perfection in this world, that good qualities are, so to speak, balanced by great defects, and that a man of judgement must take advantage of everything he can. That is why, unless corrupt practices are involved, they keep their ministers, whatever their good and bad qualities, and they prefer those they know through and through to others they could appoint; just as there are skilful musicians who prefer to play instruments whose strengths and weaknesses they know rather than others whose superiority is as yet unknown to them.

CHAPTER XXIII[106]

There is no ethical treatise, there is no history book, in which the vulnerability of princes to flattery is not severely censured. We want kings to love the truth, we want them to listen to it, to become accustomed to hearing it, and we are right to do so; but we also, to a degree, and as men do, want the opposite: we want princes to have sufficient self-regard to embrace fame, to perform great deeds, and, at the same time, to be indifferent enough to all of this to give up, of their own free will, the fruits of their labour; the same motive force ought to incline them both to deserve praise and to despise it. This is to claim a great deal on behalf of humanity; we are certainly doing men a great honour in supposing that they might exercise more power over themselves than they do over others.

Contemptus virtutis ex contemptu famae.[107] Princes who have no care for their reputation have always been idlers or pleasure-seekers who have given themselves up to easy living; they were heaps of filth animated by no virtue whatever. Cruel tyrants, it is true, have loved praise, but they did so out of odious vanity, yet another vice; they craved respect while deserving opprobrium.

In princes who are steeped in vice, flattery is a deadly poison, one that nurtures the seeds of their corruption; in princes who are virtuous, flattery is like rust: it spreads all over their fame and dulls its lustre. A man of wit and intelligence is revolted by gross flattery; he repels the clumsy flatterer. There is another sort of flattery, which employs a kind of sophistry of faults: its rhetoric minimises them; it provides reasoned arguments on behalf of the passions; it lends to severity the appearance of justice; it lends to excess so perfect an imitation of generosity that one is taken in by it; it masks debauchery with a veil of amusement and pleasure; above all, it exaggerates the vices of others in order to put up a plaque of honour to the vices of its hero. Most men submit to the flattery which suits their tastes, and which is not entirely a lie; they are incapable of correcting those who attribute to them virtues of which they themselves are already convinced. Flattery which has a sound foundation is the most subtle of all; one must be truly discerning to notice the nuances with which it enhances the truth. This sort of flattery will not cause a king go to the scaffold accompanied by poets, who should actually be his historians; it will not compose opera prologues filled with hyperbole, insipid prefaces, or grovelling epistles; it will not dazzle a hero through a bombastic recital of his triumphs; but, rather, it will take on an air of finer feeling; it will manage to introduce itself, delicately; it will appear sincere and naive. How could a great man, how could a hero, how could an intelligent prince, be vexed to hear a truth about himself which the vivacity of a friend appears to let drop? How could Louis XIV, who was aware that his very appearance was impressive to men, and who enjoyed this superiority, how could he be vexed with an old officer who, in speaking to him, trembled and stammered, and who, pausing in the middle of his speech, said to him, 'At least, Sire, I do not tremble in this way before your enemies.'

Princes who have been mere men before becoming kings can remember what, once, they were and are not so susceptible to the temptations of flattery. Those who have occupied the throne throughout their lives have always, like the gods, been fed on incense, and would die of starvation if deprived of praise.

It would seem to me, therefore, to be more reasonable and more just to pity kings rather than to condemn them. It is the flatterers, rather, and, still more, the slanderers, who deserve public condemnation and hatred, as do all those who are sufficiently enemies of the princes to hide the truth from them. But one must distinguish between flattery and praise: Trajan was persuaded, by Pliny's panegyrics, to embrace virtue; Tiberius was persuaded, by the flattery of the senators, to steep himself in vice.[108]

CHAPTER XXIV[109]

The story of Cadmus, who sowed in the earth the teeth of the dragon he had just defeated, from which was born a race of warriors who destroyed themselves, offers an emblem of what, in Machiavelli's time, the Italian princes were.[110] Their mutual perfidy and treachery caused their ruin. One has only to read the history of Italy from the end of the fourteenth to the beginning of the fifteenth centuries:[111] one finds there nothing but cruelty, sedition, violence, leagues formed to destroy one another, usurpations, and assassinations: an enormous collection, in a word, of crimes, the very thought of which fills one with horror.

If, following the example of Machiavelli, we decided to overthrow justice and humanity, we would turn the whole universe upside down; the ensuing flood of crimes would soon reduce this continent to a vast desert. It was the wickedness and barbarity of the Italian princes that lost them their states, just as Machiavelli's false principles will ruin, for certain, those who are foolish enough to follow them.

I am holding nothing back: the cowardice of some of these Italian princes, along with their wickedness, may have contributed to their downfall. It was the weakness of the kings of Naples, that, without a doubt, ruined them. But, as to politics, you can say whatever you like, you can put forward arguments, establish systems, offer examples, use every available subtlety, but you will, nevertheless, and in spite of yourself, be obliged to return to the question of justice.

I must here ask Machiavelli what he means by the following words: 'If we were to observe in a sovereign who has recently ascended the throne—which means, in other words, in a usurper—prudence and merit, we would favour him much more than we would those who owe their rank to birth alone. The reason for this is that we are much more influenced by the present than by the past; and when we find there something satisfactory, we do not look further.'

Does Machiavelli suppose that, between two men who are equally courageous and wise, a whole nation will prefer the usurper to the legitimate sovereign? Or is his comparison between a sovereign who is without virtue and one who is courageous, effective, and a violent aggressor? It cannot be the first of these; it is contrary to the most ordinary notions of common sense: it would be an effect without cause if the preference of the people was in favour of a man who had committed a violent action to make himself their master, and who, moreover, would have no greater merit than that of the legitimate sovereign.

Nor could it be the second; for, whatever qualities one ascribes to a usurper, it will be acknowledged that the violent action whereby he achieves power is an injustice.

What can be expected of a man who begins his career with a crime, unless it is against a violent and tyrannical regime? It is as though a married man suffers an infidelity on the part of his wife on the very day of their wedding: I do not think that this augurs well as to the virtue, for the rest of her life, of his new wife.

Machiavelli passes sentence on himself in this chapter. He declares that, without the love of the people, without the goodwill of the nobility, and without a well-disciplined army, it is impossible that a prince should continue to occupy the throne. The truth seems to compel him to pay it homage in this way, more or less as theologians vouch for the existence of angels that are damned, who recognise God, but blaspheme Him.

Herein lies the contradiction: to win the affection of the people and of the nobility, a prince must possess a fund of virtue; he must be humane and charitable, and must have those qualities of heart and mind that enable him to carry out the more difficult tasks of his office.

This office is like all others: men, whatever their function, never win the confidence of others unless they are just and enlightened; the most corrupt always want to have dealings with a man of integrity, just as those least capable of governing themselves rely on whomsoever is held to be the wisest. What! The most insignificant mayor, the least magistrate of a town, will need, if he wants to succeed, to be a decent and hardworking man, while royalty will be the only profession in which vice would be permitted! A prince must be as I have just described him if he is to win hearts, and not, as Machiavelli, in the course of this work, teaches him to be: unjust, cruel, ambitious, and wholly preoccupied with the task of self-aggrandisement.

Thus it is that we can see, unmasked, this man of politics, whom his own age presented as a great man, whom many ministers have recognised as the dangerous man he was, but who followed him, whose abominable maxims were given to princes to study, to whom no one has ever formally replied, and whom many politicians follow, while hoping not to be accused of doing so.

Blessed would be the man who could entirely destroy Machiavellianism throughout the whole world! I have pointed out its absurdity; it is for those who govern to persuade the world of this through their own example. They should cure the public of the false idea they have as to politics, which ought to be nothing but a system born of wisdom, but which is widely suspected of being the breviary of deceit. It is for them to banish over-subtlety and bad faith from treaties, and to strengthen honesty and candour, which, to tell the truth, are rarely found among sovereigns. It is for them to show that they are not covetous of the land of their neighbours, and that they are jealous of the preservation of their own States. A prince who wants to possess everything is like a man who gorges himself on meat without realising that his stomach cannot digest it. The prince who restricts himself to governing well is like a man who eats moderately, and whose digestion is sound.

CHAPTER XXV[112]

The question of human freedom is one of those problems that taxes to the full the minds of philosophers, and which has often brought down curses upon them from the mouths of theologians. The advocates of free will say that if men are not free, God acts through them; that it is, in other words, God, who, through the agency of men, commits murders, thefts and all manner of crimes; which is manifestly inconsistent with God's holiness. In the second place, they say that, if the Supreme Being is the father of all the vices, and the author of all iniquities that are committed, the guilty can no longer be punished, and that there can be neither crime nor virtue in the world. Now, since this frightful dogma cannot be contemplated without noticing all its contradictions, the least that one can do is to declare oneself in favour of human freedom.

The advocates of absolute necessity say, on the contrary, that God would be worse than a blind craftsman who works in total darkness if, having created this world, he did not know what ought to be done with it. A clockmaker, they say, understands the action of the smallest wheel in a watch, because he knows the movement that he has given it, and for what purpose he has done so; while God, the infinitely wise Being, would be the curious, but powerless, spectator of human actions! How could this same God, all of whose works display order, and all of which are subject to certain immutable and constant laws, have allowed men alone to enjoy independence and freedom? It would no longer be Providence, but the capriciousness of men that governs the world. Therefore, we must decide who is the automaton: the Creator or the created? It would seem more reasonable to believe that it is the being in whom weakness resides, rather than the being in whom power resides. And so, reason and the passions are like invisible chains by means of which the hand of Providence leads the human race through the events its eternal wisdom has decided upon, and which must occur in this world, in order that every individual should fulfil his destiny.

Thus it is that, in order to avoid Charybdis, we come too close to Scylla, and that the philosophers push one another into an abyss of absurdity, while the theologians cross swords in total darkness, and incur damnation devotedly, out of charity.[113] These parties wage war, more or less, as did the Carthaginians and the Romans. When the Carthaginians feared seeing Roman troops in Africa, they carried the torch of war into Italy; and when, in Rome, they wanted to get rid of Hannibal, whom they feared, they sent Scipio and all his legions to besiege Carthage.[114] Philosophers, theologians, and most of the devotees of argumentation, share the genius of the French nation: they attack energetically, but they are lost if they are reduced to defence. This is what caused some wit to say that God was the father of all sects, since he had given all of them the same weapons, as well as a good and a bad side. The question as to free will and the predestination of men is carried over by Machiavelli from metaphysics into politics; it is nevertheless a field that is quite foreign to him, and which can offer him no sustenance; for, in politics, instead of discussing whether we are free or whether we are not, whether chance or fortune can do something or whether they can do nothing, one should, correctly speaking, think of nothing but improving one's far-sightedness and wisdom.

Fortune and chance are words that have no meaning, and which, it would appear, owe their origin to the profound ignorance into which the world was sunk when imprecise names were given to effects whose causes were unknown.

What is commonly known as Caesar's fortune means, properly speaking, all those circumstances that favoured his ambitious plans. What one means when one speaks of Cato's misfortune are the unexpected ills that befell him, those reverses whose effects followed so quickly upon their causes, that he could neither, for all his caution, anticipate nor oppose them.

What is meant, when one speaks of chance, cannot be better explained than by comparing it with the throw of a die. Chance, we say, has caused my dice to show twelve rather than seven. In order to analyse this phenomenon in terms of physics, one would need eyes that were good enough to see the way in which the dice were put into the shaker, and the movement of the hand, more or less vigorous and more or less repeated, which makes the dice turn over, and move more rapidly or more slowly. These are the causes which, taken together, are known as chance.

So long as we are no more than mere men, which is to say, very limited beings, we will never be above what we call the blows of fortune. We must seize from the moment whatever chance offers; but our life is too short for us to perceive everything, and our minds are too limited to make sense of it.

There are events which will illustrate clearly that it is impossible for human wisdom to foresee everything. The first event is that of the surprise attack on Cremona by Prince Eugene, an attack concerted with all imaginable care and carried out with great valour. This is how the plan failed: the prince entered the town towards morning through a sewer, which a priest, with whom he was in collusion, opened up for him; Eugene would indubitably have been victorious, if two unforeseen things had not happened. First, a Swiss regiment, which was to have been on exercise that very same morning, was under arms earlier than expected, and resisted him until the rest of the garrison arrived. Secondly, the guide who was supposed to conduct the Prince de Vaudémont to a city gate, which Vaudémont was supposed to seize, lost his way, which meant that the detachment arrived too late.[115]

The second event I wanted to mention is that of the particular peace that the English made with France towards the end of the War of the Spanish Succession. Neither Emperor Joseph's ministers, nor the greatest philosophers, nor the most skilful politicians could have suspected that a pair of gloves would alter the fate of Europe; that, however, is precisely what happened.

The duchess of Marlborough held the office of mistress of the robes under Queen Anne in London, while her husband was winning a double reward, of fame and of wealth, while campaigning in Brabant. The duchess supported the party of her husband, the hero, while he, through his victories, upheld the position of his wife. The Tory party, which was opposed to both of them, and which wanted peace, could do nothing while the duchess was much in favour with the queen. She lost this position for a trivial enough reason. The queen had ordered some gloves, as had, at the same time, the duchess; the latter's impatience to have them made her press the glove-maker to serve her before the queen. Anne, however, wanted her gloves; a lady who disliked my lady Marlborough informed the queen about everything that had happened, and took advantage of this with such malice that the queen, from this moment, regarded the duchess as a favourite whose insolence she could no longer tolerate. The glove-maker managed to embitter the queen further, through the history of the gloves, which she, the glove-maker, related to her with venom. This episode, however insignificant in itself, was the yeast which brought about an emotional ferment, and added spice to everything that accompanies disgrace. The Tories, with Marshal de Tallard at their head, took advantage of this affair, which was a stroke of good fortune for them. The duchess of Marlborough, shortly afterwards, was disgraced, and with her fell the Whigs as well as the party of the emperor's allies.[116] This is how the most serious matters in the world unfold: Providence mocks human wisdom and pomp; causes that are frivolous and sometimes ridiculous often alter the fortunes of states and entire monarchies. On this occasion, various pathetic little women saved Louis XIV from taking a step from which he could not, perhaps, have been able to extricate himself, for all his wisdom, strength, and power; and obliged the allies to make peace in spite of themselves.

Such things happen, but I confess that they do so rarely, and that their example is not sufficient entirely to discredit prudence and prescience; they are like illnesses, which sometimes affect the health of human beings, but do not prevent them from profiting, most of the time, from the advantages of a robust constitution.

It must, therefore, necessarily be the case that those who govern should cultivate their prescience and their prudence: but that is not all. For, if they want to secure good fortune for themselves, they must learn to temper their disposition to suit every circumstance, which is very difficult.

I am speaking, in general, of only two kinds of disposition, that of a bold and vivacious man, and that of a cautious and steady man; and since physical differences underlie differences in moral character, it is almost impossible that a prince be so completely master of himself that he could take on, like a chameleon, every colour. There are centuries that favour the fame and glory of conquerors, and of those bold and enterprising men who seem to have been born to effect extraordinary changes in the world. Revolutions, wars, and, above all, the mistrust that throws sovereigns into a kind of giddy confusion, provide a conqueror with opportunities to profit from their quarrels. Even Hernán Cortés, during his conquest of Mexico, was helped by civil wars among the indigenous Americans.[117]

There are other times, in which a less troubled world seems to want nothing but steady and calm rule, and where only prudence and circumspection are required; this is a kind of blessed calm in politics which so often follows a storm; it is at such times that negotiations are more effective than battles, and that one must achieve through the pen what one could not win by the sword.

In order that a sovereign profit from every circumstance, he must learn, like a skilful pilot, to take full account of the prevailing weather.

If an army general were bold or circumspect according to the circumstances at the time, he would be virtually indomitable. Fabius undermined Hannibal with his delaying tactics; he knew that the Carthaginians were short of money and recruits, and that, without resorting to combat, it was quite enough quietly to watch their army melt away, in order to destroy it, so to speak, through starvation. Hannibal's policy was, on the contrary, to fight; his power was the result of mere chance, from which he had to derive, immediately, every possible advantage, so as to give it strength and permanency through the terror that brilliant and energetic action inspires, and by means of the resources that are derived from victory.[118]

In 1704, if the elector of Bavaria and Marshal de Tallard had not left Bavaria in order to make for Blenheim and Höchstädt, they would have remained the masters of all Swabia; for the allies, unable, for lack of victuals, to remain in Bavaria, would have been obliged to retreat towards the river Main, and to go their separate ways. It was, therefore, through lack of foresight, while there was still time for it, that the elector entrusted to the outcome of a battle what only he could preserve; this battle was for ever memorable and glorious for the German nation. His imprudence was punished by the total defeat of the French and the Bavarians, and by the loss of Bavaria and of all the land that lies between the Upper Palatinate and the Rhine.[119]

One does not usually speak about reckless people who have perished; I am speaking only of people who have been favoured by fortune. It is, in this case, as it is with dreams and prophecies: out of a thousand which were false and which we forget, we remember only the very small number that have come to pass. The world should judge outcomes by their causes, not causes by their outcomes.

I conclude, then, that a people is at risk when ruled by a prince who is bold; that such a people is continually threatened by danger; and that a circumspect sovereign, even if he is not capable of great exploits, seems born, nevertheless, to govern. The former brings risk, the latter stability.

In order that both kinds of prince should achieve greatness, they must each be born at the right time, without which their talents would be more damaging to them than profitable. Every reasonable man, and especially those who are destined by heaven to govern, ought to draw up a plan for his own conduct that is as well thought out and coordinated as is a demonstration in geometry. If such a system were followed in every way, this would be the means of achieving consistency in one's actions, and of never deviating from the objective; one could, in this way, shape every event and circumstance so as to further the achievement of one's plans; everything would contribute towards the execution of these plans.

But who are these princes for whom we claim so many rare talents? They are only men, and it is true to say that, given their nature, it is impossible for them to fulfil so many duties. One would find much more easily the phoenix of the poets and the monads of the metaphysicians than Plato's idea of man. It is right that nations should be satisfied with the efforts that sovereigns make in order to achieve perfection. The most accomplished among them will be those who least resemble Machiavelli's prince. It is only fair that we should tolerate a prince's faults, provided they are counterbalanced by good intentions and good-heartedness; we must always remember that there is no perfection in this world, and that weakness and error are the lot of mankind. The most fortunate nation is that in which a mutual tolerance between the sovereign and his subjects spreads, throughout society, that sweetness without which life is a heavy burden to bear, and the world a vale of tears rather than a pleasure-dome.

Chapter XXVI[120]

On different kinds of negotiations, and on what may be called just reasons for waging war.

We have seen, during the course of this work, how false the arguments are whereby Machiavelli has tried to deceive us by presenting, under the guise of greatness, men who are nothing more nor less than scoundrels.

I have tried throughout to strip crimes of the veil of virtue under which Machiavelli has hidden them, and to disabuse the world of the errors under which many people still labour as to the political actions of princes. I have told kings that true politics for them consists in surpassing their subjects in the exercise of virtue, so that they will not find themselves obliged to condemn in others what they have allowed themselves to be. I have also said that actions that dazzle do not suffice to establish their reputation; rather, what are needed are actions that contribute to the happiness of mankind.

I will add here two further points: one concerns negotiations, and the other the grounds for waging a war that could reasonably be called just.

The ambassadors of princes in foreign courts are in effect privileged spies, who observe the conduct of the sovereigns to whose courts they are sent; they must uncover the intentions of these sovereigns, see through their procedures, and anticipate their actions, in order to inform their masters in good time. The chief objective of their mission is to reinforce the ties of friendship between sovereigns; but instead of working for peace they are often the instruments of war. They employ flattery, cunning, and seduction to extract state secrets from ministers; they win over the weak through their cunning, the vain through their praise, and the self-interested through their gifts; they do, in short, all the evil they can, since they can sin out of duty, and are certain of impunity.

Princes must take appropriate measures against the guile of these spies. When the object of negotiation is very important, that is the moment when princes have good cause to examine rigorously the behaviour of their ministers, in order to ascertain whether Danaë's golden rain has softened their austere and virtuous behaviour.[121]

In critical times, when alliances are discussed, it is vital that sovereigns be more cautious and even more vigilant than usual. They must study carefully the nature of the things they have to promise, so that they will be able to fulfil their obligations.

A treaty that is looked at from every angle, with all its consequences explored, is quite a different matter from one that is merely considered as a whole. What had appeared to be really advantageous turns out, when examined minutely, to be nothing more than a wretched stop-gap measure, only too likely to hasten the ruin of the state. We must add to such precautions the task of explaining clearly the terms of a treaty, and here the meticulous draftsman must always take precedence over the skilful politician, so that there can be no fraudulent divergence between the letter and the spirit of the treaty.

We ought, in studying politics, to make a collection of all the mistakes which princes have made through acting in haste, for the subsequent use of those who intend to enter into treaties or alliances. The time they would need for reading such a collection would give them the opportunity to reflect, in a way that could only be salutary for them.

Negotiations are not always conducted by trusted ministers; individuals without strength of character are often sent into far-flung places, where they make proposals with a freedom all the greater because they less commit their masters personally. The preliminaries of the most recent peace between the emperor and France were conducted in this fashion, without the knowledge of the empire and the maritime powers. This agreement was reached under the auspices of a count whose estates lie on the banks of the Rhine.[122]

Victor Amadeus, the most skilful and guileful prince of his time, understood better than anyone else the art of dissembling. Europe was more than once damaged by his subtlety and guile, for example when Marshal de Catinat, in a monk's habit and on the pretext of working for the salvation of the royal soul, extricated him from the emperor's sphere of influence, and made of him a convert to the cause of France.[123] This negotiation between the king and the general was conducted with such skill, that the alliance between France and Savoy that ensued appeared to the eyes of all Europe as an unexpected and extraordinary political phenomenon.

I have offered kings the example of Victor Amadeus's conduct, not in order to justify it, far from it; my claim as to his conduct amounts to nothing more than praise of his skill and his discretion, which, when they are employed in an honourable cause, are qualities that are required, indisputably, in a sovereign.

It is a general rule that individuals of supreme merit ought to be chosen for deployment in difficult negotiations; that we need people who are not only guileful in intrigue, flexible enough to make themselves indispensable, but who have a sharp enough eye to read in the faces of others the secrets of their hearts, so that nothing escapes their gaze, and everything is revealed by the force of their reasoning.

We must not misuse guile and acuteness; they are like spices which, if too much used in a casserole, spoil the flavour, and which in the end lose that piquancy that a palate accustomed to them can no longer taste.

Probity, by contrast, is for all times; it is like a simple and natural food, which agrees with all constitutions, and which makes the body robust, without over-stimulating it.

A prince whose candour is well known will infallibly gain the confidence of all Europe; he will be fortunate without deceit, and powerful on account of his virtue alone. The peace and happiness of the state are, as it were, the centre where all political paths must meet, and this must be the aim of all its negotiations.

Peace in Europe is founded, in the first instance, on the maintenance of that wise equilibrium through which the superior strength of one monarchy is counterbalanced by the combined power of various other sovereigns. If this equilibrium were to fail, we would fear that a universal revolution would follow, and that a new monarchy would establish itself on the destruction of princes whose disunity had rendered them too weak.

The political strategy of the princes of Europe seems, then, to demand that they never neglect the alliances and treaties through which they can match the strength of an ambitious power; and that they distrust those who try to sow dissension and ill-feeling among them. Let no one forget that consul who, to demonstrate how vital unity was, seized the tail of a horse, and made fruitless efforts to pull it off; but when he pulled out one hair after another, separating them, he succeeded easily.[124] This lesson is as appropriate to sovereigns of our day as it was to the Roman legionaries; it was only their unity that could make them formidable, and could maintain peace and tranquillity in Europe.

The world would, indeed, be fortunate if there were no means, other than that of negotiation, of upholding justice and of restoring peace and goodwill between nations. People would use arguments rather than arms, and would merely dispute among themselves rather than slitting one another's throats. An unfortunate necessity obliges princes to fall back on a much more cruel course of action; there are occasions when we must protect by force of arms the freedom of people whom others unjustly want to oppress, where it is necessary to obtain through violence what iniquity does not allow to gentleness, where sovereigns must entrust the cause of their nation to the lottery of a battle. It is in one of such cases that this paradox becomes an evident truth: that a good war leads to, and secures, a good peace.

It is the objective of a war that makes it a just or an unjust war. The passions and ambitions of princes often cloud their vision, and portray to them the most violent actions in favourable colours. War is a last resort; it must be entered upon, therefore, with caution, and only in desperate cases, and it is necessary to examine carefully whether one is driven to it through an illusory pride, or by sound and solid reasons.

There are defensive wars, which are, without doubt, the most just.

There are wars of self-interest, which kings are obliged to wage in order to retain the rights on which they are being challenged; they plead, sword in hand, their own cause, and the battle decides the validity of their reasoning.

There are precautionary wars, which princes are wise to undertake. It is true that they are in fact offensive, but they are, nonetheless, just wars. When the excessive might of a power seems about to overflow, when it threatens to engulf the universe, it is wise to build dykes against it, and to check a raging torrent, while one is still capable of it. Clouds are gathering, a storm is brewing, and the lightning which presages it fills the skies; a sovereign threatened by this danger, unable on his own to ward off the storm, will ally himself, if he is wise, with all those whose interests are equally imperilled. If the kings of Egypt, of Syria, and of Macedonia had joined forces against the power of Rome, it would never have been able to overturn their might. A wisely concerted alliance, and a war undertaken energetically, would have aborted those ambitious plans whose accomplishment put the whole world in chains.

There is wisdom in preferring lesser to greater ills, as there is in choosing the most certain course of action rather than the uncertain course. It is better, then, that a prince should wage an offensive war when he has the option of choosing between an olive branch and a wreath of laurels, rather than waiting until matters become desperate, when a declaration of war could delay only by a few moments his enslavement and his ruin. It is a sound maxim that it is better to surprise rather than to be surprised; great men have always fared better by making use of their forces before their enemies have put in place arrangements likely to tie their hands and destroy their power.

Many princes have become involved in the wars of their allies through treaties, as a result of which they have been obliged to provide them with a number of auxiliary troops. Since sovereigns cannot do without alliances, since there are none in Europe who can defend themselves by their own forces alone, they undertake to give one another mutual support in case of need; which contributes to their safety, and to their preservation. Circumstances decide which of the allies gains the fruits of the alliance; a fortunate opportunity favours one of the parties on one occasion, a favourable set of circumstances helps the other contracting party at a different moment. Decency and worldly wisdom demand equally, then, the good faith of princes, that they should honour religiously the good faith required by treaties, and that they should fulfil them scrupulously; the more so since, by means of such alliances, they offer better protection to their people.

Wars, therefore, which have no other aims than to repulse usurpers, to maintain legitimate rights, to guarantee universal freedom, and to avoid the oppression and violence of ambitious men will, all of them, be just wars. Sovereigns who undertake such wars will have no cause to reproach themselves for the blood that is spilled: necessity makes them act; and in such circumstances war is a lesser evil than peace.

This subject leads me naturally to speak of those princes who, by means of an unscrupulous arrangement unheard of in antiquity, buy and sell the blood of their people; their court is like an auction house where their troops are sold to the highest bidder.

The essence of being a soldier is the defence of the fatherland; to hire soldiers out to others, as mastiffs and bulls are sold for fighting, is, it seems to me, to pervert at one and the same time the aims both of commerce and of war. It is said that one must not sell things that are sacred: eh! what is there that is more sacred than the blood of men?

As to wars of religion, if they are civil wars, they are almost always the result of some imprudence on the part of the sovereign, who has inappropriately favoured one sect at the expense of another, or has too much restrained or too much extended the public observance of certain sects. This has encouraged sectarian disputes, which flare up only briefly if the sovereign is not involved, but which become conflagrations when he feeds the fire.

To maintain strong civil government and to allow to each person freedom of conscience, in other words to be a king, and not to act the priest, is the surest means of protecting the state from the storms which the dogmatism of theologians seeks always to arouse.

Wars of religion conducted abroad are the height of injustice and absurdity. To leave Aix-la-Chapelle to go, sword in hand, to convert the Saxons, as did Charlemagne, or to assemble a fleet to propose to the sultan of Egypt that he convert to Christianity, are very curious enterprises. The crusades, and all their fury, are a thing of the past; may heaven grant that they never return!

War, in general, is such a fertile source of misfortune, its issue so uncertain, and its consequences so ruinous for a country, that a prince could not reflect long enough before engaging in warfare. The violence that soldiers inflict on an enemy country is nothing in comparison with the evils that rebound directly on the states of a prince who resorts to war; war is an act so serious, and of such great importance, that it is astonishing that so many kings should have resolved, so lightly, to take this course of action.

I am convinced that if monarchs were to see a true and faithful picture of the miseries that a declaration of war, on its own, inflicts on their peoples, they would not be oblivious to this. The imagination of monarchs is not vivid enough to offer them a true picture of ills they have not experienced, and from which their circumstances protect them. How can they imagine the taxes that burden their people, the privations suffered by the youth of their country, newly recruited into the army, the contagious diseases that afflict armies, the horror of battle, sieges that are even more murderous, the distress of the wounded whose limbs have been severed by the enemy's sword, depriving them of their only means of work and subsistence, the grief of orphans who have lost, in their frailty, their sole support through the death of their father, the loss of so many men, indispensable to the state, but harvested before their time by death?

Princes, who are only in this world to make men happy, ought to think carefully before exposing them, for vain and frivolous reasons, to everything humanity fears most.

Sovereigns who look upon their subjects as slaves expose them to risks without pity, and see them die without regret; but princes who regard other men as their equals, and who look upon their people as the body of which they are themselves the soul, are sparing of the blood of their subjects.

Finally, as I finish this work, I implore sovereigns not to be offended by the freedom with which I address them; my purpose is to tell the truth, to inspire them to virtue, and to flatter no one. The good opinion that I have of the princes who reign at this present time leads me to think them worthy of hearing the truth. It is to the Neros of this world, to rulers such as Alexander VI, Cesare Borgia, and Louis XI, it is to men such as them that one would not dare to speak the truth. Heaven be praised, there are no such men at present among the princes of Europe, and the greatest praise that can be offered them is to condemn boldly and fearlessly, in their presence, all the vices that sully royalty, and are contrary to the sentiments of humanity and justice.

3

Preface to *History of My Age*

Many people have written history, but very few have told the truth. Some chose to record anecdotes, of which they knew nothing, and imagined everything; others made compilations from newspapers; they laboured over volumes that contain nothing but a shapeless mass of rumour and popular superstition. Others compiled vacuous and prolix war journals; others still, impelled by a passion for writing, fashioned a history of events that happened several centuries before their birth. One can hardly recognise even the main events in such fictions; the heroes think, speak, and act according to the whim of the author. It is the author's own imaginings that he relates rather than the actions of those whose life he purports to be recording. None of these books is worthy of being handed down to posterity; and yet Europe is inundated with them, and there are people foolish enough to give them credence. With the exception of that wise man M. de Thou, of Rapin de Thoyras, and of two or three others at the very most, we have nothing but indifferent historians.[1] We are obliged to read them, although with considerable scepticism, and to wade through twenty passages of fallacious argumentation before finding a single interesting fact or truth. It is, in other words, a great achievement to record history truthfully; which, however, is not enough: one must also be impartial, one must write with discernment and insight, and, above all, examine and consider the subject matter with a philosophical eye.

It is not, in my view, for some student of habit and custom, nor for some Benedictine, born in the twenty-ninth century, to portray our contemporaries: to portray the negotiations, the intrigues, the wars, the battles, and all the great events that we have seen in our days grace the stage of the vast theatre that is Europe. Rather, I think, it behoves me, as a contemporary, and as an actor in these events, to offer some account to my successors of the great changes that I have seen take place in the world, and in which I have played some part. It is therefore to you, people as yet unborn, that I dedicate this work, in which I shall try to sketch in lightly everything that concerns the other European powers, and where I shall treat more fully everything that concerns Prussia, since it directly concerns my own House, which can regard the acquisition of Silesia as the occasion of its aggrandisement.[2]

This small piece of history that I am proposing to write is all the more important in that it is crowded with extraordinary and significant events. I dare to suggest, even, that, since the overthrow of the Roman empire, there has been no epoch in history more worthy of attention than that which saw the death of the Emperor Charles VI, the last surviving male of the House of Habsburg, and which produced that famous league, or plot, rather, in which so many kings conspired to bring about the ruin of the House of Austria.[3]

I will assert nothing that is not supported by evidence; the archives are my guarantors; the reports of my ministers, the letters of kings, of sovereigns, of several great men who have written to me: all this is my evidence; elsewhere I base my history on the testimony of reliable witnesses whose accounts are consistent with each other: one cannot establish the truth in any other way. The history that I offer of my campaigns will contain only a summary of their most significant events; I will not, nevertheless, be silent as to the immortal glory that so many officers won there: it is to them that I dedicate this essay, inadequate as it is, as a monument of my gratitude. It is my intention to be similarly concise in my account of matters concerning the realm of politics; I will, nevertheless, take careful note of those traits that characterise the genius of the times, as well as that of the various countries involved. I will compare the present with the past, for it is only through comparison that we arrive at sound judgements. I will dare to undertake an overall conspectus of Europe, to conduct in my mind, as it were, a military review of all these kingdoms and all these powers; and, at times, I will descend to those little details that have given rise to matters of the greatest import.

Since I am writing for posterity only, I will not be constrained by any public or personal considerations: I will declare publicly what many think privately, portraying princes just as they are, without fear of my enemies or favour towards my allies. I will speak of myself only when I cannot do otherwise; no man, whoever or whatever he is, merits the attention of future generations.

For as long as he lives, a king is the idol of his court; the great and the good flatter him, the poets celebrate him; and the public fear him, or have only little love for him. Once he is dead, the truth comes out, and jealousy often avenges itself pitilessly on the spinelessness of those who flattered him.

It is for posterity, after our death, to pass judgement on each and every one of us; during our lifetime we must ourselves be our own judge. If our intentions are pure, if we love virtue, if our hearts are not in league with the errors of our souls, and if we are certain that we have done for the good of our people everything that we could have done, that ought to be enough for us.

You will see, during the course of this work, treaties made and treaties broken; and I must, on this matter, say to you that it is our circumstances and our faculties that govern us: if our interests change, we must change with them. Our task is to watch over the happiness of our people: therefore, as soon as we sense that an alliance we have entered into spells danger or risk for them, it is for us to sever, at once, the alliance, rather than to expose our people to danger. In acting thus, the sovereign sacrifices his own best interest for that of his subjects. The annals of the whole world provide examples of this, and one can scarcely in truth act otherwise. Those who censure, severely, such conduct are people who consider that one's word, once given, is sacrosanct; they are right, and, as a private individual, I think as they do; for a man who gives his word to another, even if he had promised, without due consideration, something that turns out to be wholly prejudicial to his own interests, must keep his word, since honour prevails over self-interest. But a prince who enters into a treaty does not, as a private individual, commit himself alone, but rather exposes important states and important provinces to countless misfortunes; it would therefore be better that the sovereign repudiate such a treaty, rather than that his people perish. What would we say of a surgeon who, scrupulous to the point of folly, would be unwilling to amputate a man's gangrenous arm, just because cutting off someone's arm is in itself an evil? Is it not clear to us all that it would be much more evil to allow a man to die who could have been saved? I venture to maintain, as to this, that it is the circumstances that attend an action, it is everything that accompanies it, and everything that follows it, which should determine our judgement as to whether the action is good or bad. But how few people there are who have the knowledge to judge such a case! Human beings are like sheep; they follow their leader blindly: a wise and witty man has only to say a single word and a thousand fools will repeat it.

I cannot deny myself the satisfaction of adding here a few further general reflections on the subject of the great events that I am describing. It seems to me that there is more muddle and confusion in the most powerful states than in smaller ones; and yet the very size of the machinery of state keeps them functioning, and no one notices this internal disorder. I note, too that princes who commit their forces too far from their own frontier always suffer misfortune, because they are unable to resupply and come to the aid of troops who have ventured so far forward. I note, too, that all nations display more courage when they are fighting to defend hearth and home than when they are called upon to attack their neighbours: does not that stem from a fundamental human conviction, that self-defence, rather than attack, is just and right?

I note, at present, that the French and Spanish fleets are no match for the English, and I am astonished to recall that, during the time of Philip II, the Spanish navy was on its own superior to that of England and Holland. I observe, too, and with surprise, that all these armed navies occasion nothing but the loss of the commerce that it is their duty to protect. On the one hand, we see the king of Spain, ruler of Potosí, burdened with debt in Europe, creditor of all his crown officials, of his servants, and of the whole workforce of Madrid;[4] and on the other hand the English nation, which is throwing away all the money that thirty years of hard work have earned it. I observe the results of the Pragmatic Sanction which is turning the heads of half of Europe, not to mention the queen of Hungary who is dismembering her own provinces in order to maintain their indivisibility.[5] The war that is flaring up in Silesia is becoming contagious, and is acquiring, as it gains momentum, a further degree still of malignity. The capital of the world itself lies open to the first comer, while the pope blesses those who contribute to this, not daring to heap curses upon them; Italy has been vanquished, and is lost. Fortune is fickle: no power enjoys continuous good fortune; reversals follow rapidly upon successes. The English, like a raging torrent, are dragging the Dutch along in their wake; while these wise republicans, who sent deputies to lead the armies at the time when the greatest men of Europe, the Eugenes and the Malboroughs, were at their head, do not send any when, rather, it is the Duke of Cumberland and the Prince of Waldeck who are given the task of leading them.[6] The North flares up, and wages a disastrous war against the Swedes; Denmark stirs, complains, and grows calm again; Poland holds fast because it excites no envy. Saxony changes sides twice; on both occasions its hopes are dashed: the first time it gains nothing, and the second time it is crushed along with the other powers.[7]

What is most grievous is the terrible shedding of human blood. Europe is like a butcher's shop; there are bloody battles everywhere; you might think that the kings of Europe had decided to depopulate the earth. The complications brought on by events, moreover, have changed the causes of war; the effects continue, and the motive ceases; I believe I see players who, in the heat of the game, only abandon it either when they themselves have lost everything, or when they have ruined their opponents. If we were to ask an English minister, 'Why are you continuing with this war?', he would reply, 'So that France will not be able to afford the next campaign.' And if you put the same question to a Frenchman, the reply would be exactly the same. Let us suppose that the claims by one or other of them are correct, that two or three places on the frontier are won, that a little strip of land is acquired, and that the frontier is thereby minutely extended. All these have to be regarded as advantageous, but when we take into account the excessive cost of the war, the extent to which the people have been oppressed by taxes in order to raise such large sums of money, and, above all, the price that so many thousands of men have paid in blood to buy these victories, who would not be moved at the sight of the countless wretches who are the victims of these deadly quarrels? But if you are moved by the misfortune of an individual, if you feel pity for the catastrophe that reduces a whole family to misery, by how much the more must you feel all this when you observe the vicissitudes of the most flourishing empires and of the most powerful monarchies in Europe? This is the finest lesson in restraint that you could be offered. To be aware of the perils, the shipwrecks, the ruin caused by ambition, is to listen to the voice of experience, which calls out to you: Kings, princes, sovereigns of the future, may the story of Icarus, which shows us how severely ambition is punished, teach you to avoid, for ever, this fiery and insatiable passion.

I will go further: if a Louis XIV has suffered prodigious reverses; if a Charles XII has been almost stripped of his territories; if King Augustus was dethroned in Poland, and his son deposed in Saxony; if, finally, the emperor himself is driven out of his territories, what mere mortal would dare to believe himself spared a similar fate, would dare to risk his fortune in the face of the uncertainty of events, of the obscurities of the future, and of the unsuspected dangers that overturn, in an instant, the most shrewd, the best laid and the most ingenious plans?[8] The history of cupidity is the school of virtue: ambition breeds tyrants, restraint brings forth men of wisdom and foresight!

4

Dissertation on the Reasons
for Establishing or Repealing Laws

Those who wish to acquire a complete, as well as a wholly accurate, knowledge of the methods one must use if one is to establish or repeal laws, can do so only from history. We learn from it that every nation has had its own particular laws, that these laws have been established sequentially, and that it has always taken mankind a considerable amount of time to arrive at something that is reasonable. We learn, too, that the lawgivers whose laws have remained in force for the longest time have always been those whose aim it was to promote public happiness, and who understood, better than could anyone else, the particular character of the people whose governance they were regulating.

Such are the considerations that oblige us to go—in some detail—into the history of law itself, as well as into the ways in which laws have become established in those countries we regard as the most enlightened.

It seems probable that fathers of families were the first lawgivers: the need to establish and maintain order in their households no doubt obliged them to frame domestic laws. Since the earliest times, however, and especially when, later, men began to gather together in towns, the laws of these individual jurisdictions were found to be inadequate for a more numerous society.

The malevolence of the human heart, which remains dormant, so it seems, in solitude, reasserts itself in society; and if human intercourse, which brings together people of like character, provides companions for the virtuous, it also provides accomplices for the scoundrels.

As towns grew, so too did disorder; new vices were born, and the fathers of families, as those who had the greatest interest in suppressing them, came to a joint agreement, for their own safety, to oppose any form of dissolute living. Laws were promulgated, and magistrates appointed to ensure that these laws were observed; for, such is the depravity of the human heart, that, for the maintenance of happiness and peace, it became necessary to contain that depravity through the power of law.

The earliest laws concerned only the greatest iniquities; civil laws regulated the worship of the gods, the division of land, marriage contracts, and inheritance; while criminal laws punished severely only the most heinous crimes. In due course, however, and as further unforeseen misdemeanours came to light, these new disorders gave rise to new laws.

As towns merged with one another, republics were formed, and, because all human affairs tend to change for the worse, their governance, too, was often transformed. Weary of democracy, the people began to favour aristocracy, and even monarchical government. This latter came about in two ways: either because the people placed their trust in the evident virtue of one or other of their fellow citizens, or because, by means of some contrivance or other, an ambitious citizen usurped the sovereign power. There are few states that have not tried these various forms of government; but all of them have had different laws.

Osiris is the first lawgiver to be mentioned in secular history; he was king of Egypt, and established there his own legal system, to which even the sovereigns themselves were subject; these laws, which regulated the governance of the kingdom, also covered the conduct of individuals.

Kings earned the affection of their people only in so far as they conformed to these laws. Osiris* appointed thirty judges, the most senior of whom wore round his neck an image of Truth, hung on a chain of gold. If you were touched by this image, you had won your case.

Osiris regulated the worship of the gods, the distribution of land, and the distinctions between different kinds of people. He did not want debtors to be arrested; every subornment by rhetorical means was forbidden to lawyers. The Egyptians pawned the corpses of their fathers, depositing them with their creditors as security; but it was a matter of dishonour if these were not redeemed before their own death. Osiris believed that it was not enough to punish a man during his lifetime; he set up a tribunal whose role it was to judge them after their death, so that the stigma attached to this form of condemnation served as an incentive to encourage the living to embrace virtue.

After Egyptian law, that of the Cretans was the most ancient. Minos was their lawgiver. He claimed to be the son of Jupiter, and, in order to make his laws appear more respectable, asserted that they had been handed down to him by his father.

Lycurgus, king of Lacedaemonia [Sparta], made use of Minoan law, to which he added other laws attributed to Osiris, which he had encountered

---

*Some authors also mention Isis here.

during a voyage to Egypt. He banished from his republic gold, silver, all kinds of coinage, and all unnecessary arts and crafts; he also divided up all available land equally among the citizenry.

Lycurgus, whose intention it was to train warriors, was opposed to any display of emotion, lest it should sap his warriors' courage. To this end, he permitted the sharing of women among the citizens, so as to people the state without allowing individuals to form the sweet and tender ties of marriage; the children were all brought up at public expense. If parents could prove that their children were born with some disability, they were allowed to kill them. Lycurgus believed that a man who was not fit to bear arms did not deserve to live.

He ordered that the Helots, a kind of slaves, should till the land, and that the Spartans should occupy themselves entirely with activities that would fit them for battle.

Young people of both sexes engaged in battle; they performed their exercises naked, and in public.

He regulated their meals, and ruled that all citizens, whatever their class, should eat together.

Foreigners were forbidden to visit Sparta, lest their customs and manners corrupt those established by Lycurgus.

Thieves were punished only if they were incompetent: it was Lycurgus's intention to form a military republic, and he succeeded in this.

It was, in point of fact, Draco* who was the first lawgiver of the Athenians; but his laws were so severe that it was said of him that they were written in blood rather than in ink.

We have seen how, in Egypt and in Sparta, laws were established. Let us now look at how they were modified in Athens.

The general disorder that, at the time, prevailed in Attica, and the baneful consequences it portended, caused the people to turn to a man of such great wisdom that only he could correct so much abuse. The poor, in particular, who, because of their debts, were suffering desperately at the hands of the rich, dreamt of choosing a leader who would deliver them from the tyranny of their creditors.

During this period of disorder and dispute Solon, by universal consent, was appointed archon and chief justice. The rich, according to Plutarch,

---

*Draco imposed the death penalty for the smallest misdemeanours. He went so far as to take proceedings against inanimate objects: a statue, for example, which in falling had injured someone, was banished from the town.

accepted him gladly because he was rich, and the poor because he was a man of good will.

Solon discharged the debts of all debtors, and granted the citizenry the right to make bequests.

He allowed women whose husbands were impotent to choose another husband from among their relatives.

These same laws penalised idleness; they also acquitted the killers of adulterers; and they forbade the care and education of children being entrusted to their closest heirs.

Those who had put out the eye of a one-eyed person were condemned to lose both eyes; debauchees dared not speak in public gatherings.

Solon established no law against parricide. Such a crime seemed to him inconceivable; he believed, besides, that if he were to establish such a law, this, rather than forbidding parricide, would encourage it.

He wanted his laws to be lodged in the Areopagus; this court, founded by Cecrops, and which had originally been composed of thirty judges, was now augmented to five hundred. The Areopagus held its hearings at night; lawyers, forbidden to appeal to the emotions, pleaded their cases there clearly and simply.

Later, Athenian law was adopted in Rome; but, since the laws of the Roman empire became those of all the peoples it conquered, it will be necessary for us to expatiate further on the subject of Roman law.

Romulus was the founder and the first lawgiver of Rome; the little that has come down to us of the laws promulgated by this prince is set out below.

Romulus wanted the kings of Rome to exercise sovereign authority in matters of justice and religion; that no credence should be given to any stories that are told about the gods; that one should entertain towards them only holy and religious feelings, attributing nothing discreditable to such blessed beings. Plutarch adds that it is impious to believe that the divinity takes any pleasure in the attractiveness of mortal beauty. Romulus, himself so little superstitious, commanded, however, that nothing should be undertaken without prior consultation of the auguries.

Romulus assigned the patricians to the Senate, the plebeians to the Tribes; but he set no value on the slaves in his republic.

Husbands had the right to punish their wives by death, if they were found to be guilty of adultery or drunkenness.

Fathers had unlimited power over their children; they were permitted to let them die if they were born deformed. Parricides were punished by death. A patron who defrauded his client was considered to be an abomination. If a daughter-in-law beat her father she was left to the vengeance of the household gods. Romulus wanted the city walls to be sacred; indeed, he killed his brother Remus for having transgressed this law by jumping over the walls of the city he was founding.

This same prince established places of refuge, near, among other places, the Tarpeian Rock.

Numa added further laws to those made by Romulus; because this prince was very pious, and because his religious views were very pure, he forbade any representation of the gods in human or animal form. The result of this was that, for the first 160 years after the foundation of Rome, there were no images in the temples.

In order to promote the increase of the people, Tullus Hostilius ordained that, if a woman was brought to bed with three children at one and the same time, they should be provided for until the age of puberty at public expense.

It should be noted, too, that under the laws of Tarquin every citizen was obliged to give to the king an account of all his property, while if he failed to do so he risked being punished; that Tarquin himself regulated the gifts that each person should give to the temples; and that, among his other laws, he allowed slaves who had been freed to be accepted into the Tribes of the city. This prince's laws favoured debtors.

Such are the principal laws that the Romans acquired from their kings; Sextus Papirius made a collection of them all, which were named after him 'the Papirian code'.

Most of these laws, which had been formulated for a monarchy, were, on the expulsion of the kings, abolished.

Valerius Publicola, Brutus's colleague in the Consulate (itself one of the instruments of liberty enjoyed by Rome) was a consul who favoured the people, and who published new laws that were consistent with the kind of government he had just established.

These laws allowed the people to appeal against judgements made by the magistrates, and forbade, under pain of death, the acceptance of public office without the consent of the people. Publicola reduced taxation, and authorised the murder of citizens who attempted to establish tyrannical rule.

It was only later that lending with interest was introduced; powerful Romans charged interest at a rate of up to 12.5%. If a debtor could not repay his debts, he—and all his family—were dragged off to prison and reduced to slavery. The harshness of this law seemed intolerable to the plebeians, who were often its victims; they muttered against the consuls, the Senate proved inflexible, and the people, becoming more and more inflamed, withdrew to the

Sacred Mountain. There they talked on equal terms with the senators, and returned to Rome only on condition that their debts be cancelled, and that magistrates be created, who, through the office of the Tribunate, would be authorised to uphold the people's rights. The tribunes reduced the maximum interest rate to 6.25%, and, in the end and for some time, completely abolished lending with interest.

The two orders that, together, made up the republic of Rome were constantly forming ambitious plans whereby one of them would gain prominence over, and at the expense of, the other; this gave rise to considerable jealousy and mistrust. Various agitators who flattered the people exaggerated their own claims; while some of the younger senators, lively and passionate by nature, proud and arrogant, caused the resolutions reached by the Senate to be too harsh.

Agrarian law, which determined the division of conquered territories, caused dissension, more than once, within the republic; as, for example, in the year 267 after the foundation of Rome [133 BC]. The Senate diverted attention from these disputes by waging several wars; but the disputes flared up again and again, and continued, indeed, until the year 300 [100 BC].

Finally, Rome recognised the need for recourse to laws that would satisfy both parties in a dispute; at which point Spurius Postumius Albus, Aulus Manlius, and Publius Sulpicius Camerinus were sent to Athens, charged with the task of compiling Solon's laws. On their return, these ambassadors were elected decemvirs; they wrote down these laws, which were approved by a writ of the Senate, and, by the people, through a plebiscite. These laws were engraved on ten sheets of copper, and the following year two further sheets were added; together they formed a body of law that has become known as the Twelve Tables.

These laws limited the power of fathers; they imposed punishment on teachers who defrauded their pupils; they allowed individuals to bequeath their property to whomsoever they chose. Subsequently the triumvirs decreed that testators would be obliged to leave one quarter of their estate to their heirs; which is the origin of what we now call the Statutory or Legal Share.*

Children born posthumously, up to ten months after the death of their fathers, were declared to be legitimate. The Emperor Hadrian extended this privilege to the eleventh month.

---

*There were only two kinds of *ab intestat* heirs [in the absence of a valid will]: children and male relatives.

Divorce, hitherto unknown among Romans, first acquired legal force through the Twelve Tables; penalties were imposed on abuse, whether actual, verbal, or in writing.

Parricide, even in intent, was punishable by death.

Citizens were permitted to kill armed thieves, or those who broke into their houses at night.

Any person bearing false witness was to be thrown from the Tarpeian Rock. In criminal cases, the plaintiff had two days in which to bring his case; and the accused had three days in which to reply.* If it became clear that the plaintiff had falsely accused the defendant, his punishment was the same as that for the crime he had falsely alleged.

Such, in essence, was what the laws of the Twelve Tables contained, of which Tacitus said that they were the ultimate in good laws; to which Egypt, Greece, and everything this latter civilisation had known of perfection contributed. These laws, so equitable and just, limited the freedom of citizens only where their abuse of that freedom would have been damaging to the peace of families and the security of the republic.

The authority of the Senate, which was constantly in opposition to that of the people, the overweening ambition of the people of rank, the demands of the plebeians, which increased every day, and many other reasons that are, properly speaking, a matter for historians, once again caused violent storms. The Gracchi and the Saturnines promulgated a number of seditious laws. During the troubles caused by the civil wars, a number of ordinances were issued, which various events caused to appear and disappear. Sulla abolished the old law and promulgated new ones, laws that Lepidus destroyed. The corruption of morals, which, along with dissension in the state, gradually increased, gave rise to an infinite proliferation of laws. Pompey, elected to reform these laws, promulgated some edicts, which, however, perished along with him. During the twenty-five years of civil war and general disorder that followed, there was neither law nor custom nor justice; and this state of confusion lasted until the reign of Augustus, who, during his sixth consulate, reestablished the old laws and annulled all those that had come into being during the disorders in the republic.

Finally, the Emperor Justinian remedied the confusion created by the proliferation of laws, and ordered his chancellor Tribonius to compose a perfect legal code. Tribonius reduced existing laws to the three volumes which have come down to us as the Digest, which includes the opinions of

---

*The accused appeared as a supplicant before the magistrate, with his relatives and his clients.

the most celebrated jurists, the Codex, which in turn includes the decrees of the emperors, and the Institutes that form an abstract of Roman law.

These laws proved to be so admirable that, after the collapse of the empire, they were adopted by all the most civilised peoples, who made them the basis of their own jurisprudence.

The Romans had exported their laws to the countries they conquered. The Gauls adopted them when Julius Caesar, who had subjugated them, made Gaul a province of the empire.

During the fifth century, after the dismantling of the Roman monarchy, the Nordic races flooded into a part of Europe. These barbaric nations introduced their own laws and customs into the countries of their vanquished enemies; the Gauls were invaded by the Visigoths, the Burgundians, and the Franks.

Clovis [king of the Franks, r. 481–511] believed that he was showing generosity towards his new subjects in giving them the choice between adopting the laws of their conquerors or those of the conquered. He published the Salic law, and under the reign of his successors new laws were often created. Gundobad, king of Burgundy [r. c.473–516], made a decree whereby duelling was prescribed for those who would not hold to their solemn undertakings.

Historically, the nobility in these countries had the right to make absolute judgements, without appeal.

During the reign of Louis the Fat [r. 1108–37], royal and superior justice was established in France. We note that later Charles IX [r. 1560–84] intended to reform the judicial system and to shorten judicial process; the Edict of Moulins [1566] bears witness to this. It is remarkable that such wise laws were introduced in troubled times; but, as President Hénault says, the Chancellor de l'Hôpital was watching over the health of the fatherland.[1] In the end it was Louis XIV who arranged for all the laws introduced between Clovis's time and his own to be codified into what we now call, after him, the Code Louis [1667].

The people of Britain, whom the Romans conquered, as they did the Gauls, also adopted the laws of their conquerors.

Before they were conquered, these peoples were governed by druids, whose own rules had the force of law.

Among these peoples, fathers of families had the power of life and death over their wives and their children; all dealings with foreigners were forbidden; they slit the throats of all prisoners of war and sacrificed them to the gods.

Roman power and Roman law prevailed over these islanders until the rule of Honorius, who, by a solemn decree, restored freedom to the English in the year 410.

The Picts*, allied with the Scots, subsequently attacked them; the people of Britain, weakly supported by the Romans, and constantly under attack by their enemies, had recourse to the Saxons. The latter, after a war of 150 years, subjugated the whole island and became the masters of the people of Britain rather than their allies.

The Anglo-Saxons brought their own laws to Great Britain, the same laws that had earlier existed in Germany. They divided England into seven kingdoms, which governed themselves independently, and each of which had its own General Assembly[†], composed of nobles, of commoners, and of peasants. This particular form of government, which was, at one and the same time, monarchical, aristocratic, and democratic, has been preserved until the present time; authority is still divided between the king, the House of Lords and the Commons.

Alfred the Great gave England its first codified set of laws [in the late ninth century]. Although these were mild, Alfred was unrelenting towards magistrates who were convicted of corruption; history relates, indeed, that, in a single year he condemned to be hanged forty-four judges who had been found guilty of corrupt practices.

According to Alfred the Great's code, any Englishman accused of a crime was to be judged by his equals, a privilege that still exists in England.

After its conquest by William, duke of Normandy[†], England was transformed. This conqueror established new sovereign courts of law, one of which—the Court of Exchequer—survives to this day. These courts accompanied the king's person. He separated ecclesiastical from civil jurisdictions; and the harshest of his laws, which he published in the Norman language, was a ban on hunting, which was punishable either by mutilation or by death itself.

The kings who succeeded William the Conqueror issued different charters.

Henry I, known as Beauclerc [r. 1100–35], allowed heirs of noble birth to take possession of their inheritance, without being obliged to make some of it over to the sovereign; he even allowed members of the nobility to marry without royal consent.

---

*The Picts, peoples who came from Mecklenburg.

[†]These assemblies were called Witenagemot, or Council of the Wise, whose government took the name Heptarchy.

[†]Crowned in London in 1066.

It is also worthy of note that King Stephen [r. 1135–54] issued a charter, which not only recognised that he owed his power to the people and the clergy, but also confirmed the prerogatives of the church, and abolished the strict laws of William the Conqueror.

Subsequently, King John Lackland [r. 1199–1216] granted the charter called Magna Carta to his subjects; it consists of sixty-two articles.

These articles regulated the ways in which the fiefdoms were reconstructed. They also regulated widows' portions. Widows were, at the same time, relieved of the obligation to enter into second marriages: they could, indeed, remarry only under legal governance, with the permission of their lord. These same articles established courts of justice in permanent locations; they forbade Parliament from raising taxes without the consent of the Commons, unless their purpose was to ransom the person of the king, or to provide for his son to become a knight, or to furnish a dowry for his daughter; they required that no one be imprisoned or dispossessed or put to death, unless tried by his equals according to the laws of the kingdom; and, moreover, the king undertook neither to sell nor to refuse justice to anyone.

The Statute of Westminster that was published by Edward I [1275] was no more than a renewal of the Magna Carta, except that it forbade the acquisition of land by mortmain, and that it banished Jews from the kingdom.

Although England has many sound laws, it is perhaps the European country where the laws are the least forceful. Rapin Thoyras well observes, indeed, that, thanks to a deficiency in governance, the king's power finds itself ceaselessly in conflict with that of Parliament. They watch one another continually, either to preserve their authority or to extend it. This distracts both king and the representatives of the nation from the care they ought to be devoting to the maintenance of justice; so that this turbulent and stormy government changes its laws endlessly, by Act of Parliament, as circumstances and events require; from which it follows that England, more than any other kingdom, is in the position of needing reform of its laws.

It only remains for us to say a few words about Germany. We adopted Roman law when the Romans conquered Germania, and we continued to follow it because the emperors, when they left Italy, transferred the seat of their empire to our country. Nevertheless, each imperial area, each principality, however small, has a different common law; and these rights, over the course of time, have acquired the force of law.

Having set out the ways in which laws were established in the majority of civilised nations, we will now note that, in the countries where laws were introduced with the consent of the people, it was necessity that caused them to be adopted; while, in countries under foreign rule, it was the laws of the conquerors that became those of the conquered; but also that, at the same time, the laws were everywhere continually augmented. It is, at first sight, a matter of surprise that nations are ruled by such different jurisdictions; but any such sense of surprise disappears when it is noted that, as to the essence of these laws, they are all more or less the same. And by 'laws' I mean those laws that, to protect society, punish crime.

We note, furthermore, if we look at the practice of the wisest lawgivers, that laws must be so adjusted as to be suitable for the kind of government, and for the genius of the nation that is to adopt them; that the best lawgivers have always had, as their aim, public welfare and happiness; and that, generally speaking, those laws that are most conducive to natural justice are, with a few exceptions, the best.

Since Lycurgus was dealing with an ambitious people, he gave them laws designed to create warriors rather than citizens; and if he banished gold from his republic, this was because, of all the vices in existence, self-interest is the most inimical to military glory.

Solon said of himself that he had not given the Athenians the most perfect legal system, but the best laws that they were capable of adopting. He took into account not only the genius of the Athenians, but also the location of Athens, which is very close to the sea. For this reason he penalised idleness, encouraged industriousness, and forbade neither gold nor silver, for he foresaw that his republic could become great and powerful only if its trade and commerce flourished.

It is essential that laws be consistent with the genius of nations. If not, it would be better that they should not exist. The Romans wanted democracy, and, therefore, anything that might damage this form of government was hateful to them. This was the source of so much sedition aimed at the passage of the agrarian law, for the people persuaded themselves that through the redistribution of land some sort of social equality could be re-established. This was also the cause of frequent riots aimed at the cancellation of debt, since the creditors, who were powerful, treated their debtors, who were plebeians, inhumanely, and because nothing exacerbates differences in the condition of the people more than does the tyranny that the rich, when unchallenged, exercise over the poor.

In every country, three kinds of law are to be found: those that are concerned with politics and establish governance; those that are concerned with morals or customs, and punish criminals; and, finally, civil law, which regulates inheritance, guardianship, moneylending, and contracts. The lawgivers who establish the laws in monarchies are usually themselves sovereigns: if their laws are mild and equitable they are self-sustaining, since every individual finds them to be to his advantage; if they are harsh and tyrannical, they will soon be abolished, because they can be upheld only by force, and because the tyrant stands alone against a whole people whose only desire is to do away with these laws.

In a number of republics where individuals have been the lawgivers, their laws have succeeded only in so far as they have been able to establish an exact equilibrium between the powers of government and the freedom of citizens.

It is only in relation to laws concerning morals or customs that lawgivers agree, in general, on the same principles; except that they have been more severe in regard to one particular crime rather than another, as a result, doubtless, of their knowing to which vices their nation was most inclined.

Since laws are, as it were, a dyke erected to contain a flood of vice, they must be framed in such a way as to inspire obedience, through the fear of severe punishment; but it is nonetheless true that the lawgivers who have imposed the least severe punishment are, at least, the most humane, even if they are not the most rigorous.

It is civil law that differs most in different places. Where civil lawgivers found existing practices that had been usually introduced before their time, they did not dare abolish them, for fear of upsetting local prejudice; rather, they respected custom, which commended these laws to them; indeed, they adopted these practices, purely because of their antiquity and even when they were not equitable.

Anyone who takes the trouble to study the law from a philosophical point of view will, no doubt, find many laws that appear, at first sight, to be contrary to natural justice, but which, nevertheless, are not so. I will go no further than to instance the right of primogeniture. It would appear that nothing could be more equitable than the division of a father's estate into equal portions among all his children. Experience, nevertheless, tells us that the division of even the largest estates into many parts in time reduces wealthy families to poverty; with the result that fathers have preferred to disinherit their younger sons rather than condemn their estates to certain decline. And, for the same reason, laws that appear inappropriate and harsh to various individuals may not, in fact, be unwise, as long as they work to the advantage of society as a whole; a whole, indeed, to which any enlightened lawgiver will always sacrifice the parts.

It is the laws that concern debtors that, without doubt, demand the greatest caution and prudence on the part of those who promulgate them. If these laws favour creditors, the position of debtors becomes too difficult; some unforeseen mischance may, indeed, ruin their fortune for ever. If, by contrast, the law in question favours debtors, it damages public confidence by undermining contracts that were established in good faith.

A middle, and equitable, course, which, while upholding the validity of contracts does not overburden debtors who are insolvent, seems to me to be the philosopher's stone of jurisprudence.

We will not elaborate further on these matters. The nature of this present work, indeed, does not allow us to go into greater detail. We must confine ourselves, rather, to general reflections.

A body of perfect laws would be the masterpiece of the human mind as far as the politics of government is concerned; we would find there a unity of design and an order so precise and so proportionate that a state guided by such laws would resemble a watch, all of whose springs were made to achieve the same goal. We would find there, too, a deep knowledge of the human heart and of the genius of the nation; punishments would be tempered, so that, whilst maintaining public morals, they would be neither too lax nor too rigorous; clear and precise ordinances would avoid any recourse to litigation; such ordinances would enshrine a perfectly judged selection of all that is best in civil law, as well as a simple and inventive application of these laws to the customs and practices of the nation. Everything would be foreseen, everything would be worked out, and nothing would be subject to mishap; but perfection is not the lot of humankind.

The people would, however, have reason to be satisfied if their lawgivers considered themselves to be in the same position in relation to them as were those fathers of families who established the first laws. They loved their children; the rules which they prescribed for them had no object other than the happiness of their family.

There are very few sound laws that make the people happy; while an excess of laws overloads the legal system. Just as a good doctor does not overburden his patient with too many remedies, so the skilful lawgiver should not overburden the public with superfluous laws. An excess of medicine can be damaging, and medicines, indeed, work against each other; a country with too many laws resembles a maze, in which legal experts, and even justice itself, go astray.

In Roman times, whenever revolutions were frequent, laws proliferated; any ambitious man, indeed, who considered himself to be favoured by fortune turned himself into a lawgiver. This confusion lasted, as we have already seen, until the time of Augustus, who annulled all these unjust ordinances, and re-established the ancient laws.

In France, the number of laws greatly increased when the Franks conquered this kingdom and introduced their own laws. Louis XI [r. 1461–83] planned to combine all these laws and to establish in his empire, as he himself put it, one law and one system of weights and measures.

There are a number of laws to which men are attached because they are, for the most part, creatures of habit. Although better laws could be substituted, it would perhaps be dangerous to meddle; the confusion which this reform would introduce into the legal system might well do more harm than the new laws would do good.

This is not to deny that there are instances where reform seems absolutely necessary; which is when laws are found to be inimical to public welfare and natural justice, when they are framed in vague and obscure terms, or when, finally, they are self-contradictory either in their substance or in their language.

Let us attempt some further elucidation of these matters.

Osiris's laws on theft, for example, belong among those mentioned above. They required that those wishing to pursue a career of theft should be compelled to sign up with a leader, and that they should hand over to him immediately everything that they had stolen. Meanwhile, anyone who had suffered theft went to see the leader of the thieves in order to claim back his goods, which were restored to him, provided that the owner paid a quarter of their value. The lawgiver believed that, by this expedient, he was providing the citizens, in return for a small fee, with the means to recover what belonged to them, a system that promptly made a thief of every Egyptian. Doubtless, Osiris did not foresee such an outcome when he established this law, unless one prefers to believe that he connived in such theft, as an evil that could not be prevented, much as the government of Amsterdam tolerates street musicians, and that of Rome stylish brothels.

Moral probity and public safety would, however, require the abolition of Osiris's law, if, unfortunately, it was found to be anywhere in force.

The French have adopted a course which is in direct opposition to that of the Egyptians: the Egyptians were too permissive, the French are too severe. French law is exceptionally harsh; all housebreakers, for example, are punished by death. The French maintain, however, in order to justify themselves, that in punishing pickpockets severely they destroy the seedbed of brigands and assassins.

Natural justice ordains that there should be proportionality between punishment and crime. Major theft merits the death penalty; whereas those who are guilty of theft without violence may, to some degree, merit our compassion.

There is an infinite difference between the situation of the rich and that of the poor. The rich man abounds in good things, and is awash with excess; the poor man, abandoned by fortune, lacks even the essentials of life. If some poor wretch should steal, in order to survive, a few coins, a gold watch, or some such trifle, from a man of such grandeur that he does not notice the loss—should such a man be condemned to death? Does not common humanity demand that we temper such harshness? It is quite clear that it is the rich who have made this law. Would not, then, the poor have the right to say, 'Why is no pity shown us for our wretched condition? If you possessed any charity, if you had any human kindness, you would help us in our misery, and we would not rob you. We await your reply: is it right that all the felicity of this world should be yours, and that all its misfortunes should fall upon us?'

The Prussian legal system has established a middle course between the laxity of Egypt and the severity of France. The law does not punish common theft by imposing the death penalty; it is felt to be sufficient, rather, that the guilty be condemned to a certain term in prison. Perhaps it would be better still to introduce the Lex Talionis, a law that was observed by the Jews, and according to which the thief had to restore what he had stolen twice over; or else become the slave of the person whose goods he had taken. If we accept that a light penalty is appropriate for petty crime, we could then reserve the ultimate punishment for brigands, murderers, and assassins—so that the punishment would always fit the crime.

No law shocks humanity more than the power of life and death that fathers wielded over their children in Sparta and Rome. In Greece, a father who found himself too poor to provide for the needs of a numerous family was permitted to cause the death of the children who were in excess; in Sparta and in Rome, if a child came into the world malformed, this, in itself, authorised the father to take the child's life. We feel the full force of such barbarous laws because they are not ours; but let us consider for a moment whether we ourselves have laws that are equally unjust.

Is there not something very harsh about the way in which we punish abortion? God forbid that I should condone the frightful practice of such women as Medea, who, cruel to themselves and to the ties of blood, suffocate their progeny, without, if I dare express myself thus, allowing them even to see the light of day! But let the reader, at this point, divest himself of all his usual prejudices, and deign to give some attention to the reflections I am about to present to him.

Do not our laws condemn, too harshly, clandestine relations? Does not a young girl, born with a tender heart, and deceived by the false promises of a libertine, find herself, thanks to her gullibility, faced with a choice between the loss of her honour and the loss of the unfortunate offspring she has conceived? Is it not the law that places her in so excruciating a situation? And does not the severity of the judges deprive the state of two subjects at the same time, of the aborted child who has perished, and of the mother who could readily make up for this loss through legitimate issue? One would reply to this that foundling hospitals exist; and I know that they save the lives of an infinite number of bastards. But would it not be better to root out this evil and save so many poor little creatures who perish miserably, by abolishing the stigma which attaches to those who are themselves the innocent results of a love that is unwise and fleeting?

But nothing is more cruel than torture. The Romans tortured their slaves, whom they regarded as a kind of domestic animal. No Roman citizen, by contrast, was ever tortured.

Torture is practised in Germany on malefactors after they are convicted, in order to extract from their own lips a confession of their crimes. It is used in France to establish the facts or to uncover an accomplice. In former times the English practised ordeal or proof by fire* and by water[†]; they employ at present a form of torture less severe than the generality of such practices, but which comes to much the same thing.

I hope I may be pardoned if I here protest against all forms of torture: if, indeed, I protest on behalf of all humanity against so shameful a punishment being imposed on Christians and all civilised people, and, I dare add, against a practice that is both cruel and ineffective.

Quintilian, the wisest and most eloquent of the rhetoricians, says, while discussing torture, that it is a matter of temperament.[2] The out-and-out scoundrel denies the charge; an innocent man with a weak character admits it. A man is accused, there is evidence, the judge is uncertain, wanting further enlightenment, and this unfortunate man is tortured. If he is innocent, what barbarity to have made him suffer such martyrdom! If it is the torture that makes him bear witness against himself, what fearful inhumanity to subject to the most violent suffering, or to condemn to death, a virtuous citizen against whom there is no clear evidence, but only suspicion! Would it not be better to pardon twenty guilty people than to sacrifice one who is innocent?

---

*Ordeal by fire: a red-hot iron was put into the hands of the accused. If he was fortunate enough not to be burned by it, he was absolved; if he was burned by it, he was found guilty and punished.

†Ordeal by water: the accused was tied up and thrown into the water. If he floated, he was absolved.

Laws, surely, are established for the good of the people: must we tolerate those that place the judges in the position of systematically presiding over legal actions so gross that they revolt common humanity?

Torture was abolished in Prussia eight years ago; so that the innocent, we are confident, are not mistaken for the guilty, while justice is nonetheless done.[3]

Let us consider now various imprecise laws and procedures that are in the process of being reformed.

There was, formerly, a law in England that forbade bigamy. A man was accused of having five wives, but since the law was unclear, and since it was interpreted literally, the case fell outside the jurisdiction of the court. In order that this law be unequivocal it ought to state, clearly, that anyone who takes more than one wife should be punished, etc. In England laws that are imprecise, and that are, nevertheless, literally interpreted, have given rise to the most ridiculous abuses.*

Precise laws allow no room for wrangling. They must be understood literally. When laws are imprecise or obscure, they require recourse to the intention of the lawgiver, and, instead of reaching judgements on the facts, the task becomes that of clearly defining the law.

Wrangling and disputation are, in general, occasioned by questions of inheritance and contract; and for this reason the laws that are concerned with these matters need the greatest clarity; if one spends time in quibbling over the terms of what are essentially trifling documents, is it not far more important that the terms of the law itself be assessed with scrupulous care?

There are two traps which judges must fear: that of corruption, and that of error. Their conscience must preserve them from the former, and the lawgivers from the latter. Clear laws that offer no room for different interpretations are the first safeguard, and the clarity of the speeches that are addressed to the court the second. It is possible to restrict the speeches of the lawyers to a recital of the facts, supported by evidence, and concluding with an epilogue or a short recapitulation. Nothing is more persuasive than the eloquence of a man who is able through words to arouse and manipulate the emotions: such a lawyer takes possession of the minds of the judges; he interests them, he moves them, he carries them along, while the powerful emotions he arouses

---

*Muralt. A man had cut off the nose of his enemy: it was proposed to punish him for having mutilated a citizen; but he maintained that what he had cut off was not a body organ. Parliament declared, by decree, that the nose would be considered to be an organ. [Béat Louis de Muralt, Lettres sur les Anglais et les Français, et sur les voiages (Cologne: n.p., 1725), 71.]

create a cloud of illusion that masks the fundamental truth of the matter. Both Lycurgus and Solon forbade lawyers to use this kind of persuasion; and if we, nevertheless, meet it in the *Philippics* of Demosthenes and in the speeches *On the Crown* by Aeschines that have come down to us, we should note that they were not delivered in the Areopagus, but before the people; that the *Philippics* are deliberative in character; and that the speeches *On the Crown* are of a demonstrative rather than a judicial nature.[4]

The Romans were not as scrupulous as were the Greeks about the speeches of their orators: there is no address to the court by Cicero that is not full of passion. This causes me some distress, as we see in his defence of Cluentius that he had previously pleaded for the opposite party. Nor does Cluentius's case seem to be particularly strong; but the orator's art prevailed. Cicero's masterpiece is, without doubt, the peroration of his speech for Fonteius, which secured his acquittal even though he appeared to be guilty.[5] What an abuse of eloquence, to use its magical powers of persuasion to subvert even the soundest laws!

Prussia followed the practice of the Greeks; and if, therefore, the dangerous subtleties of eloquence are banned from addresses to the court, this is due to the wisdom of the great chancellor, one whose probity, enlightenment, and ceaseless efforts would have brought honour to the Greek and Roman republics even during those times when they most abounded in great men.[6]

There is another matter still that must be included within the obscurity of the law; this concerns the various procedures and the number of actions that litigants have to go through before bringing their cases to a conclusion. Whether it is bad laws which cause the litigants to suffer injustice, whether it is guileful advocacy that hides their rights from view, or whether it is delays, nullifying the very basis of the litigation, that cause them to lose the benefits which are their due, the end result is the same. One evil may be worse than another, but all abuses deserve reform. Anything that prolongs a case gives a considerable advantage to the rich over litigants who are poor: the rich find a way of extending the case from one action to another, they bring down and ruin their opponents, so that, in the end, they are the only parties left standing.

Formerly, in this country, cases lasted a century or more; even when a lawsuit had been found for the plaintiff by five courts, the opposing side, scornful of justice, would appeal the case to the universities, and the law professors would rewrite these judgements as they saw fit. A litigant was certainly out of luck if, among five courts of law and I know not how many universities, he could not find some souls who were mercenary and corruptible. These practices have been abolished; cases are judged, as a last resort, at the third instance, while judges are limited to a term of one year, during which they must decide even the most litigious cases.[7]

It still remains to us to say a few words about laws that are contradictory, as a result either of the terms in which they are written, or in their very import.

If, in a state, the laws are not collated into a single code, there inevitably will be some that contradict one another; and since they are the work of different lawgivers, who have not followed the same overall plan, they will lack the unity that is so essential and so necessary in all important matters.

Quintilian discusses these matters in his book *Institutio Oratoria,* while we see, in Cicero's speeches, that he often sets one law against another. We find, too, during the course of French history, edicts that are now for, now against the Huguenots. The need to collate such ordinances is all the more vital in that nothing is less worthy of the majesty of the law—which is always held to have been established wisely—than the discovery there of such obvious and manifest contradictions.

The edict against duels is wholly just, wholly equitable, and very well drafted; but it does not secure the result that the princes who drafted it sought when they issued it.[8] After a hard-fought struggle, the force of prejudice, more ancient still than the edict itself, vanquished it, while it would appear that the public, full of wrongheaded opinion, conspired tacitly not to obey it. A notion of honour, badly understood but generally accepted, defies the power of sovereigns, so that this law can remain in force only through a form of cruelty. Any man who suffers the misfortune of being insulted by some ruffian is held, the world over, to be a coward, unless he avenges this insult by putting to death its author. If a man of rank finds himself in this situation, he is looked upon as unworthy of the noble title he possesses; if he is a soldier, and does not kill his opponent, he is obliged to leave, ignominiously, the cadre in which he serves; nor will he find any alternative employment in any military service in Europe. What course of action will such an individual take if he finds himself embroiled in so thorny an affair? Will he dishonour himself by obeying the law, or will he not rather risk his life and his fortune in order to save his reputation?

The most difficult point, and one that remains to be resolved, is the need to discover some expedient which, while preserving the honour of the individual, maintains the law in all its force.

The efforts of even the greatest and most powerful of kings have done nothing to suppress this barbarous custom: Louis XIV, Frederick I, and Frederick William [I] issued strict edicts against duelling; but, even such princes achieved nothing except that duels acquired a new name and were called engagements, and that many noblemen who had been killed in this way were buried as though they had met with sudden death.

Unless all the princes of Europe meet together, and agree among themselves to regard as dishonourable all those who, in spite of the law, try to do away with themselves in single combat, unless, I declare, they agree to refuse any form of safe haven to this kind of murderer, and to punish severely those who insist on insulting their equals, either orally or in writing, or by an assault, there will be no end to duelling.

Let no one accuse me of having inherited visions from the Abbé de Saint-Pierre;[9] I see nothing impossible about individuals putting their quarrels before judges for decision, just as they put to them the disagreements which decide their fortunes. And why would princes not convene a congress for the well-being of humanity, having held so many fruitless meetings on subjects of lesser importance? As to which, I dare to maintain that this is the only means of abolishing in Europe that ill-judged notion of honour, which has cost the lives of so many decent people from whom the fatherland could have expected the greatest service.

Such, in brief, are my reflections upon the law; I have restricted myself to providing a sketch rather than a full-scale picture, but even so I am afraid of having said all too much.

It seems to me, finally, that among those nations that are only just emerging from barbarousness, strict and severe lawgivers are needed; whereas among civilised nations, whose customs are mild, lawgivers with humanity are needed.

To suppose that all men are demons, and to fall upon them with cruelty, is the vision of a wild misanthrope; to suppose that all men are angels, and to allow them free rein, is the dream of an imbecilic Capuchin. To believe that they are neither wholly good nor wholly bad, to reward their good deeds beyond their deserts, to punish their misdeeds less than they deserve, to be indulgent towards their weaknesses, and to show humanity towards all, these are the actions of a reasonable man.

5

Epistle XVIII: To Marshal Keith, on the Vain Terrors of Death and the Fears of Another Life

He is no more, this Saxon, this hero of France,[1]
Who tipped the scales against the haughty Englishman,
Laid low the Caesars' eagle for all its pride,
Left prone in his reed-bed the terrified Belgian,
And restored to the French their valour and boldness of old.

But, alas! although Mars prolonged his career in combat;
Cruel death, which, on these famous battlefields,
Preserved and respected our hero's victorious days,
And secured through his valour the destiny of France,
In the embrace of the peace, which was owed to his bravery,
Strikes him down in his bed, and makes him, while dying,
Envy the fate met in battle by
The valiant Belle-Isle[2] and the renowned Bavière.[3]
Our all-conquering hero is reduced now to dust,
Everything is destroyed, of the Saxon Achilles
Nothing is left but his illustrious name,
Sounds strung together, sterile syllables,
Which strike the delicate membranes of the ear,
Then drift and are lost in heaven's airy heights,
While the great man himself, here below, is consumed by worms.

Our regrets, and our sorrows, his memory, his fame,
His battles, where victory always prevailed,
Everything, finally, is lost; the immensity of time
Consumes at last the very names of the greatest conquerors.

But if Maurice is no more, tell me what has he to fear?
We who have lost him, it is we who must lament,
While he, a contented steersman, has reached his harbour at last.

The wise man faces death with equanimity:
It delivers us from trials and desperate ills,
Our torments end when we, too, end our days;
He who knows death neither flees it nor fears it.
It is not, believe me, the phantom we imagine,
That fearful skeleton whose all-consuming hunger
Devours the bleeding remains of men,
Harvests them throughout the universe,
And, with them, fills the dark abyss of hell.
They are mere idle dreams, these plaintive shades,
Who sink without return into those dark dwelling places,
Those places of great pain, where such trembling spirits,
Must suffer, without hope, eternal punishment;
All such fables brought from Egypt, are, like those of our forefathers,
But a frivolous heap of inflated imaginings,
Of errors bred by fancy and fear.

Ah! Let us reject, dear Keith, these unworthy terrors,
Let truth shine forth, my verses are its instrument;
Unmask yourselves, you hallowed lies,
Which are, in truth, profane,
That we may vanquish you!
Let us strip death of all those attributes,
Those secret horrors that revolt our very nature.
Does it matter that worms should feed upon our flesh?
Let us, rather, find in death merely a quiet sleep,
Sheltered from ills, undreaming, unawakened;
And even should, thereafter, that feeble spark,
That unknown atom we call the immortal soul,
Reawaken us from cold and silent death,
Challenging, thereby, the laws of our demise,
Alas! It matters not; there is nothing now
For our lifeless ashes either to hope for or to fear.

What could I have to fear from an eternal repose?
What! The God whom I adore, is he a cruel tyrant?
Could I, after my death, become the innocent victim
Of the Author to whom I owe the breath that gives me life,
And all those sweet desires of my pleasure-seeking senses?
If the human spirit is formed by the gods' own hands,

Could it be that these same gods would punish their own creation
For those very imperfections they had endowed it with?
No, my reason rejects all such sentiments.
Would a father whose heart is tender towards his children,
Would he towards us men become so harsh and strange
As to punish his son with a barbarous fate,
If this unfortunate fruit of his own fertile stock
Shocked him at birth with some deformity?
A degenerate son may indeed anger his father,
And find himself crushed by the force of his father's rage;
But what could our rage achieve against the gods?
Nothing can destroy their unending felicity.

Could the boldest provocations, born of our unruly ways,
Could such lapses offend so noble a Providence?
Re-enact, proud giants, your rebellion,
Pile up, if you can, Ossa on Pelion,
And take up fearsome arms against the sky:
You will never, not ever, harm this unshakeable throne.
Would God punish those who cannot injure him?
A god without passions, can he be roused to ire?
I know his blessings, his goodness, his clemency;
Whoever portrays him as barbarous is himself the true offender.

Ah! this soul, my dear Keith, which no one can define,
And which, after our death, a tyrant must punish,
This us that is not us, this chimera,
Disappears in the flames that physics brings.
Let the people, stupefied, respect this tale;
While we look, with steadfast gaze, upon being and nothingness.

I beg your help, divine Urania!
Endow my reason with the wings of genius,
Show to me Nature, bathed in your own bright light:
Happy the man who sees and knows your truths!

Experience, already, half-opens the gate,
I see Lucretius and Locke beckoning us on;
Come, let us follow their steps, let us reveal to mankind
Its nature, its being, and what its destiny must be;
Let us study the human mind, from its very beginning,

Throughout its progress, until we reach our ruin:
It is born, it develops, it grows with our senses,
Through which it experiences various transformations;
Our mind, like our body, is weak in infancy,
Then, in adolescence, it is thoughtless, full of fire,
Then whether laid low by ills, or strong and healthy still,
It sinks, grows feeble in decline,
And dies with us, sharing our destiny.

But the soul, which, they say, is of its nature supreme,
What! This immortal being, equal almost to the gods,
Would it leave, for us, the blessed realm of heaven?
Would it deign to unite with this frail flesh?
With this ungrateful matter, poor and perishable,
Would it witness the moments of Venus's passing joys,
And, always watchful, breathe life into a babe,
Remain shut up for nine months in the maternal womb,
A willing prisoner in a deep dark dungeon,
Only to endure thereafter every blow of fate,
To suffer heat, cold, grief, and death?

Our pride, indeed, flatters us with such a vision.
But let us now consult the disciples of Hippocrates,
Let us consider the mechanism, the interplay of forces
That move our minds, even as they do our bodies.

When the daystar, once again, completes its course,
When quiet sleep closes your eyelids
What does the soul do then? It falls asleep with you.
And when your blood, on fire, agitates your pulse,
When, its force redoubled, fever overcomes you,
Your troubled spirit, during this attack, forgets itself:
Let your blood flow out through its open channels,
Let its crimson jets, like water, soar towards the sky,
And soon the pain is gone, your lungs can breathe again,
Your errant spirit returns from its delirium.
Observe how, glass in hand, this disciple of Bacchus
Stumbles on words, which he no longer understands.
A man who has fainted, too, loses his power of thought,
His soul, at that moment oppressed by grievous ills,

Remains, as does his body, numb and dull;
But as soon as he recovers from this seizure,
When he opens his eyes, his soul, grown heavy
After a brief death, is restored to life.
Often a little blood that weighs upon the brain
Snuffs out the flame of weak reason;
If it is to think, the mind has need of organs.
If it were freed from its delicate membranes,
How could it see, feel, touch, or hear,
Think, fear, rejoice, having no memory?
This immortal atom, had it no solid matter,
Deprived of the senses, is but a stupid being;
A mere pompous name, an abstract phantom.
Can it remember the day of our birth?
Does it know how heaven unites it with matter,
And what was once its first nature?

The soul that I received, this perceptive being,
Already at birth had taught my mind most ill;
I did not bring with me the merest trace
Of what had happened in that endless space,
And during that time when my soul pre-existed me;
My memory on this matter has the right to decide.
No, my softened heart offered not a single tear
During those difficult days, during those days full of fear,[4]
When the Germans' oppressor in our fertile fields
Ravished the harvest which our own hands had sown,
When, turn and turn about, the rage of our enemies
Laid waste my exhausted fatherland,
Stole from the people, sacked the cities,
And when, displeased with us, harsh heaven
Sent, the greatest ill of all, the plague
That carried off all that was left of our people,
Made with its deadly poison the very air corrupt,
And reduced our realms to an immense desert.

All these facts I know from history,
If my mind existed then, it had no memory;
Let us then, dear Keith, judge the future by the past:
Since, before I existed, my mind had not a single thought,

So, after my death, when every part of me
Will rot and turn again to nothingness,
By the same fate it will no longer think.
No, nothing is more certain, let us be convinced:
That from the very moment when we cease to be,
Our soul's light is eclipsed.
It is in every way just like the leaping flame
That rises from the burning wood that nourishes it,
Then, once it is a cinder, sinks and slowly dies.

Yes, such is our lot, and I see with steadfast gaze
That fleeting time brings me ever closer to my end;
Should I then fear death and its unforeseen blows?
I know it will return me to the same state I was in
During the eternity that preceded my being;
Was I unhappy before my own birth?
I am bound by the laws of necessity:
My days are short-lived, my being is limited,
I foresee my own death: should I complain?

Ah! Proud mortal, listen to nature;
You will enjoy not only the favours she grants you,
For she also means to rid you of your errors,
Vanquish your prejudices, dispel your wild fancies,
And initiate you, at last, into her wise and mysterious ways:
'I myself gave you life, and it was with my consent
That your body took shape, that your days were prolonged;
The loose fibres of your being, their fragility,
All this must have taught you that your existence is frail.
You will live, if all goes well, for a moment or two.
When, out of diverse elements, I fashioned you,
I promised them then that even-handed death
Would some day repay this charitable loan:
Enjoy my blessings, but honour our agreement,
I gave you your life, and you owe me your death.
Do you want my help, also, to prolong your years?
Fear, rather, unfortunate creature, your own sad destiny:
I see you overwhelmed with pain and with ills,
With destructive grief that will gnaw at your heart;
Reduced to desiring the end of your own days,

Your hand will close your parents' eyes,
Those of your dearest friends, those even of your children,
Quite alone in the world in your declining years,
And losing every day your senses and your mind,
You will become the laughing stock of your young relatives.
Eugene and Malborough,[5] for all their great exploits,
Felt the effects of these same severe laws;
Condé, the great Condé,[6] outlived himself;
The French Augustus,[7] for all his royal crown,
Suffered misfortune in his declining years,
And saw every one of his children carried to the tomb.'

Such would be the words of our mother Nature.
Words, arrogant mortal, that must surely trouble you,
Your heart loves the world; it dazzles and it shines,
But then passes away, and with it everything vanishes.
In spite of all its dangers, you treasure life:
Your parents' love for you urges you to do so,
Your death would cause them endless mourning;
Your own concerns, too, demand attention and time;
Ah! How many grand endeavours would your death undo!
You have achieved so little, why might death not wait?

Ah! Why, wretched man, did you not seize the day?
Did you hope for immortality?
Learn that desires and hopes attend us at every age,
And that no one, in short, will complete his life's work
Before he arrives at his inevitable end.

Either sooner or later, death is always the same:
Times past simply vanish, as though they had never been,
The centuries gone by count for less than today or tomorrow.
Everything, dear Keith, is in flux; such, indeed, is the law of the universe.
Rivers, in their pride, replenish the seas,
One must fertilise the land, dry if left untilled;
If the air is too dense, balmy breezes freshen it,
While those fiery globes that traverse the skies
Take their light every day from the seasons' great star.
Nature, ever mindful, and sparing of her gifts,
Endures endless losses, but is always renewed;

From the elements themselves to all that grows here on earth
Everything alters, changes, and brings forth new life;
Matter endures, and ever changes its form,
But if the natural order makes of it one being, time rots and splits it up.

The heavens for the briefest moment have lent us light and air,
But everything must live, everything have its day;
Should we, then, be wretched if fickle Fate herself
Did not grant us a life the length of Fontenelle's?[8]
Is it for us, then, to fear death?
For us, poor wretched humans, frail playthings of destiny,
Who crawl in the mud, and whose frivolous minds,
If they did not possess the gift of speech,
Would be equal in all things to those of the animals?

Ah! Let us see in death the end of all our woes:
Angry enemies, should you take up against me vengeful arms,
Death will protect me from your insolence;
Your very anger, Great God, is rendered powerless,
And in vain does your lightning strike my memorial stone;
Death counters your blows with an eternal obstacle.
For I have seen the marvellous spectacle of the universe,
I have loved and tasted life and all its joys,
And consign, of my free will, my body to the elements.

What! Caesar, who subdued with his despotic arm
The whole known universe, Rome, its republic;
What! Virgil, author of the most sublime lines,
Newton, who divined the laws of the universe,
What more can I say? You, too, virtuous Marcus Aurelius,
An example to all mankind, my hero, my model,
All of you have suffered the finality of death!
Ah! If cruel fate did not spare even you,
Should we complain, if the weary goddess of destiny
Has just cut off the worn-out thread of all our days?

What is our destiny? Man is born to suffer,
He creates, he destroys, he loves, he watches others die,
He weeps, he takes comfort, but dies, in the end, himself:
Here, wretched humans, is your supreme happiness.
We leave behind us what is no more than a brief stay,

We live in this world as does a stranger
Who enjoys a fine and smiling landscape,
But stops at no resting place along his way.

Let us follow, dear Keith, in the steps of our forefathers,
And let us, in turn, give way to those who follow;
Everyone has his successors, and we will have ours,
Those who lament us will themselves be lamented by others.

Come now, cowardly Christians, let fears of eternal fire
Prevent you from indulging your criminal desires,
Your austere virtue is nothing more than show.
But we, who renounce all future rewards,
Who do not believe in your eternal torments,
Who have never let self-interest sully our sentiments;
It is the good of mankind, it is virtue that moves us,
It is love of duty alone that makes us flee every wrongdoing;
Let us, then, end without distress, let us die without regret,
For we leave behind a universe that overflows with our good deeds.

So, too, does the daystar, when it reaches the end of its course,
Illumine the horizon with the softest light,
While the final rays of light that it grants
Are its last sighs, which it bestows upon the universe.

Epistle XX: To My Soul (*À mon esprit*)

Harken, my soul, I can no longer stay silent,
The tales that I hear of you every day,
Your faults and your failings drive me to despair;
What! You study each day from dawn until dusk?
Urged on by an intemperate and violent desire,
You claim to be a scholar? Ah! What folly is here!
Leafing ceaselessly through some decrepit author
Who wearied the Achards,[1] whom no king has read,
You mean, imitating the Huets,[2] the Saumaises,[3]
To stuff your brain with learned nonsense?
Great heavens! A learned king! The very words make me tremble;
Could you ever have formed a more foolish plan?
That a king should know how to resolve some financial matter,
Initial a treaty, sign an enactment,
This is a lot to ask in our present time;
Could, then, more, in all conscience, be demanded of him?

A king must uphold the splendour of the throne;
Must, full of the majesty whose glamour surrounds him,
Be haughty to his neighbours, and full of disdain,
He must live on flattery, be equal in everything to the gods.
What use is learning? To know in depth
The laws of etiquette: that is perfect knowledge.
This rule of the court keeps busy those idlers
Who surround the great, and whom we call courtiers.

Yes, indeed, murmur softly and silently to the minister
Some obscure compliment on audience day,
Be a mighty hunter, be obliged to shoot game,
And always, without a blush, hear yourself praised;[4]
Hurry to the sermon, yawn throughout the play,
Be dull at supper, speak only in oracles,

And with a noble air pretend to love:
This is how a king must bore his court,
And this was the métier you had to learn.

Your pleasures, my soul, take even me by surprise;
Study, which for you has always been such pleasure,
Demeans your majesty, and diminishes your royalty.
I will go further still: to prove your madness
People say you are addicted to poetry;
Yes, you are a poet, in spite of Apollo.
Can you disown this farcical poem
In which, with venom, you demean the whole earth,
While, braving Zeus's anger, you criticise the heavens,
And, sharpening your witticisms against even Homer,
You attract a swarm of his devotees?
Do you not know that, under various guises,
They watch you pouring forth epistles and odes,
In which, like La Neuville,[5] puffing up your chest,
You preach virtue in tedious sermons?
Ignorant of the subtleties of the French language
You tear to pieces Vaugelas and d'Olivet;[6]
Ah! If Boileau still lived, perhaps, one fine morning
Your name in his verses would replace that of Cotin.[7]
So that a faint blush might rise to your cheeks
At least be ashamed of the time such a work demands,
And without dessicating your brain to no end,
Abandon the foolish pastimes of cultivated minds.

You reply, however, that, as a lover of harmony,
You are transported, in spite of yourself, by the god of genius,
That you can give free reign to your own pleasure
When the king, exhausted, allows you leisure;
And while, to amuse himself, we see many a great prince
Catch in his nets the deer that roam his lands,
You banish your woes with diverse writings,
Drowning the page in a deluge of verse!

What! When, putting to flight a deer,
Princes and hounds run in its pursuit
And find their quarry in the midst of marshy ground,

You, rather than enjoying those self-same pleasures,
Pursue at home some curious new rhyme,
The very word your wit demands, and which renders it well?
Ah! What a strange soul the heavens have given me,
So contrary to our ways, so ill brought-up,
One that, in its oddity, rebels against its own grandeur,
And claims to have opened up a new direction, its very own!
Yes! You agree with me that 'If one must always be concerned with
Trivia, which is the great occupation of courts,
You would rather abandon rank, sceptre, fatherland
And the tedious band of over-formal kings.'
Finally you add that 'Then your learned writings
Would earn respect rather than the idle scorn
Of a people full of error, of an imbecilic common folk
Who judge like a true Midas and give sentence like a Zoilus.'

I agree with you, my soul, but please do not impugn
Received opinion, which it is dangerous to attack;
I simply repeat to you, without satire,
All the rumours that are voiced about you in public.
You are mocked, above all, for the lack of gravitas
With which you season your august royalty;
There is more than one Cato who observes your every failing,
While I very often hear the whisper:
'Have we not, my friends, a most agreeable consul?'

But you always respond in your own habitual way:
'These critics are easy to confound;
And here for my part is my reply:
Have I, drunk with my own pleasures, and, as it were, ungrateful,
Neglected my duties, sacrificed the state?
Have they seen me cheat the people, dash their hopes,
Drag out endless lawsuits, muddle our finances,
Neglect treaties, and all of this in favour of the fine arts?
Have they seen me to be the last to appear on the field of Mars?
And if, in all these matters, I had shone with zeal,
If they saw me ever mindful of my duty,
Anticipating the needs of the people and the army,
How could they be so cruel as to criticise my pleasures?
I see my days pass in the bosom of innocence;

And entranced by the charms with which eloquence shines,
I have tuned my lyre to different keys.
From Horace and Maron[8] I draw my inspiration;
I do not flatter myself that I can reach their heights,
But, while below them still, I offer no complaint.
What! For all my majesty and grandeur
May I not enjoy that small freedom
That a shepherd, leading his peaceful flock,
Has in singing, at dusk, a rustic song,
At that time when shadows put to flight the sun's last rays,
And pleasure promises him a peaceful sleep?
May even Achilles, then, for all his jealous rage,
Appease his anger with his tuneful lyre,
While I, alone in all the universe, may not
Sweeten my cares and sorrows with the charms of verse?
What! Am I to be denied the springs of Permessus?[9]
But, rather, watching the grovelling crowd swell without cease,
Must I be in my place, in the middle of my court,
Flattered by fools, like the saint of the day?
Will they make me a martyr to ceremony?

Ah! Let us shake off the yoke of this tyranny.
Never mind that common sense is out of season,
I guide my steps by the light my own reason provides
And, braving the foolish notions of my critics,
I prefer above all else majestic poetry.
Since I have said so much of this, let us now compare, this once,
The laurels of Apollo and the laurels of kings.

We owe our transports to the god of genius alone.
Chance, which rules our destiny in life,
Ordains things, sometimes, so that the greatest hero
Is succeeded, sometimes, on the throne of kings,
By a stupid foetus, who, scarcely living, merely vegetates,
While the arbiter of men has, as his
Only virtue, the glamour of a title,
The sons of Apollo rise to the very heavens above.
While we dare to speak the language of the gods,
He barely speaks the language of the beasts;
Laurels, always green, have crowned our heads,

More than one king has found fame through our songs,
Our fame has never owed anything to them;
In vain does a sovereign determine our fate,
Ovid's exile in Pontus brought him no disgrace.
Once a prince, without honour, weakened on his throne,
Ends his reign, he is forgotten;
Even if his name, in some genealogical register,
Serves to designate an age in the annals of history;
Such kings, reduced to nothing now, remain for ever dead.
Whereas the subtle harmonies of our sublime verse,
Piercing the darkness and the destruction of many a century
Preserves our names and passes them to posterity;
Our deathless works, triumphant over time,
Have seen the monuments of the greatest kings perish;
Of proud Troy there remains not a trace,
Whereas three thousand years have passed, and we have Homer yet.
Since death, so fatal to all humans,
Cut short the destiny of Virgil and Augustus,
Weary of those struggles that history vaunts,
My soul, indifferent to heroic acts,
Sees there only the great deeds that every age produces;
But Virgil enchants me, and will please us still a thousand years from now:
He moves me when he paints unhappy Troy
Under the sword of the vengeful Greeks, and a prey to their flames;
He touches us with wretched Dido's love,
While lighting the torch of her funeral pyre;
What a fire, such as when he made Aeneas cross the Styx!
He guides me to the Underworld, where I see the fate
Of Anchises's descendants and of the Roman people;
I conjure with Virgil a new human race,
From the Ganges to the sea coasts where the sun goes down,
I see Octavian, blest with fortune, extending his empire.
Of the children of Apollo, you heroes, be jealous:
Caesar did everything for him, Virgil everything for us.

Let us acknowledge the origin of the powers held by kings.
Do you believe them to have been raised by a divine hand,
That their people, their state, entrusted to their care
Are but a herd of stupid beasts who must obey their commands?

Brazen crimes, the plots of traitors,
Forced men to submit themselves to masters;
Themis armed them with a vengeful sword,[10]
To inspire in men of vice a useful terror;
Others, usurping some unlawful good,
Became sovereigns by unstinting crime,
And pass for heroes amongst the ambitious.

Our origin is pure, it comes to us from the heavens;
Apollo placed us on the summit of Permessus,[11]
It is our immortality that ensures us our noble rank.

Ah! Would that the great had written only verse!
What evils would the whole world have been spared!
Caesar, less drunk with despotic power,
Would have enchanted his republic with fine verses;
The two triumvirates would not have come to pass,
Bound by ties of blood these wicked, famous, men
Wrought their vengeance on the great of Rome;
Had the hero from the North, so proud of his own valour,
More knight-errant than a sovereign or a king,
Been less enamoured of Alexander the Great,
Had he chosen as his model Horace or Pindar,
He would not have entreated the Turks and the Tartars.[12]

The Muses have always softened our ways;
Their actions are playful, their weapons are flowers;
In the quiet woods where these nymphs live,
Delicate pleasures and joys delight them;
Only the gentlest feelings can touch their hearts.'

But what am I saying? What is the use of this lengthy discourse?
What an impetuous flood of frivolous eloquence!
What a pointless abuse of the gift of speech!
It is not against me you should argue your case,
It is the whole universe that you must persuade.
It finds no sustenance in windy rhetoric.
Its critics, above all, with lively animation,
Mock your bad verses. 'But what! If they were good,
If they could charm, by modulating their tones,
If D'Argens, if Algarotti, if Maupertuis praise them,

If the French Homer himself approves them,[13]
If posterity . . .' What errors are here!
Beware, my soul, of flatterers and their poison;
Their music, more treacherous still than the Sirens' song,
May well enchant your vigils and your woes,
You should imitate, rather, Ulysses and, deaf to their song,
Reject for ever their deadly wine of praise.
Do you not know that a king, whatever he plans,
Whatever he undertakes, excels in all?
If he loves danger, battle, and risk,
To promote him yet higher Mars must be abased;
If he is strong, the flatterer will at once, without scruple,
Prove to him that only he could rival Hercules;
If his heart is easily inflamed by love,
It is for him that Ovid wrote *The Art of Love*;
If, like you, he likes to write bad verse,
Why, even Voltaire then envies his muse.
Cast off, my soul, your blindness,
Let self-love give way to judgement.
Will you find, among men, virtue without blemish?
Let us reject, without pride, three-quarters of the praises
Lavished upon us by certain men of wit;
Do you need such fulsome praise for so feeble a success?
If one day your vain and barbarous muse,
In order to praise you, compares you, modestly, with Horace,
Then the errors, all too obvious, of your writings
Will oblige you to agree how little you are worth;
And, loathing now so many and such feeble lines,
You will return to the anvil, and remake your work.
Study above all the wisdom of the ancients;
The closer you come to their refinement
The more taste you will have for their sublime works
And the more you yourself will deserve approbation.
Here is your model, and these treasures, now within reach,
Will adorn your writing and render pleasing your verse.

But since I see that you remain always unmoved,
That verse holds for you an unimaginable charm,
That, unable to stay silent, and mumbling below your breath,

Like that indiscreet confidant of Midas,
You rehearse to the reeds my frivolous pastimes;[14]
At least offer me some consolation from your mad visions;
Tell some day your faithful readers,
If you can break through the dark night of time,
Or if some stroke of fate brings you into the great world,
Tell them who this author was, whose fruitful muse
Ascended Helicon in the footsteps of pleasure,
And who wrote lines of verse to while away his leisure.

Say that my cradle lay amid the weapons of war,
That I was brought up in the thick of troubles,
Among the soldiery, without pomp and splendour,
By a stern and censorious father;
That I was the pupil of the finest captains;
That, cultivating in Sparta the gentle ways of Athens,
I was a friend of the arts rather than a true scholar,
And that, without heeding deceitful pride,
A plain and honest follower of the daughters of Memory,
I never aspired to glory and fame,
To be the most fêted of their nurslings;
Rather, knowing how to contain myself and lower my voice
I contented myself with relating my thought,
And with speaking good sense in measured prose.
Say that I have known and have suffered adversity,
But that I have, since, been numbered among the kings;
Assert unflinchingly that philosophy
Has guided my steps and reshaped my life;
Say that, while admiring the order of the heavens,
I have preferred my lyre to the tedious arts;
That, without hating Zeno, I respected Epicurus,
And followed the laws of simple Nature;
That I was able to distinguish the man from the king;
That I was strict as a king but kind as a citizen:
And, while admiring Caesar and Hercules,
I would rather have followed the virtues of Aristides.[15]
When the Fates at last, weary of their spinning,
Choose, with a snip of their scissors, to end my days,
When satire barks upon my extinguished ashes,

Say that, despising all that could be said,
By critics too harsh as to my faint and few virtues,
By fractious minds, ill-formed, morose and twisted,
That without seeking praise, and deaf to all blame,
I have preserved throughout my own peace of mind.
And that, abandoning myself to posterity,
I invite it to judge me, freely, and as it sees fit.

Preface to Extracts from Bayle's
Historical and Critical Dictionary

This *Extract* from Bayle's *Dictionary* is offered to the public in the hope that it will be favourably received. The editors have been concerned, above all, to reassemble here the various philosophical articles that appeared for the first time in this *Dictionary*, articles in which M. Bayle has achieved considerable success; we venture to assert, notwithstanding the prejudices of the school-men and the *amour-propre* of the authors of this century, that M. Bayle has surpassed, thanks to the power of his dialectic, everything produced in this genre by ancient and modern thinkers alike. One has only to compare his works with those of Cicero that survive on the *Nature of the Gods*, and with the *Tusculan Disputations*: the reader will find in the Roman orator, truth be told, an equal fund of scepticism, a greater eloquence, and a style that is more polished and more elegant. On the other hand, however, and without knowing very much about geometry, M. Bayle has particularly distinguished himself by his geometrical cast of mind: he is more concise than Cicero in his reasoning; he goes straight to the point, without amusing himself by in-dulging in squabbling, as does Cicero sometimes in the works we have just mentioned.[1] If we compare M. Bayle with his contemporaries, with, that is, Descartes and Leibniz, creative minds though they were, or with Male-branche, we will find him, we venture to assert, to be superior to these cele-brated men, not for having discovered new truths, but for having never devi-ated from accuracy and precision in his reasoning, and for having pursued the consequences of first principles. He has had the good sense, moreover, never to succumb, as did the others, to narrow or dogmatic views. Descartes and Malebranche, endowed with a lively and powerful imagination, some-times adopted the specious fictions that their minds presented to them as so many truths: one of them created a world that bore no resemblance to ours; the other, led astray by too many subtleties, confused the created with the Cre-ator, and made of man an automaton activated by the Supreme Will.[2] Leib-niz was prey to similar misapprehensions, unless one chooses to believe that he invented his system of monads and of pre-established harmony simply to amuse himself, and in order to provide the metaphysicians with a suitable subject for debate.[3] M. Bayle, whose mind was as sound as it was rigorous, has examined all the dreams of the Ancients and Moderns and, like Bellerophon in the old story, has destroyed the Chimera born of the brains of the philosophers.[4] He has never forgotten the wise precept that Aristotle instilled in his pupils: that doubt is the foundation of wisdom. He did not say, 'I wish to prove such or such a thing, whether it be true or false'; we see him, rather, always following obediently the path along which analysis and synthesis lead him.

This *Dictionary*, this truly monumental achievement of our century, has remained, up until the present moment, buried within the walls of our great libraries; its price has made its possession beyond the reach of men of letters and lovers of books who are poorly endowed with the gifts of fortune. We, however, propose to extract this treasure from its sanctuary, in order to give it universal currency. An anonymous author, who published, some years ago, *L'Esprit de Bayle*, seems already to have had in mind the project we are realising today, except that he was unable to assemble all M. Bayle's articles on philosophy, and that he included in his collection others that are purely historical in content.[5] In the collection we are offering the public, we have excluded everything that is historical in content, because M. Bayle was misled as to various facts and anecdotes, since he was relying on the good faith of various unreliable witnesses, and because it is certainly not in dictionaries that one should study history.

Our principal aim in publishing this *Extract* is to make M. Bayle's admirable dialectic more widely available. It is the very breviary of good sense, it is the most valuable reading that persons of any rank or condition could undertake; for mankind's most important task is to acquire judgement. We appeal to all those who have some knowledge of the world to bear witness to this: they will often have noticed that the reasons which have served as motives for the most important actions are entirely inadequate and frivolous.

We are not foolish enough to suppose that all one has to do in order to ensure that one's reasoning is sound is to have read Bayle; we distinguish, as one must, between the gifts that nature either grants to or withholds from men, and the perfection that art is able to bestow upon them. But is it not a great advantage to be able to provide help to people of good sense, to check the intemperate curiosity of the young, and to humble the presumption of those arrogant minds that are only too ready to yield to the temptation of dreaming up new systems? Which reader does not say to himself, when reading the refutations of Zeno's or Epicurus's systems:[6] 'What! The greatest philosophers of antiquity, those with the greatest number of adherents, have been subject to error! How much more often, then, and with how much more reason, must I be subject to error! What! If even such a person as Bayle, who spent his life in the cut and thrust of the Schools, argued, for fear of going astray, with such evident circumspection, how much more fitting it is that I should avoid being precipitate in my judgements! How, having seen so many human opinions refuted, could one fail to be persuaded that, in metaphysics, the truth is always to be found well beyond the limits of human reason? However hard you urge on your impetuous charger in this direction, you will find yourself brought to a standstill by bottomless chasms. Such obstacles, by demonstrating to you the frailty of your mind, will inspire in you a wise caution; this is the greatest fruit that one can expect to garner from reading this work.'[7]

But why waste one's time, you will object, in searching for the truth, if this truth is only to be found beyond the limits of our human sphere? My reply to this objection is that it behoves a thinking being at least to make some effort to draw closer to the truth, and that, in devoting oneself in good faith to this task, one certainly acquires from it the ability to avoid an infinity of errors. If your land does not yield much fruit, it will, at least, bear no thorns, and it will become more ready for cultivation; you will be on your guard against the subtleties of the logicians, you will adopt, without being aware of it, the spirit of Bayle, and, in discovering at first glance the shortcomings of an argument, will tread with less danger the shadowy pathways of metaphysics.

There will no doubt be, among the public, people who do not think as we do, and who will be astonished by the preference we show for the works of Bayle over the very many books on logic with which we are inundated. To which we will reply, simply, by pointing out that the principles of knowledge have, in themselves, a certain aridity which they lose in the hands of a skilful practitioner; and, since our subject leads us towards this same topic, it would perhaps be appropriate, at least where young people are concerned, for us to point out to them the different uses that orators and philosophers make of logic. The ends towards which they are working are entirely different: the orator is content with what is plausible, whereas the philosopher rejects everything except truth itself. In court, the orator responsible for defending his client does everything he can to save him: he misleads the judges, he even changes the meanings of words, so that crimes become mere weaknesses, while misdeeds become, almost, virtues; he not only obfuscates, he misrepresents those aspects of the case that are unfavourable to him; and if these ruses do not work, he has recourse to the passions, employing, in order to arouse them in his audience, the most powerful rhetorical means at his disposal.[8]

Although the eloquence deployed in the pulpit is concerned with more serious matters than is that of the courtroom, it is nevertheless conducted according to similar principles, and often causes decent souls to groan at the injudicious choice of the arguments it employs—for want of judgement, no doubt, on the part of the orator, who, unfortunately for him, provides every advantage for the argumentative and difficult people who are never satisfied by weak arguments or by pompous words. This showiness, these subtleties, these superficial arguments, none of this is acceptable in the austere and rigorous argumentation practised by good philosophers: they wish to convince only by means of evidence and truth, they examine every system of thought impartially and judiciously, they provide proofs without misrepresenting or weakening them, they employ every available argument to defend the system they are examining; after which, they make equally great efforts to attack it. Finally, they summarise the favourable or adverse probabilities; and since it is rare, in such matters, to uncover evidence that is decisive, the fear of reaching a hasty conclusion obliges them to suspend judgement. If humans are rational creatures, as the Schools assure us they are, philosophers must be more human than are their fellows; and it is for this reason that they have always been held to be the tutors of mankind; and their works, which are the very catechism of reason, cannot, for the benefit of humanity, be too widely promulgated.

8

Preface to *Abridgement of the Ecclesiastical History by Fleury*

The establishment of the Christian religion had, as do all empires, uncertain beginnings. A Jew, of doubtful parentage and a product of the dregs of society, who combined absurd ancient Hebraic prophesies with the precepts of a sound morality, to whom miracles were attributed, and who ended by being condemned to ignominious torture and death: such is the hero of this sect. Twelve fanatical followers took its message from the East and as far as Italy, winning over hearts and minds through the morality, so saintly and so pure, that they preached; and if we leave aside several miracles designed to stir people's passionate imaginings, what they taught was simply deism. This religion began to gain ground at the very time when the Roman empire was groaning under the tyranny of several monsters, who governed it one after the other. During these bloody reigns, various citizens, expecting to suffer all the misfortunes that can assail humanity, only found consolation and support against such great evils in Stoicism. Christian morality had much in common with this doctrine, which was the sole cause of the rapid progress of this religion. Ever since the reign of Claudius, Christians had formed gatherings of one sort or another, which took the form of prayer meetings among friends, and of communal suppers.[1] The heads of government, full of suspicion, and only too mindful of their own tyrannical regime, opposed all forms of assembly, all gatherings and public meetings, for fear that some plot would be hatched there, or that some bold party leader would raise the standard of revolution. Devout Christians, in their zeal, defied the Senate's measures against them; various fanatics among them disrupted the people's sacrificial ceremonies; indeed, their pious insolence drove them to the point of overturning images of the pagan gods. Others tore up edicts issued by the emperors; and there were even a number of Christians serving in the legions who refused to obey their superiors' orders. Hence came those persecutions upon which the church prides itself; hence, too, the just punishments, suffered by various obscure Christians, for disobeying the laws of the state, and for agitating against the established religion. The Christians, then, were obliged to deify their own zealots. Thanks to pagan executioners, Paradise became well populated; after these executions priests gathered up the bones of the victims, and buried them with due honour. Their tombs necessarily became the sites of miracles. The people, besotted by superstition, took to worshipping these martyrs' ashes; soon they began to erect images of the martyrs in their churches. Fake holy men, each one out-bidding the other, introduced imperceptibly the practice of invoking the saints. Feeling, however, that this practice was contrary to the Christian faith, and above all to the law of Moses, they tried to keep up appearances by making a clear distinction between the worship of God himself and the cult of idolatry. The common people, who make no such distinctions, worshipped the saints in good faith, and in their own vulgar way. Nevertheless, this dogma and this new form of worship became established only gradually, and reached its full height only towards the middle of the ninth century, after the reign of Charlemagne.

All these new dogmas became established by a similar process. In the early church, Jesus Christ had been regarded as a created person, pleasing to the Supreme Being. He does not call himself God in any chapter of the Gospels, but, rather—if one is not confused by such terms—the son of God, or son of Belial, which were proverbial Jewish expressions indicative of the goodness or wickedness of the men to whom they were applied. If the notion of the divinity of Jesus Christ gained credence in the church, it was confirmed only through the subtleties of various Greek philosophers of the Aristotelian Peripatetic sect, who, while embracing Christianity, enriched it with some of the obscure metaphysics beneath which Plato believed he had hidden various truths too dangerous to be made public.

During the adolescence of the church, during, that is, its first centuries, the most powerful men of the empire, as well as those who governed it, were pagans. The adherents of a still obscure sect could have no power; with the result that, necessarily, the government of the church took a republican form; that, generally speaking, opinions were not constrained; and that, in spite of an infinite variety of beliefs, there was communication between Christians. This is not to say that some obstinate priest or other did not, dogmatically, maintain his own beliefs and harden, indeed, his stance in the face of opposition. But such zeal was limited to specific points of dispute, and, since churchmen lacked the power of persecution, they also lacked the means of making their adversaries think as they did.

Around the beginning of the fourth century, when Constantine, for political reasons, declared himself protector of the church, everything changed.
He had barely secured the throne when he convoked an ecumenical council
in Nicaea [AD 325]. Of the fathers who composed the council, three hundred
held an opinion contrary to that of Arius; it was they who first recognised,
and declared explicitly, the divinity of Jesus Christ; they added to the creed
the words 'consubstantial with the Father' and ended by anathematising the
Arians. Thus, from one council to the next, new dogmas blossomed. It was
at the Council of Chalcedon that the Holy Spirit had its turn.[2] The fathers
who comprised this council would nevertheless have found more than one
objection to their adding a third person to the divinity of the Father and the
Son, if some priest, more cunning and more of a rascal than the others, had
not provided them with an expedient, by adding a passage, which he himself
invented for this purpose, to the beginning of the Gospel according to St
John: 'In the beginning was the word, and the word was with God and the
word was God, etc.'[3] However crude this deception might appear in our day,
it was not so at the time. The trust of the faith and the scriptures had already
passed from the people into the hands of the pontiffs; it was they who, from
among a multitude of writings, selected those they declared to be canonical.
We must add the breakup of the empire, and the wars and ravages of the barbarians, which, by destroying learning, increased brutality and ignorance; so
that we may easily be persuaded that no particular skill was needed for this
deceit, since ignorance, superstition, and stupidity had had time enough to
establish general credulity. And even if someone had dared to complain about
the intercalated passage in St John, it was easy enough to claim that the original manuscript had only recently been discovered.

When they established new dogmas, the bishops must necessarily have
noted the extent of their power and their influence. It is innate in man to exploit his advantages; so that churchmen, being human, did just that. They
manoeuvered, nevertheless, with a certain skill: they were, as it were, exposing to risk some lost child or other, who was advancing a new doctrine, one
that was consistent with their own self-interest, and which they wanted to
adopt. Next, therefore, they convoked a council, where the new doctrine was
accepted as an article of faith. Thus it was that some monk, I know not which,
discovered in a chapter of the book of the Maccabees the doctrine of purga-
tory.[4] The church embraced it, and this doctrine was to prove of greater
value to it than was the discovery of America to Spain. We must also attribute to similar manoeuverings the fabrication of false decrees, which served

as stepping stones to the papal throne, from which, ever since, popes have dictated imperiously, and to the consternation of nations, their laws.

Before attaining such heights, the church had taken on various different forms. Republican government lasted the first three centuries. After the Emperor Constantine had embraced Christianity, there arose a kind of aristocracy, headed by the emperors, the popes, and the principal patriarchs. This administration underwent, subsequently, changes such as those to which all human affairs are subject. When the ambitious find themselves vying for power and eminence, they are never slow to adopt either ruses or artifices in supplanting one another, so that the most ruthless of them prevail in time over their rivals. Such were the popes, who took advantage of the decline of the eastern empire, in order to usurp the authority of the Caesars, and to ensure that the rights of the imperial crown passed to the papal tiara. Gregory III, known also as 'the Great', was the first to attempt such measures.[5] Pope Stephen, who had similar ambitions, took several steps further in this direction. Expelled from Rome by Aistulf, king of the Lombards, he went to France where he crowned the usurper Pepin, on condition that he rid Rome of the Lombards. The pope, on his return to Rome, in order to secure the assistance he was expecting from France, wrote a letter to the king, whom he had previously crowned in the name of the Virgin, St Peter, and all the saints, in which he threatened him with eternal damnation if he did not immediately rid him of the Lombards who were overpowering him. He had given the kingdom of France, over which he had no rights, to Pepin, while, in return, Pepin had given him, so he claimed, Rome and all its possessions, which belonged, properly, to the emperors of Constantinople. Charlemagne was, subsequently, crowned in Rome by the pope; not that he believed that he owed his crown to the pontiff, but because it was said that Samuel had anointed King Saul and King David. Sovereigns wished to pay homage, through this ceremony, only to the one who, by an act of his will, raises, shakes, sustains, or overturns empires. The popes did not understand matters thus. During the reign of Louis the Pious, the son of Charlemagne, Gregory IV, setting his spiritual power above the temporal, persuaded Louis that his father had owed his throne and his empire to the Holy See. Such was the explanation that the popes, interpreters of mysteries, placed upon the consecration of sovereigns. They were held to be the vicars of Jesus Christ, they declared themselves to be infallible, and they were adored. The shadows of ignorance were growing from century to century, ever more dark. What more was needed to extend and validate the deception?

Clerical politics, always active, continued to unfold. A monk, whose name was Hildebrand, better known as Gregory VII, arrogant, austere, and audacious by nature, established the true foundation of papal majesty. He accepted no restraint, but granted himself the right to bestow and remove crowns, to proscribe kingdoms, and to free their subjects from the oath of fidelity. He acknowledged no limit to his ambition, of which we may be persuaded by considering the famous bull *In coena Domini* that he published.[6] It is from his pontificate that we must date the epoch of church despotism. His successors, subsequently, granted the clergy the same privileges that the tribunes of ancient Rome had enjoyed; they were declared to be unassailable. In order to shield them entirely from the domination of their legitimate sovereigns, the councils decided that the inferior could in no case be the judge of the superior, so that, according to the custom of the time, princes had no authority in their states over churchmen. It was by this means that the bishop of Rome secured for himself a great advantage, a militia, indeed, ready to fight under his orders in any country. However extravagant such enterprises seem to us to be, they were not so at the time. Feudal government throughout Europe was generally weak; there were powerful vassals who, born enemies of their sovereign lords, were only too eager to support the thunderbolts of excommunication that the popes hurled against their sovereign; as were the neighbouring princes, either jealous of, or hostile to, the excommunicated sovereign. And then there were priests, entirely committed to the Holy See, and independent of their temporal masters: how many ways there were of tormenting kings, and what common interests there were in providing the popes with zealous and ardent executors of their papal bulls!

We will not revisit here the quarrel between the emperors and the pontiffs on the subject of their claims to the city of Rome, or on the subject of investitures by crozier and ring; nor their disagreements, occasioned by the territories involved in the succession of the Countess Matilda.[7] No one is in any doubt that these secret disputes alone gave rise to the frequent excommunication of so many kings and emperors. There is a particular form of pride which is nurtured in the heart of an all-powerful leader; it never manifested itself more scandalously than in the conduct of Gregory VII towards the Emperor Henry IV. Closeted in his castle at Canossa with the Countess Matilda, he forced the emperor to submit to the basest and most shameful expedients before granting him absolution. We must not, however, imagine that all excommunications and papal bulls were equally injurious. They were more damaging to the emperors than they were to the kings of France, since in the Gallic countries the crown was held to be independent, and the French recognised the authority of the bishops of Rome only in spiritual matters.

However, although the popes were all-powerful, they could not prevent every excommunication of an emperor leading to civil war in Italy. Such wars often shook the pontiffs' throne; some pontiffs, driven from their capital city, and fugitives in other countries, found asylum with a sovereign who was hostile to their persecutor. It is true that they often returned to Rome triumphant, not by force of arms but through their skill, so superior was their politicking to that of the sovereigns. Nevertheless, in order not to be exposed to the vagaries of fortune, they devised schemes, which, once set in motion, were bound, in making their reign secure, to intensify their despotism. The reader expects, doubtless, that we have the Crusades in mind. In order to recruit a group of fanatics, indulgences were published; in other words, impunity for all crimes was promised to those who committed themselves to the service of the church and the holy father. In order to fight in Palestine, over which they had no claim, in order to conquer the Holy Land—something not worth the cost of the expedition—princes, kings, and emperors, followed by a countless multitude of people from all parts of Europe, abandoned their native land, and exposed themselves in distant countries to inevitable misfortune. In following such ill-concerted plans, the popes, laughing with pity at the foolish blindness of mankind, congratulated themselves on their success. During this voluntary exile of so many sovereigns, Rome met no opposition to her wishes, and as long as this frenzied madness lasted, the popes, as despots, ruled Europe. When it was noticed in Rome that a number of nations were becoming discouraged by their lack of success in the Crusades, much attention was paid to giving them new heart, through hopes of better fortune promised by some tonsured impostor or other. St Bernard was the instrument of the Holy See on various such occasions: his eloquence was ideal for increasing the poison of this wicked epidemic; he sent victims to Palestine, but was too prudent to go there himself.[8] What was the result of so many ventures? Wars which depopulated Europe, and victories no sooner won than lost. In the end, it was the Christians who opened up the breach through which the Turks entered Constantinople, and made it the seat of their power [1453].

Greater still was the moral evil produced by the Crusades. The granting of so many indulgences, the remission for crimes, all sold to the highest bidder, caused a general decline in morals; corruption grew apace; and Christian morality, so holy and pure, but now entirely forgotten, witnessed its own ruin, and on that ruin the rise of merely external worship and of superstitious practices. If the church's treasuries were exhausted, Paradise was put up for auction, which enriched the chancellery of the papal court. If the popes wanted to wage war on a sovereign with whom they were displeased, they called for a Crusade against him; they had armies, and they fought. If the Holy See wanted to ruin a prince, it declared him a heretic, and excommunicated him; this was to be a rallying-call that mobilised the whole world against him. It was through such means that the despotic yoke of the popes grew heavier. The great of the earth, exasperated by this yoke, would have liked to shake it off; but they did not dare. The authority of most of them was insecure, and the multitude of their subjects, sunk in the deepest ignorance, were gagged and bound by the fetters of superstition. Various spirits, ahead of their time, tried, in truth, to open the eyes of a bewitched populace, and to bring them enlightenment through the weak glimmerings of doubt. But the tyranny of the church made all their efforts in vain: they had to face judges who formed a party, and suffer persecution, prison, violence, and the flames that were already rising from the pyres of the Inquisition. In order to complete the picture of this age of fear and brutalisation, we must add the luxury and ostentation of the bishops, which seemed only to add insult to the wretchedness of the people; the scandalous life and atrocious crimes of so many popes, who, openly, gave the lie to the morality of the Gospels; and the remission of sins, put up for auction, which clearly proved that the church was betraying, in order to enrich itself, everything that religion holds most sacred. In the end, the pontiffs abused a power that was based on the credulity of men, just as we have seen nations abusing their sound credit. All these things accumulated, and paved the way for the Reformation.

In order that nothing be omitted, we must record a circumstance that facilitated this process. Ever since the Council of Basel, where the Emperor Sigismund deposed three popes at the same time, the Holy See feared general councils as much as previously it had favoured them.[9] The fathers had announced at Basel that the Council possessed, by divine right, the authority to correct pontiffs and to depose them. Already, during the reign of the Ottonian dynasty [919–1024], the emperors, indignant at inheriting excommunications from their predecessors, had had the good sense to make use, in their turn, of religion and of the assemblies of bishops in order to depose the bishop of Rome, and to fight him with his own weapons. Ever since the great schism of the West,[10] the bishops, too, had lost their good name; profane hands had touched this golden idol, before which the whole world had previously prostrated itself, and had found it to be made only of clay. Thereafter the Holy See feared kings, emperors, and councils; excommunications, such terrible weapons in former times, now merely rusted in the hands of the pontiffs. In other words, everything was about to change, when Wycliffe appeared in England and Jan Hus in Bohemia.[11]

This was, as yet, only the first faint dawning of the day that was to banish the shadows of darkness. Nevertheless, the cup overflowed, and even the people, vulgar and stupid as they were, overburdened with the taxes they paid to the clergy, offended by the ostentation of the bishops and by their scandalous way of life, were in a state of agitation such as usually precedes great revolutions. In the end, the sale of indulgences brought the whole process to its conclusion, and caused the Holy See to lose half of Europe, which renounced its obedience. This great spiritual revolution would certainly have arrived sooner or later, because, on the one hand, ambition knows no bounds; and because, on the other, the human spirit is capable of only a certain measure of patience, and because the pontiffs, having been, for so many centuries, in the position of deceiving the nations of Europe, thought that, by following the footsteps of their predecessors, they would run the least risk.

A monk from Saxony, brave to the point of rashness, endowed with a powerful imagination, and well able to exploit the turmoil into which the minds of his contemporaries had been plunged, became the leader of the faction that declared itself against Rome. This Bellerophon laid low his Chimera, and the magic was destroyed.[12] If we dwell upon his base and vulgar prose style, Martin Luther [1483–1546] will appear as nothing more than an impetuous monk, an uncivilised writer from a barely enlightened people. If we were to reproach him, and rightly, for the innumerable invectives and insults he lavished upon his opponents, we must nevertheless bear in mind that those for whom he wrote were roused by his imprecations, and did not understand his arguments. But if we examine the work of the reformers as a whole, we must agree that the human spirit owes part of its progress to their works; they have rid us of a number of errors that blinded the minds of our forefathers. By obliging their opponents to be more circumspect, they suppressed new superstitions that were about to appear; and because they were persecuted they were tolerant. It was under the sacred protection of this tolerance, which was established in Protestant states, that human reason was able to develop, learned men to practise philosophy, and that the limits of our knowledge have been extended. If Luther had done nothing more than free princes and peoples from the servile bondage in which the court of Rome had held them, he would have deserved to have altars put up in his name, as is done for a liberator of the fatherland; and if he had torn down only half of the veil of superstition, what gratitude truth would have owed him! The severe and critical eye of the reformers also gave pause to the fathers of the Council of Trent [1545–63], who were poised to make the Virgin the fourth member of the Trinity; nevertheless, in order to console her, they gave her the title of Mother of God and Queen of Heaven.[13]

The Protestants, who were notable for their austere virtue, forced the Catholic clergy to behave more decently. There were no more miracles; fewer saints were created; the Holy See was no longer the whore of the pontiffs, with their scandalous lives; sovereigns were protected from excommunication; the churches were less subject to interdiction; the people were no longer relieved of their oaths of allegiance; and indulgences went out of fashion. There was one further advantage that resulted from the Reformation, which was that theologians of many sects, obliged now to wage war with the pen, were forced to become better educated; the need to know made them knowledgeable. The eloquence of Greece and of ancient Rome was reborn, even if it was used only in various absurd theological disputes, which no one can fathom. Great men, nevertheless, appeared in every sect, and the pulpits, which had been filled with the idle and the ignorant, were now occupied by learned doctors of eminent merit.

Such were the benefits of the Reformation. If we compare them with the evils it caused, we must concede that the benefits that accrued from it were dearly bought. Minds throughout Europe were in ferment: the laity reexamined what they had adored, the bishops and the abbots feared the loss of their revenues, the popes the loss of their authority, and all the world caught fire. Nothing is more bitter, nor more pitiless, than theological hatred; such hatred, mixed with the politicking of sovereigns, gave rise to the wars that ravaged so many empires. Torrents of blood inundated Germany, France, and the Low Countries. It was only after victories, which were for a long time balanced on all sides, and after all the horrors of which human malice, left to its own devices and a prey to fanaticism, is capable, that, in the midst of the smoking ruins of their fatherland, Germany and Holland acquired that inestimable good: the freedom of thought. Thereafter, all of the North followed their example.

Who does not conclude, in surveying its history, that the church is the work of men? What a pitiable role men assign to God! He sends His only Son into the world; this Son is God; He sacrifices Himself in order to be reconciled with His creature; He makes Himself man in order to correct the depravity of the human race. What is the result of so great a sacrifice? The world remains every bit as corrupt as it was before His coming. Would the same God, who says, 'Let there be light'—and there was light—employ inadequate means to achieve His loving purposes? A simple act of His will would be enough to banish from the universe, for ever, moral and physical evil, to inspire in the nations whatever beliefs He pleases, and to use His omnipotence to make the nations happy. Only narrow and limited spirits would dare to attribute to God conduct so unworthy of His lovable providence, in making Him undertake, by means of the greatest miracles, a work that is not a success. These same men who hold such incoherent notions of the Supreme Being, introduce into every council new articles of faith; all of which we will see set out in this chronological abridgement, drawn from the great *History* of M. de Fleury, an author who is beyond reproach. It is the particular attribute of the works of God that they should be unchanging; the particular attribute of those of men is to be subject to vicissitude. How can it therefore be possible to regard as divine opinions that become established little by little, that can be added to, or qualified, and that change according to the desires and the self-interest of priests? How can we believe in the infallibility of those who claim to be the vicars of Jesus Christ when, judging by their morals, one would take them to be vicars of those evil beings consigned, so it is said, to the depths of torture and darkness?

We have seen popes excommunicate one another; we have seen them retract; we have seen councils that change the doctrines of earlier councils, under the specious pretext of explicating dogma. We must, then, conclude that the one or the other must have been mistaken. Why, moreover, employ the sword, fire, and persecution in order to convert nations, as Charlemagne did in Germany, as did the Spanish after the expulsion of the Moors, and as they did again in America? Does it not occur to every reader that, if a religion is true, it should be evident enough to convince us; and that, if it is false, in order to make converts, there must be persecution? We do not wish to rely on miracles that occurred so frequently in unenlightened centuries, and so rarely in enlightened times. In other words, what the history of the church offers us are examples of the politicking, the ambition, and the self-interest of priests. Instead of finding there the person of the Divinity, we see only a sacrilegious abuse of the name of the Supreme Being, which impostors—who are, moreover, revered—use as a veil to cover their criminal passions. I must take care to add nothing to this picture: I have said enough for anyone who is a thinking being, and I make no claim to spell things out for automata.

9

Essay on Self-Love, Considered as a Principle of Morality

Virtue is society's strongest bond, and the source of public peace: without it men would be like wild beasts, more bloodthirsty than lions, more cruel and treacherous than tigers or than other kinds of monster we had best avoid.

It was to soften such barbarous ways that lawgivers issued laws, that wise men taught morality, and, by demonstrating the advantages of virtue, established the value men ought to attach to it.

Philosophical sects in the countries of the East, as well as among the Greeks, while agreeing in general about the basis of their doctrines, differed, nevertheless, in the incentives they adopted to persuade their disciples to lead a virtuous life. The Stoics, in accordance with their principles, insisted on the inherent beauty of virtue, from which they concluded that we must love virtue for itself; they placed the chief happiness of mankind in its immutable possession. The Platonists said that, to practise the virtues, following the example of the immortal gods, was to come close to them and to resemble them. The Epicureans believed that a superior form of pleasure comes from the performance of the duties of morality; according to their doctrine, when properly understood, a feeling of delight and ineffable happiness is to be found in the possession of the purest virtue. In order to inspire the Jews to good and praiseworthy action, Moses promised them temporal blessings or afflictions. The Christian religion, which arose from the ruins of Judaism, used eternal punishment to suppress criminality, and encouraged virtue through the hope of eternal beatitude. Not content even with these expedients, and in the hope of attaining the highest possible degree of perfection, it claimed that the love of God alone must serve as the basis of human goodness, even if neither punishment nor reward are to be expected in another life.

We must concede that philosophical sects have produced men of the greatest merit; we also concede that Christianity has nurtured pure and saintly souls. Nevertheless, through the decline in philosophy and theology, and through the perversity of the human heart, it has come about that the various incentives to virtue have not continued to produce the good effects hoped for. How many philosophers among the pagans were philosophers only in name! You have only to glance at Lucian to be persuaded as to how little they were valued in his day.[1] How many degenerate Christians there were who corrupted the pure morality of antiquity! Greed, ambition, and fanaticism filled the hearts of those who professed the renunciation of the world, and destroyed all that simple virtue had established. History teems with such examples. In summary, with the exception of a few recluses who were both pious and useless to society, the Christians of today are no better than were the Romans of the time of Marius and Sulla; but, of course, I am restricting this parallel purely to the comparison of customs.[2]

These and similar reflections have prompted me to seek the causes that have contributed to this strange depravity among humankind. I do not know whether I am allowed to hazard my own views on matters of such importance; but it seems to me that we have been, perhaps, wrong as to the choice of motives that ought to incline men to virtue. These motives, it seems to me, had the disadvantage of not being within the reach of ordinary people. The Stoics did not perceive that admiration is a forced emotion that will not last very long; self-love allows us to applaud only with reluctance. We agree readily as to the beauty of virtue, because this avowal costs us nothing. But in agreeing to this from a desire to please rather than from conviction, we are not persuaded to improve ourselves, to overcome our evil inclinations, and to control our passions. The Platonists ought to have recollected the immense distance that lies between the Being of beings and His fragile creation. How can we ask this creature to imitate his Creator, of whom he can form only a vague and indeterminate idea, given his circumscribed and limited state? Our minds are subject to the tyranny of the senses; our reason concerns itself only with those things that our experience illuminates for us. To offer it abstractions is to lead it into a labyrinth from which it will never find the way out; whereas to present to it palpable objects of nature is to attract its attention and convince it. There are few men of sufficient genius to preserve their good sense when plunging themselves into the shadowy depths of metaphysics. In general, man is born more to a life of the senses than to one ruled by reason. The Epicureans misused the notion of pleasure, and, without meaning to, weakened the force of their doctrine by this very misuse, thus providing their disciples with a weapon to misrepresent their philosophy.

Regarding what the Christian religion thinks of as divine, and speaking of it only in philosophical terms, the Christian religion, I say, presented to the mind ideas so abstract that each catechist would have had to become a metaphysician if he were to understand these ideas; and only men born with a powerful imagination could have been chosen to be imbued with them. But few men are born with such well-organised minds. Experience proves that among ordinary people the object that is present prevails over the distant object, because it strikes the senses; the distant object affects people less powerfully; in consequence the good things of this world, the enjoyment of which is within reach, will certainly be preferred to imagined goods whose possession is envisaged confusedly, and in a distant perspective. But what shall we say about the incentives that come from the love of God in order to make man virtuous; and what shall we say about this love which the Quietists require to be independent of our fears of hell and our hopes of paradise?[3] Is such a love possible? The finite cannot conceive of the infinite; therefore we cannot form any clear idea of the Divinity; we can persuade ourselves, generally speaking, of His existence, and that is all. How can we demand of an uncultivated soul that it should love a Being that it cannot, in any way, know? Let us content ourselves with silent adoration, and restrict the promptings of our hearts to feelings of deep gratitude towards the Being of beings, in whom and through whom all beings exist.

The more we examine this matter, the more we discuss it, the more obvious it becomes that, if we are to make men virtuous, we must use a more general and simpler principle. Those who have devoted themselves to knowledge of the human heart will doubtless have discovered the expedient that we must employ. This powerful expedient is self-love, that guardian of our preservation, that author of our happiness, that inexhaustible source of our vices and our virtues, that hidden principle of all human action. It is most clearly present in the man of wit and intelligence, and it also enlightens, as to his self-interest, the most stupid of men. What could be finer or more admirable than to draw upon this source of goodness, happiness, and public felicity—even though it is a source that can also lead to vice? This admirable outcome would be secured, if this question were in the hands of an able philosopher: he would manage self-love, he would direct it towards the good, he would know how to temper one passion with another, and, by demonstrating to men that it is in their interest to be virtuous, he would make them so.

The Duc de La Rochefoucauld, who in his exploration of the human heart has unmasked so well the motive force of self-love, has used it to slander our virtues, which he considers to be only for show.[4] I, however, would like this motive force to be used to persuade men that their true self-interest lies in being good citizens, good fathers, good friends, in possessing, in short, every moral virtue; and since, in effect, this is the truth, it would not be difficult to persuade them of it.

Why do we try to capture men's minds with an appeal to their own interests when we seek to move them to follow a particular course of action, if self-interest is not, of all arguments, the most powerful and persuasive? Let us, then, use this same argument in relation to morality; let us present to men the misfortunes that will follow evil doings, and the good things that are inseparable from worthy deeds. When the Cretans cursed their enemies, they did so by urging them to give themselves over to passion and vice; this was equivalent to urging them to hurl themselves into misfortune and opprobrium.* These simple truths are capable of proof, and are well within the grasp of wise men, of men of wit and intelligence, and of the lowest of the populace.

My thesis will, without a doubt, provoke the following objection: that it is difficult to reconcile the happiness I attach to good actions with the persecution that virtue so often endures, and, still more, with the varieties of good fortune that so many perverse souls enjoy. This difficulty is easy to resolve, if we are prepared to confine ourselves to understanding by the word 'happiness' only perfect peace of mind. This peace of mind is based on our ease with ourselves, on whatever in our own actions our conscience allows us to applaud, and for which we have no reason to reproach ourselves. Now, it is obvious that such a state of mind can be present even in someone who is in other respects unfortunate; but it will never exist in a cruel and wicked heart, which, if it examines itself, can only detest itself, whatever the good fortune that it appears to enjoy.

We are not ignoring here what experience teaches us; we concede that there are countless examples of unpunished crimes, and of scoundrels who enjoy the trappings of greatness that fools admire. But do not these same criminals fear that time will unveil, in the end, a truth about them so terrible that it will uncover their shame? And as for those monsters who wore the crown, a Nero, a Caligula, a Domitian, a Louis XI, did the empty splendours that they enjoyed prevent them from hearing the condemnation of the secret voice of conscience, from being racked by remorse, and from feeling the lash of the avenging whip, which, although invisible, thrashes them and tears them apart?[5] What soul can remain at peace in such a situation? Does not that soul, rather, suffer in this life all that is most terrible in the torments of hell? It is, moreover, wholly unreasonable to judge the happiness of others by appearances alone. Such happiness can only be assessed in relation to the state of

---

*Valerius Maximus, Book VII, chapter 2.

mind of the person who is experiencing it; this state of mind varies so widely that one person may love fame, another pleasure; another, again, is attracted to trivia, yet another to matters that are thought to be important; and some even disdain and despise those things that others desire, or regard as the sovereign good.

There is, therefore, no certain rule by which we may judge what depends on a taste that is arbitrary and often capricious; whence it happens that we often complain about the happiness and good fortune of those who, in secret, groan bitterly under the burden of their afflictions. Then again, it is not in external objects, nor in the vagaries of fortune that come and go with the changing scenes of the world, that we can find felicity; we have to seek it within ourselves. There is no other felicity in this world, I say again, than peace of mind, which is why our self-interest must prompt us to seek so precious a good; and if the passions disturb it, it is they that must be tamed.

Just as a state cannot be happy while it is torn apart by civil war, so man cannot enjoy happiness if his passions are in revolt, and dispute the reign of reason. Every passion brings its own punishment; those passions that please our senses most are not exempt from this. Some bring ruin to our health; others bring cares and ceaseless anxiety; either through the disappointment of not realising the ambitious projects one had planned; or through that of not enjoying all the consideration one believes one deserves; or through the fury at not being able to take revenge on those who have insulted you; or through remorse over having borne too cruel a grudge; or through the fear of being unmasked, having committed, one after the other, a hundred villainies.

For example, the miser, ceaselessly troubled by his thirst for wealth, will employ any means whatsoever, providing he achieves his aim; but the fear of losing what it has cost him so much trouble to acquire destroys all his enjoyment in what he possesses. The ambitious man loses all sight of the present in order to propel himself blindly into the future; he is always spawning new projects; in order to attain his goals, he tramples imperiously on whatever is most sacred; the obstacles he encounters irritate and embitter him; always divided between fear and hope, he is, in point of fact, unhappy; and even when he gains possession of what he desires, he feels disgust and satiety. This state of mind inspires yet further schemes, and the happiness he seeks he never finds. Must one in so short a life form so lengthy a list of projects? The prodigal, who spends twice what he has amassed, is like the barrel of the Danaïds, which is never filled up:[6] he always has a new plan, and his many desires, which endlessly increase his needs, cause, in the end, his vices to degenerate into crimes. The tender lover becomes the plaything of the women who deceive him; the fickle lover seduces successfully only by lying, and the debauchee ruins his health while shortening his days.

But the man who is harsh, unjust, and ungrateful—what reproaches must he not bring against himself? If he is harsh he is no longer a man, because he no longer respects the rights and privileges of his own kind, and fails to recognise his fellow men as his brothers; for he has neither heart nor soul, and, feeling no compassion himself, he rejects any offered to him by others. The unjust man breaks the social covenant; he destroys, in as far as he is able, the laws under whose protection he lives; he would even revolt against the oppression he would have to suffer in order to claim the exclusive privilege of oppressing those who are weaker than he is; he sins, by using faulty reasoning; his principles are self-contradictory; and, besides, the sense of equality that nature has engraved in every heart—ought it not to rise up and oppose his unjust acts? But the most hateful vice of all, the blackest, the most infamous, is ingratitude. The ungrateful man, unaware of goodness, commits high treason against society, because he corrupts, poisons, and destroys the sweetness of friendship; he feels any offence against himself, but he feels no gratitude for any service done for his benefit; he reaches the summit of treachery by repaying good with evil. But this unnatural and degraded specimen of humanity acts against his own interests, since every individual, however high his standing, is weak by nature and cannot do without the help of his fellow men; and because the ungrateful man, excommunicated from society, has, through his ferocious insistence on securing for the future further benefit for himself, proved himself unworthy. Men must continually be told, 'You should be gentle and humane, because you are weak, and you need help; treat your fellow men with justice, so that the law may protect you in your turn against any violence on the part of a stranger. In a word, do nothing to others that you would not wish them to do to you.'

I do not propose, in this mere sketch, to go into all the arguments that self-love offers men in favour of suppressing their worse inclinations and leading a more virtuous life. The limits of the present essay do not allow this subject to be dealt with in full; I will content myself with suggesting that all those who find further incentives for the reform of human morality will perform an important service for society, and, I even venture to say, for religion.

Nothing is more true, nor more obvious, than that society could not exist or continue to exist, without the virtue and the sound morality of those who constitute it. Moral depravity, scandalous insolence and vice, contempt for virtue and for all those who practise and respect it, bad faith in business dealings, perjury, treachery, individual self-interest which prevails over that of the fatherland—all these are the precursors of the fall of states, and of the ruin of empires, since, as soon as the concepts of good and evil become confused, there can no longer be either praise or blame, either punishment or reward.

This important subject—morality—affects religion as much as it does the state. The Christian, Jewish, Muslim, and Chinese religions have, all of them, more or less the same moral code. The Christian religion, however, with its long history, still has two kinds of enemy to combat. On the one hand, there are those philosophers who, accepting only common sense and the rigorously precise reasoning that follows the principles of logic, reject the ideas and systems that do not conform to the rules of dialectic; but these are not our present concern. The others are libertines, whose corrupt morals, thanks to long practice of vice, are in revolt against the harshness of the yoke that religion wishes to impose on their passions. They reject these shackles, renounce, tacitly, any law that is inconvenient to them, and seek refuge in total unbelief. I maintain, therefore, that all the means that could be employed, in order to reform people of this sort, work, obviously, to the greater advantage of the Christian religion; and I venture to believe that human self-interest is the most powerful motive that could be employed to rescue them from their errors. Once men have been persuaded that their own good requires that they be virtuous, they will turn towards praiseworthy actions; and, since they will find themselves in effect living in conformity with the morality of the Gospels, it will be easy to persuade them to do, for the love of God, what they already have done for love of themselves; this is what the theologians call converting pagan virtues into virtues sanctified by Christianity.

But at this point another objection arises. I will, no doubt, be told, 'You are contradicting yourself; you don't think, then, that virtue is defined as a disposition of the soul that inclines it to the most perfect lack of self-interest. How can you imagine, then, that one could arrive at this perfect lack of self-interest through self-interest itself, which is precisely the disposition of the soul that is most opposed to it?' However powerful this objection may be, it is easily countered, provided one takes into account the different impulses that motivate self-love. If self-love consisted only of the desire to possess worldly goods and honours, I would have no reply to make. But its claims are not restricted to so limited a number of objects: first of all, self-love is the love of life and its preservation; next, it is the desire to be happy, next, the fear of blame and shame, next, a desire for recognition and fame, and, finally, a passion for everything that one judges to be to one's advantage; add to all of this the horror of everything we believe to be harmful to self-preservation. There is no other course open to us than that of correcting the judgement of men. What must I seek, what must I flee, in order to change this self-love from its raw and harmful state into something that is useful and praiseworthy?

The examples that we have of the greatest absence of self-interest stem from the principles of self-love. The selfless devotion of the two Deciuses,[7] who willingly sacrificed their own lives to secure victory for their country: where did this come from, if it were not from their valuing their own existence less than fame? Why did Scipio, in his first youth, at the age when passions are so dangerous, resist the temptations offered him by the beauty of his prisoner?[8] Why did he return her, still a virgin, to her fiancé, and lavish presents on them both? How can we doubt that this hero judged that his noble and generous behaviour would bring him more honour than if he had brutally satisfied his own desires? He preferred, in other words, reputation to pleasure.

How many virtuous acts, how many deeds that will for ever be celebrated, are due to nothing more than the instinct of self-love! Following a secret and almost imperceptible sentiment, men refer everything to themselves; they place themselves in the centre, where all the lines from the circumference meet. Whatever good they do, they themselves are its hidden object. The most lively sensation prevails with them over the most weak; often an evil syllogism, whose failings they do not recognise, determines their course of action. In other words, we must offer them only what is truly good, we must teach them its value, and how, by countering one impulse with another, to control their passions and to give virtue its best chance.

If it is a question of preventing a crime that is about to be committed, the best deterrent is to be found in the fear of the laws that punish this crime. It is at this point that we must arouse the love that each man has for his own preservation, in order to set it against the evil intentions that will lay him open to the most severe punishment, and even to death itself. This love of self-preservation can, also, serve to rescue the debauchee whose excesses are ruining his health and shortening his days; and similarly to recover those who are prone to fits of rage, for there are instances where such rage has brought on epileptic fits in those who were violently disturbed. Our fear of blame gives rise to effects not unlike those produced by the instinct for self-preservation. How many women owe their modesty, which we applaud, only to a desire to preserve their reputation from malicious gossip! How many men owe their lack of self-interest only to the fear of appearing in society, if they acted differently, as rogues and unfortunates! Finally, to manage skilfully the various sources of self-love, to bring home to their author all the advantages of worthy actions, this is the way to make of this source of good and evil the principal agent of merit and virtue.

I cannot resist confessing that we notice, to our shame, in the present century a strange cooling in our interest in the reform of the human heart and of human conduct. It is said in public, it is said even in print, that morality is both boring and useless; it is asserted that human nature is composed of good and evil, that this can never be changed, that the most powerful reasoning yields to the violence of the passions, and that we must let the world go on as it goes on.

But if we behaved in this way in regard to the land, if we did not cultivate it, it would, without a doubt, yield thistles and thorns, and never produce those abundant and essential harvests that supply us with food. I concede that, whatever attention we give to correcting misconduct, there will always be on earth vices and crimes; but there will be fewer of them, which is a great gain: the minds of some men will be developed and improved, and will, in their outstanding quality, even excel. Have we not seen sublime souls emerging from different schools of philosophy, men who are almost divine, who have taken virtue to the highest degree of perfection that humanity can attain? Names such as Socrates, Aristides, Cato, Brutus, Antoninus Pius, and Marcus Aurelius will always have their place in the annals of the human race, for as long as there are virtuous souls in this world. Religion has continued to produce eminent men who have excelled in their humanity and philanthropy. I do not include in this number those melancholic and fanatical recluses who have buried in religious dungeons virtues that could have been useful to their fellow men, and who have preferred to live at the expense of society rather than to serve it.

We ought to begin, today, by imitating the example of the ancients, employing every available incentive in order to improve the human race, encouraging in the schools the study of morality in preference to every other branch of knowledge, and adopting a way of teaching it that is easy to follow. Perhaps it would be no small step towards achieving this end if we were to compile catechisms from which children would learn, from their earliest youth, that, if they are to be happy, virtue is necessary and indispensable. I could wish that philosophers would be less concerned with abstruse and idle matters, and instead exercise their talents on ethics; and, above all, that their lives would serve in every way as an example to their pupils; if that were so, they would rightly deserve to be called the tutors of the human race. Theologians, too, would need to concern themselves less with explaining unintelligible dogmas;

they should be disabused of the passionate desire to explain things that are presented to us as mysteries of an order that is superior to reason. They should, instead, apply themselves with greater zeal to preaching practical morality; and, instead of giving flowery speeches, they should deliver discourses that are useful, simple, clear, and within the grasp of their audience. Men fall asleep while listening to over-subtle reasoning; they wake up when it is a matter of their own interests; with the result that, by delivering discourses that are skilful and full of wisdom, we could make self-love the champion of virtue. Recent examples, analogous to those we hope will be persuasive, could be used successfully, just as, if it were a question of encouraging an idle labourer to tend his pasture better, we would doubtless encourage him by pointing to his neighbour who has grown rich through his own labours and effort; like his neighbour, he is dependent only upon himself for his prosperity. But models must be chosen that are within the reach of those who are to imitate them; they must be appropriate for them, and not in circumstances that are disproportionate. The trophies won by Miltiades prevented Themistocles from sleeping.[9]

If great examples made such a powerful impression on the ancients why should they do so less in our days? The love of fame is innate in noble souls; this happy instinct needs only to be aroused, it needs only to be excited, and men who were previously aimless will appear before you, fervently passionate, and transformed into demi-gods. It seems to me, finally, that if the method I am proposing does not suffice to banish vice from the world, it will at least make some converts to morality, and will make fruitful those virtues that, without its help, would lie dormant. This, at the very least, will be of service to society, and it is the aim of the present piece of work.

10

Letter on Education

(LETTER FROM A GENEVAN TO M. BURLAMAQUI,
PROFESSOR IN GENEVA)

Having set out for you, in some detail, everything that concerns the government of this country, I believed that I had satisfied your curiosity, amply and in full; but I was mistaken. You find that the subject is not exhausted, you consider the education of the young to be one of the most important concerns of a good government, and you wish to be informed of the attention that is given to it in the state in which I am living. This question, which you ask of me in so few words, will attract a reply that, given the unavoidable explanations it will require of me, will exceed the limits of an ordinary letter.

I enjoy observing the young people who are growing up before our eyes; they are the future, entrusted to the care of the present generation, a new breed of men that will, in due course, replace it; they are the hope and strength of the state, which, properly directed, will perpetuate its splendour and glory. I think, as you do, that a prince who is wise will use all his powers to nurture useful and virtuous citizens in his state. My examination of the education given to the youth in different European states does not rest on examples from the present day. The many great men produced by the Greek and Roman republics have predisposed me in favour of the discipline of the ancient world, and I am persuaded that if we were to follow their methods we would create a nation possessed of more virtue and morality than are our present peoples. The education that the nobility undergoes—throughout Europe—is, without doubt, deplorable. In this country, it receives its first lessons in the paternal home, its second in the schools and universities, while its third is self-taught, since the nobility achieve independence too early—and this last is, moreover, the worst of all their lessons. In the paternal home the blind love that parents bear their children impedes their necessary correction; their mothers, above all (let it be said in passing) who tyrannise their husbands, show only boundless indulgence when it comes to matters of education. They deliver their children into the hands of servants, who both flatter and corrupt them by filling their minds with pernicious notions, notions that flourish only too well because of the profound impression they make on unformed minds. The chosen tutor is, in general, either a theologian in the making or a trainee lawyer, the kind of people, in other words, who themselves are most in need of being taken in hand. Under such skilful teachers, our young Telemachus learns his catechism, his Latin, a little geography at most, and the French language simply by hearing it spoken.[1] The father and mother applaud the little genius they have brought into the world, and, for fear of causing some upset that might blight the health of their phoenix, no one dares to reproach him. At ten or twelve years, the young gentleman is sent to some school or other, of which there is no shortage here. There are several, the Joachim School, the new academy in Berlin, that attached to Brandenburg cathedral, and that of the Kloster Berge in Magdeburg; they are, all of them, well supplied with skilful teachers.[2] The only reproach one can level at them is, perhaps, that they are concerned only with cramming their pupils. They do not teach them to think for themselves, nor do they teach them early enough to exercise their judgement; they do nothing to elevate their minds, nor to inspire in them noble and virtuous aspirations.

The young man has not taken a step beyond the threshold of the academy but he forgets everything he had learned there, because his intention was only ever to recite his lessons by heart to his pedagogue, and, no longer having any need of his new knowledge, all trace of it has been effaced by new notions and his own forgetfulness. I attribute this time wasted in college to the shortcomings of his education rather than to the frivolity of youth. Why are we unable to persuade the pupil that it is the difficulty of study itself that will turn out to be to his greatest advantage? Why do we not test his judgement, not simply by teaching him dialectic, but by persuading him to employ his own reasoning? This would be the way of persuading him that it is in his own interest not to forget what he has just learned.

Fathers either send their children, on leaving the academy, to university, or they place them in the army, or they arrange for them to obtain civil employment, or they send them off to their estates. The universities at Halle and Frankfurt an der Oder are where they usually go to complete their studies; they are staffed by professors as good as any of our time. We note with regret, however, that the study of Greek and Latin is not as popular as it was formerly. It is as though these worthy Germans have lost their taste for the profound erudition they formerly possessed, and now aim to acquire reputation and status at the least possible expense; they have taken as their example a neighbouring nation, one that is content with being merely agreeable, and will become ever more superficial.[3]

The life that, in the past, students led at university was a matter of public scandal. Instead of such places priding themselves on being the sanctuary of the Muses, they became mere dens of vice and loose living; professional swordsmen took on the role of gladiators there, the young spent their lives in disorder and excess, they learnt there everything that they should never have known, and they ignored everything that they ought to have learned. This abusive and disorderly conduct reached the point where students were being killed. This roused the government from its lethargy, and it was enlightened enough to curb this licentiousness, and to restore the institutions to their proper purpose. Since then, fathers have been able to send their children to university with every confidence that they will acquire knowledge there, and without fearing that their morals will be perverted.

In spite of this enthusiasm for reform, there remain many other abuses that require the same correction. The self-interest and idleness of the professors prevent knowledge being disseminated as widely as one would wish; they are content to perform their duties as perfunctorily as they can; they hold their lectures and seminars, but that is all. If students seek private lessons from them, they can secure these only by paying exorbitant fees, which prevents those who are not wealthy from benefitting from a public institution established to instruct and enlighten all those drawn there by their need for knowledge.

There is yet another failing: young people never themselves compose their own dissertations, theses, and disquisitions; it is an assistant master who does this, while a student with a good memory, but little talent, can win applause from this at very little cost. Is this not to encourage the young to be idle, lazy, and, in short, to teach them to do nothing? Education needs to be hard won; a student must first write, then be corrected, then rewrite his work; it is through reworking his own compositions that he becomes accustomed to thinking clearly, and expressing himself with precision. If he does not follow this method, if he does not exercise the keen memory that youth possesses, his judgement becomes rusty; he acquires knowledge, but this knowledge lacks the discernment necessary to make it useful.

Yet another failing: the authors studied are ill-chosen. It is quite right that in medicine they begin with Hippocrates and Galen, that they follow the history of this science, if indeed it is one, up until the present. But rather than adopting either Hoffmann's system, or that of some obscure doctor, why do they not study the excellent works of Boerhaave, who seems to have taken human knowledge on the subject of disease and its cure as far as the limits of our intelligence can reach?[4] The same is true of astronomy and geography. It makes good sense to cover every system, from Ptolemy to Newton; but this same good sense demands that we focus on this latter's system, which is the closest to perfection and the most free of error. There was at Halle, in earlier times, a great man, born to teach philosophy. You will guess that I am speaking of the famous Thomasius, whose method they have only to follow, and also to teach it.[5] The universities, moreover, have not, as they believe, rid philosophy of its rusty pedantry. It is true that they no longer teach the quiddities of Aristotle, nor the universals *a parte rei*.[6] 'Doctissimus, sapientissimus Wolffius' has replaced in our days that ancient hero of the schoolmen, and substantial forms have been replaced by monads and pre-established harmony, a system as absurd and unintelligible as that which has just been abandoned.[7] The professors continue, nonetheless, to repeat this farrago, because they have become familiar with its language, and because it is customary to be a Wolffian.

Finding myself one day in company with one of these philosophers, the most dogmatic, indeed, of the monadists, I ventured to ask him humbly if he had ever glanced at the works of Locke. 'I have read everything,' he replied brusquely. 'I know very well, Sir,' I said to him, 'that you are paid to know everything; but what do you think of this Locke?' 'He is an Englishman,' he replied, drily. 'Although he is English,' I rejoined, 'he seems to me to be very wise; he never loses the thread of experience in order to venture into the shadows of metaphysics; he is prudent, and he is intelligible, a great merit in a metaphysician, and I strongly believe that he might well be right.' On hearing these words, a flush spread over the features of my professor; a very unphilosophical anger suffused his face and, indeed, his whole manner, and he informed me in a voice more animated than usual that, just as each country has its own climate, so each state must have its own national philosopher. I retorted that truth is universal, and that it was greatly to be desired that as much of it as possible should come our way, even if the universities regard it as contraband. Besides which, the cause of geometry is not as well served in Germany as in the other countries of Europe. It is claimed that Germans have no head for geometry, which is certainly false: the very names of Leibniz and Copernicus prove the opposite. The reason for this, it seems to me, is that geometry lacks support, and, above all, professors skilful enough to teach it.

But I return now to the sons of the nobility, whom we last encountered when they were on the point of leaving the academies and universities. This is the moment when parents decide which course their children must take, a choice that is usually determined by chance. Most young noblemen are afraid of military life, because in this country it is a veritable school of morals: no allowances are made for young officers; they are expected to behave correctly, wisely, and decently; they are closely observed, and they have people watching over them who do not spare them. If they are beyond correction, no matter how well-connected they are, they have to leave, and can expect, thereafter, no respect. It is this, in particular, that they dislike, for, under the protection of a great name, they would prefer to indulge, without restraint, in irresponsible behaviour, to the detriment of their morals; with the result that few sons of the foremost families serve in the army. The Cadet Corps makes up for all of this; it is a nursery entrusted to the care of an officer of great distinction, who makes it his life's work to shape these young men by supervising their education, by improving their minds, by instilling in them the principles of virtue, and, in summary, by himself striving to make them useful to the fatherland.[8] Since this establishment is reserved for the minor nobility, the foremost families do not send their children there. If a father places his son in the financial world or in the law, he at once loses sight of him; the young man is left to his own devices, and chance decides what route he will take. Often, on his leaving university, the young heir is given a place in his estates, where he will discover that everything he has managed to learn is more or less useless. This, then, is the route that is, in the main, followed for the education of the young. I turn now to the evil effects that result from it.

The excessive leniency of this early education makes young men effeminate, easy-going, lazy, and cowardly. Instead of resembling the ancient German race, they might well be taken for a colony of Sybarites transplanted into our country; they wallow in idleness and sloth; they think they are in this world only to enjoy pleasures and comforts, and that men of their standing are relieved of the duty of being useful to society. From this arises what follows—their follies, their errors, the debts they contract, their debauchery, and the extravagance that has ruined in this country so many wealthy families. I concede that these failings derive as much from their age as from their education; I agree that the young are much the same everywhere, except in certain details, and I concede that, at this age, when the passions are at their most powerful, reason does not always prevail. I am persuaded, however, that a discipline that is wise, more masculine, and, when necessary, more severe, could rescue many young aristocrats from the abyss into which they are about to hurl themselves. Such moral profligacy is all the more harmful in this country, in that the rights of the first-born are not established here as they are in Austria and in the other provinces of the empress-queen [Maria Theresa]; so that it only requires one dissolute member of a family for the whole family to fall into ruin and misery. Such telling examples ought, it seems to me, redouble the care and attention that fathers devote to the correction of their children, so as to render them capable of perpetuating the distinction of their ancestors, of becoming useful subjects of the fatherland, and worthy of commanding personal respect.

It is widely believed that, in order to provide adequately for the generations to come, it is enough to have accumulated wealth for the children, to have provided them with property, and found them employment. Although these are, doubtless, the major preoccupations of all good parents, they should not restrict themselves wholly to them; their main concern must be to shape their children's morality, and to bring their judgement to maturity. I have often felt the need to exclaim, 'Fathers! Love your children! I urge you to do so, but with a love born of reason, one that is directed towards their true good. Look upon these young creatures, whose birth you witnessed, as a sacred charge, one that Providence has entrusted to you, so that, during their tender infant years, they enjoy the support that your reason provides for them. They do not, as yet, know the world; but you do know it. It is your task, therefore, to shape and mould them as is required for their own good, the well-being of your family, and that of society. I say again, shape their morality, instil in them the virtues, raise their souls on high, teach them to be diligent, cultivate their minds, so that they are thoughtful in all that they do, wise and circumspect, and so that they embrace frugality and simplicity. Entrust your heritage, then, when you die, to their sound moral principles; it will be well looked after, and your family will prosper under its care. Otherwise, from the moment of your death, dissipation and dissoluteness will reign, and if you were to be reborn in thirty years' time you would discover your fine estates to be in alien hands.' I always come back to Greek and Roman law. I believe, following their example, that sons should come of age only when they are twenty-six, and that fathers should, in one way or another, be responsible for their conduct. Thus, no doubt, the young would not be abandoned to the pernicious company of the servants; a more careful choice would, no doubt, be made as to their teachers and tutors, to whom one is entrusting one's most precious possession; the father himself would, no doubt, discipline his son, and would punish him, if need be, in order to stifle any emerging vices.

Add, to this, the introduction of various necessary reforms in the academies and the universities, so that, while the minds of youths were being filled, their powers of reasoning, which are fundamental, were not neglected; and so that fathers should take care that their children, when they come to the end of their studies, should not be corrupted by keeping bad company, especially since the earliest examples, whether good or bad, make such a powerful impression on the young as to determine, often, indelibly their character. This is one of the great pitfalls against which you must protect them. Thence comes idleness, debauchery, gambling, and every vice. The duties of fathers extend further still; I believe they ought to use, more than they do at present, considerable discernment in appreciating correctly their sons' talents, in order to steer them towards the realisation of their own particular abilities. Whatever knowledge the young may have acquired, they cannot have too much of it, no matter which route they take; the military profession demands extensive knowledge. The following absurd and unworthy assertion is often heard: 'My son does not want to pursue his studies; but he will always make a good soldier.' Yes, a foot-soldier, but not an officer likely to rise to the highest ranks, which is the only goal he ought to aim for. It happens even today that the impatience and enthusiasm of fathers give rise to another difficulty: they want for their children too rapid an advancement, they want them to rise in a single step from the lower to the highest ranks, before age has improved their ability, and brought their reason to maturity.

The law, the financial world, politics, the military, all of them, no doubt, respect noble birth; but everything would be lost in a state if birth were to be preferred to merit, a principle so misguided and absurd that a government that adopted it would suffer the most serious consequences. This is not to say that there are no exceptions to the rule, and that there are not many precocious people whose merit and talents speak for themselves; one could only wish that such examples were more common.

All in all, I am persuaded that you can make of men what you will. It is well known that the Greeks and Romans produced a considerable number of great men of all kinds, an advantage that they owed to the manly education laid down in their laws. But if these examples seem outdated, let us turn to the achievements of Tsar Peter I, who succeeded in civilising a wholly barbarous nation.[9] Why would it be impossible, then, to correct, in a civilised people, various vices due to education? It is believed, mistakenly, that the arts and the sciences undermine morality.[10] Everything that enlightens the mind, everything that increases the boundaries of knowledge, inspires the soul rather than degrading it. But that is not the case in this country. Would to God that the sciences were better loved here! It is our method of upbringing that is defective; it has only to be corrected, and one will see the rebirth of morality, of virtue, and of talent. Our effeminate youth has often reminded me of what Arminius, that proud defender of Germany, would have said if he saw this

debased, demeaned, and degraded generation of the Suebi and the Semnones;[11] but what would the Great Elector Frederick William say, he, who,
leader of a manly nation, expelled, with his men, the Swedes from his territories which they were laying waste?[12] What has become of the famous families of his time, and what are their offspring? And what will become of those
who flourish in our times? Whoever is a father must reflect on these matters,
so as to be encouraged to fulfil all the duties he owes to posterity.

I turn now to the female sex, which exercises so remarkable an influence
on the male sex. Here, one can distinguish between women of a certain age,
who have received superior education, and those who have recently entered
society; the former have knowledge, a pleasing wit, and a liveliness that is
always respectable. This contrast appeared to me so striking that I enquired
of one of my friends the reason for it. 'In the old days,' he said, 'there were
various talented women who offered board and lodging to well-born girls;
everybody was anxious to place their daughters there. It was in such establishments that the ladies of whom you speak so favourably were educated.
On the death of those who had set them up, these schools closed, and no one
has replaced them; which now obliges everyone to bring up their children at
home. Most of the methods followed are reprehensible. No attempt is made
to cultivate the minds of girls; they are left without knowledge, and without
any inspiration towards notions of virtue and honour. Their education is
commonly concerned with purely external grace, with, that is, manners and
dress; and with, in addition, a scant acquaintance with music, with whatever learning may be acquired from a few plays or novels, from dancing, and
the playing of games: there you have a summary of all the knowledge acquired
by the fair sex.'

I confess that I was surprised to discover that people of rank are bringing
up their children as actresses; these children seem to beg for public attention,
they are content merely to please, and they do not appear to seek respect and
consideration. What! Is it not their destiny to become mothers of families?
Ought we not to direct their education to this end, to inspire in them, from
the beginning, a horror of anything that could bring them dishonour, to persuade them of the useful and lasting benefits of wisdom, rather than of the
transient and fading benefits of beauty? Ought we not to give them the ability, in the fullness of time, to inculcate morality in their children? And how
can we expect this of them if they themselves have none, if a taste for idleness, frivolity, luxury, and extravagance, and if public scandal, too, prevent
them from setting a good example to their families? I must confess that the

neglect shown by fathers of families seems to me unforgivable; if their children's lives are ruined, they are the cause.

Because they are barbarians, we look with indulgence upon the Circassians. They bring up their daughters to practise all the ploys of flirtation and voluptuousness, in order that they may sell them subsequently for a better price to the seraglio of Constantinople; this is the trafficking of slaves. But if, in a free and civilised society, the foremost nobility seems to conform to this practice, and has so little self-respect that it does not recognise the opprobrium that the conduct of a daughter without morality and virtue will bring upon her family; if this is so, it is something for which their most distant posterity will reproach them, eternally. Let us be under no illusion. The dissolute conduct of women has its origin in the idle life that they lead rather than in the warmth of their temperament; spending two or three hours in front of a mirror, appraising, improving, and admiring their own charms; passing the whole afternoon in spiteful talk, then going to the theatre, then in the evening to the gaming table, then finally to supper and more gambling—does this leave them time for self-examination? Does not the boredom of this easy and idle life encourage them to pleasures of another kind, even if only in search of variety, or the experience of some new feelings?

Keeping mankind busy is the best way of protecting it from vice. Life in the countryside, simple, rural, and hard, is more innocent than that led by a crowd of idlers in the great cities. It is a well-established adage of generals that, to prevent licentiousness, disorderly conduct, and rebellion in camp, you must keep the soldier busy. Men are all alike. If we are not so foolish as to make no distinction between the licentious conduct of our fellow men and their wise and discreet behaviour, we must teach them all to keep themselves busy. A young girl may amuse herself with women's concerns, with music, and even with dancing; but we must also, and above all, apply ourselves to shaping her mind, to giving her a taste for good works, for exercising her judgement. We should encourage her to cultivate her reason by reading serious things, and persuade her that there is no shame in learning household economics. It is better that she take charge of the household accounts herself, and that she keep them in order, rather than that she contract, carelessly, debts on every side, without considering paying back what the good faith of her creditors, long ago, had advanced to her.

I must confess to you that I am often indignant when I consider the degree to which, in Europe, we misjudge this half of the human race, even to the point of denying them everything that could improve their minds. We see so many women who are not outdone by men! There are in the present century various princesses who greatly outshine their predecessors, there are ... but I dare not name them for fear of displeasing them, by offending their extreme modesty, which is the crowning glory of all their virtues. Given a more masculine, a more robust education, the female sex would outstrip our own: it possesses the charms of beauty; but are not those of the mind to be preferred?

Let us come to the point. Society cannot survive without legitimate marriage, which renews and perpetuates it. We must, therefore, nurture the young plants we are growing, so that they may become the foundation of our posterity, and in such a way that the male and the female may fulfil, equally, the duties of heads of families. It is essential that reason, intelligence, talent, morality, and virtue should serve equally as the basis of this education, so that those who have profited from it may pass it on to those to whom they give life.

Finally, so that I overlook nothing relevant to this question, I must make mention of the abuse of paternal authority that sometimes forces daughters to submit to the yoke of an ill-matched marriage. The father consults only the interests of his family, sometimes he chooses his son-in-law on a whim; or he decides upon a rich man, an aged man, or someone else who pleases him. He summons his daughter and says to her, 'I have decided, my dear, to give you Monsieur So-and-So as your husband.' His daughter, sighing, replies, 'Father, let your will be done.' We then have two people united in wedlock who are incompatible in their characters, their tastes, and their ways; troubles enter this new household from the very day that so unfortunate a bond has been created; and aversion, hatred, and scandal quickly follow. We have, in other words, two people who are thoroughly wretched; so that the principal aim of marriage has failed. Monsieur and Madame separate; they waste their possessions in the débacle, they conceive a great contempt for one another, and everything ends in misery. I respect, as much as does anyone, paternal authority, and I am not opposed to it; but I could wish that those who exercise it would not abuse it by obliging their children to marry if there is the merest mismatch between their characters and their years. Let the fathers make the choice, in accordance with their own inclination, but let them consult their children, since it is a question of an engagement on which their lifelong happiness or misfortune depends. If that does not make every marriage better, it at least removes an excuse from all those who attribute their own improper conduct to the violence that their parents have done them.

There, in brief, Monsieur, are the observations I have made concerning the shortcomings of education in this country. If you find me over-zealous as to the public good, I will take full credit for the error of which you reproach me. In demanding a great deal of men, we will at least derive something from doing so. You, who have a numerous family, and wise and careful as I know you to be, will have reflected upon the duties that fatherhood imposes on you, and you will find among your thoughts the germ of those that I have just set out. In society, we scarcely have a moment to commune with ourselves; we are content with vague ideas, we reflect even less, we follow the tyranny of fashion which extends even as far as education. We should not be surprised, then, if the results and the consequences follow the mistaken principles we act upon. I am outraged about the trouble we take to grow, in this austere climate, pineapples, bananas, and other exotic plants, but about the little care we give to the human species. People can say all they like, but one single man is more precious than all the pineapples in the universe; he is the plant we should be cultivating, the plant that deserves all our work and all our care, because he is the ornament and the glory of the fatherland.

I am, etc. . . . [13]

Examination of the *Essay on Prejudice*

I have just read a book entitled *Essay on Prejudice*. While studying it, I was greatly surprised to find that it is, itself, full of prejudice: a mixture of truths and of faulty arguments, of bitter criticisms and fanciful schemes, poured out by a zealous and fanatical philosopher. If I am to give you a faithful account of it, I will be obliged to go into some detail; however, since time is short, I will restrict myself to making a few remarks on the most important topics it raises.

I had expected to find wisdom and much sound reasoning in the work of a man who presents himself as a philosopher on every page; I had imagined I would find there nothing but illumination and evidence; but far from it. The author visualises the world rather as Plato imagined his republic to be; as, that is, capable of virtue, of happiness, and of every perfection. I venture, however, to assure him that this is not the case in the world that I inhabit, where good and evil are to be found everywhere intermingled, where both the physical and the moral worlds are marred by the imperfections that characterise them. He asserts, magisterially, that truth is made for man, and that he must be told the truth on every occasion. Such an assertion needs examination, and I will rely on experience and analogy in order to prove to him that speculative truth, far from seeming made for man, continually eludes his most painstaking investigations. Such an admission is humiliating for our self-love, but it is one that truth itself wrings from me.

Truth lies at the very bottom of a well, from which the philosophers try to recover it; while every scholar complains about the effort that it costs him to do so. If truth had been made for man, it would offer itself naturally to his gaze. He would take it in without effort, without endless reflection, without misjudgement, and the evidence for such a truth, triumphant over error, would bring conviction infallibly in its wake. It would be distinguishable, by clear signs, from error that often deceives us by appearing in this borrowed guise; there would be no more opinions, there would only be certainties. But experience teaches me quite the opposite: it shows me that no man is without error; that the greatest delusions to which the vagaries of the imagination have given birth in every age have come from the brains of philosophers; and that few philosophical systems are free from prejudice and false reasoning. It reminds me, too, of the vortices that Descartes imagined, the apocalypse that Newton, the great Newton himself, discussed, and the pre-established harmony that Leibniz, whose genius was equal to that of both these great men, invented.[1] Convinced, as I am, of the fallibility of human understanding, and impressed by the errors of these celebrated philosophers, I cry: Vanity of vanities! Oh, the vanity of the philosophical mind!

Experience, and the research it encourages, reveal mankind to be, in every century, in thrall to error, and the religious practices of nations to be founded on absurd myths, accompanied by bizarre rites and ridiculous festivals; by superstitions to which they attributed the longevity of their empire; and by prejudices that prevail from one end of the world to the other.

If we seek the causes of these errors, we find that man himself is their origin. Prejudices are the people's rationality; they are drawn, irresistibly, towards the miraculous; and, in addition, the greater part of humankind, able to subsist only by daily toil, is sunk in invincible ignorance; it has time neither to think nor to reflect. Since, therefore, men's minds are not worn down by rational thought, and since they never have to exercise any judgement, it is impossible for them to examine, according to any sound principles, those matters about which they wish to seek enlightenment, nor to follow a chain of reasoning that would disabuse them of their errors. From this comes their attachment to the religion that long custom has hallowed, and from which they cannot, without violence, be separated. It was, indeed, by force that new religious beliefs destroyed earlier religious beliefs; it was the hangman who converted the pagans, while Charlemagne brought Christianity to the Saxons, imposing his faith by fire and the sword. It would be necessary, therefore, that our philosopher, in order to enlighten the nations, preach to them with his sword in his hand. But, since philosophy renders its disciples gentle and tolerant, I flatter myself that our philosopher will think again before equipping himself with every available weapon, and before putting on the whole armour of a warrior-evangelist.

The second cause of human superstition is that tendency, that powerful inclination that draws humans towards everything which seems to them miraculous. Everyone feels this, and we cannot resist giving our full attention to the supernatural whenever we hear it discussed. It is as though the miraculous elevates the spirit; as though it ennobles our being, by opening up an immense space that enlarges the realm of our ideas, and gives free rein to our imagination, which wanders contentedly in unknown regions. Mankind loves everything that is great, everything that inspires astonishment or admiration: majestic splendour or a grand ceremony is very impressive to men; a mysterious form of worship wholly captures people's attention. If, in addition, they are assured that an invisible Divinity is present, a contagious superstitiousness takes hold of their minds, growing ever stronger, to the extent, even, of making them fanatics. These singular effects are the result of the hold that their senses have over them; for they are creatures of sentiment rather than of reason. In other words, most human opinions are based on prejudice, fiction, error, and deception. How can I reach a different conclusion than that man is born to err, that error holds sway over the whole universe, and that we scarcely see more clearly than do moles? The author must therefore confess, taking into account the experience of all the ages, that since, as we have seen, the world is awash with prejudice and superstition, truth was not made for man.

But what does this mean for our philosopher's system? I am fully expecting that he will interrupt me here, in order to warn me against confusing the truths of speculation with those of experience. I have the honour to reply that, when it comes to opinions and superstitions, we are dealing with speculative truths; and that it is with those that he has been concerned. The truths of experience are those that influence civil life, and I am persuaded that a great philosopher, such as our author, will not imagine that men will be enlightened by being told that fire will burn us, that we drown in water, that we must eat to live, that society cannot survive without virtue, and other such things as commonplace as they are well understood. But let us proceed.

At the beginning of his work, the author says that since truth benefits all men it must be communicated to them boldly and unreservedly. But in the eighth chapter, if I am not mistaken, for I am quoting from memory, he adopts a different tone, and maintains that falsehood, if it is for a particular purpose, may be permissible and useful. I hope he will be so good as to decide once and for all as to the truth or falsehood that ought to prevail, so that we may know where we stand. If I dare to hazard my own opinion alongside that of so great a philosopher, I would be of the view that a reasonable man should abuse nothing, not even truth; and there is no lack of examples to support my view. Let us suppose that a timid and fearful woman finds her life to be in danger; if one were to warn her, in an ill-considered way, of the danger in which she finds herself, her mind, troubled, agitated, and deeply distressed by the fear of death, might convey, through her blood, too abrupt a shock, and might, perhaps, hasten her demise; instead of which, if one gave her some hope of recovery, a calmer state of mind might, perhaps, help her to recover.

What would one gain from disabusing a man whose delusions make him happy? It would be a situation not unlike that where a doctor, having cured a madman, asked for his fee. The madman replied that he would give him nothing, for, during the time when he was not in his right mind, he had believed himself to be in paradise, but, having come to his senses, he found himself in hell.[2] If, when the Senate learned that Varro had lost the battle of Cannae, the patricians had shouted out in the forum, 'Romans, we are vanquished; Hannibal has totally defeated our armies!' these incautious words would have so increased the terror of the people that they would have abandoned Rome, as they did after their defeat at the battle of the Allia, and that would have been the end of the republic. The Senate, however, wisely concealed this misfortune and roused the people to the defence of their country; it recruited an army, it continued the war, and in the end the Romans defeated the Carthaginians.[3] It would seem undeniable, therefore, that we must speak truth with discretion, never inopportunely, and above all at the appropriate moment.

If I were inclined to chide the author whenever I believe I note some inaccuracy or other, I could attack him for the definition he gives us of the word 'paradox'. He claims that this word signifies every opinion that has not been adopted but which can reasonably be entertained; instead of which the ordinary meaning attached to this word is that of an opinion contrary to some truth gained from experience. I will not dwell further on this trifle; but I cannot resist pointing out to those who claim to be philosophers that their definitions must be accurate, and that they must use words only in their normal sense.

I now turn to the aims of our author. He does not disguise them, but quite clearly gives us to understand that he is against the religious superstitions of his country, that he means to abolish worship, in order to elevate natural religion upon its ruins, while at the same time putting in place a morality free of any incoherent inessentials. His intentions appear to be pure: he does not want the people to be deceived by the various fictions spread by impostors who thereby gain advantage for themselves, as do charlatans from the drugs they sell; he does not want these impostors to control the idiotic common people, nor that they should continue to enjoy the power that they hold, and which they abuse, against the prince and the state. He wants, in a word, to abolish established religion, to open the eyes of the multitude, and to help it throw off the yoke of superstition. This is an ambitious project; it remains to be seen if it is practicable, and if the author has the competence necessary to realise it.

Such an endeavour will seem impracticable to those who have made a proper study of the world, and who have examined the human heart. Everything is against it: the stubbornness with which men are attached to their everyday opinions, their ignorance, their inability to reason, their taste for the miraculous, the power of the clergy, and the means it uses to maintain that power. Thus, in a country of sixteen million souls, as in France, we must from the very beginning abandon the attempt to convert the fifteen million, eight hundred thousand souls, who remain attached to their opinions by forces that represent an insurmountable obstacle to change; there remain, then, for philosophy, two hundred thousand. This is a great many, and I would never undertake to instil the same way of thinking into so great a number of people, as different in their understanding, their minds, their judgement, and their way of looking at things, as they are in the features that differentiate their faces. Let us suppose, further, that the two hundred thousand would-be converts have received the same instruction; they will, nonetheless, all of them, have their original thoughts, their own individual opinions; there will be, among this multitude, not even two people, perhaps, who will think the same way. I will go further, and I dare, almost, to maintain that, in a state in which all prejudices were banished, not thirty years would pass before we would see the rebirth of a new set of prejudices, and that, in the end, error would proliferate so rapidly as to inundate the state. What appeals to mankind's imagination will always prevail over what engages their understanding. In other words, I have proved that error has always prevailed in the world; and since something so unchanging can be regarded as a general law of nature, I conclude from this that what has always been will always be.

We must, nevertheless, give credit to our author, whenever it is due to him. It is not through force that he proposes to bring would-be converts to the truth; he implies, rather, that he is doing no more than removing from the church the education of the young, for which it is at present responsible, in order to assign it to philosophers. This will ensure the protection of the young from those religious prejudices with which, up to the present, the schools have, since their birth, infected them. I venture, however, to point out to the author that, even if he had the power to carry out this project, such an attempt would fail. I could give as an example of this what is happening beneath his own eyes, almost, in France. Calvinists there find themselves obliged to send their children to Catholic schools; he should note that, on their return from school, fathers there lecture their children, making them repeat the catechism of Calvin, while inspiring in them a horror of popery. Not only are these things already well known, but it has now become clear that, without the perseverance of these heads of families, there would have been, for a long time now, no Huguenots in France. A philosopher may protest against such oppression of Protestants, but he must not follow such an example; for it is an act of violence to deny fathers the freedom to bring up their children as they wish; and a violent act to send these children to a school of natural religion when their fathers wish them to be Catholics like themselves. A philosopher who is also a persecutor would be a monster in the eyes of the wise man; moderation, humanity, justice, tolerance: these are the virtues that must characterise him. His principles must be invariable, and his words, his plans, and his actions follow suit.

Let us allow the author his enthusiasm for truth, and admire the skill he uses to achieve his ends. As we have seen, he is attacking a powerful adversary, the prevailing religion, that is, the priesthood that defends it, and the superstitious people who congregate beneath its standard. But if his courage in the face of so redoubtable an enemy were not, in itself, enough to display his triumph and make his victory more glorious, he chooses to provoke another enemy. Making a vigorous sally against the government, he crudely and improperly insults it, while the scorn that he displays towards it can only shock readers of good sense. Perhaps the government would have remained neutral, the peaceful spectator, merely, of the battles which this hero of truth waged against the apostles of untruthfulness; instead, he forces the government to take up arms in alliance with the church in order to oppose their common enemy. If we did not respect so great a philosopher, we would have taken this act to be a prank by some scatterbrained schoolboy, which would earn him severe punishment from his masters.

But is it only by overturning and upsetting the entire established order that one can do good for one's country? And are there not gentler means that should be adopted, used, and preferred to all others, if one wishes to serve one's country effectively? Our philosopher seems to me to resemble those doctors whose only remedy is an emetic, or those surgeons who know nothing except how to perform amputations. A wise man, one who has meditated on the ills that the church visits upon his fatherland, would no doubt make efforts to deliver it from them; but he would act with circumspection. Instead of destroying an ancient gothic edifice, he would concentrate on freeing it from the faults that disfigure it; he would discredit those absurd fictions that serve only to feed the idiocy of the public; he would set his face against the absolutions and indulgences that do nothing but encourage crime, because of the ease with which the penitent may expiate his crime, and at the same time relieve his remorse; he would speak out against all the dispensations which the church, in order to raise the greatest sums, has introduced; and against those purely external observances that replace genuine virtue with puerile mumbo-jumbo. He would speak out against those useless wasters who live at the expense of the hardworking part of the nation, against this multitude of coenobites who, suppressing all natural instinct, contribute, as far as they can, to the decline of the human race. He would encourage the sovereign to limit and restrict the enormous powers that the clergy use, culpably, against the people, and against the sovereign himself, in order to deprive the clergy of all influence in the government of the country, and to subject it to the same courts that pass judgement on lay people. In this way, religion would become a purely speculative matter, with no bearing on morality and government, superstition would diminish, and tolerance would spread more widely every day.

Let us now turn to the section in which the author discusses politics. However indirect an approach the author takes, so as to appear to be considering this matter only in the most general terms, we note that he always has France in view, and that he does not venture beyond the boundaries of that kingdom. Everything—his discussion, his critiques—relates to France, everything is relevant to France. It is only in France that judicial offices are for sale; no other state has as much debt as has that kingdom; in no other place is there so much protest against taxation. One has only to read the remonstrances of the parlement against certain financial edicts, not to mention the number of pamphlets that have appeared on the same subject; the specific complaints against the government cannot apply to any European country except France; it is only in this kingdom that revenues are collected by contractors.[4] English philosophers do not complain about their churchmen; nor have I, up until now, heard of any similar complaints from any philosopher, whether Spanish, Portuguese, or Austrian; thus it can only be in France that philosophers complain about priests. In other words, his discussion is all about his native country, and it would be difficult, or indeed impossible, for him to deny that his satire was directly aimed at it.

There are, however, moments when his anger abates, and when his mind, more tranquil now, allows him to argue more wisely. When he maintains that it is the duty of the prince to ensure the happiness of his subjects, there is universal agreement with him about this ancient truth. When he asserts that the ignorance or the idleness of sovereigns is detrimental to their peoples, he may be assured that everyone is persuaded of this. When he adds that the interests of monarchs are inseparably linked with those of their subjects, and that their fame and reputation depend upon their ruling a contented and happy nation, no one will dispute the self-evident force of his assertions. But when, with an unrelenting violence combined with the most bitter satire, he utters calumnies against his king and the government of his country, we can only take him for a madman freed from his chains and subject to the most violent fits of rage.

What! Sir Philosopher, protector as you are of morality and virtue, are you not aware that a good citizen must respect the form of government under which he lives? Are you not aware that it is quite inappropriate for an individual to insult the powers-that-be, that no one should utter calumnies against either their colleagues or their sovereigns, or anyone else, and that an author who abandons himself to the point where he employs such immoderate language is neither wise nor a philosopher?

I have no personal attachment to the Most Christian King; I have, perhaps, as much reason to complain of him as does anyone else.[5] But my indignation at the dreadful things that our author has spewed up against his king, and, above all, my love of truth—which is more powerful than any other consideration—oblige me to refute these false and revolting accusations.

Here are the accusations that the author makes: he complains that the foremost houses of France alone possess the foremost titles or marks of honour; that merit is not rewarded; that the clergy is held in too high regard, while philosophers are despised; that the ambition of the sovereign always ignites new and ruinous warfare; that mercenaries and executioners—elegant titles with which he dignifies soldiers—alone enjoy rewards and honours; that judicial offices are for sale, that the law is defective, taxation excessive, persecution intolerable, and the education of sovereigns little understood and always culpable. Here is my reply.

The interests of the state require that the prince recognise important services that are rendered to the government; and if such rewards profit even the descendants of those who have deserved well of their fatherland, this is the greatest encouragement he could offer to talent and virtue. If there are families that continue to flourish thanks to the fine actions of their ancestors, does not this encourage the public to serve their country faithfully, in order to ensure that their descendants are heaped with similar blessings? In Rome, the patrician order ranked above the plebeian and the equestrian orders; it is only in Turkey that these ranks are merged, not that things there are any the better for this. In every state in Europe the nobility enjoys the same prerogatives. The common people sometimes work their way towards a more elevated position, when, because of their genius, talent, and service, they are ennobled. This prejudice, moreover, if you wish to describe it as such, this prejudice, I say, so universally adhered to, would prevent even the king of France from sending a commoner on a mission to certain foreign courts. To refuse to render to noble birth that which is its due, is not the consequence of a philosophical freedom, but of an absurd and bourgeois vanity.

The author complains, too, that personal merit is not valued in France. I suspect that a minister has offended him, or is guilty of having denied him some allowance or other, or of not having discovered, cowering in his hovel, this wise tutor of the human race, so worthy of assisting the minister, and indeed of guiding him, in his political endeavours. You assure us, Sir Philosopher, that kings often make mistakes when choosing their aides. Nothing could be more true, and the reasons for this are easy to deduce: kings are human, and as prone to error as anyone else. Those who aspire to great office never appear before the king's eyes unmasked. It sometimes happens, no doubt, that the king allows himself to be misled; the ingenious devices, the ruses, the cabals of courtiers can, from time to time, prevail; but if the choices made by kings are not always fortunate, do not hold them solely responsible for this. Men of great talent and merit are, in every country, much more rare than could possibly be imagined by a speculative dreamer, who has nothing but theoretical notions about a world he has never known. That merit is not rewarded is a complaint heard in every country; anyone, indeed, with any presumption can say, 'I have genius and talent, but the government does not accord me the recognition I merit; therefore it lacks wisdom, judgement and justice.'

Our philosopher, next, gets hot under the collar when he comes to a subject that affects him more directly. He appears to be excessively vexed that, in his own country, the evangelists of lies are preferred to those of truth. I beg him to pause a little and to reflect—something that is perhaps unworthy of his impetuous genius, but likely, nevertheless, to assuage his anger. Let him not forget that the clergy represents a considerable entity within the state, while philosophers are isolated individuals. Let him remember what he himself, indeed, has said, that the clergy, whose power derives from the authority it has acquired over the people, and from the dangers it poses to the sovereign, must, because of the power it wields, be managed carefully. It is thus inevitable, in the nature of things, that the clergy enjoys greater prerogatives and honours than are usually granted to those who have, by their calling, renounced every ambition, and who, themselves above all human vanity, despise what the ordinary people desire so eagerly. Does our philosopher not know that it is the people, superstitious as they are, who chain the king to his throne? It is the people who oblige him to manage those recalcitrant and seditious priests, that clergy which aims to establish a state within a state, and is capable, still, of reproducing scenes as tragic as those that ended the days of Henri III and of that good king, Henri IV.[6] The prince can concern himself with established religion only if he employs tact and skill. If he bears a grudge against the edifice that is superstition, he should undermine it gradually; he would risk too much if he set about bringing it down openly. When by chance it happens that philosophers write about government without knowledge and without caution, politicians take pity on them and send them back to the first principles of their science. We must be on guard against theoretical speculation; it does not withstand the test of experience. The science of government is a science all of its own; to speak about it coherently requires long study. Either one goes astray, or one puts forward remedies that are worse than the evil complained of; and it may well happen that, in spite of having excellent good sense, one utters nothing but stupidities.

We now come to another protest against the ambition of princes. Our author is beside himself; he no longer moderates his language, but accuses sovereigns of being the butchers of their people and of sending them to war as mere cut-throats, in order to alleviate their own boredom. No doubt there have been unjust wars, no doubt blood has been shed where this could have been and should have been prevented. There are, nevertheless, cases where wars are necessary, unavoidable, and just. A prince must defend his allies when they are attacked, and, in the interests of self-preservation, he must maintain, by arms, the balance of power between the European nations. It is his duty to protect his subjects against invasion by their enemies; he is, moreover, fully authorised to maintain his own rights, including his right to succession where it is in dispute, and other similar things, by repelling, through force of arms, the injustice that has been done to him. What arbitrator do sovereigns have? Who will be their judge? Since, then, they cannot plead their cause before any court that is powerful enough to pronounce sentence on them, and to put it into effect, they fall back on the laws of nature, so that it is force of arms that decides the case. To protest against such wars, to insult the sovereigns who wage them, is to display more hatred towards kings than commiseration and humanity for the people who, indirectly, suffer. Would our philosopher approve of a sovereign who, out of pusillanimity, allowed himself to be stripped of his lands, who was prepared to sacrifice the honour, interest, and the pride of his country to the caprice of his neighbours, and who, through ineffectual efforts to preserve the peace, would lose his own person, his state, and his people? Marcus Aurelius, Trajan, and Julian were continually at war, and yet philosophers praise them; why, then, should they blame modern sovereigns for following, in this respect, their example?[7]

Not content with insulting all the crowned heads of Europe, our philosopher amuses himself from time to time by heaping ridicule on the works of Hugo Grotius.[8] I venture to think that his words on this matter will not be found to be credible, and that *On the Law of War and Peace* will survive longer than the *Essay on Prejudice*.

Learn, enemy of kings, learn, Brutus of our times, that kings are not the only ones to make war; republics have always done so. Do you not know that the republic of the Greeks, thanks to continual disputes, was ceaselessly prey to civil war? Its annals record, too, a continual succession of struggles against the Macedonians, the Persians, the Carthaginians, and the Romans, up until the time when the Aetolian League hastened its total ruin.[9] Do you not know that no monarchy has ever been more warlike than the Roman republic? If I wanted to record all its feats of arms, I should be obliged to copy its history here for you from beginning to end. Let us move now to modern republics. The Venetian republic fought against the Genoan, against the Turks, against the pope, against the emperors, and against your own Louis XII.[10] The Swiss waged wars against the House of Austria, and against Charles the Bold, duke of Burgundy;[11] and, if I may borrow one of your noble expressions, do they not, more butchers than are the kings of Europe, sell their citizens as mercenaries to the princes who are waging war? About England, another republic, I will say nothing; you know from experience whether or not England is at war, and how she wages it.[12] The Dutch, ever since the foundation of their republic, have involved themselves in all the troubles of Europe. Sweden has waged as many wars in her time as a republic as she undertook while she was a monarchy. As to Poland, I need only ask you what is happening there at present, what has happened there during the present century, and whether you believe that she has enjoyed constant peace.[13] All the governments of Europe, and of the whole universe indeed, with the exception of the Quakers, are therefore, according to your criteria, tyrannical and barbarous. Why, then, should only monarchies be accused of what they have in common with republics?

You speak out against war. It is, indeed, in itself deadly; but it is an evil not unlike those other curses ordained by heaven, which we must suppose to be necessary for the ordering of this universe, because they occur periodically, and because no century until now has been able to boast that it is exempt from them. If you want to establish perpetual peace, you will have to be transported to another, an ideal world, where thine and mine are unknown, where princes, their ministers, and their subjects are all free of passion, and where reason generally prevails; or else commit yourself to the projects of the late Abbé de

Saint-Pierre;[14] or, if that is repugnant to you because he was a priest, you must simply accept things as they are; for in this world we must expect that there will be wars, as there have always been, from the time when men's actions were first recorded and handed down.

But for now, let us see if your vague and excessive criticisms of the French government have any foundation. You lodge the accusation against Louis XV, but without naming him, that all the wars he waged were unjust. But please do not imagine that it is enough to make such assertions with effrontery and impudence; assertions need proof, or, great philosopher though you wish to appear, you will go down as an infamous slanderer. Let us look into the details of the case, so that we may decide if the reasons that caused Louis XV to wage the wars he undertook were legitimate or not. The first which comes to mind is that of 1733. His father-in-law was elected king of Poland. The Emperor Charles VI, in league with Russia, opposed this election. The king of France, unable to reach Russia, attacked Charles VI in order to support the rights of his father-in-law, who was twice elected to the same throne; and, being unable to prevail in Poland, he procured Lorraine for King Stanisław in compensation.[15] Would one condemn a son-in-law who comes to the aid of his father-in-law, a king who supports the right of a free nation to make elections, a prince who wishes to prevent various powers from taking upon themselves the right to give away kingdoms? Unless one were to be carried away by animosity and implacable hatred, it would be impossible to condemn the conduct of this prince.

The second war began in 1741, caused by a dispute over the succession to the House of Austria, whose emperor, Charles VI, the last male of that house, had just died. It is certain that the famous Pragmatic Sanction, upon which Charles VI was founding his hopes, could not remove the rights to succession of the houses of Bavaria and Saxony, nor inflict the least damage on the pretensions that the House of Brandenburg nurtured towards various duchies of Silesia.[16] It was very likely that, at the beginning of this war, a French army, sent at this point into Germany, would make Louis XV the arbiter of the case at issue between these princes, and would oblige them to accept, amicably, his wishes as regards this succession. What is certain is that, given the role that France had played in the Peace of Westphalia, she could not play a finer nor a greater role than the above. But since ill-fortune, and all manner of events, combined to disrupt these plans, must we blame Louis XV because part of this war went badly? Should a philosopher judge a plan only by its outcome? It is easier to trade insults thoughtlessly than to think carefully and to reflect upon what one means. What! This man, who presents himself at the beginning of his work as a zealot for truth, is no more than a villain, given to every exaggeration, who, in order to heap abuse upon sovereigns, compounds his wickedness with lies.

I turn to the war of 1756.[17] The author of the *Essay on Prejudice* must himself have many prejudices, and a great deal of bitterness against his country, if he does not agree in good faith that it was England that forced France to take up arms. Is this bloody and barbarous tyrant, whom you paint in such dark colours, recognisable as the peace-loving Louis XV, who displayed a truly angelic patience and moderation before declaring war on England? Of what can we reproach him? Could one claim that he ought not to have defended himself? My dear friend, you are either ignorant, or brainless, or an arrant slanderer: choose as you will. But a philosopher you are not.

So much for sovereigns.* But let no one imagine that the author is kinder towards other sorts and conditions of men; everyone is the butt of his sarcasm. But this is nothing compared with the scorn and the insults he heaps upon the military. According to him, soldiers are the worst dregs of society. But it is in vain that our arrogant philosopher tries to deny their worth; since we will always need to defend ourselves, we will always recognise their merits. Will we allow this brainless man to insult the most noble task in society, that of defending one's fellow citizens? Scipio, you who rescued Rome from the hands of Hannibal, and who subdued Carthage; Gustavus, the great Gustavus, the protector of German liberty; Turenne, the sword and shield of your fatherland; Marlborough, whose arms maintained the balance of power in Europe; Eugene, the prop and stay, the power and glory of Austria; and Maurice, the last hero of France![18] Free yourselves, noble shades that you are, free yourselves from the bonds of death and of the tomb! With what astonishment will you hear how, in this century of paradox, your efforts and your actions are insulted—those efforts and actions that have earned you, rightly, immortality! Will you recognise your successors as the mercenary executioners—elegant epithet!—depicted by these sophists? What will you say on hearing a cynic, more impudent than Diogenes himself, barking from the bottom of his barrel, and railing against your dazzling reputation, whose splendour offends him?[19] What can they avail, these impotent insults against you, you whose names are bathed in glory; and against the universal acclamation of all the ages, whose tribute you still enjoy? And you, who follow in the foot-

---

*This information has been provided by a soldier, who is indignant at the silence of his colleagues, in order that the philosophers will not interpret their silence as a tacit acquiescence in the stupidities that these philosophers have enjoyed themselves, for some time now, in imparting. [Author's note]

steps of these true heroes, may you continue to imitate their virtue, and to despise the idle clamour of a demented sophist, a self-styled apostle of truth, who spews out nothing but slander, lies, and insults.

Unworthy windbag! Do you need to be taught that the arts, crafts, and professions can flourish only in peacetime, under the protection of the force of arms? Have you not seen, during the wars that have been waged in your time, that, while the intrepid soldier stands guard on the frontiers, the farmer is waiting to gather in the harvest, the abundant fruit of his labours? Do you not know that, while the warrior is exposed on land and sea to a death he either inflicts or suffers, the merchant, undistracted by such concerns, continues with his flourishing business? Are you so stupid that you have not noticed that, while the generals and the officers, whom your pen treats so unjustly, were braving the rigours of every season and the harshest fatigues, you yourself were composing peacefully, in your wretched little house, the rhapsodies, the twaddle, the impertinences, the follies that you shower upon us? What! Could it be said that you will muddle every sound notion, and claim, by means of crude sophisms, that the prudent measures that wise governments put in place are questionable? Ought it to be necessary to prove in the present century that, without the brave soldiers who defend kingdoms, these countries would fall prey to the first occupying force?

Yes, Sir so-called Philosopher, France maintains great armies. Nor does she any longer endure those times of confusion and trouble when she was tearing herself apart in civil war, a kind of war more pernicious and cruel even than are foreign wars. It seems that you regret those times when powerful vassals, in league with one another, could hold out against a sovereign who had insufficient forces to oppose them. No, you are not the author of the *Essay on Prejudice*; this book could only have been written by some party chief of the League, restored to life, who, breathing again the spirit of faction and disorder, attempts to rouse the people to rebellion against the legitimate authority of the sovereign.[20] What would you have said if, during the course of the last war, it so happened that the English reached the gates of Paris? With what venom would you have unleashed your anger against the government that had provided so poorly for the safety of the kingdom and of the capital! And you would have been right. Why, then, thoughtless man, intoxicated by your dreams, are you trying to blacken and vilify these true pillars of the state, this army which is respected by the people, who owe it the greatest gratitude? What! These intrepid defenders who sacrifice themselves for the fatherland, would you envy them the honours and distinctions they so justly deserve? They have bought them with their blood, they have gained them by risking their peace of mind, their health, and their lives. Unworthy man that you are!—who seeks to vilify their merits, to deprive them of the glory, of the rewards that are their due, and to stifle the feelings of gratitude which the public owes them!

Do not imagine, for a moment, that it is the military alone who have cause to complain of our author. There is no rank or condition in the kingdom that is immune from his barbs. He tells us that the judiciary in France is venal. We have known that for a long time. If we are to discover the origin of this abuse we must, if I am not mistaken, go back to the time when King John was imprisoned by the English, or, even better, to the imprisonment of Francis I.[21] France found itself in honour bound to free its king from the hands of Charles V, who only wanted to restore his freedom if certain conditions were met. Since the Treasury was exhausted, and since no sum could be found that was considerable enough for the ransom of the king, recourse was had, in order to buy back the freedom of this prince, to the dire expedient of putting up for sale all judicial offices. The almost continual wars that followed the release of Francis I, the internal unrest and civil war that flared up during the reign of his descendants, all this prevented successive monarchs from discharging the debt, of which they are still, even now, making repayment. It is the misfortune of France that, even in our days, Louis XV finds himself in a position no better than that of his ancestors, which has prevented him from repaying the creditors the considerable advances they had granted the throne during those calamitous times.

Should we, then, blame Louis XV, if this ancient abuse has not yet been abolished? No doubt, the power of making decisions on the fortunes of an individual should not be something that can be acquired by money; but it is rather the authors of this situation, who alone are responsible for it, who should be blamed for it, and not a king who is innocent of it. Although these abuses persist, the author will, nevertheless, be obliged to confess that one cannot, in truth, accuse the Parlement of Paris of prevarication, and that the venality of judicial offices has had no influence on its administration of justice.[22] Let the author complain—opportunely—about the confusing number of laws that exist, and which vary from province to province, but which, in a kingdom like France, ought to be clear and uniform. Louis XIV wanted to undertake legal reform; but all manner of obstacles prevented him from completing this work.[23] Our author ought to know, then, if he does not already, and ought also to understand, if he can, the infinite difficulties and repeated obstacles that face those who try to alter practices hallowed by custom. We would have to go into the minutest details if we were to understand

the close connections between the different things that the passage of time
has forged, and which cannot be altered without consequences worse still than
the evil one is trying to remedy; this is a case of which it can truly be said,
that criticism is easy, but art is difficult.

Step forward, if you please, Sir, controller-general of finance, and you too,
gentlemen from the world of finance, it's your turn. The author, filled with
ill humour, is raging against taxes, against the collection of public monies,
against the burdens that the people bear and which, they claim, oppress them,
against tax-farmers, against the administrators of all such revenues, whom he
roundly accuses of embezzlement, of misappropriation, and of robbery. This
is all very well, so long as he can prove it. But, since, in reading him, I always,
in the face of his perpetual exaggerations, exercise caution, I suspect him of
an infinite degree of overstatement, employed with the intention of vilifying
the government. His words 'barbarous tyrant', a notion inseparable in his
mind from royalty, and which he applies, whenever he can, indirectly to his
own sovereign, make me suspect him of bad faith. Let us consider, then,
whether he knows what he is talking about, and if he has taken the trouble
to examine thoroughly the matters in question. Whence come these huge
debts that burden France? What were their origins? It is widely known that
a large part of them date from the reign of Louis XIV, and were incurred during the War of the Succession, which was the most just of all the wars he
undertook.[24] Subsequently, the Duke of Orléans, the regent of the kingdom,
flattered himself that he had disposed of them by means of the system that
Law had proposed to him.[25] In carrying this system to excess he destroyed
the kingdom, and the debts were only partly settled and not wholly extinguished. After the death of the regent, and under the wise administration of
Cardinal Fleury, time healed some of the kingdom's ancient wounds.[26]

But the wars that flared up subsequently obliged Louis XV to enter into
new debts. Good faith and the maintenance of public credit demand that
these debts be honoured, or at least that the government should pay the interest on the debt in full. If the ordinary revenues of the state are taken up in
financing its current expenditure, where, if not from the people, is the king
to find the sums necessary to pay the interest on the debt, or the portions of
the debt that fall due for repayment? And since, by long-established practice
in this country, the collection of certain rents and new taxes has passed into
the hands of contractors, the king finds himself more or less obliged to use
their services. No one denies that, where finance is concerned, tax inspec-
tors and collectors, of whom there are perhaps too great a number, may commit misappropriation and theft, and that the people are sometimes right in

complaining of the harshness of their exactions; but how do you prevent such things in a kingdom as vast as France? The bigger a monarchy, the more abuse there will be; even if the number of supervisors were equal to the number of tax collectors, these officials, through yet further tricks and ruses, would succeed, again and again, in pulling the wool over the watchful eyes of those charged with bringing to light these tricks and ruses.

If the intentions of our author had been honourable, if he had really understood the causes of the ruinous spending of the state, he would have warned, with moderation, of the need for the state to be more economical in its military expenditure, and of the need to be rid of those businessmen who, by illicit means, enrich themselves while the state grows poorer; and of the need to ensure that procurement contracts, as has sometimes happened, are not undertaken at twice their true value. And, finally, he could and should have suggested that reducing all the excessive pensions and expenses of the court would be a means, worthy of the attention of a good prince, of alleviating the burden of taxation. If he had adopted a more moderate tone, his advice could well have made some impression; but insults merely irritate, and persuade no one. Let him, then, propose ways and means of paying off the debt without both damaging public trust and trampling upon the people, and I will say to him that he will soon be appointed controller-general of finance.

A true philosopher would have considered, impartially, whether numerous armies, maintained during times of peace, whether wars, costly as they are today, are more, or less, effective than was the previous custom of hastily arming the peasantry whenever a neighbour seemed to pose a threat, and of supporting this militia through pillage and robbery, without granting it regular pay; and of dismissing it in peacetime. The unique advantage of this arrangement was that the military cost nothing in times of peace, but that, when the call to arms sounded, every citizen became a soldier, whereas, at present, these roles are separate: the farmer and the manufacturer each continues his own work, without interruption, while that section of the citizens destined to defend the others performs its duty. If our great armies, maintained during their operations at the expense of the state, are costly, this at least brings with it the advantage that wars can last only eight or ten years at the very most, and that the consequent exhaustion of resources makes sovereigns more disposed in certain cases to preserve peace than they would be by inclination. It thus follows from our modern practice that our wars are shorter than those of our forebears, less ruinous to the lands that provide the theatre of war, and that we owe to the great expense that wars involve those brief moments of peace that we enjoy, and which, moreover, the exhaustion of the great powers will probably lengthen.

I will go further. Our philosopher, that enemy of kings, insists that sovereigns do not owe their power to divine authority. We will not quibble about this; after all, he is so rarely right that it would be a sign of ill humour on our part to contradict him when the probabilities are on his side. The truth is that the Capetian dynasty usurped power, the Carolingians took possession of it by cunning and artifice, while the Valois and the Bourbons obtained the crown by right of succession. We would, moreover, surrender to him such titles as 'images of the Divinity' or 'God's representatives', which one attributes to kings so improperly. Kings, like the rest of us, are men; they do not enjoy the exclusive privilege of being perfect in a world where nothing is so. They bring to the throne, upon which an accident of birth has placed them, their timidity or their resolution, their energy or their idleness, their vices or their virtues; and in a hereditary monarchy it must of necessity be the case that princes with very differing characters succeed one another. One cannot with justice claim, when one is not perfect oneself, that princes have no faults. What perspicacity would we display in saying that this or that individual is good for nothing, greedy, extravagant, or debauched? None—no more than is displayed in reading out loud the house-names one sees as one walks about a town. A philosopher, who must know that the essence of things never changes, will not amuse himself by criticising an oak tree for not bearing apples, a donkey for not having the wings of an eagle, or a sturgeon for not having the horns of a bull. A philosopher will not exaggerate evils that are real but difficult to remedy; nor will he go about shouting, 'Everything is evil!', without saying how everything could be good. His voice will not trumpet forth sedition, will not be a rallying call for the malcontents, nor provide an excuse for rebellion. He will, rather, respect those customs that are established and sanctioned by the nation, by the government, by those who comprise it, and by those who depend on it. This is what the peace-loving Du Marsais believed, who is credited with composing a libellous essay two years after he was dead and buried.[27] But the true author of this libel could only be a schoolboy, as socially inexperienced as he is confused. But what else can I say? What! In a country where the author of *Telemachus* himself raised and educated the successor to the throne, there can be such an attack on the education of princes![28] If our schoolboy were to reply that there is no longer a Fénelon in France, he must blame the sterility of our century for this, and not those who are responsible for the education of princes.

These are, in substance, my general remarks on the *Essay on Prejudice*. Its style seemed to me boring, because it is nothing but a monotonous rant, during which the same ideas are repeated again and again, too often in exactly the same terms. In the midst of this chaos I did nevertheless find various details that are better than the rest. However, in order to make of this work a useful book, one would have to remove the repetitions, the conceits, the false reasoning, the errors, and the insults: which would reduce it to a quarter of its present length. But what have I learned from my reading of this book? What truths has the author imparted to me? That all churchmen are monsters, who should be stoned; that the king of France is a barbarous tyrant; that his ministers are arch-rascals, his courtiers cowardly rogues who grovel at the foot of the throne; the great and good of the kingdom ignoramuses who are steeped, moreover, in arrogance (but wait! let him at least except the Duc de Nivernois!);[29] the French field-marshals and officers, mercenaries and executioners; the judges, infamous and corrupt; the bankers, Cartouches and Mandrins;[30] the historians, the corrupters of princes; the poets, poisoners of the public; and that there is no one, in the whole kingdom, who is wise, praiseworthy, or entitled to respect, with the exception of the author and his friends, who have glorified themselves with the title of *philosophes*.

I regret the time that I have wasted in reading this work, and the time I am wasting in giving you an account of it.

London, April 1770.

12

Critical Examination of *The System of Nature*

The System of Nature is a work that, on a first reading, has great appeal; its faults, which are artfully hidden, become apparent only after several re-readings. The author has been skilful in obscuring the consequences of his principles, in order to distract the scrutiny of the critic; the illusion he creates, however, is not powerful enough to prevent our noticing certain inconsistencies and contradictions into which he is often led; and our observing, too, that some views he expresses are contrary to his system but seem to be wrested from him by the force of truth. The issues in metaphysics that he discusses are obscure, and fraught with the greatest difficulties. To lose one's way is pardonable when one enters a labyrinth in which so many others have gone astray. It would appear, however, that this shadowy path can be followed with less risk if one doubts one's own judgement, if one remembers that in speculation of this kind, the guidance of experience deserts us, and that all that remain to us are probabilities, more or less strong, on which we may base our opinions. This consideration is in itself quite enough to inspire restraint and humility in every philosopher who wishes to establish a system; our author, apparently, does not think so, since he prides himself on being dogmatic.

The principal subjects that he treats in this work are:

1. God and nature;
2. fatalism;
3. religious morality, compared with the morality of natural religion; and
4. sovereigns, the cause of all the misfortunes that states suffer.

As to the first subject, the reasons the author gives for rejecting the Divinity are a little surprising, in view of the importance of this matter. He says that it costs him less to accept blind matter, prompted to act through movement, than to have recourse to an intelligent cause acting by itself; as if that which costs him less trouble to accept were closer to the truth than that which costs him difficulty to explain. He admits that it is his indignation at religious persecution that has made him an atheist. But are these reasons enough to determine the views of a philosopher: laziness and emotion? So naïve an admission can only inspire distrust in the reader: indeed, how could one believe him if he makes up his mind on the basis of such frivolous motives? I can only suppose that our philosopher sometimes yields, too self-indulgently, to his imagination, and that, struck by the contradictory definitions that the theologians offer of the Divinity, he confuses these definitions, which cannot withstand the scrutiny of good sense, with an intelligent nature that must necessarily govern the continued existence of the universe. The entire world gives proof of this intelligence; you have only to open your eyes to be convinced of this. Man is a thinking being produced by nature; it must therefore be the case that nature is infinitely more intelligent than he is, or else nature would have bestowed on him perfections she does not possess herself; which would be a formal contradiction.

If thought derives from our human constitution, it is certain that nature, infinitely better organised than man, who is an imperceptible part of the great whole, must possess intelligence to the highest degree of perfection. Blind nature, as the agent of movement,[1] can produce only confusion, and since its actions are unplanned it could never achieve any predetermined ends, nor produce any of those masterpieces that human wisdom must admire, whether they are infinitely small or infinitely great. The ends that nature has set itself in all its works manifest themselves so clearly that we are forced to recognise a supreme first cause, possessed of the highest possible intelligence, which necessarily presides over nature. When I consider man, I see him at birth the most feeble of all the animals, unable to attack or to defend himself, incapable of withstanding the rigours of the seasons, and always vulnerable to being devoured by ferocious beasts. To compensate for the frailty of his body, and so that the species should not die out, nature has endowed him with an intelligence superior to that of all other creatures, an advantage through which he acquires by art what nature appears to have denied him. The lowest of the animals contains within its body a laboratory more skilfully constructed than that of the most proficient chemist; it produces fluids, which sustain and renew its being, which are absorbed into its constituent parts, and which prolong its life. How could this marvellous system, so necessary for the preservation of all animate beings, be born of a crude and brutish first cause, which would work its great wonders without even noticing this? But we need not go to these lengths to confound our philosopher and destroy his system; a mite's eye, a blade of grass are enough to demonstrate to him the intelligence of the craftsman. I will go further; I believe that, even if we accept, as he does, a blind first cause, it could be proved to him that the creation of species would become uncertain, and that they would degenerate randomly into diverse and bizarre beings. It is only, therefore, the immutable laws of an intelligent nature which, among this endless procreation, could invariably maintain the species in their entire integrity. The author attempts in vain to delude himself; truth, more powerful than he is, compels him to say that nature assembles within its immense laboratory materials enough to form new creations; that it acts, therefore, in pursuit of a considered end; nature, therefore, is intelligent. Even if we are of little good faith, it is impossible to object to this truth; even those objections that are based on physical and moral evil cannot overturn it: the eternity of the world destroys this difficulty. Nature is, therefore, without contradiction, intelligent, always acting in conformity with the eternal laws of weight, movement, gravitation, etc., which it would know neither how to destroy nor to change. Although our reason proves to us the existence of this Being, although we catch glimpses of it, although we guess at some of its works, we will never know it well enough to define it, and every philosopher who attacks the phantom created by the theologians is in effect battling against Ixion's cloud,[2] without even coming close to that Being of whose existence the whole universe serves as proof and witness. It is doubtless very surprising that a philosopher as enlightened as our author should take it into his head to give credence to these ancient errors concerning germless reproduction through degeneration; he quotes the English doctor Needham, who, deceived by a false experiment, believed that he had created some conger eels.[3] If all this were true it would argue for the operation of a nature that is blind; whereas, on the contrary, it is refuted by all experiments. Can we really believe that this same author accepts the reality of a universal flood? How absurd: a miracle that could not be accepted by any geometrician, and which could not in any way be consistent with his system! The waters that covered our whole world, were they created deliberately? What an immense depth they must have had in order to tower over the highest mountains! Were they subsequently annihilated? What became of them? What! He closes his eyes in order not to see an intelligent Being presiding over the universe, a Being whom all nature reveals to him; and he also believes in the most irrational miracle that it is possible to imagine! I must confess that I cannot conceive how so many contradictions could be reconciled within a philosophical mind, nor how, while composing his work, the author did not notice any of this himself. But let us proceed.

He has copied, almost literally, the theory of fatalism which Leibniz expounds and upon which Wolff has made a commentary.[4] I believe that, if we are to understand one another, we must define the concept of freedom. I understand by this word every act of our will that we ourselves decide upon without constraint. Do not imagine that, in departing from this principle, I mean to oppose—in general and in every particular—the theory of fatalism; I seek nothing but truth, I respect it wherever I find it, and I bow to it whenever I am shown it. If we are to consider the question correctly, we must reproduce the author's principal argument. All our ideas, he says, come from our senses and as a consequence of our physical constitution. All our actions are therefore necessary. We agree with him that we owe everything to our senses, and to our sense-organs; but the author ought to have noticed that our received ideas give way to new combinations. In the first of these operations, the mind is passive; in the second, it is active. Invention and imagination work on objects that our senses have taught us to know; for example, when Newton was learning geometry, his mind was passive, and he collected ideas; but when he arrived at his astonishing discoveries, he was more than a mere agent, he was a creator. It is important to distinguish the different ways in which the human mind functions: it is a slave where impulse dominates, but it enjoys perfect freedom where the imagination is active. I therefore agree with the author that there is a certain causal chain that acts upon man and frequently rules him. Man acquires at birth his temperament, his character, along with the seeds of his vices and virtues, a part of his very being which he can neither suppress nor augment, his talent or genius, or his sluggishness and incapacity. Whenever we allow ourselves to be carried away by the ardour of our passions, necessity, victorious over our freedom, triumphs; whenever the force of reason tames these passions, freedom prevails.

But is man not wholly free when he is offered different courses of action, which he considers, inclining towards one or the other, and which, finally, he decides upon by choice? The author will no doubt reply that necessity determines his choice. I believe that I glimpse in this reply a misuse of the term 'necessity', its confusion with the notions of cause, motive, and reason. Without doubt nothing happens without a cause, but not every cause is a necessary cause. No doubt, a man, unless he is a madman, will make decisions on the basis of reasoning which relates to his self-love; I repeat, he would not be free, but raving mad, if he were to do otherwise.[5] Freedom, then, is like wisdom, reason, virtue, health: something that no human being possesses entirely, but only intermittently. We are, in some ways, the victims of the rule of fate; and, in other ways, free and independent agents. Let us follow Locke. He is wholly convinced that, when his door is shut, he is not empowered to go out of it, but, when it is open, he is free to act as he sees fit.[6] The more we try to get down to the essence of this matter, the more complicated it becomes;

we succeed, through over-subtlety, in making it so obscure that we no longer understand ourselves; it is, above all, an irritation for the adherents of fatalism that their active lives are in constant contradiction with the principles of their speculative theory.

The author of *The System of Nature,* having exhausted all the arguments that his imagination offers him to prove that fatal necessity puts in chains, and entirely governs, men in all their actions, ought then to conclude that man is merely a kind of machine, or, if you like, a puppet operated by the hands of a blind puppeteer. Nonetheless, he rails against priests, against governments, and against education; he believes, then, that the men occupied in these spheres are free, while proving to them that they are slaves. What an absurdity! What a contradiction! If everything happens by necessity, then advice, instructions, law, penalties, and rewards become superfluous and, indeed, useless; it is as though you said to a man in chains: break free from your bonds. You might just as well preach to an oak tree, in an attempt to persuade it to change itself into an orange tree. But experience shows us that it is possible to succeed in correcting men's faults; we must, then, of necessity, conclude that men enjoy, in part at least, freedom. Let us, then, be content with the lessons of experience, and not accept a principle that we contradict ceaselessly in our actions.

The theory of fatalism leads to the direst consequences for society; if we accept it, Marcus Aurelius and Catiline, and the Président de Thou and Ravaillac, would all be of equal merit.[7] We should not regard men as mere machines, some made for vice and others for virtue, incapable of being, of their own volition, meritorious or the opposite, and consequently of being punished or rewarded; this would undermine morality and good behaviour, the very foundations on which society is built. But whence comes this love that, in general, all men have of freedom? If freedom were an ideal entity, how could they recognise it? It must, then, be the case that they have had some experience of it, that they have felt it; it must, therefore, be the case that freedom exists in reality; it would otherwise be unlikely that they could love it. Whatever Calvin, Leibniz, the Arminians, and the author of *The System of Nature* may say, they will never persuade anyone that we are nothing but mill-wheels, which a necessary and irresistible cause, according to its own whim, sets in motion. All these errors into which our author has fallen come from the frenzy of the systematic mind; his opinions were fixed from the outset; he encountered phenomena, circumstances, and small details which could fit in with his theory. But in generalising his ideas, he found other patterns and truths of experience which contradicted his theory; as to these last, by twisting them and doing them violence, he adjusted them, as well as he was able, so as to be consistent with the rest of his system. It is obvious that he did not neglect any evidence that could strengthen the case for his dogmatic fatalism, while at the same time it is clear that he gives the lie to it throughout the whole course of his work. As for me, I think that, in such a case, a true philosopher ought to sacrifice his self-esteem to the love of truth.

But let us turn now to the section that is concerned with religion. One could accuse the author of intellectual sterility, and of great maladroitness, because he maligns the Christian religion for faults that it does not have. How can he claim with any truth that the Christian religion is the cause of all the ills of the human race? He could have expressed himself more clearly simply by claiming that human ambition and self-interest have used this religion as an excuse for bringing trouble to the world and satisfying the passions of men. What can one take, in good faith, from the morality of the Decalogue? If there were in all the Gospels this one precept only, 'Do not do to others what you would not wish them to do to you,' we must agree that these few words contain the essence of all morality. And did not Jesus preach forgiveness, charity, and humanity in his fine Sermon on the Mount? Law, then, should not have been confused with its abuse, things written with things done, or true Christian morality with the debased version of the priests. How then can our author accuse the Christian religion itself of causing the decline of morality? But he could accuse the clergy of substituting faith for the social virtues, practices that are merely external for good works, light penances instead of conscientious remorse, indulgences that they sell instead of the need for amendment of life. He could reproach them for absolving people from their oaths, and for suppressing and doing violence to their consciences. These criminal abuses invite us to rise up against those who introduce and authorise them; but by what right can our author do so, he who supposes men to be machines? How can he reprimand a tonsured machine, whom necessity has forced to be a deceiver, to act a part, and to scoff at the credulity of ordinary people?

Let us leave the theory of fatalism aside for one moment, and consider things as they really are in the world. The author ought to know that, whatever the religion, the law, and the government of a state, there will always be, among the great number of its citizens, people who are more or less scoundrels; the greater part of the population is everywhere little given to reasoning, prone to indulge in floods of emotion, and more inclined to vice than drawn to goodness; the most we can expect of good government is that, under it, serious crime occurs more rarely than it does under bad government. Our author ought to know that to exaggerate is not to reason, that calumny discredits a philosopher, just as it does an author who is not a philosopher, and that, when he is angry, which does sometimes happen, we could apply to him what Menippus said to Jupiter: 'You are reaching for your thunderbolt; there-fore you must be in error.'[8] There is, doubtless, only one morality. It sets out what individuals owe each other reciprocally; it is the foundation of society; under whatever government, under whatever religion one finds oneself, it ought to be the same; the morality of the Gospels, taken in all its purity, would, if practised, be useful. But if we accept the dogma of fatalism, there is no longer morality or virtue, and the whole edifice of society crumbles. It is incontestable that our author's aim is to overturn religion: but he has chosen the most difficult and circuitous route to achieve this. The following is, or so it seems to me, the most natural route for him to have followed: he should have attacked the historical element of religion, the absurd fairy tales upon which the whole edifice is built, its still more absurd traditions, more fool-ish, more ridiculous, indeed, than the most extravagant creations of pagan-ism.[9] This would have been the way of proving that God has not spoken, it would have been the way of freeing men from their foolish and stupid credu-lity. The author had another, shorter, route to this same end. Having set out the arguments against the immortality of the soul that Lucretius expounds with such power in his third book, he ought to have concluded that, since everything comes to an end for man when this life ends, and since there re-mains to him nothing to fear or to hope for after his death, there can be no relationship between man and the Divinity, who can neither punish nor re-ward him.[10] Without this relationship, there is no longer either worship or religion, and the Divinity becomes for man nothing more than an object of speculation and curiosity. But what peculiarities and contradictions there are in the work of this philosopher! Having, with great labour, filled two volumes with proofs of his theory, he confesses that there are very few men capable of accepting and holding fast to it. We might suppose, then, that, blind as he thinks nature to be, he acts without reason, and only an irresistible necessity makes him compose a work that could plunge him into the greatest dangers, without him or anyone else being able to derive the least benefit from it.

Let us turn now to the sovereigns, whom the author has, curiously, taken it upon himself to decry. I venture to assure him that the clergy have never uttered to princes the stupidities he ascribes to them. If it should happen that they speak of kings as representations of the Divinity, this is doubtless done in a wholly hyperbolical sense, since the intention here is to warn them through this comparison not to abuse their authority, but to be benevolent and just, in keeping with the common view we form of the Divinity in every nation.[11] The author seems to believe that there are treaties between sover-eigns and the clergy, whereby princes promise to honour and give authority to men of the church, on condition that they preach submission to the people.

I venture to assure him that this is an idle notion, that nothing is more erroneous, nor more ill-conceived, than this so-called pact. It is very probable that the priests try to validate this view, in order to gain status and to give themselves a role to play; what is certain is that sovereigns, thanks to their credulity, their superstition, their ineptitude, and their blindness where the church is concerned, give cause for suspicion that they themselves share such an understanding; but everything in the end depends on the character of the prince. When he is weak and bigoted, the priests prevail; if he is so unfortunate as to be an unbeliever, the priests plot against him, and, for want of anything better, slander him and blacken his reputation.

I turn once again from these little blunders to the prejudices of the author; how can he accuse kings of being responsible for the poor education of their subjects? He imagines that it is a political principle, that it is better that a government rule an ignorant populace rather than an enlightened nation. This seems a little like the ideas of a college rector who, confined within a narrow compass of speculation, knows neither the world, nor governments, nor the elements of politics. No doubt all governments of civilised peoples concern themselves with public education. What, then, are the colleges, the academies, the universities with which Europe teems, if they are not establishments dedicated to the instruction of the young? But to claim that the prince of a large state is responsible for the education that every father of a family gives to his children, that is the most ridiculous claim that has ever been made. There is no need for a sovereign to rummage in the affairs of families and to meddle with what goes on in private houses, which can only result in the most odious tyranny. Our philosopher writes down whatever presents itself to his pen, without examining its consequences, and he is certainly amusing himself when he describes, politely, the courts as hotbeds of public corruption; which makes me, in truth, ashamed of philosophy. How can one exaggerate to such an extent? How can one utter such stupidities? Some less vehement spirit, some wiser man, would have been content merely to point out that, the more populous a society is, the more refined are its vices; and that the more opportunities there are for the passions to express themselves, the more active they are. One would allow Juvenal, or some professional satirist, the comparison between courts and 'hotbeds of public corruption',[12] but a philosopher . . . I will say no more. If our author had been, for six months, a community administrator in the little town of Pau in the Béarn, he would have a better appreciation of men than he would ever have learned from his idle theorising. How can he imagine that sovereigns would encourage their subjects to commit crime: what good would it do them to oblige themselves to punish such malefactors? It happens from time to time, no doubt, that various rogues evade the rigours of the law; but this never arises from any settled intention to encourage violent crime by offering the criminal the hope of impunity; we must attribute this kind of case to excessive indulgence on the part of the prince. It happens, no doubt, in every government, that some guilty people, through intrigue, corruption, or the support of powerful protectors, find a way to evade the punishments they have deserved; but in order to prevent such ploys, intrigues, and corruption, a prince would need to possess the omniscience that theologians attribute to God.

When it comes to government, our author stumbles at every step. He imagines that it is necessity and wretchedness that drive men to commit the most serious crimes. But this is not the case. In every country, men who are neither lazy nor good-for-nothing can find, through work, enough to live on. In every state, the most dangerous men are those who are dissipated or prodigal; their excessive appetites soon exhaust their resources, and they are driven to extreme lengths, and subsequently forced to resort to expedients of the lowest, the most odious, and the most infamous kind. Catiline and his gang, the supporters of Julius Caesar, the rebels or frondeurs stirred up by Cardinal de Retz, and those who followed the fortunes of Cromwell, were all of them people of the kind that could not settle their debts, nor restore their tattered fortunes, except by overturning the state whose citizens they were.[13] Among the foremost families of the state, spendthrifts plot and act like rogues; while among the people the idle and the dissipated end by becoming bandits, and by committing the most serious assaults against the security of the state.

After the author has proved beyond all doubt that he knows neither men, nor how they should be governed, he echoes Boileau's satirical rantings against Alexander the Great,[14] he inveighs against Charles V and his son Philip II, although it is clear, beyond any doubt, that it is Louis XIV against whom he bears ill will. Among all the paradoxes maintained, with the greatest self-satisfaction, by the so-called philosophers of our day, the vilification of the great names of the previous century seems to be that which is closest to their hearts. How could their own reputations be enhanced by their exaggerated account of the shortcomings of a king who, in his greatness and splendour, outshone them all? The shortcomings of Louis XIV are, moreover, well known, and these so-called philosophers do not even have the trivial merit of being the first to discover them. A prince who reigns for only eight days will doubtless display some shortcoming or other; is it not, then, more likely that a monarch who has spent sixty years of his life on the throne will be found to have shortcomings? If you were to set yourself up as an impartial judge, and if you were to examine the life of this great prince, you would have to agree that in his kingdom he did more good than ill. If we were to offer a detailed apology of him, it would fill a whole volume; I will confine myself here to the principal issues. You might well, then, attribute his persecution of the Huguenots to the shortcomings of the age, to the superstitions in which he had been brought up, and to the unwise trust he placed in his confessor; you might well attribute the burning of the Palatinate to the harsh and haughty disposition of Louvois.[15] Louis XIV may scarcely be reproached further, except in regard to several wars he undertook out of vanity and arrogance. You cannot, however, deny him his role as champion of the fine arts. France owes him its manufacturing and its trade; it owes him, too, the extension of its noble frontiers, as well as the high regard that France enjoyed in Europe in his time.[16] Pay homage, then, to his admirable and truly royal qualities. Whoever, nowadays, wishes to denigrate sovereigns must attack their feebleness, their idleness, and their ignorance; they are for the most part more weak than ambitious, and more vain than masterful.

The author's true opinions about government reveal themselves only towards the end of his work, where he tells us that, in his view, subjects should have the right to depose their sovereigns when they are no longer content with them. It is in order to bring this about that he expostulates against the large armies that could present some obstacle to this right; you might think you were reading La Fontaine's fable of the wolf and the shepherd.[17] If ever the futile ideas of our philosopher could be realised, the forms of government in all the states of Europe would first need to be recast, which seems to him to be a mere bagatelle. It would be necessary also, which seems to me impossible, that these subjects, who have set themselves up as the judges of their master, should be wise and equitable, that the pretenders to the throne should be without ambition, and that neither intrigue, nor plotting, nor a spirit of independence could prevail; it would require also that the dethroned royal family should be totally eradicated; otherwise the seeds of civil war would be sown, and party leaders would always be ready to take charge of factions in order to cause trouble for the state.[18] A further consequence would result from this form of government: that candidates for, and pretenders to, the throne would continually arouse and stir up the people, and turn them against the prince, fomenting sedition and revolt, flattering themselves that, by these means, they would improve their fortune and achieve power; so that such a government would be continually exposed to civil wars, which are a thousand times more dangerous than foreign wars. It is to avoid such difficulties that rules of succession have been adopted and established in many European states. It has become obvious that elections bring trouble in their wake, and there is anxiety, too, as is only natural, that jealous neighbours might profit from so favourable an opportunity to conquer and lay waste the kingdom. The author could easily have enlightened himself as to the consequences of his theories; he had only to cast his eye on Poland, where each election of a king becomes a time of civil and foreign war.

It is quite erroneous to believe that there can ever be perfection in human affairs; the imagination can create such chimeras, but they will never be realised. Since the dawn of time nations have tested every form of government; history abounds with them; but there is none that is not subject to difficulty.[19] Most nations have, nevertheless, accepted the order of succession that obtains in ruling families, because, given the choice they had to make, it was the least bad option. The evil that results from this system derives from the fact that it is impossible that, in a family, talents and merit should be transmitted uninterruptedly from father to son over a long succession of years; and that it sometimes happens that the throne is occupied by princes unworthy of this role. But even in this case, there remains the resource of skilful ministers, who, thanks to their abilities, are able to remedy the damage that is no doubt caused by the ineptitude of the sovereign. The obvious advantage that follows from this arrangement is that princes born to occupy the throne are less arrogant and vain than the upstarts who, puffed up with their new status, and disdainful of those who were formerly their equals, take pleasure in making them feel, on every occasion, their superiority. But take note, in particular, that a prince who is certain that his children will succeed him is likely to fulfil his duties with much more enthusiasm, since he believes that he is working for his family, and for the great benefit of the state that he sees as his patrimony; whereas, in states with elections, sovereigns think only of themselves, of what can last during their lifetime, and of nothing more; they try to enrich their families, and they allow everything to decline in a state that, in their eyes, is a precarious possession, which they will be obliged some day to give up. If anyone wishes to be persuaded of this, he has only to consider what happens in the ecclesiastical principalities of Germany, in Poland, and even in Rome, where the baneful results of elective monarchy are only too evident. Whatever course one takes in this world will prove itself subject to difficulties and often to terrible drawbacks. It is therefore necessary, if one believes oneself clear-sighted enough to enlighten the public, to avoid, above all, proposing remedies worse than the ills that are complained of; and, when one can do nothing better, to abide by ancient custom and, above all, established law.

13

Dialogue of the Dead between Madame de Pompadour and the Virgin Mary

THE VIRGIN Welcome, my little darling. But whatever brings you here?

POMPADOUR It's high time you learnt, my little darling, the appropriate terms to use when you have the honour to address a person of my standing. A wretched little Jewess, who gave birth in a stable, along with oxen and asses, must certainly call me Madame; it's the very least she can do.

THE VIRGIN Very well! If you absolutely insist on this, you will be Madame. But have you forgotten the great role I played in Edom, and the even greater role I now play, here in heaven?

POMPADOUR Yes indeed, I remember very well the story of Bluebeard and the donkey-skin.

THE VIRGIN Which is to say?

POMPADOUR That, as to your rank and status, opinions differ very considerably. The general view is that the Council of Trent accords you honours that you don't possess.[1] The common people, imbeciles that they are, call you Queen of Heaven; people of good sense shrug their shoulders; and the philosophers make fun of all this.

THE VIRGIN What? Impertinent little creature that you are, who manoeuvred your way into heaven in spite of all that fraud and contraband, you who deserve to burn in hell for all eternity for all your mischief-making: how dare you look me in the face while uttering such insolent remarks?

POMPADOUR Calm down, Madam Virgin! Do you think I am the only person whose amorous entanglements might be mentioned here? Don't push me too hard, or I'll recall various entertaining songs that were doing the rounds in Jerusalem during your time there.

THE VIRGIN What a deceitful creature you are! I know nothing of the stupid things you are saying.

POMPADOUR You would understand them very well if you cared to remember a certain Roman soldier called Penter. You were in love with him . . .

You're blushing . . . ! Everyone knows, make no mistake of it, that you lived with him on the most intimate terms, and that he is believed to be the father of . . .

THE VIRGIN I will take no more of this. What? Can it be possible that such stupidities should be bandied about, without my Divine husband striking down with lightning the impious creatures that spread them abroad? If only He would unleash upon them all the scourges that hell can inflict—plague, famine, and war—so as to destroy the present human race, which is worse even than that which He drowned in times past in the Great Flood! The entire universe must be full of encyclopae-dists.[2] Everything is lost if even such a whore as you are dares to say such vile things to me.

POMPADOUR Oh! This is too much. I admire the nobility with which you express yourself; but, since I find myself in such low company, let us not mince our words. Speaking, then, as one whore to another, the difference between us is that I was the whore of a great king, and you of a wretched Roman soldier.

THE VIRGIN Just a moment! Were not the Abbé Bernis and Monsieur . . . & Monsieur C . . . forerunners of your Most Christian Majesty?[3] And if you had not taken the white flowers, half of the city of Paris would have worked alongside you to adorn your lover's head.[4] That was all your doing. As for me, I have lived so chastely that I was a virgin both before and after giving birth.[5]

POMPADOUR Oh! As to virginity, Madame, I can certainly claim it as much as you can, and perhaps more. I had, with Monsieur d'Étioles, only one daughter, a delicate little thing, while you had two boys:[6] and, as you know, boys are terrible destroyers of virginity. They say that your older boy be-came famous.

THE VIRGIN Alas, yes! He was hanged; but it was that that made His fortune.

POMPADOUR It was that very thing that put me off having boys.

THE VIRGIN You have no sublimity of soul. It was His being hanged that is the mystery.

POMPADOUR You look for mysteries where there are none. Is it in any way surprising that the son of a carpenter, or of a Roman soldier, should be hanged for having tried to stir up the people? Miserable little Jewess that you are, forget all this nonsense. Accept that God is beyond our reach; He does not beget, He is invisible, and infinite; an immensity separates Him from us, vile creatures that we are. You could not have been, nor have you been, visited by Him, as I was, really and truly, by Louis XV.

THE VIRGIN Don't you know, then, that He sent the Holy Ghost to me, and that it was through the Holy Ghost that the celestial seed was implanted in me?

POMPADOUR What you say fills me with horror. It is blasphemy.

THE VIRGIN In that case you understand nothing.

POMPADOUR It is as though the French king had sent the Duc d'Aguin to me on his behalf, to request that I bestow my favours upon him; but this comparison is, nonetheless, false; for the Duc d'Aguin exists; he is well known.[7] Whereas your Holy Ghost is an adjunct to the Godhead, one that owes its existence to Plato's brain and to various imbecilic Jews, who invented a triple God, and adopted these Greek chimeras as truth.

THE VIRGIN It astonishes me, Madame, to see you overturning, simply to amuse yourself, the very foundations of your own faith, and of that religion which the death of my Son gave to the world.

POMPADOUR Is it not enough that tedious fictions such as these should have ruled the world for fourteen centuries, and is it not high time that men emerged from their blindness? Things that appear marvellous may dazzle for a while; but in due course they suffer the same fate as do all lies, and, when exposed to the light of truth, simply vanish.

THE VIRGIN In which case would I no longer be Queen of Heaven?

POMPADOUR Your standing and the high regard in which you were held established this title, but they no longer hold good. As for me, I was, really and truly, more queen of France than you were queen of heaven. I am no longer queen, and must reconcile myself to this. But during my time, and as the fancy took me, I made and unmade ministers, I appointed ambassadors and generals, and I declared war and peace.

THE VIRGIN As was clear for all to see from the noble war you waged in Germany and, at sea, against the English.[8] It is said, Madame, that your foot-soldiers were everywhere defeated; and that, of the eighty ships that you had beneath your command, not even six survived that were seaworthy.

POMPADOUR Wisdom and good fortune do not always go hand in hand: sometimes even a small misfortune is enough to upset the best-laid plan. Still, it was always I who ruled; it was my imprimatur that issued imperial orders to the whole of France; whereas your immaculate suzerainty has never decided anything, either in heaven or on earth. Besides which, my Most Christian lover did not make love to me through his ambassadors, but, quite simply, in the usual way, as everyone does. But, returning to the point in question, I suggest that, once and for all, you renounce your appalling Jewish fairy-tale, which is nothing more nor less than a terrible blasphemy. Don't forget that it is the greatest possible impiety to attribute to the Being of Beings a love that is not chaste, not to mention adulteries that recall the debaucheries of which the Jupiter of the Gentiles was accused. You ought to die of shame for having profaned the name of God, for having used so revered a name in order to draw a veil over misdeeds easily pardoned as a series of human frailties.

THE VIRGIN You're a fine one to speak of adultery! You, who have committed it twice and three times over. It was d'Étioles's wife, was it not, who expelled Stanisław's daughter from the bed of your Most Christian man?[9]

POMPADOUR I cannot but acknowledge that it was so; but what can ambition not achieve? Born in exile in Hamburg,[10] sent back to France as a result of various intrigues, I was married off to a banker; at which point I caught sight of the throne, it was offered to me, and I took it; anyone else would have done the same thing.

THE VIRGIN One may be tempted by a god; but as to a king—that's not nearly good enough.

POMPADOUR Let us not profane the Divinity, by bringing Him into our conversation. Let us rather, Madame, restrict ourselves to human affairs; you to your Joseph or your Penter, I to my d'Étioles, or to my Most Christian lover.

THE VIRGIN It is certain that this Most Christian Majesty has a very un-Christian mistress, who deprives me even of the satisfaction I used to enjoy, that my perfect greatness still impressed the world.

POMPADOUR Let us console one another as best we may, Madame; for, as you can see only too well, our moment is over, since neither you nor I is now queen in this land.

THE VIRGIN My whole misfortune stems from the fact that the Council of Trent has lost its credibility among men. I see only too well that this marvellous system must be abandoned in favour of a return to sad reality. In other words, I am sacrificing in the interests of truth a fiction that earlier pleased me so much.

POMPADOUR You are losing nothing but idle fancies.

THE VIRGIN That is quite true. Abdication always costs one dear, even if what one loses is no more than a dream.

POMPADOUR Whereas I have left the world with good grace, and without succumbing to despair.

THE VIRGIN But how did you find your way here?

POMPADOUR My lover has an infallible recipe whereby a soul can avoid pur-
gatory and hell and go directly to heaven.

THE VIRGIN And how does he manage this?

POMPADOUR He sent a confessor to me when I was dying; and, thanks to
the absolution he gave me, which served as my passe-partout, I arrived here
without hindrance. My lover preserves this recipe very carefully so that he
can use it himself when the occasion arises. But, as for us, sinners as both
of us are, let us henceforth live in peace. There can be no jealousy between
us as to our charms, and since, moreover, we practised the same profession,
let us be of mutual support to one another, and let us try to make life here
bearable.

THE VIRGIN Yes indeed, that is the very best thing we could do, especially
since in this place quarrels are forbidden. Let us go and find some company. Would you like me to introduce you to Mary Magdalene?

POMPADOUR Gladly, since we are all fellow professionals, and as long as I
have the upper hand.

THE VIRGIN Here there is no upper hand nor the opposite, no formal nor
casual introductions. Death is the great leveller: you are all of you equal,
with the sole exception of myself.

POMPADOUR There you go again, reverting to your past illusions.

THE VIRGIN I admit it. It is difficult to lose one's misapprehensions. Besides which, you must know that a certain Greek claims that the love of
glory is the last passion of the sage.[11]

POMPADOUR Let us not concern ourselves any more with Greeks and sages;
we have nothing in common with them. And so, for want of anything better, let us go and join Mary Magdalene.

14

Essay on the Forms of Government
and the Duties of Sovereigns

If we go back to the most distant antiquity, we find that the peoples of whom some knowledge has come down to us led a pastoral life, and formed no social groups: what the book of Genesis records about the history of the patriarchs provides sufficient witness of this. Before the time of the small Jewish nation, the Egyptians must have been similarly scattered in family groups in those lands that the Nile did not flood; and some centuries must, doubtless, have elapsed before this river, now tamed, allowed the indigenous people to gather in small villages. We learn from Greek history the names of the founders of towns, and of the lawgivers who were the first to bring them together in groups; this nation remained primitive for a long time, as did all the inhabitants of our globe. If the annals of the Etruscans, of the Samnites, of the Sabines, etc. had come down to us, we would certainly learn that these peoples lived in isolated family groups before being brought together and united. The Gauls were already forming associations of peoples at the time when Julius Caesar conquered them. But it appears that Great Britain had not reached that stage of development when Caesar arrived there for the first time with his Roman legions. During the era of that great man, the Germans could only be compared with the Iroquois, the Algonquins, and other similar primitive peoples; they lived from hunting, fishing, and the milk of their herds and flocks. A German would think he was demeaning himself if he tilled the soil; he used for such tasks the slaves he had acquired in war; besides, the Hercynian Forest covered, almost entirely, the vast area of land that now comprises Germany. The population could not increase in number, because of the lack of adequate food; and this is, doubtless, the true cause of those huge movements of the peoples of the North, who surged southwards in search of cultivable land and a less rigorous climate.

It is astonishing to imagine that the human race lived for so long in an utterly primitive state, without forming itself into societies; and we must earnestly seek what it was that moved them to unite in social groupings.

Doubtless, the violence and pillage of other neighbouring hordes gave these isolated small groups the idea of joining with other families to secure their possessions by means of a shared defence. Such is the origin of law, which teaches social groups to prefer the general good to their individual interests. Thereafter, no one without fear of punishment dared seize another's goods, no one dared threaten the life of his neighbour, but must respect his neighbour's wife and possessions, and regard them as sacred objects; while, if the society as a whole found itself under attack, everyone must hasten to save it. This important truth, that we must behave towards others as we would wish them to act towards us, becomes the basis of law and of the social covenant; thence comes love of one's country, seen as the guardian of our happiness. But since law could not be upheld or implemented without a regulator who ceaselessly watched over it, magistrates came into being, whom the people elected and obeyed. We must never forget that the preservation of law was the sole reason for persuading men to accept authority: that is the true origin of sovereignty. The magistrate was the first servant of the state.[1] When these emerging societies had reason to fear their neighbours, it was the magistrate who armed the people, and flew to the defence of the citizens.

The universal human instinct, which encourages men to secure for themselves the greatest possible happiness, led to the formation of different kinds of government. Some believed that, in giving themselves over to the leadership of various wise men, they would find this happiness; hence came aristocratic government. Others preferred oligarchy. Athens and most Greek republics chose democracy. Persia and the Orient bent the knee to tyranny. The Romans had kings for some time; but they became wearied of the violence of the Tarquins, and changed their form of government to an aristocracy. Soon, exhausted by the harshness of the patricians, who oppressed them with usury, the common people left Rome and only returned after the Senate had granted powers to the tribunes elected by the people to protect themselves against the violence of the patricians; subsequently the people virtually became the seat of supreme authority within the state.[2] One usually branded as tyrants those men who seized power through violence, and who, with only their whims and their passions to guide them, overturned the fundamental laws and principles that society had established for its own preservation.

But, whatever the wisdom of the lawgivers and of the leaders who first brought the people together, however worthy their institutions, not one of these governments was able wholly to maintain its integrity. Why? Because men are imperfect, as are, consequently, their works; because citizens, driven by their passions, allow themselves to be blinded by self-interest, which always destroys regard for the general good; and because, finally, there is no stability in this world. Under aristocratic government, abuse of authority on the part of the principal citizens of the state, is, in general, the cause of the revolutions that follow. Democracy in Rome was overturned by the people themselves; the plebeian masses, blinded, allowed themselves to be corrupted by ambitious citizens who subsequently enslaved them and deprived them of their liberty. This is the fate that England must expect if its lower chamber does not put the true interests of the nation above the infamous corruption that is destroying it. As for monarchical government, many different kinds have been seen. The feudal government of the past, which was some centuries ago almost universal in Europe, had been established by the barbarian conquests. The general who commanded a barbarian horde appointed himself sovereign of the conquered country, and divided its provinces among his chief officers; they were, in fact, subjects of the paramount lord, and they provided soldiery for him if he required it; but, since some of these vassals became as powerful as their leader, states within the state came into being. This was the seedbed for civil wars, which caused misfortune for society in general. In Germany, these vassals became independent; they were crushed in France, in England, and in Spain. The only example that remains to us of this abominable form of government is to be found in the Polish republic. In Turkey, the sovereign is a despot; he can, with impunity, commit the most revolting atrocities; but, again, by a vicissitude common enough among barbarous nations, or through just retribution, it often happens that he is, in turn, strangled. As to truly monarchical government, it is the worst or the best of all, depending on how it is administered.

We have noted that citizens only granted pre-eminence to one of their own kind in return for services they expected of him. These services consist in upholding the law, in seeing that justice is scrupulously observed, in opposing, by every available means, the corruption of morals, and in defending the state against its enemies. The magistrate must watch over the cultivation of land; he must ensure a plentiful supply of food for the people, and encourage industry and commerce; he is like a permanent sentinel whose task it is to be ever watchful of neighbouring states, and of the movements of the enemies of the state. We require of him that, with foresight and prudence, he should in time establish relationships, and choose allies that are most favourable to the interests he is pursuing. From even so brief an exposition, we can see what detailed knowledge each of these tasks demands. To this should be added a profound study of the characteristics of the country that the magistrate must govern, and a thorough knowledge of the genius of the nation, since, if he errs out of ignorance, the sovereign is held to be as guilty as he would be if he erred out of malice: the former are faults committed out of laziness, the latter are the vices of the heart; but the evil that results is the same for society.

Princes, sovereigns and kings are not, then, clothed in supreme authority in order that they may immerse themselves with impunity in debauchery and luxury. They have not been raised above their fellow-citizens so that, in their pride, they may vaunt themselves in self-representation, and insult, scornfully, simple morality, poverty, and misery. They are not the heads of the state in order that they may keep about them a pack of wasters whose idleness and uselessness encourage every vice. The bad practices of monarchical government stem from many different causes, whose source is the character of the sovereign. So a prince with a weakness for women will allow himself to be ruled by his mistresses and his favourites. These latter, abusing the power that they exercise over the prince's mind, will make use of this influence in order to commit injustice, to protect those devoid of morals, to sell public offices, and other such misdemeanours. If the prince, out of idleness, delivers the helm of state into mercenary hands, by which I mean his ministers, one of them will steer to the right, the other to the left. No one will follow an overall plan, and each minister will overturn what he finds, however good it is, in order to become a creator of novelties, and to realise his own fantasies, to the detriment, often, of the public good. Subsequent ministers will, in turn, hurry to reverse these arrangements, with no more constancy than their predecessors, only too happy to be considered as creative.

Thus, this sequence of changes and variations allows no project time to put down roots. From this there arises confusion, disorder, and every vice of a bad administration. Its corrupt apologists have a ready excuse, by means of which they disguise the evil of these perpetual changes. And, since such ministers are content if no one is looking into their conduct, they are very careful not to set an example by dealing severely with their subordinates. Men are attached only to what belongs to them; the state does not belong to these ministers; they have not truly, therefore, its welfare at heart; everything is done without any sense of commitment, or with a kind of stoical indifference, from which stems the decline of justice, of the financial position, and of the military. This government, formerly monarchical, has degenerated into a veritable aristocracy, where the ministers and the generals direct matters according to their whims, at which point there is no longer any overall system; everyone follows his own notions, and the central point, the unifying point, is lost. Just as all the springs of a watch work together to the same end, which is that of measuring time, so the springs of government must be wound up in the same way, so that all the different parts of the administration work together equally for the greater good of the state, an important objective of which one must never lose sight. Besides, the personal interests of ministers and generals are usually wholly opposed to one another, and sometimes prevent the implementation of a better policy, because the individual minister or general did not propose it himself. But the evil reaches its zenith if some perverse souls manage to persuade the sovereign that his interests are different from those of his subjects, at which point, without knowing why, the sovereign becomes the enemy of his people. He becomes, through refusing to listen, harsh, severe, and inhumane, for, since the principle from which he departs is false, its consequences must also necessarily be so. The sovereign is attached by indissoluble ties to the body of the state; consequently he himself feels, with true sympathy, all the evils that afflict his subjects, just as society suffers equally, all the misfortunes that affect its sovereign. There is only one good, which is that of the state as a whole. If the prince loses some of his provinces, he is no longer in a position to help his subjects to the extent he could in the past; if misfortune has forced him to contract debts, it is the poor citizens who must repay them; if, however, the people are few in number, if they are sunk in misery, the sovereign is deprived of every resource. These are truths so incontestable that there is no need to dwell on them further.

So, to recapitulate, the sovereign represents the state; he and his people form a single body, which can only be happy in so far as concord unites them. The prince is to the people he governs what the head is to the body: he must see, think, and act on behalf of the whole community if he is to procure for it all the benefits that it might enjoy. If one chooses to prefer monarchical to republican government, the verdict for the sovereign is clear: he must be active and honourable, and must summon all his strength to fulfil the task that is required of him. The following are my ideas as to the nature of his duties.

He must acquire a precise and a detailed knowledge of the strengths and weaknesses of his country, its financial resources and its population, its economy, its trade, its law, and the character of the nation he is to govern. Its laws, if they are to be good laws, must be clearly drafted, so that manipulative litigants can neither turn them to their own advantage nor use the letter rather than the spirit of the law to determine the fortunes of individuals arbitrarily and irregularly. Legal procedures must be as brief as possible, in order to avoid ruin for litigants who would otherwise spend in needless costs what, in justice and in good law, is no more than their due. This aspect of government cannot be watched over too closely, in order that every possible barrier be put in place against the greed of judges and excessive self-interest on the part of lawyers. Every person must be held to their duties by visitations that take place from time to time in the provinces, where anyone who believes himself injured may bring his complaint before the commission, and where corrupt officials must be severely punished. It is perhaps superfluous to add that the punishment should never exceed what the crime merits, that violence should never be used in the place of law, and that it is better that a sovereign be too indulgent than too severe. Because any individual who does not act out of principle behaves inconsistently, it is especially important that the magistrate, who watches over the well-being of the people, should act according to an established system, whether in politics, war, finance, commerce, or law. For example, a mild and biddable people does not need severe laws, but laws that are consistent with its character. The underlying rationale of these systems must always be the greater good of society; the principles ought in each case to suit the situation of the country, its long-established customs, if those are good, and the genius of the nation.

In politics, for example, it is a well-known fact that the most obvious, and therefore the best, allies are those whose interests coincide with ours, but who are not such close neighbours that we find ourselves involved in discussion with them as to our different interests. Sometimes bizarre events give rise to unexpected alliances. We have seen in our time nations who have always been rivals, and even enemies, and who yet march under the same flag; but such cases rarely occur and will never serve as examples. The latter alliances can never be anything but temporary, whereas the former, entered into for mutual benefit, are the only alliances that are likely to last. In the situation in which Europe finds itself today, all the princes have armed forces, some of them pre-eminent powers with the capability of crushing the weak. Prudence demands, in this situation, that alliances should be formed with other powers, either to secure support in case of attack, or to check the dangerous projects of enemies, or to support, with the aid of these allies, justified claims against opponents. But this is not enough; we must have eyes and ears among our neighbours, and above all among our enemies, who will report faithfully what they have seen and heard. Men are wicked; we must above all guard against being taken by surprise, since everything that takes us by surprise discountenances and alarms us, something that never happens when we are prepared, however troubling the event we are expecting. European politics are so deceptive that the best informed can be duped, if they are not always alert and on guard.

Military doctrine must also be based on principles that are sound and founded on experience. This requires knowledge of the genius of the nation, its capabilities, and of how far its economy should be risked in taking on the enemy. Nowadays we are prevented from using the practices of the Greeks and the Romans in warfare. The discovery of gunpowder has completely changed warfare. Victory now depends upon superior firepower. Military exercises, rules, and tactics have been recast in order to conform to this situation, and recently the massive use of large amounts of artillery that encumber armies forces us in turn to adopt this system, both to maintain our own positions and to attack the enemy's, if important considerations demand it. In other words, these many new refinements have changed the art of war so fundamentally that nowadays it would be unpardonably bold for a general, imitating leaders such as Turenne, Condé, or Luxembourg, to risk entering into a battle following the dispositions that those great generals made in their day.[3] In those times victories were achieved by courage and strength; now the artillery decides everything, and the skill of the general consists in making his troops approach the enemy without being destroyed before beginning to attack it. In order to secure this advantage, he must silence the guns of the enemy through his own superior firepower. But one thing that will remain permanent and unchanging in the art of war is *castramétrie*, the art, that is, of dominating the largest part of a given terrain to one's advantage. If further new discoveries are made, the generals of the day will have to take account of these new factors and make changes to our strategy where correction is needed.

There are states which, given their location and their constitution, are, inevitably, maritime powers. These include England, Holland, France, Spain, and Denmark. They are surrounded by sea, and the distant colonies that they possess require them to have ships, in order to maintain communication and commerce between the mother country and her distant dominions. There are other states, such as Austria, Poland, Prussia, and even Russia, some of which could dispense with a navy. Others, still, would commit an unforgiveable political error if they divided their armed forces in order to deploy at sea resources of which they have a vital need on land. The size of the armed forces that a state maintains must be in proportion to the resources of its enemies; they must be equal in strength, or the weaker is in danger of being worsted. We may object, perhaps, that the prince must count on the help of his allies. This would be possible, if the allies were as they ought to be; but their enthusiasm may only be lukewarm, and it would certainly be a mistake to count on others rather than on oneself. If frontiers are so situated that they can be protected by fortifications, these must, at all costs, be built, and no effort should be spared in making them perfect. France has set an example of this, and has on various occasions profited from it.

But neither political nor military affairs can prosper if the public finances are not managed in the best possible way, and if the prince himself neither practises economy nor is prudent. Money is like a magic wand, which can work wonders. Grand political schemes, the upkeep of the armed forces, the best intentions for the relief of the people, all of these remain dormant if there is no money to bring them to life. The thrift of the sovereign is all the more likely to be useful to the public good, because if he has insufficient funds in reserve, either to finance a war without burdening the people with excessive taxation, or to come to the aid of citizens in times of calamity, then all these costs fall on his subjects, who find themselves penniless in times of misfortune when they have the greatest need of help. No government can do without taxation; whether it be republican or monarchical, it has the same need. It is essential that the official in charge of all public works should have enough to live on, that the judges be paid, so as to prevent them from corruption, and that the soldiery be provided for, so that it commits no violence for lack of the means of subsistence. It is necessary, too, that the people appointed to manage the public finances should be sufficiently well rewarded, so that they are not obliged, through need, to deal with public money improperly. These various expenditures require considerable sums of money, to which must be added some monies put aside annually for exceptional circumstances. Note, however, that these charges are something that must necessarily be borne by the people. The great art lies in raising these funds without trampling on the citizens. For taxes to be equitable and not arbitrary, there must be registers of property or cadastres, which, if they are correctly drawn up, impose the charges proportionately, according to the means of individuals. This is very necessary, because it would be an unforgiveable financial error if taxes, maladroitly apportioned, were to discourage the farmer from working; he must, after paying his dues, still be able to live in some comfort, he and his family. Far from oppressing the foster-fathers of the state, we should be encouraging them to cultivate their land properly; therein lies the true wealth of the country. The land produces our most essential food supplies, and those who work it are, as we have already said, the true foster-fathers of our society.

It may be objected, perhaps, that Holland subsists without its land providing it with even a hundredth part of what it consumes. My answer to this objection is that it is a very small state, where commerce makes up for agriculture; but the more extensive a government is, the more the rural economy needs to be encouraged.

Indirect, or excise, taxes are another kind of tax that is levied on towns. They need to be handled skilfully in order not to weigh too heavily upon the provisions most necessary for life, such as bread, small beer, meat, etc., that most affect soldiers, working men, and craftsmen. Otherwise it would follow, to the detriment of the people, that labour costs would rise, as a result of which goods would become so expensive that sales abroad would be lost. This is what is happening now in Holland and in England. These two nations, having contracted immense debts during the recent wars, have created new taxes in order to pay the interest on the debts. But since, by their clumsiness, they have weighed down their workforce, they have almost destroyed their industry. Hence, with the high prices in Holland being further increased, these republicans are having their bedlinen made in Verviers and Liège, and England has lost its considerable sales of wool in Germany. In order to make good such damage, the sovereign must often reflect on the condition of the poor, put himself in the place of a peasant or of a handworker, and say to himself, 'If I had been born into that class of citizen, whose capital is the work of their hands, what would I want from the sovereign?' It is the sovereign's duty then to put into practice what good sense tells him. There are, within most of the states of Europe, provinces where the peasants, tied to the land, are the serfs of the gentry, their masters; this is the most unfortunate of all conditions, and the one that most disgusts humanity. It is certainly the case that no man was born to be the slave of his fellow men. We detest, and reasonably, such abuses, and we believe that all that is necessary to abolish this barbarous custom is our wish to do so. But this is not so, for the custom derives from ancient contracts agreed between the possessors of land and those who work it. Agriculture depends on the services rendered by the peasantry; in wishing to abolish at a stroke this abominable system, we would entirely overturn the agricultural economy, and it would be necessary to compensate the nobility, in part, for the loss of revenues it would suffer.

We come next to the question, no less important, of industry and commerce. If a country is to continue to flourish, it is above all necessary that the balance of trade should be to its advantage: if it pays out more for imports than it earns through exports, it is inevitable that it will, from year to year, become impoverished. Imagine a purse that contains one hundred ducats. If every day you take from it one ducat, and put nothing back, at the end of a hundred days the purse will, as you will agree, be empty. Here are the ways of preventing this loss: make manufactured goods from all the raw materials that you possess, put foreign materials to work in order to gain the cost of labour, and work at low cost in order to secure overseas sales. As for trade, it depends on three things: on the excess of your own commodities, which you export; on the commodities of your neighbours, from which you profit by selling them; and on the foreign goods that you need and that you import. It is on these products that we have just mentioned that the commerce of a state must depend; this is what it is capable of, in the nature of things. England, Holland, France, Spain, and Portugal have possessions in the two Indies, and have more extensive resources, thanks to their mercantile marines, than have the other kingdoms. To make the most of the advantages one has, and to undertake nothing that is beyond one's powers—such is the counsel of wisdom.

It remains for us to speak of the best means of maintaining, without fail, the abundance of food supplies, of which society has an indispensable need if it is to flourish. The first requirement is to ensure good cultivation of the land, the reclamation of all the areas that are capable of yield, and an increase in the number of cattle in order to ensure more milk, butter, cheese, and manure. We must, moreover, keep an exact record of the number of bushels of different kinds of grain, harvested in good, mediocre, and bad years. We must deduct consumption from this total, and, from this result, ascertain what is superfluous (the export of which must be permitted), or what is lacking, and which needs to be procured. Every sovereign who is committed to the public good must ensure that the granaries are plentifully supplied, in order to make up for a poor harvest and to prevent famine. We have observed in Germany, after the poor harvests of 1771 and 1772, the misfortunes that Saxony and the provinces of the empire suffered because such a necessary precaution had been overlooked. The people were reduced to grinding oak bark, which served them as a foodstuff. This wretched food hastened their death; a number of families, unaided, perished; there was universal devastation. Others, pale, ashen, and emaciated, fled their country, to seek help elsewhere. Such a sight aroused compassion; a heart of stone would have been touched by it. How the officials concerned must have reproached themselves on seeing these calamities without being able to offer any remedy!

We now move on to another matter, which is perhaps equally interesting. There are few countries whose the citizens all hold similar views on religion; their views are often entirely divergent; some of them form themselves into what are called 'sects'. So, the question arises: must all citizens think the same way, or may each citizen be permitted to think as he pleases? There are, as to the first, grave politicians who will say to you, 'Everybody must be of the same opinion, so that there is no dispute among the citizenry.' Whereupon, the theologian opines, 'Whoever does not think as I do is damned, and it is not proper that my sovereign should be king of the damned; they must, then, be roasted in this world, so that they fare all the better in the next.' To which we can only reply that in no society does everyone think alike; that most Christian nations ascribe to God human attributes; that most Catholic nations are idolatrous, because no peasant—I am wholly persuaded of this—knows the difference between the exalted adoration of the Holy Trinity and the worship of the Virgin Mary; he adores in good faith whatever image he invokes.[4] There are, in other words, in every Christian sect, a number of heretics; everyone, moreover, believes what seems to him to be probable. You can compel, by violence, some poor wretch to repeat a certain form of words that, in his heart, he does not agree with; in other words, the persecutor has gained nothing. But, if we return to the early origins of society, it would appear that the sovereign has no right to determine the thinking of his subjects. One would have to be insane to imagine that men have ever said to a fellow man, 'We are raising you above ourselves, because we like to be slaves, and we are giving you the power to direct, as you will, our thoughts.' On the contrary, they said, 'We need you to uphold the laws we wish to obey, to govern us wisely, and to defend us; we demand of you, moreover, that you respect our freedom.' The verdict, here, is clear, and cannot be appealed; and this tolerance, moreover, is so favourable to the society in which it is established that it ensures the good fortune of the state. Once every form of worship is tolerated, everything is peaceful; whereas persecution has given rise to the bloodiest, the longest, and the most destructive civil wars. The least of the evils of persecution is to cause the persecuted to emigrate; there have been in France provinces whose population has suffered from, and which still feel the effects of, the revocation of the Edict of Nantes.[5]

These are, in general, the duties that a prince must fulfil. If he is never to fall short in them, he must recall, often, that, like the least of his subjects, he is a man; if he is the highest judge, the most senior general, the foremost financier, or the first minister of the land, this is not merely in order to represent these positions, but so that he may fulfil the relevant duties. He is no more than the first servant of the state, obliged to act with probity, with wisdom, and with total disinterest, as if at any moment he were to be held to account for his administration by his subjects. He is guilty, therefore, if he squanders the people's money, the revenues from tax, on luxury, ostentation, and dissolute living: he, whose duty it is to uphold the morality that is the guardian of law, whose duty it is to improve the nation's education, and not to pervert it by bad example. One of his most important tasks is the preservation, in its entirety, of morality. The sovereign can contribute a great deal to this by recognising and rewarding those citizens who have acted virtuously, while holding in contempt those whose depravity and disgraceful behaviour no longer causes them even to blush. The prince must roundly condemn every dishonest and ignoble act, and withhold recognition from those who are incorrigible. There is yet another interesting matter of which we must not lose sight, and which, if it were to be neglected, would do irreparable harm to public morality: this is when the prince gives too much recognition to people who lack merit but possess great wealth. Such honours, inappropriately bestowed, confirm the public in the popular prejudice that, in order to receive public recognition, it is enough to be rich. Whereupon, self-interest and greed loosen the bridle that was restraining these people; everyone wants to accumulate wealth; they resort to shameful ways of acquiring it; corruption prevails, takes root, and becomes widespread; men with talent, men of virtue, are despised, and the public respects only those bastard sons of Midas, whose extravagance and ostentation dazzle it.[6] To protect the morals of the nation from such perversity and excess the prince must always take care to honour only personal merit, and to display nothing but contempt for opulence without morals or virtue. Moreover, since the sovereign is, properly speaking, the head of a family made up of citizens, since he is the father of his people, he must on every occasion serve as a last refuge for the unfortunate, he must be a father to orphans, must help and comfort widows, must have as much compassion for the merest wretch as for the foremost courtier, and must distribute alms to those who are deprived of all help, and can be assisted only through his benevolence.

The foregoing follows the principles we established at the beginning of this essay, and sets out precisely the notion we must have of the duties of a sovereign, and of the only way in which monarchical government can be good and beneficial. If a number of princes conduct themselves differently, we must attribute this to their lack of reflection on their position and on the duties that derive from it. They carry a burden whose weight and importance they do not recognise, and they go astray for want of knowledge, for, in our times, ignorance is responsible for more errors than is wickedness. This sketch of a sovereign will, perhaps, appear to critics to be the model laid down by the Stoics, the idea of the sage which the Stoics imagined, who never existed, and whom only Marcus Aurelius came close to embodying.[7] We would like to think that this feeble essay would be capable of creating more Marcus Aureliuses; this would be the finest reward that we could expect, and one that would at the same time be a benefit to humanity. We must nevertheless add, that a prince who followed the laborious course of action that we have set out would never attain total perfection, because, with the best will in the world, he could be mistaken in his choice of those he employed to administer public business; because matters could be presented to him in a false light; because his orders would not be implemented faithfully; because wrongdoing would be covered up in order that it would not come to the prince's notice; because his employees would be harsh, headstrong, and too unbending and arrogant in their management of affairs; and finally because, in a large country, the prince cannot be everywhere. Such, therefore, is, and will be, our destiny here below, that we will never attain that degree of perfection that the happiness of nations demands, and that, when it comes to government, as to everything else, we must content ourselves with what is least imperfect.

ACKNOWLEDGEMENTS

This project could only come to fruition thanks to the generous support of the recently established Research Center Sanssouci, based next to Frederick's palaces at the Sanssouci Park and funded by the University of Potsdam and the foundation running the formerly royal palaces and gardens, Stiftung Preußische Schlösser und Gärten Berlin-Brandenburg (SPSG). I am grateful to its directors, Iwan-Michelangelo D'Aprile of the University of Potsdam and Jürgen Luh of the SPSG, for their keen interest in this endeavour and their encouragement.

Angela Scholar brought her substantial experience of translating eighteenth-century French prose to bear on Frederick's complex writings. Her dedication to the task and meticulous work deserve a very large measure of gratitude. The translator herself would like to thank Michael Scholar, her husband and amanuensis, and her sons, Tom, Richard, and John Scholar, for their support during her work on the translation.

A grant from the REF Strategic Fund of the Humanities Division at the University of Oxford enabled Shiru Lim to conduct a final round of comparison between the translation and the original texts. I am very grateful to her for the eagle-eyed perusal of the texts, and to Julia Smith and Hollie Press at Oxford's History Faculty for all their help. A grant from Magdalen College, Oxford, funded the indexing.

Nicholas Cronk, Anthony La Vopa, John Robertson, and Hamish Scott, as well as the reviewers for Princeton University Press, all provided indispensable comments on an earlier draft of the Introduction. Their generous feedback has substantially improved the piece, as well as the project as a whole.

I was fortunate enough to work on this edition in close collaboration with the Voltaire Foundation at Oxford. My colleagues at this unique editorial and research centre—especially Nicholas Cronk and Gillian Pink—were exceptionally helpful with material concerning Voltaire, Frederick's intellectual interlocutor over more than forty years. Ruggero Sciuto assisted me with comments concerning the Baron d'Holbach.

An embryonic version of the ideas explored in the Introduction was presented in April 2018 at the annual Quentin Skinner Lecture in Modern Intellectual History at the University of Cambridge. The subsequent discussion of Frederick and his works contributed significantly to my work on this edition. For their comments and queries, I am particularly grateful to Thomas Biskup, Richard Bourke, Tim Hochstrasser, Andrew Kahn, Shiru Lim, Isaac Nakhimovsky, Jürgen Overhoff, Michael Sonenscher, and—last but not in any way least—Quentin Skinner, who endowed the series and provided invaluable advice.

Ben Tate at Princeton University Press supported this project from its inception with useful advice, great enthusiasm, and constant encouragement. I am deeply grateful to Ben for all his help. For the smooth production of the edition, I would like to thank Nathan Carr and Francis Eaves.

AVI LIFSCHITZ, DECEMBER 2019

NOTES

1. DISSERTATION ON THE INNOCENCE
OF ERRORS OF THE MIND

Frederick composed this text in summer 1738 after reading Voltaire's *Éléments de la philosophie de Newton*, which had appeared a few months earlier. The crown prince sent a copy to Voltaire on 30 September 1738, accompanied by a letter on the epistemological ramifications of Newton's worldview (Letter D1621 in *OCV* 89:304–7). He chose not to publish the *Dissertation*: it was first printed in vol. 6 of Frederick's *Œuvres posthumes*, ed. Jean Charles Thibault de Laveaux (Berlin: Voss and Decker, 1788). The text is translated from *OFG* 8:33–50.

1. Philante is a figure in *Les Caractères, ou Les Moeurs de ce siècle* (1688) by Jean de La Bruyère (1645–96), a collection of maxims and moral portraits inspired by an ancient treatise by Theophrastus. Frederick possessed at least three different editions of La Bruyère's work.
2. Nicolaus Copernicus (1473–1543), the renowned Renaissance astronomer whose heliocentric theory in *De revolutionibus orbium coelestium* (*On the Revolutions of the Heavenly Spheres*, 1543) offered an alternative to Ptolemaic astronomy. Voltaire saw Copernicus as a forerunner of Newton, and called Frederick 'un prince copernicien' (a Copernican prince) early on in their correspondence (Voltaire to Frederick, April 1738, in *OFG* 21:219). Tycho Brahe (1546–1601) was a renowned observer of planetary motions. His 'errors' consisted in attempting to combine Copernicus's insights with elements of the geocentric Ptolemaic system.
3. Joshua 10:12–13.
4. The notion that the inhabitants of Malabar (in south-western India) calculated correctly the orbits of planets while assuming that the sun revolved around a local mountain is usually traced back to the so-called *Malabar Correspondence*. It is based on questions by the Protestant missionaries Bartholomäus Ziegenbalg (1682–1719) and Johann Ernst Gründler (1677–1720), followed by the replies of indigenous correspondents. Ninety-nine letters were included in the volumes of the *Halle Reports* (*Hallesche Berichte*, 1714 and 1717), which were quickly translated into English and French.
5. A reference to a maze-like structure of King Minos of Crete. According to Greek mythology, at its centre lay the mighty minotaur (a creature combining the features of a man and a bull). When the Athenian Theseus attempted to slay the minotaur, Minos's daughter Ariadne provided him with a thread to trace his route within the labyrinth so as to find safely his way out.

6. This is actually a quotation from Virgil, *Georgics* II.490: 'Blessed is he who has succeeded in learning the laws of nature's working': Virgil, *Eclogues. Georgics. Aeneid: Books I–VI*, trans. H. Rushton Fairclough, revised by G. P. Goold, Loeb Classical Library (Cambridge, MA: Harvard University Press, 2014), 170–71. Frederick admired the Epicurean poet Lucretius throughout his life.

7. A reference to debates over the preceding decades between modernisers of ancient atomic theory such as Pierre Gassendi (1592–1655), adherents of the physics of René Descartes (1596–1650), and the followers of Isaac Newton (1643–1727). Frederick and Voltaire counted themselves among the last group.

8. *Le moine bourru*, a wandering ghost of a monk, was a popular figure in early modern French folklore, especially in the Advent season.

9. Icarus was the son of Daedalus, the craftsman who built King Minos's labyrinth in Crete (see note 5 above). Minos imprisoned Daedalus and his son in the labyrinth for assisting Ariadne and Theseus in slaying the minotaur. Both father and son managed to escape the maze, using wings of wax fashioned by Daedalus. Not heeding his father's advice, Icarus flew too close to the sun: his wings melted and he drowned in the sea below.

10. It is not known whether the ancient sceptic Pyrrho of Elis (c.360–c.270 BC) was connected to Aristotle's Lyceum in Athens.

11. Plato's Academy in Athens became, at a later stage, a centre of radical scepticism, which Pierre Bayle distinguished from more moderate Pyrrhonism: *Dictionnaire historique et critique*, 5th edn (Amsterdam, Leiden, The Hague, and Utrecht, 1740), 731–36. See Frederick's preface to an edition of Bayle's *Dictionary* in this volume (pp. 125–28).

12. This group of mythological heroes, named after their ship, the *Argo*, accompanied Jason to Colchis in the Caucasus in search of the Golden Fleece.

13. Pharamond, a legendary Frankish king of the early Middle Ages, was the protagonist of a chivalric novel by La Calprenède, *Faramond, ou L'histoire de France* (7 vols, 1661–70) and of the theatre play *Pharamond* (1736) by Louis de Cahusac, a copy of which Frederick possessed. Roland is the hero of the medieval epic poem *Chanson de Roland*, probably composed between 1040 and 1115. Amadis and Gandalin are figures in the fourteenth-century Spanish chivalric romance *Amadís de Gaula*. (See also *Anti-Machiavel*, chapter VIII, p. 30. (Page numbers given for *Anti-Machiavel* in these notes refer to the translation in this volume.)

14. For another reference to David's character, see *Anti-Machiavel*, chapter XIX, p. 55. Frederick admired the entry on the biblical king in Pierre Bayle's *Dictionnaire historique et critique* of 1697 (see his letter to Voltaire, 25 November 1765, *OCV* 113:416–18). Bayle's article on David was included in the collection of entries from his work, to which Frederick wrote a preface (see pp. 125–28 of this volume).

2. ANTI-MACHIAVEL, OR A STUDY OF MACHIAVELLI'S *THE PRINCE*

Frederick's *Anti-Machiavel* originated in the intensive correspondence he conducted as crown prince with Voltaire. In early 1738, Voltaire sent Frederick a few chapters of his work in progress *Le Siècle de Louis XIV* (begun in 1732, published in 1751). Frederick replied that while he was enchanted by the account, Machiavelli should be struck off its list of great authors. In March 1739, Frederick informed Voltaire that he was thinking of composing a work on Machiavelli's *The Prince*; Voltaire strongly encouraged the crown prince to embark on the project. In December 1739, Frederick sent Voltaire the first twelve chapters of his refutation of Machiavelli. Although uncertain about the benefits of publishing the work, in April 1740 Frederick entrusted the *Anti-Machiavel* to Voltaire, who went on to commission a publisher in The Hague. After his accession to the throne (31 May 1740), Frederick changed his mind and ordered Voltaire to withdraw the manuscript from the publisher; Voltaire replied that he could not stop the press. The first edition was published in September 1740 by Van Duren in The Hague and Mayer in London, including only some of Voltaire's modifications, which were meant to temper the vehemence of Frederick's attacks on the church and foreign powers. Voltaire published the revised version a few weeks later in The Hague with a competitor of Van Duren; in the nineteenth century, a manuscript version was discovered in Berlin and published by J.D.E. Preuß. The translated text follows the original edition, which was the most widely reprinted, translated, and read version of the *Anti-Machiavel* in eighteenth-century Europe (*OFG* 8:65–184).

1. Nero (37–68), who arranged the murder of his mother Agrippina and forced his tutor Seneca to commit suicide, eventually took his own life following a military rebellion. Caligula (12–41) was murdered by the Praetorian Guard following a reign that became identified with arbitrary and cruel government. Usually regarded as a less corrupt emperor, Tiberius (42 BC–AD 37, successor to Augustus) was still portrayed in negative terms by Tacitus and Suetonius. More positively described by ancient historians were Titus (39–81), especially praised for his apt and generous response to an eruption of Vesuvius and a large fire in Rome (in 79 and 80); Trajan (53–117), who led military expansion while implementing philanthropic social programmes in the empire; and Antoninus (or Antoninus Pius, 86–161), renowned for his peaceful and effective rule.
2. The title in Machiavelli's *The Prince*: 'How many forms of principalities there are, and how they are acquired'.
3. The title in Machiavelli's *The Prince*: 'Of hereditary principalities'.
4. Francis I (Franz I Stephan, 1708–65), Holy Roman Emperor from 1745 until his death, was forced in 1737 to exchange the Duchy of Lorraine for the

Grand Duchy of Tuscany as part of the terms concluding the War of the Polish Succession (1733–35). The former king of Poland, Stanisław Leszczyński, became duke of Lorraine (see also pp. 20, 30, 42 of this text). Frederick refers here to the citizens' affection for Francis's father, Leopold of Lorraine (1679–1729). As crown prince of Brandenburg-Prussia, Frederick avidly followed the War of the Polish Succession. He provides detailed accounts of the war in his historical writings, and refers to it profusely in this text.

5. The title in Machiavelli's *The Prince*: 'Of mixed principalities'.

6. Pope Alexander VI (Rodrigo Borgia, 1431–1503) was usually held as a paragon of nepotism and libertinism for fathering children by different mistresses and using the papacy to pursue familial gain, partly through his support of the military campaigns of his son, Cesare Borgia (1475–1507). Machiavelli's frequent references to the latter as a ruthless 'new prince' account for Frederick's recurrent condemnations. Galeazzo Maria Sforza (1444–76), duke of Milan from 1466, renowned as a patron of the arts and for his cruel manner of governing, was assassinated by three aristocrats; Ludovico Sforza (1452–1508), duke of Milan from 1494, was captured by the French in Novara in 1500; the houses of York and Lancaster fought over the English throne in the Wars of the Roses of the fifteenth century.

7. Stanisław Leszczyński (1677–1766) was imposed by Charles XII of Sweden in 1704 on the Polish nobility as king of Poland, but lost the crown in 1709 once Sweden was defeated by Russia at the battle of Poltava. Stanisław was crowned again in 1733 with French support (his daughter was married to Louis XV), only to be deposed during the War of the Polish Succession (1733–35), becoming duke of Lorraine as part of the peace settlement. (See note 4 above.)

8. The title in Machiavelli's *The Prince*: 'Why the kingdom of Darius, conquered by Alexander, did not rebel after Alexander's death against his successors'.

9. Armand Jean du Plessis, cardinal de Richelieu (1585–1642) served as chief minister to Louis XIII of France from 1624 until his death. He was succeeded in this role by Cardinal Jules Mazarin (or Mazzarino/Mazzarini, 1602–61), who served as chief minister to Louis XIII and the young Louis XIV from 1642 to 1661. The early modern French parlements were provincial appellate and administrative courts rather than legislative bodies. Among their responsibilities was the official registration of new laws in their respective provinces, which they sometimes used as occasions to express disagreement with the crown (via 'remonstrances').

10. The title in Machiavelli's *The Prince*: 'How one should govern cities or principalities, which used to live under their own laws before being conquered'.

11. The title in Machiavelli's *The Prince*: 'Of new states, acquired by one's own arms and force'.

12. All traditionally regarded as creators of new polities: Moses, lawgiver of ancient Israel; Cyrus II of Persia (c.590–530BC), founder of the Achaemenid

empire; Romulus and Remus, mythical founders of Rome; Theseus, founder-hero of Athens; Hiero II (c.303–215 BC), king of Syracuse.

13. Muhammad (c.570–632), founder of Islam; Manco Cápac, founder and ruler of Inca civilisation according to chronicles and myths, probably in the thirteenth century; Odin (Wodan), a major god in Germanic and Norse mythology.

14. The Jesuit settlements (or 'reductions') for indigenous peoples in Paraguay had become, by the eighteenth century, semi-autonomous and economically successful, before the expulsion of the Jesuits from the Spanish empire in 1767. Their relative independence was also mocked by Voltaire in *Candide, ou l'optimisme* (1759).

15. John of Leiden (1509–36), a millenarian Anabaptist leader, proclaimed himself king of Münster in 1534. Following a siege of the town, he was captured and tortured to death.

16. Oliver Cromwell (1599–1658), lord protector of the Commonwealth of England, Scotland, and Ireland from 1653 to 1658, following the execution of King Charles I and the establishment of a commonwealth in 1649. In 1658–59 Cromwell was succeeded as lord protector by his son Richard (1626–1712), who lost the confidence of the army and was forced to resign before the restoration of the monarchy under Charles II in 1660.

17. Sabbatai Zevi (1626–76) declared himself the Jewish messiah and led a messianic movement in the Ottoman empire. He eventually converted to Islam.

18. Pepin the Short (c.714–68) forced the last Merovingian king, Childeric III, into exile in a monastery and proclaimed himself in 751 king of the Franks, thereby establishing the Carolingian dynasty. Henri I, duke of Guise (1550–88), was the founder of the Catholic League that tried to thwart the accession of the Protestant Henry of Navarre to the French throne (as Henri IV); King Henri III arranged the duke's assassination in December 1588.

19. Hiero II (c.306–215 BC), was tyrant of Syracuse in Sicily from c.270 to 215 BC.

20. John III Sobieski (1629–96) was elected king of Poland in 1674, following several military victories; Gustav Vasa (1496–1560) became king of Sweden in 1523, after leading a rebellion against Denmark. The Antonines were the Roman emperors Antoninus Pius (r. 138–61) and his successor Marcus Aurelius (r. 161–80), although the epithet was sometimes extended to earlier or later emperors. Antoninus Pius and Marcus Aurelius, whose reigns were characterised by relative peace and prosperity, were among the 'five good emperors' of the Nerva-Antonine dynasty (see also note 1 above). Frederick frequently modelled himself in public after Marcus Aurelius, renowned for composing the *Meditations*, a compilation of reflections along Stoic lines.

21. The title in Machiavelli's *The Prince*: 'Of new principalities, acquired through the arms and fortune of others'.

22. François de Salignac de La Mothe-Fénelon (1651–1715), a French arch-bishop, theologian, and royal tutor, author of *Télémaque*, a didactic novel (see the Introduction to this volume (hereafter 'Introduction'), pp. xxiii–xxiv).

23. Augustus II 'the Strong' (1670–1733), elector of Saxony and king of Poland, whose death triggered the War of the Polish Succession (1733–35). Known for his physical prowess and numerous children, many of whom were born out of wedlock.

24. Jacques-Bénigne Bossuet (1627–1704), bishop of Meaux, court preacher to Louis XIV and apologist for absolutist monarchy by divine grace, renowned for his sermons (see Introduction, pp. xxi–xxii); Esprit Fléchier (1632–1710), bishop of Nîmes and eloquent author of sermons and panegyrics; Pliny the Younger (61–c.113), Roman magistrate and author who composed orations praising the Emperor Trajan.

25. The title in Machiavelli's *The Prince*: 'Of those who have acquired a principal-ity by wickedness.'

26. Agathocles (361/360–289 BC), was the son of a potter who seized control of Syracuse and ruled it tyrannically after a coup; Oliverotto Euffreducci (da Fermo, c.1475–1502), a military leader (*condottiero*) and Cesare Borgia's sometime accomplice, was murdered by the latter in Senigallia alongside other former allies.

27. Figures in the early modern chivalric romances *Amadís de Gaula* and *Orlando Furioso*. Frederick possessed French editions of both books and read them as a child.

28. Voltaire argued, in his *Histoire de Charles XII* (1731), that the adventurous Swedish king was inspired by Quintus Curtius's first-century account of Alex-ander the Great; Frederick makes a similar assertion in his own account of Charles XII (*OFG* 7:84). Abdolonymus (or Abdalonymus) was made king of Sidon by Alexander the Great, an episode compared by Frederick to the eighteenth-century installation of Stanisław Leszczyński on the Polish throne (see note 7 above). At the battle of Gaugamela or Arbela (331 BC) Alexander the Great defeated Achaemenid Persia; the battle of Poltava (July 1709) sig-nalled Sweden's decline as a great European power, due to Charles XII's de-feat by Peter I of Russia.

29. Probably a reference to *Cartouche, or the Robbers* (1722), the English version of a popular French comedy of the previous year by Marc-Antoine Legrand (1673–1728).

30. In the Sicilian Vespers, an uprising at Easter 1282 against Charles of Anjou, Si-cilian rebels massacred his French troops. During the French Wars of Religion, Protestant (Huguenot) leaders were assassinated on the eve of St Bartholomew's day, 23–24 August 1572, alongside thousands of their co-religionists.

31. Dionysius I of Syracuse (c.430–367 BC), who assumed power in a coup, was renowned for his violent and cruel manner of government. Louis XI of France

(1423–83) became a symbol of intense diplomatic activities and subterfuge; Ivan II Vasilyevich (1530–84) was the Russian tsar commonly known as Ivan the Terrible. For Tiberius and Nero, see note 1 above.

32. The title in Machiavelli's *The Prince*: 'Of the civil principality'.

33. The title in Machiavelli's *The Prince*: 'How the strengths of all principalities ought to be measured'.

34. An allusion to Ernst August I, duke of Saxe-Weimar (1688–1748), whose troops Frederick inspected in 1730 at Mühlberg.

35. In Greek mythology, Salmoneus, king of Elis, identified himself with Zeus (Jupiter). He had brass items tied to his chariot to create a thunder-like effect and torches thrown into the air to imitate lightning.

36. The title in Machiavelli's *The Prince*: 'Of ecclesiastical principalities'.

37. Cf. Lucretius, *De rerum natura* (*On the Nature of Things*), I.101: 'Tantum religio potuit suadere malorum' (So powerful was religion/superstition in inspiring evil deeds).

38. See note 6 above.

39. Leo X (Giovanni de' Medici, 1475–1521), pope from 1513 until his death.

40. The title in Machiavelli's *The Prince*: 'Of the different sorts of army, and of mercenary troops'.

41. Leonidas, king of Sparta, led the Greek alliance in the battle of Thermopylae against the invading Persians (480 BC).

42. Probably Frederick William I of Brandenburg-Prussia (1688–1740), Frederick's father (see Introduction, pp. ix–xii).

43. Frederick effectively criticises here the moderated phrasing in the French translation he read ('le faire sortir de ce monde'), whereas Machiavelli had clearly referred, in the original Italian, to the general's killing ('ammazzarlo'). Frederick used *Le Prince*, an edition published by Henri Desbordes in Amsterdam in 1696. Francesco Bussone, count of Carmagnola (c.1382–1432) was a military leader in the service of Milan and later Venice. He was assassinated by the Venetians when they suspected he had deliberately prolonged the wars against Milan.

44. The title in Machiavelli's *The Prince*: 'Of auxiliaries, mixed troops, and one's own'.

45. In the War of the Spanish Succession (1701–14), a frequent point of reference for Frederick.

46. Frederick IV of Denmark (1671–1730), Frederick Wilhelm I of Brandenburg-Prussia (1688–1740, Frederick II's father), and Peter I of Russia (1672–1725).

47. An allusion to Stanisław Leszczyński and the War of the Polish Succession (see note 7 above).

48. 1 Samuel 17:38–40.

49. The title in Machiavelli's *The Prince*: 'Of military matters concerning a Prince'.

50. André-Hercule de Fleury (1653–1743), a French cardinal and chief minister to Louis XV; Francisco Jiménez de Cisneros (1436–1517), a Spanish cardinal and statesman; Pope Clement XII (Lorenzo Corsini, 1652–1740).

51. Under King Gustavus Adolphus (1594–1632), Sweden became one of the great European powers, especially during the Thirty Years' War (1618–48); Henri de La Tour d'Auvergne, vicomte de Turenne (1611–75), one of France's most renowned generals in the seventeenth century, fell at the battle of Salzbach in 1675; John Churchill, first duke of Marlborough (1650–1722), was a British general and statesman who won a series of major battles in the War of the Spanish Succession (1701–14); Prince Eugene Francis of Savoy-Carignano (1663–1736) was renowned for his military prowess in Habsburg service against the Ottoman empire and, in alliance with Marlborough, against France in the War of the Spanish Succession.

52. Francis Stephen, duke of Lorraine until 1735, grand duke of Tuscany from 1737, and Holy Roman Emperor Francis I from 1745 (see note 4 above). The episode Frederick refers to took place in 1737, near Kolar in Serbia.

53. The title in Machiavelli's *The Prince*: 'Of the things for which men, and especially princes, are praised or blamed'.

54. Louis XII of France (1462–1515) was involved in the Italian wars but also famous for governing moderately with the collaboration of the estates. Domitian (51–96) is usually portrayed as a tyrant due to his frequent clashes with the Roman Senate. For Trajan, see note 1 above, and for Louis XI, note 31.

55. Pope Innocent XI (Benedetto Odescalchi, 1611–89) enacted reforms in the Vatican, including measures against nepotism. On Alexander VI, see note 6 above.

56. The title in Machiavelli's *The Prince*: 'Of generosity and meanness'.

57. Greek artists of the fifth century BC.

58. The comparison between the necessity of luxury in large states and its detrimental effects in small, usually republican polities, is also made in Voltaire's *Défense du mondain* (1737). Voltaire discussed this work with Frederick shortly before the composition of *Anti-Machiavel*. See Introduction, pp. xxvii–xxxii..

59. Francis I of France (1494–1547), renowned for fostering the French Renaissance through his generous support of the arts. At the battle of Pavia (February 1525), he suffered a major defeat by the forces of his rival Charles V, Holy Roman Emperor and king of Spain; Francis I was taken hostage and transferred to Madrid for several months.

60. Cosimo de' Medici (1389–1464), banker and statesman, established his family's prominence in Florentine politics.

61. The title in Machiavelli's *The Prince*: 'Of cruelty and clemency, and whether it is better to be loved than feared'.

62. Machiavelli quotes a passage from Virgil's *Aeneid* I.563–64: 'Res dura et regni novitas me talia cogunt / moliri, et late fines custode tueri.' ('Stern necessity and

the new estate of my kingdom force me to do such hard deeds and protect my frontiers far and wide with guards': Virgil, *Aeneid I–VI*, trans. Fairclough, 281 [see note 6 to *Dissertation on the Innocence of Errors of the Mind*, above]). The subsequent allusion is to Voltaire's successful play *Œdipe* (1718).

63. The title in Machiavelli's *The Prince*: 'How princes should keep their word.'

64. Another allusion to Voltaire's play *Œdipe* (1718), III.1: 'Un seul mot, un soupir, un coup d'œil nous trahit.' (*OCV* 1A:204).

65. Felice Peretti (1521–90), from 1585 Pope Sixtus V, was a reforming pope of the Counter-Reformation. Philip II of Spain (1527–98) was the son and heir of Charles V, and a defender and promoter of Catholicism whose rule witnessed the Dutch rebellion and the creation of an independent Dutch republic (1581), as well as the defeat of the Spanish Armada by the English fleet in 1588. For Cromwell, see note 16 above.

66. Machiavelli refers to the mythical centaur Chiron. The half-human, half-beast creature was entrusted with the nursing of Achilles and other heroes, who thereby learned to use characteristics of both natures.

67. Cartouche is the criminal protagonist of the play Frederick refers to in his chapter VIII (see note 29 above).

68. This maxim was, however, attributed by early modern historians to King John (Jean) II of France (1319–64), also 'John the Good' (Jean le Bon).

69. The venue of public executions in Paris (today Place de l'Hôtel de Ville).

70. Luis Méndez de Haro y Guzmán (1598–1661), Spanish statesman and adviser to King Philip IV; Abraham de Fabert (1599–1662), French military leader and engineer. On Mazarin, see note 9 above.

71. Probably a reference to French positions during the War of the Polish Succession (1733–35). In his *History of the House of Brandenburg*, Frederick complained that both France and Austria neglected the interests of their allies in the Treaty of Vienna (1738) which concluded the war (*OFG* 1:194).

72. The title in Machiavelli's *The Prince*: 'How princes should avoid being despised and hated.'

73. The reference is actually to Augustus II 'the Strong' (1670–1733), elector of Saxony and king of Poland: see note 23 above.

74. The Roman noblewoman Lucretia was, according to the traditional story, violently raped by the son of the last king of Rome, Lucius Tarquinius Superbus. This led to a popular rebellion, the overthrow of the monarchy, and the subsequent establishment of the Roman republic (c.510 BC).

75. On the French parlements, see note 9 above.

76. For Marcus Aurelius, see note 20 above; Gordian I (c.159–238) and Gordian II (c.192–238), father and son, ruled the Roman empire as co-regents for twenty days in 238, known as 'the year of the six emperors'.

77. Ancient historians claimed that Claudius (10 BC–AD 54) was poisoned to death by his wife Agrippina, who wished to enthrone her son Nero (on Nero

and Caligula, see note 1 above). Galba, Otho, and Vitellius succeeded one another in AD 69, 'the year of the four emperors': their reigns were all undermined by rebellions and competing claims to authority. Galba (3 BC–AD 69) was assassinated by Praetorian Guards, Otho (32–69) committed suicide, and Vitellius (15–69) was murdered by the troops of Vespasian (9–79), his successor. Didius Julianus (133/7–93), was made emperor after bribing the Praetorian Guard, and murdered shortly afterwards, in 193, 'the year of the five emperors'.

78. Constantine I ('the Great', c.272–337) disbanded and abolished the Praetorian Guard in 312 in part due to the role it had played in appointing emperors, murdering and extorting favours from potential candidates.

79. Theodosius I (347–95) consolidated the empire, overcame internal strife, and strengthened the status of Christianity as state religion in the Roman empire by abolishing pagan practices and traditions. Under Justinian I (c.482–565), the Eastern Roman empire conquered large swathes of the former Western empire from the Ostrogoths and other tribes; he commissioned the codification of Roman law in the *Corpus Iuris Civilis*.

80. Augustus (Gaius Octavius, 63 BC–AD 14), the first Roman emperor (from 27 BC) after a long civil war that effectively put an end to republican rule in Rome.

81. Commodus (161–92) was portrayed in antiquity as a despotic megalomaniac, obsessed with a cult of his own personality; he was strangled to death in his bath as part of a conspiracy to end his reign. Caracalla (188–217) was murdered by one of his soldiers at the instigation of the praetorian prefect Macrinus (c.165–218). Severus Alexander (c.208–35) was assassinated along with his mother by his troops, who hailed Maximinus Thrax (c.173–238) as emperor. The latter, a provincial of low social status, was murdered by one of his soldiers in 238, the 'year of six emperors', following a protracted conflict with the Senate and several mutinies.

82. Pupienus (c.165–238), one of the contenders for the imperial throne in the 'year of the six emperors', was assassinated by the Praetorian Guard alongside his co-regent Balbinus. Probus (c.232–82), a successful military leader, was murdered by disaffected soldiers. Diocletian (c.244–311) enacted wide-ranging administrative reforms and stabilised the empire after a long period of crisis. Valentinian (321–75) was generally considered a competent military leader and emperor.

83. For Galeazzo Sforza, see note 6 above; on Cromwell, note 16. According to medieval chronicles, Samo established the first union of Slavic tribes, c.623, and governed it until his death (c.658). Piast (sometimes Piast the Wheelwright) was the ninth-century legendary founder of the Piast dynasty of Poland.

84. Widukind, leader of the Saxons in the late eighth century and a major adversary of Charlemagne (c. 747–814), king of the Franks; Otto I (912–73), Holy Roman Emperor from 962.

85. Septimius Severus (c.145–211), a Roman military leader, deposed and killed his predecessor Didius Julianus (see note 77 above), fought off rival claimants to the imperial throne, and subsequently embarked on a series of military campaigns.

86. The title in Machiavelli's *The Prince*: 'Whether building fortresses, and other things frequently done by princes, are useful or not'.

87. The Dutch stadtholder and prince of Orange became in 1689, as William III, king of England, Scotland, and Ireland (co-reigning with his wife Mary) following the 'Glorious Revolution' and the deposition, in 1688, of the Catholic James II.

88. In Greek mythology, the Danaïdes were the fifty daughters of Danaus, king of Argos. On their wedding night, all but one of the Danaïdes murdered their husbands; they were punished by having to carry water for all eternity in a barrel full of holes (or a similarly leaking device).

89. Agrippa Menenius Lanatus, Roman consul in 503 BC, was credited with convincing the plebeians to terminate their secession and return to Rome by means of the 'parable of the belly and the members', as related by Livy (II.32). Different body organs (the plebeians) resented the belly (the Senate) for idly enjoying food that they had to gather through hard work. They soon learned, however, that without digestion by the belly they would be left malnourished and dysfunctional. Versions of the fable appear in Shakespeare's *Coriolanus* and in La Fontaine's *Fables*.

90. A reference to confrontations between French and Austrians armies in Brabant during the Nine Years' War (1688–97) and the War of the Spanish Succession (1701–14).

91. 'The conqueror of India' is Alexander the Great; 'the arbiter of Poland' refers to the Swedish king Charles XII. About both, see note 28 above.

92. François Henri de Montmorency-Bouteville, duke of Luxembourg, (1628–95), a French general who fought in the wars against the Dutch in the 1660s and 1670s, and in the Nine Years' War. Claude Louis Hector, duke of Villars (1653–1734), marshal-general of France from 1702, one of Louis XIV's most important generals in the War of the Spanish Succession. On Charles XII of Sweden, see notes 7 and 28 above; on Eugene and Marlborough, note 51.

93. The title in Machiavelli's *The Prince*: 'How a prince should act in order to be esteemed'.

94. Ferdinand II of Aragon (1452–1516), king of Aragon who, through his marriage to Isabella of Castile, laid the foundations for a united Spanish kingdom. Bernabò Visconti (1323–85), ruler of Milan who was involved in numerous wars and eventually murdered by his relatives.

95. Related in Quintus Curtius Rufus, *Histories of Alexander the Great*, VII.8.

96. In Cicero's *Pro Ligario* (based on a legal case of 46 BC), XII.

97. This is a reference to Frederick's ancestor, 'the Great Elector' Frederick William I of Brandenburg. Frederick seems, however, to be mistaken. When Sweden invaded Brandenburg in 1675, the Great Elector did try to secure Moscow's help (to no avail). Local troops eventually defeated the Swedes without Russian assistance at the battle of Fehrbellin (June 1675).

98. Pericles (c.495–429 BC), initiated extensive building projects on the Acropolis; under his leadership, literature and the arts flourished in Athens.

99. Cicero (106–43 BC), the Roman republican statesman who was proscribed and murdered by the triumvirate of which Octavianus (later Augustus) was a member, is renowned for composing political and philosophical treatises as well as numerous speeches and letters. Ovid (43 BC–c.AD 17), author of the *Metamorphoses*, a significant source of ancient mythology, was banned by Augustus to a remote province by the Black Sea. Horace (65–8 BC), renowned author of the *Satires* and *Odes*, fought for the republic in his youth, but later extolled Augustus's reign. Like Horace, Virgil (70–19 BC), author of the *Aeneid*, belonged to the circle around Maecenas, Augustus's adviser and friend who fostered the arts.

100. Pierre Corneille (1606–84), Jean Racine (1639–99), and Molière (Jean-Baptiste Poquelin, 1622–73), the most renowned playwrights of Louis XIV's reign; Nicolas Boileau-Despréaux (1636–1711), poet and critic; René Descartes (1596–1650), widely regarded as one of the founders of modern philosophy, spent much of his life in the Netherlands rather than in France; Charles Le Brun (1619–90), court painter to Louis XIV; François Girardon (1628–1715), renowned painter and professor at the Royal Academy of Painting and Sculpture. Louis XIV's forces crossed the Rhine in 1672 into Dutch territory; Brandenburg-Prussia was allied with the Netherlands. According to the Duc de Saint-Simon, General de Marsin showed the French commander at the battle of Turin (1706), the Duc d'Orléans, a royal edict prohibiting any initiative beyond besieging the Piedmontese capital—which prevented the French from pursuing Austrian forces further afield. The flourishing of the arts as a marker of national greatness was the theme of Voltaire's *Le Siècle de Louis XIV* (1751); early chapter drafts were sent to Frederick in the late 1730s.

101. In *Pro Archia poeta*, Cicero's defence in 62 BC of Aulus Licinius Archias, a poet accused of falsely claiming to be a Roman citizen. This quotation appears in Voltaire's dedication to Madame du Châtelet at the outset of his play *Alzire* (1734).

102. Lorenzo de' Medici (1449–92, 'the Magnificent'), renowned for his support of artists such as Botticelli, Ghirlandaio, and Michelangelo, and authors including the philosophers Marsilio Ficino and Giovanni Pico della Mirandola.

103. Probably a memorised passage misattributed by Frederick to Marcus Aurelius.

104. The title in Machiavelli's *The Prince*: 'Of princes' secretaries'.

105. For Frederick's view of this pope, see also chapter XVIII (note 65 above).

106. The title in Machiavelli's *The Prince*: 'How flatterers should be avoided'.
107. 'Contempt of virtue arises from the contempt of fame': a variation on a maxim in Tacitus, *Annales* IV, ch. 38 ('Nam contemptu famae contemni virtutes').
108. Pliny the Younger (c.61–c.113), a lawyer and magistrate, renowned for his letters to the Emperor Trajan (among other addressees). On Trajan and Tiberius, see note 1 above.
109. The title in Machiavelli's *The Prince*: 'Why the princes of Italy have lost their states'.
110. The mythological founder and first king of Thebes.
111. Probably a reference to the period from the late fourteenth to the early sixteenth centuries.
112. The title in Machiavelli's *The Prince*: 'How powerful fortune is in human affairs, and how it can be resisted'.
113. Scylla and Charybdis are the mythical sea monsters based on opposite sides of the Strait of Messina, between Sicily and Calabria. Circumventing one brought sailors too close to the other; the challenge was to identify a route that steered clear of both.
114. In the Second Punic War (218–201 BC).
115. At the battle of Cremona (31 January–1 February 1702), during the War of the Spanish Succession (1701–14), between a French contingent headed by Marshal Villeroy and Austrian forces led by Prince Eugene of Savoy (see note 51 above) and Prince de Vaudémont.
116. A peculiar perspective on the tensions between Queen Anne (1665–1714) and her erstwhile favourite Sarah Churchill, duchess of Marlborough (1660–1744) and wife of the statesman and general John Churchill, first duke of Marlborough (note 51 above). The Churchills were dismissed in 1711. Camille d'Hostun de La Baume, comte de Tallard (1652–1728) was a French military leader who, taken prisoner of war at the battle of Blenheim (1704), stayed in England until 1711. The elderly Churchill rejected Frederick's account.
117. Hernán Cortés (1485–1547), Spanish conqueror of Mexico (1519–21) and governor of New Spain.
118. Quintus Fabius Maximus Verrucosus (c.275–203 BC), or Fabius Cunctator (the Delayer), exhausted Hannibal's resources by employing this tactic in the Second Punic War (218–201 BC).
119. The anti-French alliance, led by the Duke of Marlborough and Prince Eugene of Savoy (note 51 above), won a decisive victory over French and Bavarian forces at the battle of Blenheim (13 August 1704) during the War of the Spanish Succession.
120. The title of the last chapter of Machiavelli's *The Prince* is 'An exhortation to liberate Italy from the barbarians'. Frederick departs here from his free commentary on the content of Machiavelli's chapters. A manuscript version of this chapter was discovered in Berlin in 1876; it is included in some modern

editions of the text. The translation above follows the printed edition which was widely known in the eighteenth century (reproduced in *OFG* 8:176–84).

121. In Greek mythology, Danaë, daughter of King Acrisius of Argos, was impregnated when Zeus, in the form of golden rain, penetrated the subterranean chamber in which her father had imprisoned her, fearing death by the hand of her child. She gave birth to Perseus.

122. Johann Friedrich Alexander zu Wied-Neuwied (1706–91) participated in the preliminary negotiations over the Peace of Vienna (1738), which officially concluded the War of the Polish Succession (1733–35).

123. Towards the end of the Nine Years' War (1688–97), Victor Amadeus II, duke of Savoy, left the Grand Alliance and negotiated separately with France.

124. A reference to Quintus Sertorius (c. 123–72 BC), a Roman general. The story is related differently in Plutarch's *Life of Sertorius*.

3. Preface to *History of My Age*

Histoire de mon temps is the title Frederick gave, in 1775, to the final version of his account of the first two Silesian Wars. Its version of 1746, with the preface translated here, was meant to become part of Frederick's history of his dynasty. The preface highlights Frederick's philosophy of history and his views on the practice of its writing. Some sections of the king's account of earlier Prussian history were published in the proceedings of the Berlin Academy in the late 1740s, followed by authorised editions of the *Mémoires pour servir à l'histoire de la maison de Brandebourg* in 1751 and 1767. Unlike the king's history of his predecessors, however, his account of the Silesian Wars—prefaced by the translated text—remained unpublished in his lifetime. A second preface was written in 1775; the text first appeared in a mutilated form in 1788, in a posthumous edition of the king's works. The translation follows the version restored from original manuscripts in *OFG* 2:v–xii.

1. Jacques Auguste de Thou (1553–1617), a French magistrate and historian whose multi-volume history of his times (*Historiae sui temporis*, 1604–1608) covered the French Wars of Religion and was criticised by devout Catholics. Paul de Rapin de Thoyras (1661–1725), an exiled French Huguenot, published in 1724 a large *History of England* (*Histoire d'Angleterre*), which was a popular reference work on English history before David Hume's project (1754–61).

2. In the First Silesian War of 1740–42, part of the wider War of the Austrian Succession (see Introduction, pp. xii–xiv).

3. The Habsburg ruler and Holy Roman Emperor Charles VI (1685–1740) made various attempts to secure the succession of his daughter Maria Theresa (1717–80), most notably by issuing the Pragmatic Sanction, allowing the inheritance of the Habsburg lands by female offspring. Charles's death on 20 Oc-

tober 1740 gave rise to the War of the Austrian Succession (1740–48), in which Charles Albert of Bavaria (1697–1745) fought Austria with French support and was elected Holy Roman Emperor (1742–45)—the first non-Habsburg to bear the title since the fifteenth century. Frederick, who acceded to the Prussian throne in May 1740, exploited the vulnerability of Charles by launching in December of the same year a war in which he conquered Austrian Silesia (see Introduction, p. xiii).

4. Philip V of Spain (1683–1746); Potosí (in Bolivia) was a major centre of Spanish silver mining.

5. A reference to Maria Theresa of Austria: see note 3 above.

6. A comparison of the War of the Spanish succession (1701–14) with the War of the Austrian Succession (1740–48). On Prince Eugene and the Duke of Marlborough, see note 51 to *Anti-Machiavel*. Prince William Augustus, duke of Cumberland (1721–65) and Charles August Frederick of Waldeck and Pyrmont (1704–63) led, largely ineffectively, Dutch and allied troops in the War of the Austrian Succession.

7. In the First Silesian War, Saxony changed its affiliation in summer 1741 from Austria to France (Frederick's ally), before returning to the Austrian fold in further conflicts.

8. On Charles XII of Sweden, see *Anti-Machiavel*, notes 7 and 28. Augustus II ('the Strong') of Saxony was deposed in Poland by the Swedes in 1704, and was restored to his Polish throne by Russia in 1709. The reference to his son Augustus III (1696–1763) seems to be mistaken: he was not deposed in Saxony. The mentioned emperor is Charles Albert of Bavaria (see note 3 above), who—as the Holy Roman Emperor Charles VII—was chased out of Bavaria in the War of the Austrian Succession and rarely gained control over his territories.

4. DISSERTATION ON THE REASONS FOR ESTABLISHING OR REPEALING LAWS

The *Dissertation* was written in late 1749 and read at the Berlin Academy of Sciences and Belles-Lettres on 22 January 1750 by Claude-Étienne Darget (1712–78), Frederick's reader and secretary. Although the *Dissertation* was composed shortly after the publication of Montesquieu's *De l'esprit des lois* (1748), there is no conclusive evidence that Frederick had read or possessed a copy of Montesquieu's work before composing this treatise. The king first referred to *De l'esprit des lois* in a letter of April 1753 (*OFG* 20:43).

The *Dissertation* appeared in the limited edition of *Œuvres du philosophe de Sans-Souci* (1750; see the editorial preface below to *Epistle XVIII: To Marshal Keith*). In 1751, it became publicly accessible in the proceedings of the Berlin Academy for the year 1749 (*Histoire de l'Académie Royale des Sciences et Belles Lettres, année 1749* [Berlin: Haude & Spener, 1751], 375–415). A slightly revised version appeared in an edition of Frederick's *Mémoires pour servir à l'histoire de la maison de Brandebourg* (Berlin: Voss, 1767), 104–54. This latest edition was used by J.D.E. Preuß in *OFG* 9:9–37, and is translated here. The Berlin Academy version features marginal notes with Frederick's sources as well as footnotes. The original references have been marked in the translated text with asterisks; the editor's annotations are numbered, as elsewhere in this volume.

1. Michel de l'Hôpital (1507–73) oversaw the legal system as chancellor of France between 1560 and 1568. Charles-Jean-François Hénault (1685–1770) was a poet, playwright, and historian, whose *Abrégé chronologique de l'histoire de France* (1744) Frederick used here.

2. Quintilian, *Institutio oratoria* V.4 and V.10. See *The Orator's Education*, vol. 2 (Books III–V), ed. Donald A. Russell, Loeb Classical Library (Cambridge, MA: Harvard University Press, 2001), 330–31 and 400–401.

3. Frederick issued a cabinet order to this effect a few days after his accession, on 3 June 1740, further extended in another decree of August 1754.

4. The *Philippics* are speeches against Philip II of Macedon, delivered by the Athenian statesman and orator Demosthenes (384–322BC; see also *Anti-Machiavel*, chapter IX). Aeschines (c.390–314BC), who opposed Demosthenes's political stance, tried to prosecute Ctesiphon, an orator who had suggested rewarding Demosthenes with a golden crown for his services to the state. In the ensuing quarrel, Aeschines delivered his oration *Against Ctesiphon*; it was Demosthenes who replied with *On the Crown* (330BC).

5. Aulus Cluentius Habitus, defended by Cicero in 66BC, was accused by his mother of poisoning her husband Oppianicus; a few years earlier, Cluentius himself claimed he had been poisoned by his stepfather. Marcus Fonteius was a Roman statesmen and military leader who, after governing Transalpine Gaul (c.74–72BC), was accused of corruption but probably acquitted thanks to Cicero's spirited defence.

6. Samuel von Cocceji (1679–1755) was entrusted by Frederick with reviewing Silesian law after the annexation of the Austrian province and, subsequently, reforming the Prussian legal system.

7. Frederick issued an edict to this effect in summer 1746.

8. Legislation against duelling was enacted in France and various states of the Holy Roman Empire after the Thirty Years' War.

9. Charles-Irénée Castel de Saint-Pierre (1658–43), a French diplomat and author, who proposed a system of international arbitration in his *Projet pour rendre la paix perpétuelle en Europe* (1713). Saint-Pierre reviewed Frederick's first published work in *Réflexions sur l'Anti-Machiavel de 1740* (1741), and even travelled to Berlin to meet Frederick. The king, however, refused to engage with the ageing author and his project for perpetual peace.

5. Epistle XVIII: To Marshal Keith, on the Vain Terrors of Death and the Fears of Another Life

This poem and the following one, rhymed in the French original, were parts of *Œuvres du philosophe de Sans-Souci*, a collection of odes and philosophical poems entrusted by Frederick to a close circle of confidants and not intended for public consumption. A first version was printed confidentially in 1749 at the Berlin palace, followed by a three-volume edition of 1750 and a new version in 1752, revised by Voltaire (who resided in Potsdam from 1750 to 1753). As the *Epistle* begins with a reference to the death of Maurice de Saxe (November 1750), the text was probably composed between the second and third versions of the *Œuvres*.

Following a decade of public curiosity about *Œuvres*, they were published in January 1760 in Paris and Lyon with the blessing of the government of France, Frederick's adversary in the Seven Years' War (1756–63). Aware of the potential reputational damage, Frederick rushed to publish an extended, authorised edition (*Poësies diverses*, 1760) in which he modified some of the more radical points. The current poem was presented, by means of a new subtitle, as a mere imitation of Book III of Lucretius's *De rerum natura*; 'lâches chrétiens' (cowardly Christians [p. 115 in this translation]) now became 'mortels craintifs' (timid mortals) and, in a later edition, 'lâches humains' (cowardly human beings). The translated text follows the original version, as reproduced in *OFG* 10:226–37.

The addressee of the poem, James Francis Edward Keith (1696–1758), was a Scottish Jacobite nobleman in exile, who offered his military services first to Russia and, from 1747, to Frederick. He died from a fatal injury suffered during the battle of Hochkirch (1758). Keith's elder brother, George (1692/3–1778) also served Frederick; both brothers were close friends of the king.

1. Maurice de Saxe (1696–1750), a Saxon general in French service during the War of the Austrian Succession (1740–48, encompassing the First and Second Silesian Wars). Between 1745 and 1747, French armies under his command inflicted several defeats in the Low Countries on a British-Austrian-Dutch military alliance. As Frederick recounts below, despite his military exploits, Maurice de Saxe died of fever in his bed.
2. Louis Charles Armand Fouquet, chevalier de Belle-Isle (1693–1747) died while leading a French charge on Piedmontese forces at the battle of Assietta during the War of the Austrian Succession.
3. Emanuel François Joseph, comte de Bavière (1695–1747), a Bavarian general in the French army during the War of the Austrian Succession, who died in action at the battle of Lauffeldt.
4. A reference to the Thirty Years' War (1618–48).

5. Prince Eugene of Savoy (1663–1736), a general in the Austrian and Imperial armies, one of the most renowned early modern military leaders; John Churchill, first duke of Marlborough (1650–1722), the English general and statesman who led, together with Prince Eugene, the allied forces against France in the War of the Spanish Succession (1701–14). References to these generals can also be found throughout Frederick's *Anti-Machiavel* (see, e.g., notes 51 and 115 to *Anti-Machiavel*, above).

6. Louis II de Bourbon, prince of Condé (1621–86, also known as the 'Grand Condé' and until 1646 as the Duc d'Enghien), was a French general who led his forces to victory in battles during the Thirty Years' Wars and Louis XIV's Dutch campaigns. He also played a leading role in the Fronde (1648–53), the aristocratic rebellion against the government of Cardinal Mazarin.

7. Louis XIV of France (1638–1715).

8. Bernard Le Bovier de Fontenelle (1657–1757), perpetual secretary of the Parisian Academy of Sciences (1697–1740), a nonagenarian when Frederick wrote the poem.

6. Epistle XX: To My Soul (*À mon esprit*)

While this ode was composed in 1749, it featured as the last 'Epistle' in *Œuvres du philosophe de Sans-Souci*. For its publication history, see the editorial preface above to *Epistle XVIII: To Marshal Keith*. It is probably modelled on 'Satire IX' by Nicolas Boileau-Despréaux (1636–1711), which addresses the author's soul in a similar manner. Boileau, poet and theoretician of aesthetics, was also appointed Louis XIV's court historian. The text is translated from *OFG* 10:248–58.

1. Antoine Achard (1696–1772), born in Geneva, was from 1724 a learned pastor at a French Calvinist church near Berlin; he became member of the Berlin Academy in 1743.

2. Pierre-Daniel Huet (1630–1721), French bishop and prolific scholar.

3. Claude Saumaise (1588–1653), French biblical and classical scholar.

4. For Frederick's critique of hunting as a royal and aristocratic pastime, see *Anti-Machiavel*, chapter XIV (pp. 43–6).

5. Anne-Joseph-Claude Frey de Neuville (1693–1774), a French Jesuit renowned for his eloquent sermons and obituaries.

6. Claude Favre de Vaugelas (1585–1650), French grammarian and one of the first members of the Académie française, author of *Remarques sur la langue française, utiles à ceux qui veulent bien parler et bien écrire* (Paris, 1647); Pierre-Joseph Thoulier d'Olivet, French translator, editor, and grammarian, an active contributor to the dictionary of the Académie française. This is a pun on a passage in Molière's *Les Femmes savantes* (1672), Act II, scene 7: 'It est vrai que l'on sue à soufrir son discours / Elle y met Vaugelas en pièces tous les jours.'

7. Charles Cotin (1604–81), French poet and scholar, one of Boileau's critics who are mentioned in the latter's 'Satire IX'.

8. A reference to the Roman poet Virgil (Publius Vergilius Maro, c.70–19BC).

9. Permessus was a stream on the slopes of Mount Helicon, apparently sacred to the god Apollo.

10. Themis, a female titan in Greek mythology, represented justice, order, and sometimes also philosophy.

11. Mount Parnassus was probably meant here.

12. Charles XII of Sweden (1682–1718), whose career was analysed in essays by Voltaire and Frederick. See also *Anti-Machiavel*, chapter VIII (p. 30).

13. Jean-Baptiste de Boyer, marquis d'Argens (1703–71), Francesco Algarotti (1712–64), and Pierre Louis Moreau de Maupertuis (1698–1759), president of the Berlin Academy, belonged to the intimate circle of Frederick's friends and advisers at the time he composed this ode. The 'French Homer' is Voltaire.

14. In some versions of the Greek myth of Midas, the Phrygian king was endowed with donkey's ears after he dared to dispute the superiority of Apollo's music-making. Midas tried to hide the fact, but his barber whispered the secret into a hole he dug in the ground. A thick tangle of reeds grew on this spot, chanting the secret whenever the wind blew through it.

15. An Athenian statesman and general (c.530–c.464BC), known as 'the Just' for his virtuous conduct. Frederick could read an account of his life in an edition of André Dacier's translation of Plutarch's *Parallel Lives* (*Les vies des hommes illustres de Plutarque* [Amsterdam, 1735]); a copy was kept in his library.

7. Preface to Extracts from Bayle's *Historical and Critical Dictionary*

The *Dictionnaire historique et critique* (1697) by Pierre Bayle (1647–1706), a French Huguenot refugee in the Netherlands, was one of the most influential works in the European Enlightenment. The sceptical, analytical treatment of various ideas, personalities, and events was usually confined in the *Dictionnaire* to the voluminous footnotes (often much longer than the main text). As early as 1742, Frederick wrote to his confidant Charles-Étienne Jordan (1700–45) from the battlefield that he was Bayle's student in whatever concerned reason (*OFG* 17:237). The king edited a selection of articles from the *Dictionnaire* together with his adviser Jean-Baptiste de Boyer, marquis d'Argens (1703–71); it was printed in 1765 by the Berlin publisher Voss. A second, extended version was published by Voss in 1767; the translation is made from the preface to the second edition, reproduced in *OFG* 7:141–47.

1. In the five *Tusculan Disputations* (*Tusculanae disputationes*, c.45BC) Cicero popularised Greek philosophy for Roman audiences, focussing mostly on Stoic

(and partly on Platonic) ideas; *On the Nature of the Gods* (*De natura deorum*, c.45 BC) is Cicero's discussion of Hellenistic theology and metaphysics.

2. René Descartes (1596–1650) argued that the cosmos was a plenum containing circling bands (vortices) which determined the orbits of planets. Newtonian physics had undermined and replaced this theory by the mid-eighteenth century; among the most renowned popularisers of Newtonianism were Voltaire and Frederick's associates Francesco Algarotti (1712–64) and Pierre Louis Moreau de Maupertuis (1698–1759; president of the Berlin Academy from 1746 until his death). According to the theory of occasionalism elaborated by Nicolas Malebranche (1638–1715), God was the cause for, and the agent of, the correlation between sensations and volitions in human beings.

3. Gottfried Wilhelm Leibniz (1646–1716) developed his metaphysics mostly in *Discours de métaphysique* (1686), *Théodicée* (1710), and *Monadology* (1714). As crown prince, Frederick was influenced by Christian Wolff (1679–1754), who followed and updated Leibniz's philosophy on major topics; after launching his correspondence with Voltaire, Frederick changed his mind and viewed both Leibniz and Wolff as largely dogmatic metaphysicians. See also note 7 to *Letter on Education*, below.

4. In Greek mythology, Bellerophon, son of Glaucus, king of Corinth, slew the fire-breathing monster Chimera while riding his winged horse Pegasus.

5. While abridgements and shorter editions of Bayle's *Dictionnaire* abounded in the eighteenth century, none bears this title. Frederick's sister Wilhelmine wrote to Voltaire in 1752 that the king had wished to write a treatise with this title, probably a reference to the project that would eventually be published in 1765. (Wilhelmine of Bayreuth to Voltaire, 12 June 1752, Letter D4910 in *OCV* 97:76–77)

6. Zeno of Citium (c. 332–c. 262 BC) and Epicurus of Samos (c. 341–c. 270 BC), respective founders of the renowned Hellenistic philosophical schools of Stoicism and Epicureanism.

7. On the epistemological humility occasioned by the limits of human understanding, see also Frederick's *Dissertation on the Innocence of Errors of the Mind* (pp. 1–12 above).

8. See also Frederick's critique of legal rhetoric in *A Dissertation on the Reasons for Establishing or Repealing Laws* (pp. 103–5 above).

8. PREFACE TO *ABRIDGEMENT OF THE ECCLESIASTICAL HISTORY BY FLEURY*

This is Frederick's preface to *Abrégé de l'Histoire ecclésiastique de Fleury. Traduit de l'anglais*, published in two volumes in May 1766 in Berlin (and, of course, not translated from English). The identity of the author of the 'abridgement' itself, allegedly based on Claude Fleury's popular *Histoire ecclésiastique* (20 vols, 1691–1720), has not been fully ascertained. Voltaire, among others, assumed it was Jean-Martin de Prades (c. 1720–82), a Catholic theologian persecuted in France who found refuge in Prussia in 1752. The identity of the author notwithstanding, what Voltaire called the 'violent preface' came to represent the king's attitude to Christian theology and the history of the church (Voltaire to Villevieille, 18 July 1766, Letter D13430 in *OCV* 114:326–27). Frederick studied closely Fleury's *Histoire ecclésiastique* in summer 1762 during the siege of Schweidnitz (Świdnica in Silesia). The text is translated from *OFG* 7:149–64.

1. On Claudius and his successors, see also *Anti-Machiavel*, chapter XIX (note 77).
2. Frederick probably meant to refer here to the First Council of Constantinople (381), where this issue was discussed, rather than the Council of Chalcedon (451).
3. Possibly also a reference to 1 John 5:7 (in the King James Version: 'For there are three that bear record in heaven, the Father, the Word, and the Holy Ghost: and these three are one.')
4. Probably a reference to 2 Maccabees 12:41–46.
5. It is to Pope Gregory I that the title is usually applied.
6. This papal bull was first issued officially by Urban V in 1363 and recurrently confirmed by his successors. Hildebrand of Sovana, or Pope Gregory VII from 1073 to 1085, is widely renowned for his quarrel with the Holy Roman Emperor Henry IV, whom he excommunicated and dethroned three times in the Investiture Controversy over the rights of emperor and pope in relation to one another.
7. A reference to disputes between empire and papacy over the lands formerly controlled by Matilda of Tuscany (1046–1115), a supporter of Pope Gregory VII in his conflict with Henry IV.
8. Bernard of Clairvaux (c. 1090–1153) preached for the eventually failed Second Crusade (1147–49/50).
9. Probably a mistaken reference to the Council of Constance (1414–18).
10. The split between two, later three concurrent popes, based in Rome and Avignon (1378–1417).
11. John Wycliffe (c. 1330–84) and Jan Hus (c. 1370–1415), critics of the popes and clerical politics, have been widely regarded as precursors of the Reformation.
12. See note 4 to 'Preface to Extracts from Bayle's *Historical and Critical Dictionary*', above.
13. For Frederick's views on the Virgin, see also *Dialogue between Madame de Pompadour and the Virgin Mary* in this volume.

9. ESSAY ON SELF-LOVE, CONSIDERED
AS A PRINCIPLE OF MORALITY

On 11 January 1770, this essay was read at a public meeting of the Berlin Academy of Sciences and Belles-Lettres; Frederick sent personal copies to Voltaire and d'Alembert. It was published by Voss in Berlin 1770, and appeared in the same year in the belated proceedings of the Academy for 1763. Original notes are asterisked; the text is translated from *OFG* 9:99–114.

1. Lucian of Samosata (c. 120–after 180) composed satirical dialogues and treatises ridiculing, among others, philosophers, orators, and traditional tales about the gods. Frederick possessed his works in French translation.
2. Gaius Marius (c. 157–86 BC) and Lucius Cornelius Sulla (138–78 BC) were the main opponents in the Roman civil war of 88–87 BC.
3. Quietism, a Catholic strand influential in France and southern Europe in the seventeenth and eighteenth centuries, usually advocated the annihilation of one's self-regarding sentiments for a pure love of God irrespective of any rewards or punishments. It was condemned in 1699 by Pope Innocent XII; among its renowned French adherents was Fénelon (see Introduction, pp. xxiii–xxiv).
4. François de La Rochefoucauld (1613–80), author of *Réflexions, ou Sentences et maximes morales* (1664–65). Frederick possessed several editions of La Rouchefoucauld's *Maxims*, which emphasised the power of self-love and the passions in human affairs.
5. See notes 1 (Nero and Caligula), 31 (Louis XI), and 54 (Domitian) to *Anti-Machiavel*.
6. See note 88 to *Anti-Machiavel*.
7. Publius Decius Mus and his son of the same name, Roman consuls and generals, dedicated themselves and the armies they confronted to the gods of the underworld in order to secure Rome's triumph. They died, respectively, in 340 BC (at the battle of Vesuvius in the First Latin War) and 295 BC (in the Third Samnite War).
8. Victorious over New Carthage in Spain (209 BC), Scipio Africanus is said to have released an exceptionally beautiful Carthaginian hostage, reuniting her with her fiancé, who was one of the enemy leaders.
9. Miltiades (c. 550–489 BC), Athenian military leader who played a central role in the battle of Marathon (490 BC) against the Persians. Themistocles (c. 524–459 BC) is renowned for his victory in the battle of Salamis (480 BC) over the Persian fleet.

10. LETTER ON EDUCATION

This treatise was published in 1770 by Voss in Berlin with *Lettre sur l'éducation* on its title page, although the text itself starts under the title *Lettre d'un Génevois à M. Burlamaqui, professeur à Genève* (p. 3 of the original). It is, therefore, framed as a report on Prussian affairs sent by a Berlin-based Genevan to his late compatriot Jean-Jacques Burlamaqui (1694–1748), a renowned theorist of natural law and international relations. The composition of the text is probably linked to Frederick's attempts to reform Prussian education in the wake of the Seven Years' War and the foundation of the Academy of Nobles, or Military Academy, in 1765 in Berlin. The text is translated from *OFG* 9:131–47.

1. On Telemachus, the eponymous princely hero of Fénelon's bestselling novel (1699), see Introduction, pp. xxiii–xxiv.
2. The 'academy' referred to here is the military Academy of Nobles, established in 1765 in Berlin.
3. A frequent contemporary allusion to France.
4. Friedrich Hoffmann (1660–1742), a medical author and professor of medicine at the University of Halle, also served between 1709 and 1712 as court physician to Frederick I. Herman Boerhaave (1668–1738), an innovative physician and professor of medicine at the University of Leiden, was the mentor of Enlightenment authors such as Albrecht von Haller (1708–77) and Julien Offray de La Mettrie (1709–51), the physician-turned-radical philosopher who found refuge in 1748 in Frederick's Prussia.
5. Christian Thomasius (1655–1728), natural law theorist and professor of law at Leipzig and later at Halle, pioneered lecturing in German instead of Latin and advocated a reform of academic teaching.
6. A reference to the medieval scholastic dispute between realists and nominalists over the existence of universals as distinct from individual instances.
7. 'The most learned, wisest Wolff', a reference to Christian Wolff (1679–1754), who elaborated in a series of Latin and German treatises central themes in Leibnizian philosophy—although he did not consistently agree with Leibniz. The latter argued that monads were the mind-like basic units of the universe and that material and immaterial substances (for example, bodies and minds) did not directly interact with one another: they were pre-programmed to act as if they causally impacted one another ('pre-established harmony'). The young Frederick was initially impressed by some of Wolff's works, but his correspondence with Voltaire distanced him from the German philosopher. Upon his accession in 1740, Frederick recalled Wolff to the Prussian University of Halle, from which he had been expelled in 1723 by Frederick William I (see Introduction, pp. x, xii, xxvii–xxviii).
8. Johann Jobst Heinrich Wilhelm von Buddenbrock (1707–81), a Prussian general and military educator who was a close associate of Frederick.
9. On Peter I of Russia (1672–1725), see also notes 28 and 46 to *Anti-Machiavel*.
10. This was the main thesis of Jean-Jacques Rousseau's *Discourse on the Sciences and the Arts*, which won the prize contest of the Dijon Academy in 1750. Frederick wrote his own *Discourse on the Utility of the Sciences and the Arts for the State* in 1772 (*OFG* 9:195–207).

11. Arminius (c.17BC–AD21), head of the Cherusci, led a coalition of Germanic tribes to victory over Roman legions in AD9 at the battle of Teutoburg Forest. The Suebi and Semnones were Germanic tribes mentioned in Julius Caesar's *Commentaries on the Gallic War* (c.50BC) and Tacitus's *Germania* (AD98).

12. Frederick William (1620–88), elector of Brandenburg and duke of Prussia, has been regarded as 'the Great Elector' due to his military and diplomatic achievements, including the victory over Swedish forces at the battle of Fehrbellin (1675). See also note 97 to *Anti-Machiavel*.

13. The text concludes with a truncated form of an eighteenth-century letter ending ('I am, Sir, your most humble servant . . .').

11. EXAMINATION OF THE *ESSAY ON PREJUDICE*

This is Frederick's response to *Essai sur les préjugés, ou De l'influence des opinions sur les mœurs et sur le bonheur des hommes, ouvrage contenant l'apologie de la philosophie*, allegedly published in London (actually in Lausanne) in 1770 by 'Mr. D. M.'. In the eighteenth century, it was regarded as a posthumous work by Du Marsais (see note 27 below); its author is now widely considered to be Paul-Henri Thiry, baron d'Holbach (1723–89). The reply is one of Frederick's most pessimistic statements on the prospects of widespread Enlightenment and the perfectibility of human affairs, an attitude also manifest in his contemporary correspondence with d'Alembert, where the king argued that 'credulity, superstition, and the timid fears of feeble minds will always prevail among the majority of the public' (Frederick to d'Alembert, 8 January 1770, *OFG* 24:520–23). D'Alembert defended the possibility of the gradual extension and increase of Enlightenment beyond a small circle of philosophers. The exchange resulted in a prize contest at the Berlin Academy in 1780 on 'whether it is useful for the people to be deceived'. Frederick sent this text in May 1770 to d'Alembert and Voltaire; it was published in 1770 by Voss in Berlin (despite the final reference to London). The text is translated from *OFG* 9:149–75.

1. On the alleged errors of Descartes and Leibniz, see notes 2 and 3 to the 'Preface to Extracts from Bayle's *Historical and Critical Dictionary*', above. Frederick also refers here to Isaac Newton's posthumously published *Observations upon the Prophecies of Daniel and the Apocalypse of St John* (1733).

2. A similar anecdote appears in *Dissertation on the Innocence of Errors of the Mind*, pp. 9–10 above.

3. At the battle of Cannae (216BC), during the Second Punic War, a Carthaginian army under Hannibal won a decisive victory over larger Roman forces (led by the consuls Lucius Aemilius Paullus and Gaius Terentius Varro; see also Frederick's references to the Punic Wars in chapters XVII and XXV of *Anti-Machiavel*). In 390/387BC, Gallic tribes defeated Roman armies at the battle of the Allia, which resulted in the sack of Rome by the Gallic Senones.

4. On the parlements of France, see note 9 to *Anti-Machiavel*.

5. France was one of Prussia's mighty enemies in the Seven Years' War (1756–63).

6. Both Henri III of France (1551–89) and his successor Henri IV (1553–1610) were assassinated by fanatical Catholics. See also chapter IV of *Anti-Machiavel*.

7. On the emperors Trajan and Marcus Aurelius, see notes 1 and 20 to *Anti-Machiavel*. Julian (331/2–63) was the last non-Christian Roman emperor, who tried to restore traditional Roman practices. After successful campaigns against Germanic tribes in Europe, he died at the battle of Samarra during his invasion of the Sassanid empire. Julian also composed philosophical works in Greek.

8. Hugo Grotius (1583–1645), a Dutch humanist who wrote treatises on natural law, international law, and theology. Especially renowned for his works *Mare liberum* (*The Free Sea*, 1609) and *De jure belli ac pacis* (*On the Law of War and Peace*, 1625), of which Frederick possessed two editions.

9. The Aetolian League was a confederation of cities and tribes in central Greece, formed around the middle of the fourth century BC, mostly to oppose increasing Macedonian power.

10. On Louis XII of France, see note 54 to *Anti-Machiavel*.

11. Charles the Bold, duke of Burgundy (1433–77) was killed in battle by the Swiss forces allied with Lorraine, which he tried to dominate as a link between Burgundy and his possessions in the Low Countries.

12. Due to the power of Parliament, England was considered a republic to some extent by various eighteenth-century authors. See also chapter XIX of *Anti-Machiavel*, where Frederick argues that in England, 'Parliament is the arbiter between the people and the king, and the king has unlimited powers to do good, but none to do harm' (p. 56). In the Seven Years' War (1756–63), Britain acquired major French territories in North America and southern Asia.

13. From 1768 to 1772, Poland was embroiled in civil war between the Bar Confederation and King Stanisław Poniatowski, allied with Russia. At the end of the conflict, in the First Partition of Poland (1772), Prussia, Russia, and Austria seized considerable territories of the Polish-Lithuanian Commonwealth.

14. On Saint-Pierre, see note 9 to *Dissertation on the Reasons for Establishing or Repealing Laws*.

15. On these events in the War of the Polish Succession (1733–35), see notes 4 and 7 to *Anti-Machiavel*. Louis XV of France (1710–74) was married to Maria Leszczyńska (1703–68), daughter of Stanisław Leszczyński (1677–1766), king of Poland in 1704–09 and 1733–36.

16. On the War of the Austrian Succession (1740–48), encompassing the first two Silesian Wars, see Introduction, pp. xii–xiii.

17. On the Seven Years' War (1756–63), see Introduction, pp. xiii–xiv.

18. On Scipio, see *Anti-Machiavel*, chapters XVII and XXV; for Gustavus Adolphus, Turenne, Marlborough, and Eugene, note 51 to *Anti-Machiavel*. On Maurice de Saxe, see note 1 to *Epistle XVIII: To Marshal Keith*.

19. Diogenes of Sinope or Diogenes the Cynic (c.412–c.323 BC), critic of the social and political conventions of his day, lived in a large barrel or a ceramic container, and is said to have acted impudently towards Alexander the Great when the latter visited Corinth.

20. The Holy League, or the Catholic League of France, was formed in 1576 by Henri I, duke of Guise, to oppose French Protestants and drive them out of the kingdom. It played a major role in the subsequent civil conflict and inspired the assassin of King Henri III (see note 6 above).

21. King John (Jean) II of France (1319–64), also 'John the Good' (Jean le Bon), was captured by English forces at the battle of Poitiers (1356). On Francis I, see note 59 to *Anti-Machiavel*.

22. See note 9 to *Anti-Machiavel*.

23. *Dissertation on the Reasons for Establishing or Repealing Laws*, p. 94 above.

24. The War of the Spanish Succession (1701–14). See also *Anti-Machiavel*, chapters X and XXV.

25. Philippe II, duke of Orléans (1674–1723), ruled France from 1715 to 1723 as regent of the kingdom during Louis XV's minority. John Law (1671–1729), a Scottish economist and banker, founded in 1716 a bank that effectively became the first national bank of France, financing state debt by issuing paper money, and a joint-stock company with a monopoly over French trade in North America. The 'Law System' collapsed in 1720, a few months after the regent appointed Law finance minister (contrôleur général des finances), following increased speculation and a breakdown in public confidence; the disgraced Law had to flee France.

26. See *Anti-Machiavel*, note 50.

27. César Chesneau Du Marsais (1676–1756), philosopher of language and author of numerous entries in Diderot and d'Alembert's *Encyclopédie*, where the article 'Philosophe' was based on his renowned essay (1743) of the same title. In the eighteenth century, the *Essay on Prejudice* was considered as a posthumous work by Du Marsais; see the introduction to this text. (Frederick made here an error concerning the date of Du Marsais's death.)

28. On Fénelon, see Introduction, pp. xxiii–xxiv.

29. Louis-Jules Barbon Mancini-Mazarini, duc de Never or Nivernois (1716–98), a great-nephew of Cardinal Mazarin, was a French diplomat, author and poet, member of the Académie française, Académie des inscriptions et belles-lettres, and the Royal Society of London. In 1756, he spent two months on a diplomatic mission in Prussia.

30. On Cartouche, see notes 29 and 67 to *Anti-Machiavel* (chapters VIII and XVIII). Louis Mandrin (1725–55) led a band of smugglers before his arrest and public execution. His exploits enjoyed widespread popularity in eighteenth-century Europe.

12. CRITICAL EXAMINATION OF
THE SYSTEM OF NATURE

The System of Nature (*Système de la nature*), elaborating various aspects of radical materialism and atheism, was published in 1770 by Baron d'Holbach, the probable author of the *Essay on Prejudice* (see the preface to the previous text). On its title page it was misleadingly attributed to a long-deceased author, Jean-Baptiste de Mirabaud (1675–1760), who served as perpetual secretary of the Académie française (1742–55). Frederick sent this text to Voltaire and d'Alembert in summer 1770, but refused to publish it (unlike his critique of the *Essay on Prejudice*). It first appeared in the 1788 edition of the king's *Œuvres posthumes*. The text is translated from *OFG* 9:177–94.

1. Or 'assisted by movement': in earlier editions, both variants ('aide de mouvement' and 'aidée de mouvement') can be found.
2. In Greek mythology, Ixion, a Thessalian king, coveted the goddess Hera, Zeus's wife. Zeus sent him a cloud in the shape of Hera, with which he coupled. As a punishment, Ixion was bound to a fiery wheel for all eternity.
3. John Turberville Needham (1713–81) was widely believed to have provided evidence of spontaneous generation via microscopic observations. Needham, a Catholic priest, rejected d'Holbach's materialist interpretation of his scientific work. His refutations were included in *Idée sommaire, ou Vue générale du système physique et métaphysique de M. Needham sur la génération des corps organisés* (Brussels, 1781).
4. See note 7 to *Letter on Education*, above.
5. See also Frederick's *Essay on Self-Love, Considered as a Principle of Morality*, in this volume.
6. John Locke (1632–1704) argued in *An Essay Concerning Human Understanding* (1690) that the notion of 'free will' was mistaken, for freedom should be ascribed to agents rather than to their will. Locke's example refers to a locked room: 'Again, suppose a man be carried, whilst fast asleep, into a room, where is a person he longs to see and speak with; and be there locked fast in, beyond his power to get out; he awakes, and is glad to find himself in so desirable company, which he stays willingly in, i.e. prefers his stay to going away; I ask, Is not this stay voluntary? I think nobody will doubt it; and yet being locked fast in, it is evident he is not at liberty not to stay, he has not freedom to be gone. So that liberty is not an idea belonging to volition, or preferring; but to the person having the power of doing, or forbearing to do, according as the mind shall choose or direct.' (Locke, *Essay*, II.xxi.10)
7. On Marcus Aurelius, see note 20 to *Anti-Machiavel*. Lucius Sergius Catilina (108–62BC), anglicised as Catiline, a Roman patrician who led a conspiracy

to overthrow the republic. On de Thou, see note 1 to 'Preface to *History of My Age*'. François Ravaillac (1578–1610) assassinated Henri IV in Paris on 14 May 1610.

8. Probably a reference to Cyniscus's retort to Zeus in Lucian's dialogue *Zeus Catechized* (Lucian II: *The Downward Journey or The Tyrant, Zeus Catechized* [. . .], trans. A. M. Harmon, Loeb Classical Library (Cambridge, MA: Harvard University Press, 1915, 59–87).

9. See, in this volume, Frederick's own 'Preface to *Abridgement of the Ecclesiastical History by Fleury*'.

10. Book III of Lucretius's Epicurean poem *De rerum natura* (first century BC), one of Frederick's favourite ancient texts. See, along these lines, the king's *Epistle XVIII: To Marshal Keith* in this volume.

11. See also the concluding section of *Examination of the* Essay on Prejudice, p. 177 above.

12. Frederick possessed French translations of the *Satires* by Persius (first century AD) and Juvenal (early second century AD).

13. Jean-François Paul de Gondi, cardinal de Retz (1613–89), initially opposed the crown in the Fronde, the civil conflicts in France (from 1648 to 1653).

14. On Boileau, see the editorial preface, above, to Frederick's ode *To My Soul*.

15. François-Michel le Tellier, marquis de Louvois (1641–91), French secretary of state for war under Louis XIV.

16. Voltaire provided a similar assessment of the Sun King in his *Siècle de Louis XIV* (1751; *OCV* 11–13).

17. In this fable, the wolf vows never to devour sheep—only in order to change his mind once he observes the shepherds themselves eating lamb.

18. Cf. *Anti-Machiavel*, chapter III.

19. See Frederick's *Essay on the Forms of Government and the Duties of Sovereigns*, in this volume.

13. DIALOGUE OF THE DEAD BETWEEN MADAME DE POMPADOUR AND THE VIRGIN MARY

Frederick reported to d'Alembert on this dialogue in a letter of 16 December 1773, highlighting its risqué nature (*OFG* 24:682–83). The king did not wish to send it via the usual postal services, entrusting a copy to Friedrich Melchior Grimm, who delivered several months later personally a parcel from Frederick to d'Alembert in Paris. The latter confirmed his receipt of the dialogue and his satisfaction in a letter of 31 October 1774 (*OFG* 24:706–7). After Frederick's death, manuscript copies of the dialogue went missing: most posthumous editions did not include it among the king's several dialogues of the dead, except for a single French edition published in London in 1789 by George Robinson, probably edited by Thomas Holcroft

(1745–1809). Holcroft, who also translated for Robinson the multi-volume *Œuvres posthumes* by Frederick, explained that this dialogue remained untranslated as it would have offended too many readers. A rare copy of the uncensored London edition was identified in the late 1990s by Gerhard Knoll. Following his detective work, tracing the dialogue's history in Frederick's literary estate and outside it, the dialogue was published in 1999 in a bilingual French/German edition. The text is translated from the second, extended edition of Frederick II, *Totengespräch zwischen Madame de Pompadour und der Jungfrau Maria*, ed. Gerhard Knoll (Berlin: Berlin Verlag, 2000), 15–19.

1. Among other issues, the post-Reformation Council of Trent (1545–63) reaffirmed the veneration of the Virgin Mary. See also Frederick's 'Preface to *Abridgement of the Ecclesiastical History by Fleury*', pp. 136–37 above.

2. A reference to the *Encyclopédie, ou dictionnaire raisonné des sciences, des arts et des métiers* (Encyclopedia, or a rational dictionary of the sciences, arts, and crafts), published in France between 1751 and 1772. Several of Frederick's contacts, including Voltaire, contributed entries to the project; one of its co-editors, d'Alembert, was especially close to Frederick. D'Alembert spent summer 1763 in Potsdam and Berlin, and corresponded frequently with the king (see also the editorial preface above to Frederick's *Examination of the Essay on Prejudice*). Madame de Pompadour was thought to support the *Encyclopédie* behind the scenes.

3. François-Joachim de Pierre, cardinal de Bernis (1715–94), archbishop of Albi and French diplomat who served as foreign minister in 1757–58. Renowned also as poet and author of epigrams, member of the Académie française, Bernis won Madame de Pompadour's friendship and patronage, although she eventually turned against him.

4. Probably a reference to leucorrhoea (*fluor albus*), a venereal infection.

5. Frederick's close associate and adviser, Jean-Baptiste de Boyer, marquis d'Argens (1703–71), discussed early Christian views of the Virgin in a long note in his *Déffense du paganisme par l'empereur Julien, en grec et en françois. Avec des dissertations et des notes pour servir d'éclaircissement au texte et pour en réfuter les erreurs* (Berlin: Voss, 1764), 186–205. Similar views are expressed in d'Argens's earlier work *Lettres juives* (1735–37).

6. Charles-Guillaume Le Normant d'Étioles (1717–99), financier and Madame de Pompadour's husband. In 1741 the couple had a son, who died soon after his birth, and in 1744 a daughter, Alexandrine, who lived until 1754.

7. Probably Frederick's idiosyncratic spelling for the Duc d'Ayen (Louis de Noailles, duc d'Ayen, from 1766 duc de Noailles) (1713–93), a general and confidant of Louis XV.

8. The Seven Years' War (1756–63).

9. Maria Leszczyńska (1703–68), daughter of Stanisław Leszczyński—king of Poland and later duke of Lorraine—was queen consort of France as Louis XV's
wife.

10. This seems to be Frederick's invention: Madame de Pompadour was born and
baptised in Paris in December 1721.

11. A potential reference to Aristotle's *Nicomachean Ethics* IV.3. See also Frederick's *Essay on Self-Love, Considered as a Principle of Morality* in this volume.

14. Essay on the Forms of Government and the Duties of Sovereigns

The *Essay* was composed by Frederick in August 1777 and printed by Decker in Berlin in a handful of copies for the king's use. Voltaire and d'Alembert received copies
of the *Essay* immediately; in 1781 Frederick gave a copy to the Prussian minister
Ewald Friedrich von Hertzberg (1725–95). It became widely accessible in posthumous editions of the king's work. The text is translated from *OFG* 9:221–40.

1. See also *Anti-Machiavel*, chapter I (p. 15).

2. On this episode, see also *Dissertation on the Reasons for Establishing or Repealing Laws* in this volume, pp. 91–2.

3. All seventeenth-century military leaders. On Turenne and Luxembourg, see
notes 51 and 92 to *Anti-Machiavel*; On the prince of Condé, see note 6 to
Epistle XVIII: To Marshal Keith.

4. See also Frederick's 'Preface to *Abridgement of the Ecclesiastical History by
Fleury*' in this volume.

5. The Edict of Nantes (1598), in which Henri IV granted French Calvinists
(Huguenots) limited religious and civil rights in the Catholic kingdom, was re-
voked in 1685 by Louis XIV (in the Edict of Fontainebleau). Frederick's ancestor, the Great Elector Frederick William (1620–88), offered Huguenots set-
tling in Brandenburg-Prussia substantial privileges.

6. The mythical King Midas of Lydia was endowed by Dionysus with the power
to turn everything he touched into gold. See also note 14 to *Epistle XX: To My
Soul*.

7. See note 20 to *Anti-Machiavel*.

INDEX

absolutism, viii, xi, xiv, xix, xx, xxi, xxxv.
  See also Enlightened Absolutism
Académie des inscriptions, 236n29
Académie française, 228n6, 236n29, 237, 239n3
Academy of Sciences, Paris, 228
Academy of Sciences and Belles-Lettres, Berlin,
  xii, 224, 225, 226, 228, 228n1, 229n13,
  230n2, 232, 234
agriculture, xxv, 63, 203; societies based on,
  xxiii, xxvii, 63
amour-propre, xxxiii, 125. *See also* self-love
animals, 44, 45, 114, 180
Anti-Machiavel, xxxii, xxxiii, xxxv, xxxvi,
  212nn13 and 14, 213, 218n58, 225nn6 and
  8, 226n4, 228nn6 and 4, 229n12, 231n1,
  232nn5 and 6, 233n9, 234nn12 and 3, 235nn4,
  6, 7, 10, 12, 15, and 18, 236nn21, 24, 26 and
  30, 237n7, 238n18, 240nn1, 3 and 7; Saint-
  Pierre's response to, 226n9
antiquity, xxii, xxxiv, 16, 27, 36, 80, 98, 127,
  140, 195
Aristotle, 7, 126, 130, 152, 240n11
armies, xxv, 16, 19, 22, 26, 33, 34, 35, 36, 39, 40,
  42, 58, 60, 61, 80, 81, 84, 85, 135, 163, 173,
  176, 188, 201, 221n90, 227n1, 228n5, 232n7,
  234n3; of auxiliary troops, 41–42, 79; com-
  prising foreigners or mercenaries, 38–41; and
  discipline, 19, 36; in peacetime, 16, 19, 33.
  See also military, the
artillery, 36, 60, 201
arts, the, ix, xxvi, xxvii, xxx, xxxii, xxxiii, xli,
  38, 46, 63, 64, 65, 123, 155, 173, 222n100,
  233n10
asylum, xii, 134
Augustus (Roman emperor), 56, 64, 93, 99,
  120, 220n80, 222n99
Augustus II of Saxony, 28, 54, 55, 86, 216n23,
  219n73, 225n8

Austria, xiii, xiv, xl, 153, 172, 201, 219n71,
  225nn3, 5 and 7, 235n13; House of, 83,
  170, 171
authority: of the Caesars, 132; clerical, 158,
  185; divine, 177; of the law, 55; papal, 134,
  135, 137; paternal, 158; political, xix, 52;
  princely, 133; royal, vii, xv, xviii, xx, xxii;
  sovereign, 54, 90, 173, 196, 197; supreme,
  xxxvii, 196, 198
authorship (Frederick's), ix, xvii, xxx, xxxv

battlefield, 43, 107
Bayle, Pierre, xxiv, 125, 126, 127, 212nn11 and
  14, 229, 230n5, 234n1
beer, 203
Berlin, ix, x, xii, xiii, xxxviii, xxxix, xl, 150, 213,
  223n120, 226n9, 227, 228n1, 229, 230, 233,
  233n2, 239n2
Berlin Academy. *See* Academy of Sciences and
  Belles-Lettres, Berlin
Bible, the, xxi, xxii, xxvii, xxix, xxx, 44
bishops, 36, 131, 134, 135, 136, 137
Bodin, Jean, xxi
books, 126; on history, 14, 42, 82; on logic, 127
borders, xxxix, 16, 23, 63, 173, 188, 201, 219n62
Bossuet, Jacques-Bénigne, xxi, xxii, 216n24
Brandenburg, ix, xii, xiii, xiv, 150, 222n97;
  House of, 171
Brandenburg-Prussia, x, xi, xii, xiii, xiv, xxxviii,
  xl, 222n100, 240n5

Caesar, Julius, xxxvii, 22, 40, 45, 54, 61, 62, 72,
  94, 114, 120, 121, 123, 187, 195
Calvinism, x, xxiv, xlii,
calvinists, 164, 240n5
Catherine II, Empress of Russia, viii, xv